JV6483 .D354 2004
RGC
33663003577166
Guarding the golden door :
American immigration policy
and immigrants since 1882

P9-DEN-492

D0015013

DATE DUE

DEC 1 5 2005	
MAR 0 3 2006	
JUL 0 7 2006	
NOV 1 2 2007	
OCT 11 2010	
MAY 1 0 2011	
SEP 1 4 2011	
NOV 0 7 2011	
NOV 0 5 2012	

BRODART, CO.   Cat. No. 23-221-003

ALSO BY ROGER DANIELS

*The Politics of Prejudice: The Anti-Japanese Movement in California
and the Struggle for Japanese Exclusion*

American Racism: Exploration of the Nature of Prejudice
(with Harry H. L. Kitano)

The Bonus March: An Episode of the Great Depression

Concentration Camps, USA: Japanese Americans and World War II

The Decision to Relocate the Japanese Americans

*Concentration Camps, North America: Japanese in the United States
and Canada during World War II*

Asian Americans: Emerging Minorities
(with Harry H. L. Kitano)

*Asian America: Chinese and Japanese in
the United States since 1850*

*Coming to America: A History of Immigration
and Ethnicity in American Life*

Prisoners Without Trial: Japanese Americans in World War II

Not Like Us: Immigrants and Minorities in America, 1890–1924

Debating American Immigration
(with Otis Graham)

American Immigration: A Student Companion

Guarding the Golden Door

Guarding the Golden Door

AMERICAN IMMIGRATION POLICY

AND IMMIGRANTS SINCE 1882

Roger Daniels

🖐 HILL AND WANG

A DIVISION OF FARRAR, STRAUS AND GIROUX

NEW YORK

Hill and Wang
A division of Farrar, Straus and Giroux
19 Union Square West, New York 10003

Copyright © 2004 by Roger Daniels
All rights reserved
Distributed in Canada by Douglas & McIntyre Ltd.
Printed in the United States of America
First edition, 2004

Library of Congress Cataloging-in-Publication Data
Daniels, Roger.
  Guarding the Golden Door : American immigration policy and immigrants since 1882 /
Roger Daniels.— 1st ed.
      p.   cm.
Includes bibliographical references (p.   ) and index.
  ISBN 0-8090-5343-8 (alk. paper)
  1. Immigrants—Government policy—United States—History. 2. Immigrants—United
States—History. 3. United States—Emigration and immigration—Government policy—
History. 4. United States—Emigration and immigration—History.   I. Title

  JV6483.D36 2003
  325.73—dc21

                                                                    2003007714

Designed by Jonathan D. Lippincott

www.fsgbooks.com

1   3   5   7   9   10   8   6   4   2

AUSTIN COMMUNITY COLLEGE
LIBRARY SERVICES

To the memory of
Harry H. L. Kitano
(1926–2002)
Friend, Activist, Scholar

Contents

List of Tables and Charts

Tables

Charts

Acknowledgments

I have been engaged in the crafting of this book for almost two decades. The first published artifact was an essay in a journal issue dedicated to John Higham in 1986.* When I first wrote about immigration law at the beginning of the '60s, I could not have imagined in my wildest dreams that within four decades some 25 million legal immigrants would come to America. It is obviously impossible to acknowledge all the intellectual debts that I have piled up during those years.

Many of those debts are recognized in the notes, but a number of the most pressing are recorded here. This book's dedication to Harry Kitano is not just an act of friendship. In a collaboration of almost four decades, resulting in four books and three academic conferences without a single harsh word, I learned about another discipline and another America.

My home base, the University of Cincinnati, provided much free time and other support, and a succession of department chairs—most recently Barbara Ramusack—have been responsive to many of my needs.

A number of my fellow immigration historians have answered queries and made comments. Dave Reimers, in particular, was always willing to share his unparalleled knowledge of recent immigration. Marian L. Smith, the historian at the Immigration and Naturalization Service, was more than

*"Changes in Immigration Law and Nativism since 1924," *American Jewish History* (Dec. 1986): 159–80.

forthcoming, and is a model public historian. She not only answered myriad questions, but sometimes posed important questions, with answers, that I did not have the wit to ask.

My students, undergraduate and graduate, heard early versions of much of what is presented here and their reactions and questions have significantly helped to shape the final result.

At Hill and Wang, Elisabeth Sifton quickly welcomed and sharpened my proposal, and Thomas LeBien was a meticulous and probing editor who consistently provided wise counsel. Every chapter carries his fingerprints and is better for them. Production editor JoAnna Kremer, copyeditor Cari Luna, proofreader Teddy Rosenbaum, and editorial assistant Kristina McGowan led a team that produced edited copy and advance proofs at a speed that dazzled someone who works mostly with university presses.

Last, but in no way least, I proclaim my eternal debt to Judith Mandel Daniels, who has vetted and improved everything that I have published during our marriage, which is, not coincidentally, coeval with my scholarly publishing career. Unfortunately the blame for the errors that must exist cannot be pinned on any of these accomplices, so as the saying goes, I claim responsibility.

PART I

The Golden Door Closes and Opens, 1882–1965

CHAPTER ONE

The Beginnings of
Immigration Restriction, 1882–1917

In the beginning Congress created the Chinese Exclusion Act. Like much of what Congress has done about immigration since then, it was conceived in ignorance, was falsely presented to the public, and had consequences undreamt of by its creators. That May 1882 statute, which has long been treated as a minor if somewhat disreputable incident, can now be seen as a nodal point in the history of American immigration policy. It marked the moment when the golden doorway of admission to the United States began to narrow and initiated a thirty-nine-year period of successive exclusions of certain kinds of immigrants, 1882–1921, followed by twenty-two years, 1921–43, when statutes and administrative actions set narrowing numerical limits for those immigrants who had not otherwise been excluded. During those years a federal bureaucracy was created to control immigration and immigrants, a bureaucracy whose initial raison d'être was to keep out first Chinese and then others who were deemed to be inferior.

The most comprehensive historical work on American immigration policy posits a different periodization, distinguishing between "the development of a regulatory system" in 1883–1913 and a period that went "from regulation to restriction" in 1913–29.[1] This seems to me to make a false distinction: in fact each narrowing of the grounds of admission to the United States made subsequent narrowings easier. The same would be true in reverse, when restrictions were progressively relaxed from 1943 on. In the decades following World War II, even as the immigration laws and regulations were loosened and made less discriminatory, the second generation of immigration historians tended to assume that immigration would never again be a major factor in American life. From a vantage point at the beginning of the twenty-first century, however, it now appears that the period of intense restriction, which eventually resulted in very small numbers of immigrants, was a temporary rather than a permanent alteration in a general pattern.

The clearest way to demonstrate the apparent continuity of immigration patterns in modern American history is to examine the percentage of foreign-born residents in the country, whom the census began to count only in 1850 vis-à-vis the gross number of immigrants admitted. The data show that between 1860 and 1920, a period when almost every aspect of American life was transformed, the incidence of immigrants in the American population was remarkably stable: in seven successive censuses, about one American in seven was foreign-born, the actual percentages varying only between 13.2 and 14.7 percent. The total number of resident immigrants grew steadily from 1850 to 1930, but their incidence in the population began to decline in 1910 and hit a low of 4.7 percent—less than one American in twenty—in 1970. This was well after immigration had begun to grow again, but the drop in incidence continued due to the high mortality among foreign-born because so many were old and so few immigrants had arrived in the previous four decades.* Because of depression, war, and immigration policy, fewer immigrants came to the United States between 1931 and 1971—7.3 million—than had arrived in the single decade 1901–10, even though the population in 1970 was more than twice as large as that in 1910. Since 1970 the number and incidence of immigrants have risen, but that incidence is still well below traditional levels. The commonly held perception that America is receiving an unprecedented proportion of immigrants is false.

---

*One tends to forget that many foreign-born spend most of their lives in the United States: my mother, for example, came in 1900 as a babe in arms and was recorded as foreign-born in every census until her death. After her naturalization in 1937 she was recorded as a foreign-born naturalized citizen.

TABLE 1.1

FOREIGN BORN IN THE UNITED STATES, 1850–2000

Year	Number (in millions)	Percentage
1850	2.2	9.7
1860	4.1	13.2
1870	5.6	14.0
1880	6.7	13.3
1890	9.2	14.7
1900	10.4	13.6
1910	13.6	14.7
1920	14.0	13.2
1930	14.3	11.6
1940	11.7	8.9
1950	10.4	6.9
1960	9.7	5.4
1970	9.6	4.7
1980	14.1	6.2
1990	19.8	7.9
2000	21.1	11.1

Source: U.S. Census data. A most useful analysis is in Campbell J. Gibson and Emily Lennon, "Historical Census Statistics on the Foreign-Born Population of the United States: 1850–1990," Population Division Working Paper No. 15, Washington: U.S. Bureau of the Census, February 1999.

TABLE 1.2

IMMIGRATION, 1851–2000

Years	Number (in millions)
1851–60	2.6
1861–70	2.3
1871–80	2.8
1881–90	5.2
1891–00	3.7
1901–10	8.8
1911–20	5.7
1921–30	4.1
1931–40	0.5
1941–50	1.0
1951–60	2.5
1961–70	3.3
1971–80	4.5

Years	Number (in millions)
1981–90	7.3
1991–00	9.1
Total	63.4

Source: Immigration and Naturalization Service, *2000 Statistical Yearbook of the Immigration and Naturalization Service*, Washington: GPO, September 2002, Table 1, p. 15.

What has changed, however, have been American attitudes toward immigration and immigrants. One issue that this book explores is the dualistic attitude that most Americans have developed toward immigration and immigrants, on the one hand reveling in the nation's immigrant past and on the other rejecting much of its immigrant present.

That the United States, along with a number of other "settler societies," is a nation of immigrants goes almost without saying.[2] Despite this, most historians do not accord either immigration or immigration policy the attention these topics deserve, and the space allocated to them in most textbooks is both cursory and spasmodic. Most still maintain the old invidious distinction between the earlier "colonists" and the later "immigrants."

The founding fathers knew that continued immigration was vital to help fill their largely empty new nation. Thomas Jefferson's list of complaints against King George III in the Declaration of Independence included the charge that the king had "endeavored to prevent the population of these States . . . obstructing the laws for the naturalization of foreigners [and] refusing to pass others to encourage their migration hither." Eleven years later the authors of the Constitution clearly had immigration in mind when they provided that Congress should "establish a uniform rule of naturalization" (Article I, Section 8) and made immigrants eligible for all federal offices save president and vice president. They also protected the foreign slave trade, a major source of immigration, by prohibiting interference with it for twenty years (Article 1, Section 9). When that period expired, Congress, at President Jefferson's invitation, promptly made that trade illegal, but did not interfere with either the domestic slave trade or slavery itself. The approximately 50,000 slaves smuggled into the United States after 1808 became the first illegal immigrants.

President George Washington and all his successors through John Tyler took it as a given that continued immigration was vital for the health of the nation. While none made as blunt a declaration as the nineteenth-century Argentine statesman Juan Bautista Alberdi, who insisted that "to govern is to populate," their endorsements were unambiguous. Washington, addressing an association of Irish immigrants just after the battle of Yorktown, said:

> The bosom of America is open to receive not only the opulent and respectable stranger, but the oppressed and persecuted of all nations and religions, whom we shall welcome to participate in all of our rights and privileges, if by decency and propriety of conduct they appear to merit the enjoyment.[3]

The anti-immigrant legislation of the John Adams administration in the late 1790s—the infamous Alien and Sedition Acts—was not so much an effort to restrict immigration as a desperate but vain attempt to keep Federalism in power and Jeffersonians out. Federalists generally opposed only those immigrants who they thought might vote for Jefferson. Apart from that episode, a pro-immigrant consensus long prevailed, a consensus well described in President John Tyler's 1841 message to Congress: "We hold out to the people of other countries an invitation to come and settle among us as members of our rapidly growing family."[4]

Thus for the first sixty years, and beyond, immigration and naturalization laws were minimal. Congress quickly enacted a 1790 statute specifying that naturalization was restricted to "free white persons."[5] The obvious intention was to bar the naturalization of blacks and indentured servants. (The French constitution of 1789 had similarly barred the suffrage of persons "in livery.") This naturalization act, as amended, was used later to bar the immigration of Asians, but there is no evidence that Congress had Asians in mind in 1790, and, in fact, a number of Asians were naturalized in the middle decades of the nineteenth century, at least one of them at the behest of the federal government.[6] And the first statute dealing directly with free immigration was not enacted until 1819, when Congress ordered, as part of a statute dealing with import duties, that every vessel entering an American port deliver a manifest of passengers being landed to the collector of customs for that district.[7] No other immigration statutes were enacted until after the Civil War.

The political elites' positive consensus about immigration and absence of legislative regulation does not mean that immigration was universally popular. Many Americans had long held hostile feelings toward immigrants in general and certain types of immigrants in particular—a position that has come to be known as nativism. The historian John Higham, its premier explicator, has defined it as "intense opposition to an internal minority on the grounds of its foreign (i.e., 'un-American') connections."[8] I will use the word more broadly to describe persons, organizations, and movements that oppose immigration or the amount of immigration on whatever grounds, and I shall use it often in the plural.*

American nativisms are older than the United States. For example, early in the eighteenth century a Boston mob tried to prevent the landing of Protestant Irish and later in the century that transplanted Bostonian Benjamin Franklin published one of the first nativist tracts. His *Observations Concerning the Increase of Mankind* (1751) had as its main target the burgeoning German immigration in Pennsylvania, but also demonstrated a broad, if to us curious, racism.

> Why should the Palatine boors be suffered to swarm into our Settlements, and by herding together establish their Language and Manners to the Exclusion of ours? Why should Pennsylvania, founded by the English, become a Colony of *Aliens*, who will shortly be so numerous as to Germanize us instead of us Anglifying them, and will never adopt our Language or Customs, any more than they can acquire our Complexion.

Franklin's comments are typical of American complaints against immigrants irrespective of time and place: they have bad habits ("Palatine boors"); they are clannish ("herding together"); they don't speak English ("their Language"); and they are going to take over ("Germanize us instead of our Anglifying them"). These are the arguments used against Italians, Jews, and others a hundred years ago, and may be heard today against "Mexicans, Latinos, Hispanics, etc." The targets have changed, but the complaints remain largely the same. Their gravamen is simply this: they are not like us.

Franklin went on to demonstrate the degree to which notions of race are relative rather than absolute. He noted that the number of "purely white People in the World is proportionately very small," but his notion of who was white was strangely narrow. Most Europeans were not white but, according to him, "swarthy": in this category he mentioned Spaniards, Ital-

---

*That we use the same words, "nativist" and "nativism," to describe a whole range of behaviors illustrates one of the problems that historians of discrimination and prejudice face. There is a real difference between burning down Catholic churches and convents, as happened in the 1830s and 1840s, and keeping Catholics from buying homes in certain neighborhoods through restrictive covenants, as occurred in the twentieth century until these were declared unconstitutional by the Supreme Court in *Shelly v. Kramer* (1948), yet both can be categorized as nativistic. That is why I employ the little-used plural—nativisms.

ians, French, Russians, Swedes, and Germans except for the Saxons, "who with the English, make the principal Body of White People on the Face of the Earth."

Finally, Franklin proposed an explicitly racist immigration policy: "Why Increase the Sons of Africa, by Planting them in America, where we have so fair an Opportunity, by excluding all Blacks and Tawneys, of increasing the lovely White and Red?"[9] Yet, although Franklin can justly be called a founding father of American nativism, he was a father with no intellectual children. And it should be noted that this theme does not recur in Franklin's writings and that the forty-five-year-old American had not yet been abroad when he wrote these sentences. In his old age he encouraged immigration from the European continent.*

No concerted anti-immigrant movement developed in America until almost a century later. But when many thousands of desperately poor Catholic Irish immigrants began arriving at East Coast ports in the mid-1840s, many of them fleeing the consequences of the terrible potato famine that killed more than a million Irish, the pro-immigration consensus was weakened. (Many of the immigrants had been subsidized to emigrate by Irish landlords and the British government.) In reaction, Massachusetts and New York passed laws taxing and otherwise impeding immigrants. These were appealed to the Supreme Court, which struck them down in the *Passenger Cases* of 1849, ruling that: 1) although the Constitution said nothing about immigration directly, it was clearly "foreign commerce," which the Constitution explicitly reserved to Congress; and 2) Congress's jurisdiction was preemptive so that even in the absence of any federal legislation, state governments could not regulate immigration.[10]

Immigration had been growing very quickly in the antebellum decades. In the 1830s, 600,000 came, 1.7 million arrived in the 1840s, and 2.6 million in the 1850s, which amounted to a 433 percent increase over two decades. About a third of the immigrants were Irish, almost all of them Catholic, and another third were German, a large segment of whom were Catholics. Irish immigrants went largely to the northeastern United States, many entering through Boston and New York, with a substantial minority entering via Canada. Almost all Irish settled in cities as far south as Baltimore and as far west as Cincinnati: large numbers of them moved into new

---

*Nativists in the mid-nineteenth century did try to appropriate another founder as their intellectual ancestor, fabricating the legend that, at a crucial stage of the revolution—the precise place varies— George Washington ordered that "only native Americans be placed on guard tonight."

urban occupations such as policemen, firemen, and horse-car drivers, as well as unskilled labor. Unlike the Irish, almost no Germans settled in New England; most entered through New York, which supplanted Philadelphia as the chief immigrant port in the 1820s. German settlement in the East was concentrated between New York and Baltimore, but a growing minority settled within the area between St. Louis, Cincinnati, and Milwaukee, which scholars have called the "German Triangle." Many Germans came seeking farms and found them, while large numbers were skilled craftsmen.

The frustration of Protestant nativist groups over the increasing immigration and the growing crisis over slavery were the preconditions for the first anti-immigrant mass movement in American history. In the 1830s and 1840s violent anti-Catholic riots occurred, primarily in New England and Philadelphia: in 1834, just outside Boston, a mob burned down an Ursuline convent; and in Philadelphia during the 1840s a number of mobs attacked Catholic churches. No organization accepted responsibility, as we say today, but by the early 1850s a new political movement had been born, directed largely against immigrants.

The Know-Nothings, as contemporary opponents and later historians called them, were members of a secret Protestant fraternal organization, the Order of the Star-Spangled Banner, whose members had to be native-born white Protestants who took an oath to "[resist] the insidious policy of the Church of Rome, and all other foreign influences against the institutions of our country, by placing in all offices in the gift of the people, whether by election or by appointment, none but native-born Protestant citizens." Members of the Order were instructed to reply "I know nothing" to any questions about the organization.

It had a meteoric rise, growing from just forty-three members to more than a million in a little over two years. A million white males represented almost one-eighth of the nation's potential electorate (in 1852 just some 6 million men voted for president). It is therefore no surprise that anti-immigrant candidates did well in the elections of 1854 and 1855, electing eight governors, more than a hundred congressmen, the mayors of Boston, Philadelphia, and Chicago, and thousands of other local officials. Many states enacted anti-immigrant statutes in this period. In Massachusetts, for example, naturalized citizens were denied the vote until two years after they became citizens, an act that particularly outraged Abraham Lincoln. The movement's national agenda included lengthening the period required for naturalization from five to fourteen years, various proposals to limit immigration, and a constitutional amendment barring foreign-born citizens from holding any public office.[11]

Emboldened by its electoral success, the Order formed the American Party and in 1856 ran ex-President Millard Fillmore for president on a platform that ignored the slavery issue but included anti-immigrant planks. Fillmore got more than 800,000 votes, some 20 percent of the electorate, but carried only the state of Maryland. The American Party collapsed and, by 1860, so had the Know-Nothing movement. The Civil War years, in which immigrant soldiers fought for both the Union and the Confederacy, often in ethnic regiments or smaller units, ended, for a time, the anti-immigrant furor. The Know-Nothings did not achieve any of their agenda, but they serve as an exemplar of one kind of anti-immigrant movement: one whose major objection to immigrants is their religion.

The depression-scarred 1890s saw a minor reprise of organized anti-Catholicism. The short-lived American Protective Association, founded in Iowa in 1887 by a still-obscure man named Henry Bowers, had its greatest appeal in the rural Midwest and the Pacific Northwest. Its political agenda was similar to that of the Know-Nothings, but it had little national impact and faded with the return of relative prosperity around 1900.[12] Yet, religious prejudices against Catholics and Jews continued to be an important element of many subsequent anti-immigrant movements, though never again at their core. In the post–Civil War years that core was provided first by race and then by ethnicity.

The adoption of the Fourteenth Amendment in the summer of 1868 with its unambiguous initial sentence — "All persons born or naturalized in the United States, and subject to the jurisdiction thereof, are citizens of the United States and of the State wherein they reside" — established, for the first time, a national citizenship and made citizens of former slaves who had been born in the United States, and left those who had been born in Africa or the West Indies ineligible to citizenship.[13] Quite logically, Congress took up the question of amending the naturalization law, basically unchanged since 1790, which still limited eligibility to "free white persons."[14]

Had Congress amended the naturalization statute in 1866 it might well have simply dropped "white" as well as "free" from the new statute, but events in 1868, 1869, and early 1870 brought the issue of Chinese immigration into national prominence. This, along with the turmoil of Reconstruction helped to focus anti-immigrant sentiments on race rather than religion.[15]

Chinese had begun to immigrate to California and the American West in significant numbers in the 1850s. They came like thousands of others from Europe, Latin America, and the rest of the United States, seeking gold. Almost all came from the area around Canton and were young men seeking "riches": consular reports indicated that for many the goal was to return with $400 and that by mid-decade some had already achieved it. In the tradition of previous Chinese migrants within Asia, they called themselves "guests": since the Chinese characters for California also mean "gold mountain," those in California were "gan sam hack" or gold mountain guests. Students of immigration usually call such immigrants "sojourners" and note that there have been numerous sojourners among immigrants to America since the seventeenth century.

The census of 1870 recorded more than 60,000 Chinese, three-quarters of them in California and almost all of them men. As late as 1867, California Republicans were still willing to pass a resolution "in favor of voluntary immigration . . . from whatever nationality it may come," but after losing the gubernatorial election in that year, partially because their opponents had labeled them as pro-Chinese, they vied with other parties in the virulence of their anti-Chinese expressions.[16]

The following year the Senate ratified the Burlingame Treaty with China, which recognized "the inherent and inalienable right of man to change his home and allegiance" and "the mutual advantage of . . . free migration," although the treaty specified that "nothing contained herein shall be held to confer naturalization . . . upon the subjects of China in the United States."[17]

The completion of the Union-Central Pacific Railroad at Promontory Point, Utah, in May 1869, threw some 10,000 Chinese railroad builders onto the California labor market and pushed the Chinese immigration issue to the top of western workingmen's political agenda. Although there had been legal and extra-legal discrimination against Chinese almost as soon as the first immigrants got off the boat, the major phase of the anti-Chinese movement in California dates from that time. In the same month the golden spike was driven, Henry George, a radical reformer and economic theorist, raised, perhaps for the first time anywhere, the bogus specter of the invasion of the United States by an Asian army, what came to be called the Yellow Peril. In a front-page article in the New York *Tribune*, the "prophet of San Francisco" warned that:

> The 60,000 or 100,000 Mongolians on our Western coast are the thin edge of the wedge which has for its base the 500,000,000 of Eastern Asia . . . The Chinaman can live where stronger than he would starve. Give him fair play and this quality enables him to drive out stronger races . . . [Unless Chinese immigration is checked] the youngest home of the nations must in its early manhood follow the path and meet the doom of Babylon, Nineveh and Rome . . . Here plain to the eye of him who chooses to see are the dragon's teeth [which will] spring up armed men marshaled for civil war. Shall we prohibit their sowing while there is still time or shall we wait until they are firmly embedded, and then try to pluck them up?[18]

In the South many had a different reaction. Faced with the problems of reinserting the freedmen into the Southern labor system, some Southern businessmen and planters fantasized that indentured Chinese labor might allow them to set up a new system of slavery. They tried to disguise their efforts as a kind of missionary enterprise, arguing that by bringing Chinese to America they would be

> falling in with the apparent leanings of Providence, and while we avail ourselves of the physical assistance these pagans are capable of affording us, endeavor at the same time to bring to bear upon them the elevating and saving influence of our holy religion, so that when those coming among us shall return to their own country, they may carry back with them and disseminate the good seed which is here sown, and the New World shall thus in a double sense become the regenerator of the Old.[19]

With the help of the Dutch-born labor contractor Cornelius Koopmanschap (1828–82), perhaps a thousand or so Chinese laborers were sent from the West Coast to the South in the early 1870s, the largest group of whom worked on the Alabama and Chattanooga Railroad. Although Chinese workers were never a significant factor in the Southern economy, the discussions of this scheme in the press helped make Americans more aware of the Chinese question.[20]

Against this background of growing hostility and attention to the issue of Chinese in America the Massachusetts radical Republican senator, Charles Sumner, in an April 1870 speech delivered just after the ratification of the Fifteenth Amendment, announced his intention to go one step further on the road to true democracy and ensure that the word *white* was eliminated from the naturalization laws. This drew a reaction from Frank Pixley, a San Francisco lawyer and Republican politician (later notorious as an anti-Chinese demagogue). Though he supported the Fifteenth Amendment and African American suffrage in California, he opposed naturalization and citizenship for Chinese. "This is not the question of the African whom our forefathers brought here and who had generations of ancestors born upon the soil," Pixley wrote Sumner. "This is a question of bringing a new people here, and are we not planting the seeds of an evil which may develop to our great and permanent injury?" Pixley admitted that "as a class Chinese are intelligent," and he believed, erroneously, that all of them could read and write and were mere sojourners who did "not acquire lands or real property," also that among "the multitudes of Chinese women in our state there is not a wife or virtuous female in their number."[21]

Such criticism did not faze Sumner and he may not have answered Pixley, but the San Francisco attorney's letter prefigured the debate that took place in the Senate that summer. The issue of color-blind naturalization was not a new one. Sumner had introduced bills removing the word "white" from the naturalization statutes in 1868 and 1869, but neither had come to a vote and the issue of Chinese naturalization had not been raised. His chance to force the issue came in July 1870, when the Senate had under consideration two similar bills "to amend the Naturalization Laws and to punish crimes against the same." Their object was to prevent election frauds perpetrated by unnaturalized or illegally naturalized voters—who presumably voted Democratic. On July 2 Sumner moved to add, as a new section of one of them, the text of a bill he had previously introduced that would strike out the word "white" wherever it appeared in acts of Congress relating to naturalization, "so that in naturalization there shall be no distinction of race or color."

In his brief remarks that day he spoke of the denial of rights to African Americans and made no direct mention of Chinese, although a number of Republican senators, including William M. Stewart of Nevada and George Henry Williams of Oregon, raised the specter of hordes of incoming Chinese and massive Chinese suffrage. Williams, an Oregon Republican, moved a further amendment: "*Provided,* that nothing in this Act shall be construed to authorize the naturalization of persons born in the Chinese Empire." When Oliver P. Morton (R-IN) remarked that "the whole Chinese problem" was involved and called for caution and reflection, Sumner countered that it "simply opens the question of the Declaration of Independence." Thus was the issue of Chinese naturalization—and behind that of Chinese immigration—joined for the first time in Congress.

Sumner rose to the occasion. In the ensuing debate, conducted on the Fourth of July, Sumner made his defense of Chinese naturalization.

> Senators undertake to disturb us . . . by reminding us of the possibility of large numbers swarming from China; but the answer to all this is very obvious and very simple. If the Chinese come here, they will come for citizenship or merely for labor. If they come for citizenship, then in this desire do they give a pledge of loyalty to our institutions; and where is the peril in such vows? They are peaceful and industrious; how can their citizenship be the occasion of solicitude?

As was his wont, Sumner made direct and personal replies to the arguments of his opponents. After reading aloud from the Gospel of St. Matthew's account of Peter's triple denial of Jesus of Nazareth, Sumner analogized that "thrice has a Senator [Stewart of Nevada] on this floor denied these great principles of the Declaration of Independence. The time may come when he will weep bitterly."

In answer to Williams of Oregon, who had argued that color-blind naturalization would give "millions of heathens and pagans power to control our institutions," Sumner answered, "Fearlessly we may go forward and welcome all comers, for there can be no harm here; the heathens and pagans do not exist whose coming can disturb our institutions. Worse than any heathen or pagan abroad are those in our midst who are false to our institutions." Later he insisted that the "peril" to the "Republic" existed only "in imagination; it is illusion, not a reality."

On what had become the Chinese issue—no other Asian group was mentioned—Sumner did not prevail. In a confusing parliamentary situation, his amendment was first rejected, then accepted, then reconsidered, and twice again rejected, on votes of 30–14 and 26–12. But Sumner's struggle for African naturalization did bear fruit. An amendment by an Ohio-born Republican from Alabama, the former brevet major general of Ohio Volunteers Willard Warner, to extend naturalization to "aliens of African nativity and to persons of African descent" was narrowly adopted by votes of 21–20 and 20–17. A motion by Lyman Trumbull (R-IL) to extend naturalization "to persons born in the Chinese Empire," was defeated 31–9, and the amended bill passed, 33–8, with Sumner voting in the affirmative.[22] For the next seventy-three years Chinese and other Asians were the only persons genetically ineligible to American citizenship, and some Asians remained ineligible until 1952 when the McCarran-Walter Act made the naturalization statutes color-blind.

Thus most Reconstruction Era Republicans took the position that the Californian Pixley had: that naturalization rights should be accorded to Africans and foreign-born African Americans, but not to Chinese. Frederick Douglass, on the other hand, understood that an important principle had been defeated: the great African American leader congratulated Sumner for being "in the right place on the Chinese question. As usual you are in the van, the country in the rear."[23] Sumner's brief fight for Chinese rights was quickly forgotten by contemporaries and many historians.*

In 1870 the census counted 63,000 Chinese in the country and in 1880 found 105,000. In that year more than 70 percent of all American Chinese lived in California and a mere 3 percent lived in all the territory east of Denver. Males outnumbered females by a little more than twenty to one.

Originally drawn to the mines of the Sierra Nevadas, Chinese were driven from them by the violence of white miners and deliberate discrimination by the state of California, which levied a heavy foreign-miners tax collected almost exclusively from Chinese. They were largely employed in humble occupations, although a significant number were merchants and other entrepreneurs. But even as Sumner spoke on the ninety-fourth anniversary of the Declaration, an event in the western part of his home state was helping to stimulate anti-Chinese activity in the eastern United States.

On June 13, 1870, in North Adams, Massachusetts, seventy-five Chinese workmen brought from San Francisco under three-year contracts arrived on a train and were escorted by thirty policemen to the shoemaking factory of Calvin T. Sampson. He had brought them in to replace his striking shoemakers, members of the Knights of St. Crispin, the shoemakers union, then America's largest trade union.[24] Although Chinese labor never became a significant factor in Eastern industrial labor—only two other instances are known—the incident had significant repercussions. In August the National Labor Union, the first national labor federation of the post–Civil War period, changed its policy about immigration. The previous year its convention had resolved that "voluntary Chinese emigrants ought

---

*Sumner's most distinguished modern biographer, David H. Donald, can find no place for it in his two-volume biography, although it was treated by some of his predecessors.

to enjoy the protection of the laws like other citizens." Now, with Crispin and California delegates in attendance, it resolved that "the presence in our country of Chinese laborers in large numbers is an evil . . . and should be prevented by legislation."[25]

For the labor movement this was a Rubicon: from then until the very end of the twentieth century its basic stance was anti-immigrant, and although most of its leaders and its academic apologists claim that the opposition was based completely on economic grounds, racism was a major factor. By the early twentieth century not only business unionists like Samuel Gompers but also socialists like Morris Hillquit and Victor Berger were virulent opponents of Asian immigration: the latter insisted that the United States and Canada must remain "White Men's countries."[26]

Yet, despite the efforts of Western congressmen—often with border states and Southern allies—to erect legislative barriers to Chinese immigration, Congress was reluctant to do so. In his 1874 annual message, President Ulysses S. Grant weighed in against the Chinese, claiming that the "great proportion" of Chinese were involuntary contract laborers—and thus illegal immigrants—and that an even worse evil were Chinese women, almost none of whom "perform any honorable labor, but . . . are brought for shameful purposes." He went on to say that "if this evil practice can be legislated against" it would be his "pleasure" to enforce it.[27]

The next year, 1875, Congress passed the so-called Page Act—for Horace F. Page (1833–90) then a first-term California Republican congressman. It created two classes of illegal immigrants—persons under sentence for crimes other than political and women "imported for purposes of prostitution" and made the importation of "any subject of China, Japan, or any Oriental country" without their consent a felony. Rhetorical sections of the statute and remarks made during the congressional debate made it clear that the bill was really aimed at Chinese women.* Though historians have long treated it as an ineffective legislative way station on the road to exclusion, recent scholarship focusing on the act's administration has shown that it was, in fact, an effective inhibition on the immigration of Chinese women.[28]

The same Congress that passed the Page Act also authorized a joint congressional committee to investigate Chinese immigration; this took testi-

---

*Curiously, Grant, nine months *after* he signed the Page Act, called Congress's attention to the "evil" of the "importation of Chinese women." Richardson, *Messages*, 7:355.

mony in the Palace Hotel in San Francisco just before and after the presidential election of 1876. By that time both national political party platforms inveighed against the Chinese, the Republicans a little tentatively—it is "the immediate duty of Congress to investigate the effects of the immigration and importation of Mongolians"—while the Democrats unreservedly denounced "the policy which tolerates the revival of the coolie-trade in Mongolian women held for immoral purposes, and Mongolian men to perform servile labor."[29]

The majority report of the joint congressional committee claimed that the Pacific Coast had to become "either American or Mongolian," and insisting that there was "not sufficient brain capacity in the Chinese race to furnish motive power for self-government" and that "there is no Aryan or European race which is not far superior to the Chinese." It urged the president to get the Burlingame Treaty modified and Congress to legislate against "Asiatic immigration."[30] The report was presented to Congress while it was settling the disputed election of 1876, so no immediate action was taken. After much debate the next session of Congress, just before it went out of existence, passed the so-called fifteen passenger bill which barred any vessel from bringing more than fifteen Chinese immigrants. A sticking point was the existing Burlingame Treaty, which some wanted to override totally while others wanted to wait for a diplomatic renegotiation. The bill also instructed the president to notify the Chinese that portions of the treaty were abrogated, which passage of the bill would have accomplished.

Rutherford B. Hayes responded with a reasoned veto message that accepted the desirability of stemming Chinese immigration. He argued that the Chinese manifested "all the traits of race, religion, manners, and customs, habitations, mode of life, segregation here, and the keeping up of the ties of their original home . . . [which] stamp them as strangers and sojourners, and not as incorporated elements of our national life."[31] But, he insisted, there was no emergency to justify unilateral abrogation of the treaty, which could have disastrous consequences both for American merchants and for missionaries in China. He promised that there would be a renegotiation of the treaty.

Somewhat protracted diplomatic renegotiations of the treaty were completed by the end of 1880, and the new treaty was ratified and proclaimed in October 1881. It gave the United States, unilaterally, the rights to "regulate, limit, or suspend" the "coming or residence" of Chinese laborers, but it allowed Chinese subjects "proceeding to the United States as teachers, students, merchants, or from curiosity, together with their body and household servants, and Chinese laborers now in the United States to go and come of their own free will and accord."[32]

The subsequent session of Congress passed a bill suspending the immigration of Chinese laborers for twenty years. President Chester A. Arthur vetoed it, arguing that "It may be that the great and paramount interest of protecting our labor from Asiatic competition may justify us in a permanent adoption of this policy; but it is wiser in the first place to make a shorter experiment, with a view hereafter of maintaining only such features as time and experience may command."[33] Congress responded by re-passing the bill with a ten-year suspension, and Arthur signed it into law on May 6, 1882.[34]

This law prohibited the entry of Chinese laborers—defined as "both skilled and unskilled laborers and Chinese employed in mining"—after August 4, 1882, and it provided that any Chinese who was in the country on November 17, 1880, the effective date of the Sino-American Treaty, or had come between that date and August 4, 1882, had the right to leave and return. American certificates would be issued, free of charge, to any Chinese who left the United States and wished to return. Every Chinese, other than a laborer, had to have a certificate of identification supplied by the Chinese government either in English or with an English translation. The law, as opposed to the treaty, did not spell out who was entitled to enter the United States, although it did specify that diplomats and other officials of the Chinese government doing government business and their body and household servants were admissible. Fines for bringing Chinese in illegally could run as high as $1,000 per individual, and vessels landing Chinese illegally were liable to seizure and condemnation.

Thus, what is commonly called the Chinese Exclusion Act—its proper title is "To Execute Certain Treaty Stipulations Relating to Chinese"—became law. The typical textbook gives it only a sentence or two, but it merits a much more extensive treatment. Viewed from the perspective of the early twenty-first century, the Exclusion Act is clearly the pivot on which all American immigration policy turned, the hinge on which Emma Lazarus's "Golden Door" began to swing toward a closed position. It initiated an era of steadily increasing restrictions on immigration of all kinds that lasted until 1943, when, under special circumstances, the Chinese exclusion laws were repealed.

The enforcement of Chinese exclusion was problematic from the beginning. The federal government had no immigration bureaucracy and its enforcement fell first to customs officials. The Chinese American community, which had successfully applied to the state and federal courts for protection from various discriminatory state statutes and municipal ordinances, now appealed to the federal courts for protection from this federal law. The courts upheld the principle of exclusion but did rule that, as the law was written, it affected only Chinese coming from China and that Chinese entering from anywhere else—for practical purposes this meant Canada, Cuba, or Mexico—were not affected by it. In 1884 the original act was amended to bar the entry of *any* Chinese person except as otherwise authorized. Other problems involved the efficacy of the new certificates, which, despite identifying photographs, were sometimes used for entry by persons other than those to whom they were issued. (Fingerprinting did not come into use for another few decades.)[35]

Meanwhile, although the Chinese American population was beginning a long period of decline, anti-Chinese agitation and violence continued throughout the West: some of the worst outrages, such as the Rock Springs, Wyoming, massacre of 1885, followed rather than preceded the exclusion act. A new treaty with China was negotiated in 1888 that would have extended the bars against Chinese laborers for twenty years, with an extension of an additional twenty years if neither side renounced the treaty. But in the ratification process the Senate added several conditions, one of which would have cancelled all the outstanding return certificates. This China refused to accept, and the treaty was never in effect.

Congress then passed the so-called Scott Act, named for Representative William L. Scott of Pennsylvania, who was also Grover Cleveland's campaign manager, which unilaterally cancelled the certificates although the treaty prescribing them was still in effect.[36] Unlike Hayes, who had been punctilious about treaty obligations, President Cleveland signed it into law a little more than a month before the 1888 election. He took the unusual step of justifying his doing so in a message that failed to mention the certificates. He did note that some of the provisions of the act had been agreed to by the Chinese government and supported his position by asserting that the "experiment of blending the social habits and mutual race idiosyncrasies of the Chinese laboring classes with those of the great body of the people of the United States [has] proved by the experience of twenty years . . . in every sense unwise, impolitic, and injurious to both nations."[37]

Attorneys for Chinese interests challenged the Scott Act in federal court because it was a clear violation of the 1881 treaty, but the courts upheld the government in the *Chinese Exclusion Case* and established the rule of law that in case of conflict between acts of Congress and treaties, which were each the law of the land, whichever came later should prevail.[38]

In May 1892, as the original term of exclusion was about to expire, Congress passed the Geary Act, which extended exclusion for another ten years and placed harsh and unprecedented restrictions upon Chinese persons living in the United States. Reversing the normal presumption, it stated that "any Chinese person or person of Chinese descent" was deemed to be in the country illegally unless he or she could demonstrate otherwise. It also denied the right of bail to Chinese aliens in habeas corpus proceedings, and required all Chinese in the United States to get a certificate of residence, a kind of internal passport, within a year (that is by May 1893) or be deported.[39]

Chinese American organizations so mobilized their community that only a little over a tenth of the Chinese in the United States registered, a remarkable act of passive resistance. Actively the community leadership, perhaps aided by the Chinese government, employed three prominent constitutional lawyers to challenge the law. The case was expedited directly to the Supreme Court immediately after the registration deadline ran out. At the time the case was heard, in May 1893, only some 13,000 Chinese had registered, and more than 90,000 had not. The nominal plaintiffs were three alien Chinese laborers who had been residents of New York City since before the first exclusion act and had been ordered deported for lack of a certificate. Two, Fong Yue Ting and Wong Quan, had refused to register. The third, Lee Joe, tried to register but was denied a certificate because his witnesses were Chinese and the law required "at least one credible witness other than Chinese" to attest to prior residence.

Despite impressive briefs and arguments that convinced three justices, five justices supported the government and upheld the law. Justice Horace Gray, for the majority, held in the case of *Fong Yue Ting v. United States* that the three Chinese, like other resident aliens, were entitled

> to the safeguards of the Constitution, and to the protection of the laws, in regard to their rights of persons and property, and to their civil and criminal responsibility [but insisted that the Constitution could not shield them if

Congress decided that] their removal is necessary or expedient for the public interest.

In a pale paraphrase of Taney's Dred Scott decision, Gray wrote that "it appears impossible to hold that a Chinese laborer acquired under any of the treaties or acts of Congress, any right, as a denizen or otherwise, to be and remain in this country, except by license, permission and sufferance of Congress."[40] Although the particular case involved Chinese, the case was governing for unnaturalized immigrants. They were—and are—more or less at the mercy of Congress.

While some anti-Chinese enthusiasts on the West Coast expected mass deportations to ensue, nothing of the sort happened. Secretary of the Treasury John G. Carlisle estimated that mass removal of all 90,000 uncertified Chinese would cost the country at least $7.2 million: his annual budget for immigration enforcement was $25,000. Both he and Attorney General Richard Olney instructed their subordinates to refrain from taking action.[41] At about the same time Secretary of State Walter Q. Gresham assured Yang Yu, the Chinese minister, that in its next session Congress would moderate the measure so that Chinese might register.[42] Such an act was indeed passed in November 1893, giving Chinese six additional months to register.

Altogether about 105,000 Chinese eventually applied for and received certificates, so that they could not only remain in the United States but also could, once again, leave the country and return. But the 1893 act added new barriers for Chinese in exempt classes, particularly those whom the immigration service came to call "treaty merchants." For example, the law provided that any "Chinaman" trying to enter on the grounds that he was a returning merchant had to provide affidavits or other evidence from "two credible witnesses other than Chinese" that what he said was true.[43]

The annexation of the Hawaiian Islands in 1898 had extended the exclusion laws there where they affected a Chinese community that numbered 25,000 in 1900. As the time for the expiration of the 1892 act neared, Congress enacted a statute extending the existing legislation "until otherwise provided by law" and expanded its scope to all of the American empire that had been acquired largely in the Spanish-American War of 1898.[44] It is instructive to note that this act was signed by President Theodore Roosevelt, who would later protest vehemently against anti-Japanese agitation.

The foregoing is no more than a capsule history of the Chinese Exclusion acts, but it is important to understand the many ways in which the act shaped not only the lives of Chinese Americans but also the culture of the organization that was, in large part, created to enforce it, the immigration service of the United States.

When the Chinese Exclusion Act was passed there were probably about 125,000 Chinese living and working in the United States. That number dropped steadily until it just exceeded 60,000 in the census of 1920. Then it began to rise slowly and had reached almost 78,000 in 1940, a bare majority of whom were recorded as U.S. citizens. Although a standard complaint against Chinese immigrants in the United States was that they failed to adapt to American conditions, the community had very quickly learned how to use American law and lawyers to protect their rights in state and federal courts. These lawyers were not usually hired by the individual defendants but by communal associations, particularly the so-called Six Companies, which evolved into the Chinese Community Benefit Association. Legal scholars have discovered more than 10,000 habeas corpus cases involving Chinese litigants in the state and federal courts in California alone.[45] These cases helped to set the parameters of American immigration law and to establish the rights of all aliens. Chinese American community leaders had developed a great respect for the efficacy of the American legal system until it failed to protect them from the Geary Act in 1893. Although the community still took cases to court and Chinese Americans remained, on a per capita basis, the most persistent litagators in the United States, it increasingly resorted to illegal expedients to evade the law.

I will give two examples. Between the Sino-American Treaty of 1881 and the immigration act of 1924, Chinese merchants enjoyed a special status, for they could come and go as they wished, and they could bring family members to the United States to join them. Who was a "merchant"? The 1893 statute defined a merchant as "a person engaged in buying and selling merchandise, at a fixed place of business, which business is conducted in his name, and who during the time he claims to be engaged as a merchant, does not engage in the performance of any manual labor, except as is necessary in the conduct of such business as a merchant."[46]

One can find in the archives of the immigration service partnership agreements that show literally dozens of partners for rather small businesses that cannot have supported so many persons, even frugal Chinese immigrants. But the courts generally ruled, in the absence of evidence to the contrary, that all such partners were merchants with treaty rights. And these merchants could bring in wives, which increased the number of Chinese American women whose children, born in the United States, were native-born U.S. citizens with all the legal rights of citizenship thanks to the Fourteenth Amendment.

The decentralized and erratic nature of birth registration in the United States enabled some Chinese men in the 1890s to acquire citizenship fraudulently. And then in 1906 a natural catastrophe—the great San Francisco earthquake and fire—destroyed the city's vital statistics, which made it even easier for increasing numbers of young men to claim and secure U.S. citizenship. Among the rights that they could exercise was the right to leave the country and reenter with impunity. Although we speak of Chinese American society as a bachelor society—in 1910 the gender ratio was still larger than 14 to 1—until after World War II probably most Chinese men in the United States were married, but their wives were in China unable to join them.[47] Sociologists speak of such unions as "mutilated marriages": Chinese Americans call the female partners "living widows." Chinese men who had successfully established American citizenship could visit China and get married. Any resulting offspring were derivative American citizens who could enter the United States, although their mothers—aliens ineligible to citizenship—could not. Each visit to China by an adult male citizen created at least one "slot" in which he could have fathered a child. Some years after the birth should have occurred, a school-age boy or young man would join his "father."

An incredible percentage of the children thus putatively fathered were sons. Of course there were some Chinese men who brought their own sons into America. Others, however, brought in other men's sons, whom the community called "paper sons." There were also a few "paper daughters," but the vast majority of Chinese who entered as derivative citizens were male.[48] There is no way of ascertaining how many paper sons and other illegal Chinese immigrants gained entry during the Exclusion Era, 1882–1943; we only know the official figure of almost 95,000 legal individual entries of alien Chinese during that era. Many of those were returning immigrants, and some of them reentered more than once. The entries average some 1,500 a year, which comes to about four every day over a sixty-year period. Averages can be misleading, of course: relatively few could enter after 1924 and in the 1930s the average was below 600 annually. And one should note that the immigration of Chinese women was particularly affected by the 1924 law. Prior to its passage about 150 alien Chinese women had been entering annually—that is, 10 percent of the total. Between 1924 and 1930 there were none. A 1930 statute relaxed the ban and for the next decade about sixty women a year were able to enter.[49] In a final demographic observation, it should be noted that in 1940, for the first time, the census recorded that a slight majority of Chinese in the continental United States were citizens—40,000 citizens and 37,000 aliens, but that includes an indeterminate number of "paper sons."

The discriminatory way in which Chinese were treated—today we would call it ethnic profiling—can be seen in the operating assumptions at the two chief immigrant inspection facilities: New York's Ellis Island, established in 1892, and San Francisco's Angel Island, established in 1910. The latter is sometimes called "the Ellis Island of the West," but that is a misnomer. Ellis Island, in its heyday, existed to facilitate immigration, and most of the people who passed through it did not even spend the night there. The medical examinations were largely perfunctory, except for those who had visible physical handicaps,[50] and the rejection rate over most of its existence as a receiving station was in the neighborhood of 1 percent. Angel Island, on the other hand, existed to isolate and to impede the immigration of Chinese and, to a much lesser extent, Japanese and other Asians. Most Chinese applicants for admission were subjected to intense cross-examination; physical examinations were relatively thorough for all Chinese and included taking stool samples. Most of the recent literature about Angel Island stresses the difficulties and rejections, but even there rejection was a minority phenomenon. The currently available records do not permit precision, but perhaps 50,000 came in while perhaps 9,000 were barred, a rejection rate of about 18 percent.[51]

The experience of enforcing the Chinese exclusion laws was clearly a major influence in the formation of the immigration service's culture. Its officers were not fools: they came to understand very quickly that they faced a community conspiracy and that many of the Chinese people who came before them for admission were attempting to commit fraud. Most of them concluded that Chinese were "born liars" and could not be trusted under any circumstances. They seem not to have been able to understand that Chinese, whose business ethics were impeccable, found it perfectly acceptable to lie to them. As a result they tended to treat all Chinese entrants as if they were criminals.

It was relatively easy for these attitudes to shift from Chinese to other immigrants, particularly since a whole series of immigration commissioners drawn from the ranks of trade unions came to their posts with built-in prejudices against immigrants and persistently urged Congress to enact further restrictions. The actions of the federal courts further increased the power of immigration officials to make arbitrary decisions about who could and could not enter the United States. In the words of Lucy Salyer:

> The doctrines providing the foundation for immigration law arose out of struggles on the West Coast among Chinese immigrants, government officials, and federal judges over the enforcement of the Chinese exclusion laws. Though on the margins of society, Chinese immigrants in their resistance to exclusion laid claim to principles and practices—habeas corpus, due process, evidentiary rules, judicial review—that were at the heart of Anglo-American jurisprudence. Officials were faced with the choice of extending those core principles to Chinese, with the practical effect of undermining exclusionist aims and the symbolic effect of recognizing Chinese as functional, if not formal, members of the society with legitimate claims to its cherished legal heritage. Rejecting that option, government officials instead persuaded Congress and the Supreme Court that the nation's gates could be effectively guarded only if they were allowed full authority and discretion over immigration policy without interference from the federal courts. Ironically, in their efforts to secure the door against Chinese immigration, officials undermined the very principles they accused the Chinese of subverting. The immigration law resulting from this struggle stood at odds with one of the most esteemed Anglo-American legal principles—the rule of law.[52]

This contributed to create a bureaucracy unlike most other federal bureaucracies. While the Department of Agriculture spoke for farmers, the Department of Labor spoke for working people, and the Forest Service looked out for the trees, the immigration service, which became the Immigration and Naturalization Service (INS) in 1933, lobbied against the interests of legal immigrants, especially those of color and those who seemed to them un-American.

CHAPTER TWO

The 1920s: The Triumph of the Old Nativism

After the Chinese Exclusion Act there followed, piecemeal, a series of restrictions that by the end of World War I limited the immigration policy of the United States in eight distinct ways. The excluded categories were: contract laborers; Asians (except for Japanese and Filipinos); certain criminals; persons who failed to meet certain moral standards; persons with various diseases and disabilities; paupers; some radicals; and illiterates.

In August 1882, less than three months after passing the Chinese Exclusion Act, Congress enacted the first general immigration law.[1] A brief, relatively simple measure, it placed a fifty-cent head tax on incoming ship passengers to defray immigration expenses; those who walked or took a train from Canada or Mexico did not have to pay. Then as now, Congress intended to run immigration on the cheap, making the immigrants themselves foot the bill for the costs associated with immigration; in many years the fees collected outstripped costs. The law also made the Secretary of the Treasury supervisor of "the business of immigration"—already responsible for customs, he could use existing inspectors—and authorized him to contract with state boards to do what administering and processing of immigration there was. In New York, which had long had such a board, immigrants were ushered through Castle Garden, on the East River near the southern tip of Manhattan.* Charged with examining all immigrants, the boards

---

*After the decision to create a federal facility on Ellis Island, the state and federal governments had a falling-out, so from 1890 to the opening of Ellis Island in 1892, immigrants were processed in the nearby federal Barge Office. See George J. Svejda, *Castle Garden as an Immigrant Depot* (Washington: GPO, 1968); and Thomas M. Pitkin, *Keepers of the Gate: A History of Ellis Island* (New York: New York University Press, 1975).

were ordered to refuse admittance to "any convict, lunatic, idiot, or any person unable to take care of himself or herself without becoming a public charge." That last provision, transmuted in 1891 into "paupers or persons likely to become a public charge" or the "LPC clause," would become a major factor in early immigration restriction. Originally intended to keep out persons physically and mentally unable to take care of themselves, it eventually barred the able-bodied poor.

The Secretary of the Treasury was to establish rules and issue instructions "not inconsistent with law," a mandate that gave him and his successors considerable latitude in managing immigration. He was directed to establish regulations for the return of foreign convicts to "the place from whence they came" and to see that the shipowners who brought them bore the costs. The 1882 law exempted persons convicted of political crimes: they were admissible. Two decades later Congress would begin passing legislation barring the admission of foreign radicals.

Congress then addressed the question of contract labor. An 1864 law, partially inspired by a fear of a shortage of skilled labor due to the Civil War, allowed employers to contract with immigrant journeymen, advancing them passage money for a set period of employment. It also enabled employers to sue to get their money back if the contracts were not fulfilled. After its repeal in 1868, such contracts were legal but unenforceable. How many contract journeymen immigrated is unknown, but trade unionists were convinced that many did. Particularly active in lobbying for legislation barring contract laborers were the Knights of Labor and its Grand Master Workman Terence V. Powderly.

The first law forbidding the entry of contract laborers, the Foran Act, was enacted in 1885 with perfecting amendments adopted two years later.[2] The act made it "unlawful" for any individual or firm to import or otherwise arrange for the importation of workers and provided that such workers, like convicts, be "sent back from whence they came." It further made all such labor contracts null and void, and fined employers $1,000 per contract worker, but forced the government to sue in federal district courts, an act which was not much resorted to. More effectively it made ship captains who brought in contract laborers liable for a fine of $500 for each individual and imprisonment for up to six months.

And, as continues to be the case with employer sanctions, there were numerous exceptions. The most significant enabled employers to bring in foreign skilled workers if and when native "skilled labor" could not be obtained, and "personal and domestic servants" without any qualification. (There was no shortage of agricultural workers, so they were not then included.) Also exempted were actors and other performers, ministers of any religious denomination, persons belonging to any "recognized profession," and professors "for colleges and seminaries." And, in what may have been the most used loophole of all, the statute provided that:

> nothing in this act shall be construed as prohibiting any individual from assisting any member of his family to migrate from any foreign country to the United States, for the purpose of settlement here.[3]

Surviving immigrant letters testify, as do various posters and other documents in European museums and archives, that widespread recruiting continued after 1885. While it is impossible to quantify illegal contract labor, we do know that between 1892 and 1907 about a thousand persons a year were refused admittance because they were deemed to be contract laborers.

In 1891 Congress added "polygamists" to the excluded category — European Mormon converts, not Muslims, were the target — and refined the language about what kinds of crimes made a person ineligible to enter.[4] Also, the 1891 act for the first time made things that happened after immigration grounds for expulsion: anyone who became a public charge "within one year after his arrival" was deemed, retroactively, to have entered in violation of the law.

But more important, in 1891, Congress, increasingly concerned about immigration, established exclusive federal control over immigration, ending the long collaboration with state boards and commissions. It created the office of Superintendent of Immigration (salary $4,000, half that of a cabinet officer), and gave him twenty-seven subordinates, including one inspector for each of twenty-four inspection stations. Immigrants were to be examined by physicians in the Marine Hospital Service or by those under contract. Still under the supervision of the Secretary of the Treasury, the newly established Bureau of Immigration began to operate the immigrant receiving station at Ellis Island in 1892. Since, in this era and beyond, some 70 percent of all enumerated immigrants entered through New York, Ellis Island became synonymous with immigration, and many American families now "remember" that their immigrant ancestors came through Ellis long before the station existed. In 1895 the chief of the Bureau received the title of Commissioner General of

Immigration. Thus, a little more than a century after the founding of the republic, during which more than 16 million immigrants had entered the country, the United States finally had an immigration service.*

Although historians have long focused on the importance of the 1890s, they have not generally paid much attention to immigration. They should. Also a part of "the watershed of the 1890s,"[5] attitudes toward immigration underwent an important transition that was shaped by the contemporary economic crisis and the growing apprehension that many or most of the contemporary immigrants were of the wrong sort. To be sure, a similar rise of anti-immigrant feeling took place in the 1840s and 1850s, and another would occur in the late 1980s and early 1990s, but neither equaled the movement begun in the late nineteenth century, which sustained itself for four decades and culminated in the Immigration Act of 1924.

This end-of-century anti-immigrant feeling reflected the great increase in the number of immigrants, even though the relative incidence of immigrants in the population was remarkably constant. Between 1871 and 1901, 11.7 million persons are recorded as immigrating to the United States. That is considerably more than immigrated to the United States and the British North American colonies in the seventeenth, eighteenth, and the first seven decades of the nineteenth centuries combined, but fewer than the 12.9 million who came in the first fourteen years of the twentieth century. In addition, the United States Immigration Commission's massive 1911 report making a case for major restriction captured the existing prejudices that stigmatized the so-called new immigrants[†]—Southern and Eastern Europeans, largely Italians, Jews, and Poles—as follows:

> The old immigration movement was essentially one of permanence. The
> new immigration is very largely one of individuals, a considerable proportion
> of whom apparently have no intention of permanently changing their resi-

---

*It is not possible to pinpoint the growth in the 1890s. Many of the records either burned in the disastrous fire that destroyed the first Ellis Island immigration facility on June 14, 1897, or were deliberately discarded during the Eisenhower administration. But, once established, the service grew quickly: by the end of fiscal 1906 the Bureau had more than twelve hundred employees.

†The phrase was popularized by Francis Amasa Walker (1840–97), a director of the census and president of MIT for the last fifteen years of his life. Interestingly, it was the census of 1890, the same census that triggered Turner's frontier thesis essay, that suggested this position to him. See Walker, "Immigration," *Yale Review* I (1892): 131–35, and "Restriction of Immigration," *Atlantic Monthly* 67 (1896): 822–29.

dence, their only purpose in coming to America being to temporarily take advantage of the greater wages paid for industrial labor in this country.[6]

The distinction, long made by nativists, was given intellectual respectability by commentators such as Lord Bryce, who, in his *The American Commonwealth* (1888), could sneer that "new immigrants, politically incompetent" were easily corruptible.[7] Others used the term as part of a calculated program to change American immigration policy. The most effective such group was the Immigration Restriction League.[8]

The League, founded in 1894 by recent Harvard graduates, was never a mass organization. Today it would be called a right-wing think tank. It may have been the first organization that sought to influence and "educate" both elites and the wider public with a specific legislative agenda in mind. Led by Boston Brahmins and wannabe Brahmins who found "their" city more and more firmly in the grip of Irish and Irish American politicians, the League's goal, as described by historian Barbara Miller Solomon, was to save "the nation by preventing any further inroads on Anglo-Saxon America by strangers."[9]

The most important of the League's founders was Prescott F. Hall (1868–1921), who, after graduation from Harvard Law School, devoted most of his life to restricting immigration: even Barbara Miller Solomon is at a loss to explain the source of his "mania about aliens." He believed that the American people had to decide whether they wanted their country "to be peopled by British, German, and Scandinavian stock, historically free, energetic, progressive, or by Slav, Latin, and Asiatic races [this latter referred to Jews rather than to Chinese or Japanese] historically down-trodden, atavistic and stagnant."[10] In addition to Hall's lifelong association with the League, he became, around 1906, chairman of the Immigration Committee of the Eugenics Section of the American Breeders Association.[11]

While Hall and his associates favored a drastic restriction, for tactical reasons the League's first major lobbying efforts were for a literacy test. Three years before the League was formed, Henry Cabot Lodge (1850–1924), a Republican member of the House from Massachusetts who had earned a history Ph.D. from Harvard and who would become the League's chief legislative spokesman, introduced in 1891 an unsuccessful bill to institute a literacy test as a qualification for admission, thus setting off a legislative struggle that went on for twenty-six years.[12]

Subsequent Congresses saw other literacy-test bills introduced amid rising political concern about immigration. In 1892 the national platforms of both parties inveighed against pauper, criminal, and contract immigration, while in 1896 the GOP called for legislation "to exclude from entrance to the United States those who can neither read nor write."[13] In the lame-duck session of the 54th Congress, which met after William McKinley's victory over William Jennings Bryan in 1896, an immigration bill containing a literacy test passed by a vote of 205 to 35 in the House and 34 to 31 in the Senate. Grover Cleveland vetoed it on March 2, 1897, two days before leaving office, characterizing the bill as "illiberal, narrow, and un-American." He remarked further, in typical Bourbon Democrat fashion, that:

> It is infinitely more safe to admit a hundred thousand immigrants who, though unable to read and write, seek among us only a home and an opportunity to work than to admit one of those unruly agitators and enemies of governmental control who can not only read and write, but delights in arousing by unruly speech the illiterate and peacefully minded to discontent and tumult.[14]

Most contemporary observers expected, in view of the GOP platform and the election results, that a literacy test would be quickly enacted. A recent chronicler of immigration law, E. P. Hutchinson, found it "surprising" that a literacy test was not passed in 1897–98 "in view of the strong sentiment that had built up in and out of Congress for restrictive immigration" and the presence of "a favorably disposed resident of the White House."[15] What he and others have failed to note is not only that McKinley had very carefully not endorsed a literacy test: in his acceptance letter he noted the need for legislation "as will secure the United States from invasion by the debased and criminal classes of the Old World" and in his inaugural he had insisted only that "against all who come here to make war upon [American institutions and laws] our gates must be promptly and tightly closed."[16]

Lodge, promoted to the Senate in 1893, dropped a literacy-test bill into the hopper at the first opportunity in the short March session, but it was not acted on. The Senate did take it up in the regular session that began in December and passed a literacy-test bill in January 1898. But that bill was a somewhat weaker measure than either the one that Lodge had introduced or the one passed in the previous Congress. Those bills had each called for excluding "all persons physically capable and over 16 years of age who cannot read and write the English language or some other language." This was amended, over Lodge's protest, to "read *or* write." The Senate then passed the bill by a vote of 45 to 28. With this vote, a dramatic change from the narrow 34 to 31 margin the year before, the literacy test seemed certain to become law.

But on two separate occasions the House defeated motions to consider the bill.[17] It is clear that the Republican leadership, almost certainly with the agreement or encouragement of the White House, wanted to kill the bill without having to take a public stand against a measure that had been endorsed in the party platform and was probably supported by a majority of the voting public. This studied inaction clearly suited the manufacturing interests of the country who had contributed spectacularly to McKinley's campaign. They were intent on having abundant supplies of unskilled workers on hand: literacy was not a requirement for most of the jobs at the bottom levels of the manufacturing labor force.

Had Lodge's bill passed the House and been signed into law, the United States would have been the first nation to use an educational qualification to deter unwanted immigration. Instead, that "honor" went to the British colony of Natal in southern Africa, where in July 1897 the legislature, in order to inhibit immigration from India, passed Act 14 of that year, "To place certain Restriction on Immigration." The law required anyone entering Natal to have £25 and knowledge of a European language, with that knowledge to be judged by an immigration officer. This became known as the "Natal formula" and was used elsewhere in the empire. The most notorious example was in Australia where the "white Australia" policy of 1901 allowed the immigration officer to choose the language or languages in which any unwanted immigrant might be examined. The law was used to keep out non-whites and European radicals.[18]

Prior to its eventual enactment by Congress in 1917, a literacy test was nearly adopted in 1903 and 1907, recommended in the 1911 report of the United States Immigration Commission, passed by successive Congresses in 1913, 1915, and 1917, vetoed by Presidents William Howard Taft and Woodrow Wilson, with Wilson's 1917 veto being overridden. All of that activity occurred in the Progressive Era, when economic concerns were not as paramount as they were in the Gilded Age. As E. N. Saveth and others have demonstrated, most progressives were not particularly sympathetic to either labor or immigrants.[19] The successful bill and its consequences will be discussed later in this chapter, but I want to discuss the presidential vetoes here.

Taft's 1913 veto was essentially an economic argument, although it noted that illiteracy was usually due to a lack of opportunity rather than a lack of ability. Most of his message consisted of the written opinion of his Secretary of Commerce and Labor, Charles Nagel, whose thesis was—and is—all but a mantra for employers and their spokesmen: "the natives are not willing to do the work the aliens come over to do."[20]

President Woodrow Wilson's veto two years later no doubt surprised readers of his popular five-volume A History of the American People (1901–02). As Wilson's biographer Arthur S. Link noted, it was history written from a "conservative point of view."[21] President Wilson was not embarrassed by the tomes' neo-Confederate point of view about the Civil War and Reconstruction—he continued to propagate it as president, instituting segregation among federal employees and praising the film The Birth of a Nation, a glorification of the Ku Klux Klan, as "history written with lightning."

But his expressed opinions about recent immigrants and immigration proved a political liability. Professor Wilson had written of the

> multitudes of men of the lowest class from the south of Italy and men of the meaner sort out of Hungary and Poland, men out of the ranks where there was neither skill nor energy nor any initiative of quick intelligence; and they came in numbers which increased from year to year, as if the countries of the south of Europe were disburdening themselves of the more sordid and hapless elements of their population.[22]

As president, however, most of Wilson's actions on immigration, beginning with his appointment of Anthony Caminetti,* a second-generation Italian American who had been a militant anti-Japanese legislator in California, as Commissioner General of Immigration and his 1915 veto of the literacy test were of a pro-European immigrant nature. Without mentioning any economic argument, Wilson wrote that literacy tests

> are not tests of quality or of character or of personal fitness, but tests of opportunity. Those who come seeking opportunity are not to be admitted unless they have already had one of the chief of the opportunities they seek, the opportunity of education.† The object of such provisions is restriction, not selection.[23]

---

*Caminetti later distinguished himself as a radical-hunter in tandem with A. Mitchell Palmer and J. Edgar Hoover. See Michael Magliari, "Anthony Caminetti . . . , 1854–1923," ANB.
†The notion that any significant number of immigrants came seeking education for themselves, rather than for their children, is not to be taken seriously.

Cleveland, Taft, and Wilson, each in his own way and for his own reasons, harked back to a traditional view of immigration, a view that, by the turn of the century if not sooner, was probably no longer held by a majority of the American electorate. A number of factors—economic, political, and intellectual—surely contributed to the change in public opinion. Before considering 1917, a critical year in the history of immigration policy, it is appropriate to discuss the events that helped shape that opinion, not the least of which was the creation of the immigration service itself.

The passage of the 1891 Immigration Act and the opening the next year of the immigration station on Ellis Island mark the real beginning of an immigration service and one that grew rapidly. Unlike most federal bureaucracies, which serve as advocates for their constituencies—agriculture for farmers, labor for working people, the Children's Bureau for children—the immigration service has seen its primary mission as protecting America from the harmful effects of immigrants and immigration. No individual was more important in imprinting this attitude than McKinley's appointee, Terence V. Powderly, the second Commissioner General of Immigration, who served from 1897 to 1902.

Powderly, best known as the Grand Master Workman of the reformist Knights of Labor, is the only person to be a nationally known figure prior to being appointed as chief immigration bureaucrat. He got the job chiefly due to his vigorous campaigning for McKinley during the 1896 campaign. Powderly's tenure set a precedent: all subsequent Republican presidents until Nixon appointed labor leaders as Commissioners General of Immigration or Secretaries of Labor. Unlike Powderly, most were time-serving hacks.[24]

As head of the Knights and as Commissioner General Powderly's chief concern about immigration was contract labor, especially the contract labor of skilled workmen. Powderly believed, with some justification, that large numbers of skilled contract laborers were brought in as cabin passengers who were not normally examined and did not pass through special immigration facilities. At Powderly's instruction, his inspectors sometimes grilled middle-class cabin passengers: as a *New York Times* headline put it, in an age when middle-class citizens expected and usually received respect from officials, "Cabin Passengers Questioned Offensively by United States Commissioner General Powderly's Order."[25]

More significant, Powderly was a persistent advocate of all kinds of additional immigration restriction, and although he repeatedly denied any form of prejudice toward European immigrants, time and again he stated his belief that British, German, and Scandinavian immigrants made the best Americans. To be sure, such statements were often preceded or followed by positive remarks about some North Italians or Poles.[26] Like most labor leaders of the period, he was implacably hostile to all Asian immigrants. His Democratic predecessor, Herman Stump (1837–1917), had reported, for fiscal 1897, that:

> [T]he number of Japanese to arrive during the fiscal year was 1,296, as compared with 1,110 for the preceding year. These immigrants were reported to be intelligent, thrifty, possessed of small sums of money, and most of them desired to engage in agricultural pursuits.[27]

Three years later, when exactly the same kinds of Japanese were entering, Powderly complained of

> the large increase in Japanese immigration . . . [and argued that], unless checked, it will produce serious trouble in the Pacific States, where such aliens are used as cheap laborers to take the place of white workingmen.[28]

Many, if not most, of the 12,000 Japanese immigrants that year came from newly annexed Hawaii, not Japan, and their profile was similar to that described by Stump. Few of them were in competition with the native-born white workingmen whom Powderly saw as his constituency, as almost all of the Japanese toiled in agriculture, on railroad construction and work gangs, and in domestic service.

Powderly, and most of his immediate successors, used their annual reports as another opportunity to argue for greater immigration restriction. In his 1900 report he cited immigrant literacy even though it was not a requirement of the law, reporting that 93,576 immigrants had been admitted who could neither read nor write, and an additional 2,097 who could read but not write. This amounted to just over a fifth—21.3 percent—of the immigrants admitted that year. Powderly's immediate successor, Frank P. Sargent, who served from 1902 to 1908, provided a whole laundry list of proposed "reforms." In addition to a literacy test, which was de rigueur for immigration officials, he wanted to keep out "moral perverts," the disabled, and all immigrants traveling alone under seventeen or over sixty years of age unless they had relatives in the United States able to provide for them.

Further, he was convinced that both land borders needed to be more heavily guarded.* Sargent also began an almost unbroken tradition of asking for more staff and complaining about increasing immigration from Mexico. Citing the concentration of immigrants in states like New York and Pennsylvania as a cause of their failure to assimilate, he expressed the hope that, somehow, immigrants could be shunted to states such as Arkansas and Mississippi.[29]

To be sure, everyone in the immigration service wasn't anti-immigrant. Fiorello La Guardia, the most famous person ever to work at Ellis Island— he was an interpreter there between 1907 and 1910—persistently championed immigrants, then and later. In a memoir written four decades later, he remembered the crowded conditions and the heartbreak caused by rejection at the very door to the promised land. Unwittingly, he contributed to the commonly held notion that great numbers of people were rejected in those years of high immigration. "Several hundred immigrants daily," he wrote, "were found to be suffering from trachoma, and their exclusion was mandatory." If several hundred was as many as three hundred, that would mean 110,000 yearly exclusions just at Ellis Island for trachoma alone. Yet, in the four years of La Guardia's employment, rejections at all points of entry from all causes totaled 13,000, 11,000, 10,000, and 24,000.[30]

One of the reasons for the failure of the literacy test to be enacted was the return of confidence with the end of the depression of the 1890s— "Every barn in Kansas," Ray Stannard Baker reported from the former hotbed of Populism and Bryanism, "has a fresh coat of paint"—and the triumph in the Spanish-American War. In the course of the latter the United States acquired an overseas empire. Three parts of that empire—Hawaii, Puerto Rico, and the Philippines—had large populations of people of color. Each of them was treated quite differently as far as citizenship, and thus immigration, was concerned.[31]

A national debate about whether the Constitution and the Bill of Rights would prevail in the conquered territory attended the birth of America's overseas empire. A popular form of the question was, "Does the Constitution follow the flag?" In language often punctuated by racist rhetoric[†] the

---

*There was no formal Border Patrol until 1924.

†In a case involving the legality of a tariff on goods from Puerto Rico, the Court showed that it, too, was in the grip of the "Anglo-Saxon complex," opining *in dicta* that "in overseas possessions inhabited by alien races, differing from us in religion, customs, laws, methods of taxation, and modes of thought, the administering of government and justice, according to Anglo-Saxon principles, may for a time, be impossible . . ." *Downes v. Bidwell* at 182 U.S. 287.

Supreme Court ruled that it did not in a series of fourteen separate decisions, usually referred to as the *Insular Cases*, handed down between 1901 and 1904. While a cynic could remark that whether or not the Constitution followed the flag the Supreme Court followed the election returns, more restrained commentators have pointed out that, while the justices' opinions were far from intellectually consistent they do show that, as a group, they wanted to give the executive and Congress wide discretion in foreign affairs, a stance not unfamiliar to twenty-first-century court watchers.[32]

The citizenship of the inhabitants of America's new acquisitions was governed by statute. Hawaii, for example, was annexed in 1898 by joint resolution of Congress—an 1897 treaty of annexation could not get approval of two-thirds of the Senate—and was treated, in law, as any other American territory.[33] The so-called Organic Act of 1900 declared that "all persons who were citizens of the Republic of Hawaii on August twelfth, eighteen hundred and ninety eight, are hereby declared to be citizens of the United States and citizens of the Territory of Hawaii."[34] Thus, for example, Hawaii's strict contract labor laws no longer applied and the United States' Chinese Exclusion acts did. At the time of annexation more than half of the islands' population was Japanese, and about a quarter was Chinese: few were citizens of Hawaii, but thousands of them, mostly Japanese, were enabled to migrate farther east to California. In addition, of course, thanks to the Fourteenth Amendment, every person born in Hawaii after annexation was a birthright citizen. Thus the United States would soon have tens of thousands of citizens of Asian ancestry.

This unintended consequence of annexation soon became clear to Congress, which repeatedly refused to admit Hawaii as a state. The territorial legislature began its petitions to Congress for statehood in 1903, the first of at least eighteen such efforts, and in 1919 the first of many bills to admit Hawaii failed to pass Congress. Hawaii more than met the normal requirements for statehood—size of population, system of government, etc.—but Congress could not stomach the idea of a state with a non-white majority. As Ernest H. Gruening, who served as director of the Division of Territories and Island Possessions in the Interior Department from 1934 to 1939, remembered, Representative John E. Rankin (D-MS) turned to him during a 1937 congressional hearing in Honolulu and said, "Mah Gawd, if we give them folks statehood we're lahkley to have a senator called Moto."*[35] Hawaii's admission was delayed until 1959.

---

*Rankin's reference was to a series of films based on the character Mr. Moto, a Japanese detective/

The Philippines and Puerto Rico were ceded to the United States by Spain on December 10, 1898, in the Treaty of Paris, which formally ended the Spanish-American War. Puerto Rico's status was initially governed by the Foraker Act of 1900. It established that, except for persons who chose to preserve their allegiance to Spain, Puerto Ricans were citizens of Puerto Rico and "entitled to the protection of the United States."[36] They were thus not United States citizens, but nationals. A similar status was established for Filipinos. By the time Woodrow Wilson became president in 1913, a consensus was emerging that the Philippines and Puerto Rico should be treated differently. The Jones Act of 1916 committed the United States to granting independence to the Philippines at some future but unspecified date. Thus Filipinos remained, for a time, American nationals. The next year Puerto Ricans were made American citizens; those who wished to maintain Puerto Rican or any other citizenship had to file an affidavit to do so.[37] In terms of citizenship, what was extended to Puerto Rico in 1917 was applied to the Virgin Islands in 1917, to Guam in 1950, and to the Northern Mariana Islands in 1976. Conversely, the Philippine example was followed in the case of American Samoa, whose residents remain American nationals, but without the promise of independence.[38] The immigration implications of the Filipinos' status as nationals will be discussed later.

Between 1903 and 1917 the United States made a succession of accretional changes in immigration administration, naturalization procedures and law, and immigration policy. These actions culminated in the immigration act of 1917, which codified all previous law and added the much debated literacy test, the first general restriction that applied to all immigrants.

The administrative changes first transferred the Bureau of Immigration from the Treasury to the newly created Department of Commerce and Labor (1903), expanded the functions of the Bureau into a Bureau of Immigration and Naturalization (1906), and moved the Bureau to the Department of Labor when the latter was separated from Commerce and divided it into separate Bureaus of Immigration and Naturalization, each with its own commissioner (1913).[39]

---

secret agent, created by the novelist John P. Marquand. Typically, Hollywood cast a Caucasian actor in the part, the Hungarian-born Peter Lorre.

A 1906 statute regularized the previously haphazard naturalization procedures, providing that "no alien may be naturalized or admitted as a citizen of the United States who cannot speak the English language" and
barred anarchists and polygamists from naturalization.[40] The changes in
immigration law and policy were not only much more numerous, but they
also involved both Congress and the president. Reacting to the assassination of President McKinley by a native-born American anarchist with the
"foreign-sounding" name Czolgosz, Congress for the first time tried to
monitor the opinions of immigrants by barring "anarchists, or persons who
believe in or advocate the overthrow by force or violence the government of
the United States or of all government or of all forms of law, or the assassination of public officials" and barred the naturalization of any such
person.[41]

Growing concern over Japanese immigration on the West Coast triggered a mini–international crisis that involved a president, Theodore Roosevelt, in an immigration matter to an unprecedented degree. Had Japan
been weak, as China then was, Roosevelt would not have bothered and
some kind of Japanese exclusion on the Chinese model, or worse, would
surely have been enacted in the first decade of the century. But Japan was
a rising power, having defeated Russia in the Russo-Japanese War of
1904–05. So, in 1906, it was diplomacy and not primarily legislation that
dealt with the crisis set off by the actions of the San Francisco School Board
and the attempted actions by the California legislature.

Although there had been a sprinkling of Japanese immigration in the
post–Civil War decades, there were, as late as 1890, a mere 2,000 Japanese in the continental United States, a little more than half of them in
California. By 1900 there were nearly 25,000 — 10,000 in California —
many of them secondary migrants from Hawaii. In the next ten years the
national total grew to nearly 75,000, with some 40,000 in California. There
had been flurries of anti-Japanese activity and nonfatal violence, most of
it by workingmen, in San Francisco and Fresno in the early 1890s, but
after 1900 a powerful anti-Japanese movement developed all along the
Pacific Coast.

San Francisco was the epicenter of the movement, which stretched
from Vancouver, British Columbia, to San Diego. The first anti-Japanese
mass meeting was held in San Francisco in May 1900, and later that year the
national Populist Party added an anti-Japanese plank to its platform and the

American Federation of Labor urged Congress to extend to Japanese the existing bars against Chinese laborers. In February 1905, in the midst of the Russo-Japanese War, the most prestigious newspaper in California, the *San Francisco Chronicle*, launched a crusade against Japanese immigrants. The state legislature quickly followed with a March resolution asking Congress to "limit and diminish" further Japanese immigration, and in May delegates from sixty-seven organizations, mostly associated with labor unions, formed the Asiatic Exclusion League. In San Francisco Japanese restaurants and other businesses were boycotted, picketed, and vandalized. By late summer and early fall of 1906 unprovoked assaults against Japanese pedestrians were frequent in San Francisco and not unknown elsewhere.

The worst single anti-Asian violence of this era north of Mexico* occurred in Vancouver, British Columbia, at a time of heightened racial tension in the Pacific Northwest. On September 7, 1907, a Saturday night, a large anti-Japanese mass meeting in Vancouver developed into a full-fledged riot. A mob of at least 1,000 persons invaded and looted Chinatown without opposition and then turned to Nihonmachi, the Japanese quarter centered on Powell Street. Here it met serious resistance from Japanese, who used fists, sticks, rocks, and knives in a successful defense. No firearms were involved and the injuries on each side were slight, and eventually the Canadian government paid property damages to Japanese and Chinese claimants.

Nothing so violent happened in the United States. Rather, a year before the Vancouver riot, the San Francisco School Board on October 6, 1906, ordered all Japanese students in its public schools to attend the segregated school for Chinese that had been operating in Chinatown since 1885. The move was little noticed outside of the Bay Area until garbled versions of the order appeared in Tokyo newspapers, causing a sensation.

In Washington, Theodore Roosevelt was furious. Although the federal government had made no public response to the California legislature's previous anti-Japanese resolutions, the president, more than a year before the school board's action, had privately instructed his minister in Tokyo to inform the Japanese government that "the American government and the American

---

*Mexico had a vicious anti-Chinese movement. In one night in 1911, revolutionary soldiers and a mob killed 303 unarmed Chinese men, women, and children in the city of Torreón. See Leo M. Dambourges Jacques, "The Chinese Massacre in Torreón (Coahuila) in 1911," *Arizona and the West* 16 (1974):233–46.

people" had no sympathy with the anti-Japanese agitation and that "while I am President" Japanese would be treated "exactly like . . . other civilized peoples."[42] Similarly, in a little-noted passage of his 1905 annual message to Congress, after some routine identification of unworthy and unwelcome immigrant groups, he seemed to embrace the old pro-immigrant consensus.

> It is unwise to depart from the old American tradition and to discriminate for or against any man who desires to come here and become a citizen, save on the ground of that man's fitness for citizenship . . . We cannot afford to consider whether he is Catholic or Protestant, Jew or Gentile; whether he is Englishman or Irishman, Frenchman or German, Japanese, Italian, Scandinavian, Slav, or Magyar.

In contrast to his placing the Japanese on his A-list, Roosevelt then devoted a paragraph to justifying continued exclusion of Chinese labor, claiming—and perhaps believing—that even the Chinese government did not want them to come.[43]

In his next annual message, a little more than a month after the school board news broke, Roosevelt focused on the Japanese in a way that was impossible to ignore. After a platitudinous paragraph about treating all immigrants and nations fairly—nothing about Chinese here—the president continued:

> I am prompted to say this by the attitude of hostility assumed here and there toward the Japanese in this country. This hostility is sporadic and is limited to a very few places. Nevertheless it is most discreditable to us as a people, and it may be filled with the gravest consequences to the nation.

After more platitudes and soft-soap about a half-century of friendly relations and the outrageous claim that the "overwhelming mass of our people cherish a lively regard and respect for the people of Japan" Roosevelt got down to business.

> But here and there a most unworthy feeling has manifested itself toward the Japanese [such as] shutting them out of the common schools of San Francisco [and] mutterings against them in one or two other places, because of their efficiency as workers. To shut them out from the public schools is a wicked absurdity . . . I recommend to the Congress that an act be past [sic]*

*Widely read and highly intellectual TR was an abominable speller and insisted upon certain simplified spellings.

specifically providing for the naturalization of Japanese who come here intending to become American citizens.

He complained further that the federal government could not properly protect the rights of aliens and asked for unspecified legislation to enable it to do so. To emphasize the seriousness of the matter in his eyes he warned that it was preposterous that

> the mob of a single city may at any time perform acts of lawless violence which would plunge us into war . . . It is unthinkable that we should continue a policy under which a given locality may be allowed to commit a crime against a friendly nation.[44]

The proposal that the right of naturalization be granted to Japanese was a one-time event, not to be repeated by an American president until Truman seriously proposed it in 1949. Although Roosevelt had read the pertinent passage to the Japanese Ambassador before delivering the message, just two months after the message, when Japanese negotiators suggested a trade— Tokyo would accept a cutoff of immigration if Washington would grant naturalization for those already in the United States—Secretary of State Elihu Root instructed the American side that this was not an option because "no statute could be passed or treaty ratified" which included naturalization.[45]

Shortly after the school board news broke, Roosevelt sent Victor H. Metcalf, the only Californian in the cabinet, to investigate. Born in upstate New York and educated at Yale, Metcalf (1853–1936) had practiced law in Oakland, California, since 1879. A three-term Republican congressman before entering the cabinet as Secretary of Commerce and Labor in 1904, Metcalf had evinced little sympathy with the anti-Japanese agitation. Back in May 1905 he had told reporters that he was not concerned about Japanese immigration and attributed the problem to white men who were not willing to do the work in the fruit districts.[46] In mid-December 1906, Metcalf's careful report was transmitted to Congress by the White House. Apart from the recommendation that strict age/grade limits be set—there had been complaints that some nearly grown men were in lower classes with little white girls—Metcalf's report found the complaints unjustified and the segregation policy—which was never put into effect—reprehensible.

> All the considerations which may move a people, every consideration of duty in the consideration of our treaty obligations, every consideration of more or less close friendship with the Empire of Japan, would unite in demanding, it

seems to me, of the United States Government and all of its people, the fullest protection and the highest consideration for the subjects of Japan.[47]

Metcalf's report was just what Roosevelt wanted, and in further negotiations with San Francisco officials, the California congressional delegation, and the Republican governor in Sacramento, the school board rescinded its segregation order and Roosevelt promised federal action tantamount to exclusion. Thus school segregation was removed permanently from the roster of issues between Japan and the United States. Few commentators note that, in a few rural school districts around Sacramento, where Japanese pupils outnumbered whites, segregated schools existed unchallenged by both Japan and the United States. Since no one made an issue of them, Tokyo, which was well informed about the conditions of Japanese American life, simply turned a blind eye.

The school issue settled, Roosevelt and Root now had to deliver what they had promised the Californians without offending Japan. Complicated but low-key negotiations resulted in what is called the Gentlemen's Agreement, not actually a single document but a series of six notes exchanged between the two countries in late 1907 and early 1908.[48]*

Only the initial piece of the puzzle wound up on the statute books. With the prior agreement of Tokyo, Root himself drafted a clause that was inserted into the conveniently pending immigration act of 1907. It gave the president authority to bar entry to the United States of any alien carrying a passport valid for any place other than the continental United States. While seemingly universal in application, it was aimed at alien Japanese in Hawaii, many of whom had such passports valid only for Hawaii.[49]

The essence of the agreement was that Japan would not issue passports good for the continental United States to laborers, skilled or unskilled, but that passports could be issued to "laborers who had already been in America and the parents, wives and children of laborers already resident there." The agreement, which was scrupulously observed by both sides for sixteen years, had serious unintended consequences. What neither side apparently realized was that large numbers of single Japanese men resident in the United States and Hawaii would bring over wives, many of them so-called "picture brides," women married by proxy to men they had never

---

*Foolishly the State Department suppressed these documents until 1939, although normal publication of the documents for those years took place in 1910 and 1912. This secrecy was a factor in the unilateral abrogation of the Gentlemen's Agreement by Congress in 1924.

seen, a procedure legal in Japanese law. These newly married couples, not surprisingly, began to produce children born on American soil and thus U.S. citizens. After the Chinese exclusion acts, total Chinese American population shrank for more than four decades. After the Gentlemen's Agreement, Japanese American population grew rapidly. Intended by both sides as a device to ease tensions, the Gentlemen's Agreement managed to exacerbate them. It was, however, vital for the nascent Japanese American community.

Meanwhile the course of piecemeal immigration restriction continued even as legal immigration hit its all-time high: between 1905 and 1914 almost 9.9 million immigrants were enumerated entering the United States, more than in any ten-year period before or since. The act of 1907—which contained Root's handiwork—codified existing immigration law, increased the head tax to four dollars, and, most significantly, authorized what became the United States Immigration Commission, sometimes known as the Dillingham Commission, for its chair and instigator, Senator William P. Dillingham. The president, the Speaker of the House, and the president pro tem of the Senate each appointed three of its nine members. It was the first large-scale U.S. government study of immigration. In existence between 1907 and 1910, the Commission published its massive report in forty-one volumes in 1911. While highly useful to scholars, the data gathered by the Commission was used—and misused—to substantiate its prejudged conclusion, namely that the immigrants then coming to America, chiefly from Eastern and Southern Europe, were inferior in education, ability, and genetic makeup to most of those who had come previously. Therefore, in addition to the literacy test it recommended that a new and generally restrictive and ethnically discriminating immigration policy be instituted: "the limitation of each [race] arriving each year to a certain percentage of that race arriving during a given period of years." The year before World War I broke out in Europe, Dillingham introduced a plan to limit immigration by establishing national quotas that would set maxima, not provide minima. Not acted upon in 1913, the report became a major impetus to immigration restrictions occurring in 1917, 1921, and 1924.[50]

The war in Europe interrupted normal migration streams. During fiscal 1916 the total number of immigrants dropped below 300,000, fewer than half of them from Europe. Since more than 125,000 had left the country during the year, net immigration was just over 150,000. It had been 900,000 in the last pre-war year. Although logic might suggest that immigration be left alone under the circumstances, Congress, reflecting the nation, was in a hyper-nationalistic mood in February 1917. When Woodrow Wilson again vetoed the literacy-test provision, Congress overrode him with votes to spare: 287–106 in the House and 62–19 in the Senate. That a popular president with majorities in both houses could be so little regarded by Congress just three months after his reelection is testimony to the strength of anti-immigrant feeling.

The law enacted in 1917 was the first significant general restriction of immigration ever passed. All future immigrants "over sixteen years of age, capable of reading" would have to be literate, although, in the case of family immigration, if the husband were literate the wife need not be. In addition, mothers, grandparents, widowed or unmarried daughters of a literate male alien, or one already living here, need not be literate. The 1917 version of the test law defined literacy as being able to read any recognized language including Hebrew and Yiddish. (Extreme nativists wanted an English-only law, but Congress never seriously considered that option.) The law also created an "Asiatic barred zone." By using degrees of latitude and longitude, South and Southeast Asians were added to the list of those denied entry, but peoples of the Russian Far East and Asians from Persia (Iran) west were admissible if otherwise qualified. At the time the major practical effect was to cut off immigration from India. The law also expanded, by adding criteria, the kinds of mental, physical, and moral "defects" that were grounds for exclusion, made the existing antiradical provisions more severe, and raised the head tax to $8.[51]

Despite the more than two decades of struggle it engendered, the literacy test, when finally enacted, had little effect. During the last year in which it was the major statutory bar to immigration (July 1920–June 1921) more than 800,000 immigrants entered the country and 250,000 returned home.* About 1.5 percent of the number of all entrants, nearly 14,000 persons, were excluded or deported on one ground or another. Only a tenth of these, a mere 1,450 persons, were kept out by the much heralded literacy test. Rising standards of education in Europe had pulled most of the teeth the law might once have had. Despite its eventual uselessness as a deterrent, the passage of the 1917 act was an important nodal point in the movement to restrict immigration. It showed the restrictionists that they could

---

*The 800,000 figure would not be reached again until 1989.

command majority support and the law's failure to restrict even became an added argument that more needed to be done.

As noted, the 1917 act strengthened the antiradical provisions of immigrant law. It also made, for the first time, immoral or criminal behavior or espousal of certain kinds of radicalism by immigrants within five years *after* they came to America grounds for deportation. In addition, the time limit for retroactive deportation under the "LPC clause" was extended from three to five years. The numbers of persons deported was not, in this era, a significant percentage of immigrants—only in 1926 were as many as 10,000 persons deported—but the regularly expressed desire of congressional majorities to expel persons thought undesirable was symbolic of the country's growing nativist propensities.

The drive toward preparedness and war in 1917 fueled nationalistic xenophobia, and the wartime disregard for civil liberties was flagrant. The post-war reaction to the Bolshevik Revolution, increased domestic radicalism, and the disillusionment engendered by the obvious failure of certain American war aims helped push anti-immigrant sentiment to perhaps its highest peaks in American history. Added to this, there was the short but severe post-war depression: for all of 1921 recorded unemployment averaged almost 12 percent of the labor force. Many of the unemployed were ex-servicemen, and the image of a stream of immigrants taking jobs from former doughboys was used by nativists to whip up further anti-immigrant hysteria.

We now know that immigration after WW I did not reach pre-war levels, but the impression at the time was that not only were vast numbers of foreigners flooding the land but that innumerable hordes of ignorant, penniless Europeans were about to descend upon America. These and their fears fueled the post-war Red Scare, what Assistant Secretary of Labor Louis F. Post called the "deportations delirium of 1920," helping to create the preconditions for the broader restrictionist movement to come.[52]

Some, but by no means all, of the restrictionists were overtly anti-Semitic, and the unrelated facts that many of the deported radicals were Jewish and that more than 100,000 Jews from Central and Eastern Europe had entered during 1920 was used as a special bugaboo. Albert Johnson, a Republican representative from Hoquiam, Washington, who chaired the House Committee on Immigration, used excerpts from American consular reports to argue that the country was in danger of being swamped by "ab-

normally twisted" and "unassimilable" Jews, "filthy, un-American* and often dangerous in their habits."[53] During the lame-duck session of Congress
following the 1920 election of Warren Harding, Johnson's committee formally proposed a two-year suspension of all immigration to give the lawmakers time to recast the immigration laws. Within one week the full
House overwhelmingly adopted the suspension idea, 296–42, but cut it to
fourteen months. The Senate was not so easily stampeded. In addition, one
of its more influential members, William P. Dillingham, was still in the
Senate (he would die in 1923). Dillingham reintroduced his quota plan
and steered it quickly through the Senate.

Although clearly aimed at reducing immigration from Eastern and
Southern Europe, Dillingham's plan contained elements of fairness and
equity that would later be lost. His bill would neither affect the existing bars
against Asians nor apply to immigrants from the Western Hemisphere.
There would be limits for Europeans that would allow the migration of only
5 percent of the number of foreign-born from each country that had been
listed in the 1910 census. This would have produced a maximum annual
quota of 600,000 persons, although the assumption was that many of the
quota spaces—some of those allocated to the British Isles, for example—
would not be used. Dillingham's proposal originally gave the Secretary of
Labor discretion to admit aliens in excess of quota if it was considered necessary for humanitarian purposes, but that was removed by amendment in
the Senate.† Like the Johnson bill for which it was a substitute, it was an
emergency measure of one year's duration.[54]

Although there were complaints from hard-core restrictionists that the
bill was too generous, it passed the Senate easily. The House reluctantly accepted the quota principle, but lowered the annual percentage to 3 percent, reducing the number of annual quota spaces to some 350,000,
although the assumption that many of them would not be used still applied.
Aliens under the age of eighteen who were children of U.S. citizens were
exempt from quota limitation and other close relatives of citizens or resident aliens who had filed for citizenship papers received preference within

---

*It is instructive to note how, in the course of a quarter-century, the appellative "un-American"
changed from being used to describe the opponents of immigration to describing the immigrants
themselves.
†Had such a clause been on the books in the 1930s, when Frances Perkins was Secretary of Labor,
the sordid story of American refugee policy would surely have been different. The amendment was
made by Ellison D. (Cotton Ed) Smith of South Carolina.

the quotas. Intellectuals, artists, and members of learned professions received special status: if there were quota spaces, they used them, but if there were not they could enter anyway. The Senate agreed to the House reduction and the measure went to President Wilson just before he left office. Wilson killed it with a pocket veto, but only seventy-six days later during the special session of the new Congress called by Harding, a quite similar measure became law. The only change of substance was a provision adding to those exempt from numerical restriction persons who were seeking admission solely because of religious persecution, but they had to meet all other requirements. The bill was so uncontroversial that it went through the House without recorded vote and passed the Senate by 78–1. The 1921 act was a benchmark in immigration restriction: it marked the first time that a numerical cap had been legislated.

In May 1922, the one-year measure was extended for two additional years.[55] This set the stage for a major debate in the spring of 1924, just months before the presidential election. The act that marked the greatest triumph of nativism was passed in May 1924, before the nominating conventions. The GOP platform endorsed the new law; the Democrats, badly divided, could only reiterate their habitual opposition to "Asiatic immigration." In 1928, however, the party that ran "the hero of the cities," Al Smith, would resolve that "laws which limit immigration must be preserved in full force and effect."[56]

The importance of the 1924 act is hard to overemphasize. I have never seen an accurate description of it in a general American history textbook, although it is discussed in almost all of them.[57] To understand it one must be aware of the historical context and of the issues that were contested. In 1924 it was a foregone conclusion that there would be a permanent restriction of immigration. Although the short-lived post-war depression was over, fears about job-stealing and the lowering of the standard of living by immigrants willing to work cheap were still shaping the national mood. The nation was also gripped by xenophobia and a rejection of Europe. Most important, perhaps, was the beleaguered feeling of so many old-stock Protestant Americans. Immigrants and their non-Protestant cultures, they felt, represented a serious and sustained challenge to American values. The struggles in the 1920s between the old America and the new, struggles over prohibition, over immigration, and over modernity itself, have led John Higham to dub the decade the "tribal twenties."[58] Many who then spoke for the majority were keenly aware of the potential influence of the immigrants and their children, who, in 1920, already comprised more than a third of the total population and whose incidence in the electorate was growing. No other issue so completely encapsulated the spirit of the decade as immigration restriction did.

The 1920s was also the first decade in which women possessed the vote and the Cable Act, or Married Woman's Act, of 1922 ended the automatic granting and revoking of women's citizenship because of their marital status. Prior to 1922 an alien woman who married a citizen or whose husband became naturalized automatically became an American citizen. Conversely, any female citizen, native-born or naturalized, who married an alien was divested of her citizenship. This automatic granting and divestment of citizenship ended as Congress declared that "the right of any woman to become a naturalized citizen of the United States shall not be denied or abridged because of her sex or because she is a married woman." However, despite the principle cited above, the law also provided that "any woman citizen who marries an alien ineligible to citizenship"—in other words an Asian of any nationality—"shall cease to be a citizen of the United States." Of course, a male citizen could marry an alien female Asian with no legal disability: no federal law ever penalized male citizens for their marriages. The section denaturalizing some Asian American women was repealed in 1930: its most numerous victims had been young Japanese American women citizens who married older Japanese American aliens.[59]

The general debate on immigration law in 1924 was never a question of whether immigration should be restricted further, but rather, how severely and in what additional ways immigration should be curtailed, and which kinds of immigrants should be allowed to enter. Prior to 1924 dislocations caused by WW I and the limitations from 1921 on had already changed the patterns of immigration significantly, as Table 2.1 shows. European immigration, which had run at about 87 percent of all immigration in the five years immediately before the war, ran at about 64 percent of all immigration in the five years after. Nonquota immigration from the Western Hemisphere, almost all of it from Canada and Mexico, increased absolutely and relatively. Between 1910 and 1914 the 500,000 New World immigrants represented about one-tenth of all immigrants. About two-thirds of them were from Canada, one-sixth from Mexico and another sixth from the rest of the hemisphere. During 1920–24, the 800,000 New World immigrants made up three-eighths of all immigrants. Canadians were three-fifths of this total, Mexicans almost three-tenths, while the rest of the hemisphere provided only an eleventh.

TABLE 2.1
IMMIGRATION FROM THE NEW WORLD,
1910–14 AND 1920–24

Year	Total Immigration	New World	%	Canada	Mexico
1910	1,041,570	89,534	8.6	56,555	18,691
1911	878,587	94,364	10.7	56,830	19,889
1912	838,172	95,926	11.4	55,990	23,238
1913	1,197,892	103,907	8.7	73,802	11,926
1914	1,218,480	122,695	10.1	86,139	14,614
—	—	—	—	—	—
1920	430,001	162,666	37.8	90,025	52,316
1921	805,228	124,118	15.4	72,317	30,758
1922	309,556	77,448	25.0	46,810	19,551
1923	522,919	199,972	38.2	117,011	63,768
1924	706,896	318,855	45.1	200,690	89,336

Source: U.S. Department of Commerce, *Historical Statistics of the United States*, Series C 88–144, Washington: GPO, 1957.

Four major issues were fought out in the 1924 debate. First, should the quota system be based on the newly available 1920 census and what percentage should apply; second, should the New World remain outside of the quota system; third, should the special arrangement about Japanese immigration, the Gentlemen's Agreement, be allowed to stand; and fourth, what kind of a "permanent" system of immigration control should be established. The first three issues were of immediate relevance. Moderate restrictionists wanted to make the 1921 law permanent, move the baseline to the latest available census, keep the Western Hemisphere quota-free, and either continue the Gentlemen's Agreement or give Japan a quota. The severe restrictionists wanted a nonvariable and smaller quota, to extend the quota to the New World, and to bar Japanese along with other Asians. The latter persuasion, as we shall see, won the first and third arguments but lost the second. Other issues, some of them quite significant, were largely ignored in the congressional debates. As would often be the case with immigration legislation, Congress did not fully understand the implications of the legislation it passed.

The baseline of the quota system was pushed back to the census of 1890 and the percentage was lowered from 3 to 2 percent. The reasons for this were frankly stated: from the restrictionists' point of view, too many Eastern and Southern Europeans were coming in under the existing law and updating to the 1920 census would have let in even more. Albert Johnson, leader of the extreme restrictionist forces in the House, calculated that, instead of the 42,000 Italian and 31,000 Polish annual quota spaces that would result if the 1921 law were updated, a 2 percent quota based on the 1890 census—some called it the "Anglo-Saxon census" as it preceded the era of heaviest immigration from eastern and southern Europe—would cut the numbers to 4,000 Italians and 6,000 Poles. In terms of total numbers, 2 percent of the 1920 foreign-born white population would have produced an annual quota of some 270,000; the adopted 1890 base provided a quota of some 180,000.

No numerical limitation was placed on Western Hemisphere immigration, partly because many Southwestern and Western legislators insisted that their regions needed Mexican agricultural labor. Congress did, however, narrow the Western Hemisphere exemption. Whereas the existing law exempted from quota limitation anyone who had lived for five years anyplace in the hemisphere, the 1924 law exempted only persons born in its independent nations, plus Canada, Newfoundland, and the Canal Zone.[60] Persons born in other European colonies in the New World—most of the Caribbean islands—were admissible as quota immigrants charged to the quota of the mother country. Those removed from the quota-free category were almost all black.

The Senate seemed to be ready to insist on some kind of special arrangement for the Japanese, primarily because of Japan's growing economic and military importance. Either the Gentlemen's Agreement could be continued, or, conversely, Japan could be given a quota. Under the Gentlemen's Agreement an average of some 7,700 Japanese, mostly women, had been entering annually since 1920, while under the quota system Japan would have been entitled to a quota of 100 annually. But Senator Henry Cabot Lodge (R-MA), in the last major act of a long political career, stampeded the Senate into believing that a note from the Japanese Ambassador to Washington, stating that "grave consequences" would result if the Gentlemen's Agreement were unilaterally abrogated, was a threat to the United States. The agreement was voided and the proud Japanese were shut out under the formula that no "alien ineligible to citizenship" could enter the United States as an immigrant. It was safe to use this formula as the Supreme Court in the 1922 case of Ozawa v. U.S. had ruled that the 1870 statute restricting naturalization to "white persons and persons of

African descent" was constitutional and that Japanese were not "white persons."[61]

In addition to the Western Hemisphere natives noted above, nonquota immigrants in the 1924 law included: wives and unmarried children of United States citizens under eighteen years of age (husbands of United States citizens were added only in 1928, and then only if the marriage had taken place before June 1, 1928); previously admitted immigrants returning from a visit abroad; any minister of any religious denomination or professor of a college, academy, seminary, or university and his wife (but not husband) and unmarried children under eighteen; bona fide students; and women who had previously lost their citizenship by marriage or from the loss of citizenship by their husbands. And finally, the long-established rights of Chinese "treaty merchants" and their families to domicile within the United States were reaffirmed.[62]

For the first time, visas and photographs were required of all immigrants, which involved the consular service of the Department of State directly in the regulation of immigration. There was a $9 charge for visas, which, added to the $9 head tax, meant an outlay of $18 to enter. While this sum was hardly a major deterrent to immigrants who were paying for an Atlantic passage, it was significant to Mexican immigrants, who were long used to casually crossing and recrossing the border. The act also required reentry permits, at $3 each, for aliens leaving the country and wishing to return, which also encouraged Mexicans to come and go informally.

The statutory requirement of a visa, which had to be obtained at an American consulate, was felt to be most important by restrictionists. It was, in their terminology, a way of controlling immigration at the source and it gave considerable discretionary authority to individual consular officials. There is no thorough study of how the consular service actually regulated the issuance of visas, but it is quite clear that officials such as Wilber J. Carr, who directed the consular service from 1909 to 1937, saw their roles to be gatekeepers, and that Carr and many of his subordinates were nativists.[63] There is also a great deal of anecdotal evidence that individual consuls often used their authority to impose their own agendas. George Messersmith, who was Consul-General in Antwerp in 1925, was sure that what America needed was immigrants who were "not only imbued with the idea of bettering [their] own condition, but also with the determination to overcome obstacles" like the first settlers of America. In the same year, an obscure American consul in Plymouth, England, concerned that some husbands were using emigration as a way of avoiding family responsibilities, instituted a policy of requiring the wife's consent if the husband applied for a visa without asking for visas for his family.[64] The administration of the law gave wide exclusionary latitude to consular officials. Of course, immigrants sometimes were able to pick and choose among consuls. In Nazi-era Germany, for example, Jewish visa applicants soon learned which consuls were more likely to approve visas.

In the distribution of quota visas under the 1924 law, family reunification was given great importance. The concept, which has become a staple of American immigration policy, had been pioneered in the restrictions against Chinese and Japanese and later used to vitiate the effects of the literacy test. Fifty percent of the quota of each nationality was to be made available to fathers and mothers of U.S. citizens who were twenty-one years of age or older, and husbands of U.S. citizens. (Wives of citizens, as noted, were what the law called exempt from numerical limitation. After 1928, when some husbands were made nonquota immigrants, those married after May 31, 1928, remained quota immigrants. These clauses mark a little-noticed way in which the rights of female United States citizens were inferior to those of male citizens.) Reflecting the influence of the farm bloc, preference within that 50 percent was also given to immigrants "skilled in agriculture," and their wives and children under eighteen years of age. The remaining half of each national quota, plus any unused portion of the first half, was earmarked for some family members of legal resident aliens in the United States, their children under twenty-one years of age and their wives, but not their husbands. Any remaining quota spaces were to be used by other quota immigrants of that nationality. Unused quota spaces from one nationality could not be transferred to any other nationality. And, typifying the spirit of the law, the burden of proof that someone was in fact eligible for entry was placed upon each immigrant; previously, at least in theory, the burden had been on the government to demonstrate ineligibility.

For the future, Congress mandated a "scientific" study of the origins of the American people as of 1920 to serve as a base for a new "national origins system" that would govern immigration after July 1, 1929. The total number of quota spaces from then on was to be reduced to about 150,000. Based on that study, the president was to promulgate national quotas by Executive Order.[65] In one section of the law, the one usually quoted, the method of making that determination seems reasonably fair. "National origin" was to be determined by calculating "the number of inhabitants in continental United States in 1920 whose origin by birth or ancestry" is attributable to each nation. But the next section, not usually cited, excludes from "inhabitants in the United States in 1920" the following: any immigrants from the New World and their descendants; any Asians or their descendants; the descendants of "slave immigrants"; and the descendants of "American aborigines." If anyone requires evidence that Congress regarded the United States as a "white man's country," this clause—subdivision "d" of Section 11 of the Immigration Act of 1924—provides it.[66]

Congress thus wrote the assumptions of the Immigration Restriction League and other nativist groups into the statute book of the United States. President Calvin Coolidge, who signed the bill into law, had published as vice president an article entitled "Whose Country Is This?" In it he made clear his adherence not only to the theory of Nordic supremacy but also to the notion that intermarriage between "Nordics" and other groups produced deteriorated offspring. The chief author of the law, Albert Johnson, justified it three years later:

> Today, instead of a well-knit homogeneous citizenry, we have a body politic made up of all and every diverse element. Today, instead of a nation descended from generations of freemen bred to a knowledge of the principles and practice of self-government, of liberty under law, we have a heterogeneous population no small proportion of which is sprung from races that, throughout the centuries, have known no liberty at all . . . In other words, our capacity to maintain our cherished institutions stands diluted by a stream of alien blood, with all its inherited misconceptions respecting the relationships of the governing power to the governed. It is out of appreciation of this fundamental fact . . . that the American people have come to sanction—indeed demand—reform of our immigration laws. They have seen, patent and plain, the encroachments of the foreign-born flood upon their own lives. They have come to realize that such a flood, affecting as it does every individual of whatever race or origin, can not fail likewise to affect the institutions which have made and preserved American liberties. It is no wonder, therefore, that the myth of the melting pot has been discredited . . . The United States is our land . . . We intend to maintain it so. The day of indiscriminate acceptance of all races has definitely ended.

Whatever one may think of Johnson's racial theories, which in slightly different form soon became the official ideology of Nazi Germany, most Americans desired the goal he sought and attained: drastic restriction of immigration. And it is easy to see that, in a frontierless democracy, some kind of restriction of immigration was not only inevitable but desirable. The real tragedy is not that the United States restricted immigration, but that it did so in a blatantly racist way that perpetuated old injustices and created new ones, which endured for decades.

Immigration, of course, went on, and at a higher rate than most restrictionists had assumed. Table 2.2 shows actual immigration for the remainder of the decade. During that period immigration averaged almost 300,000 a year as opposed to nearly 600,000 annually in the first four years of the decade and close to 900,000 in the decade 1900–1910. Curiously enough, among the greatest European beneficiaries of the new law were the very Germans with whom the United States had been at war a few years previously. German immigration ran at almost 45,000 annually for the period, more than at any time since the early 1890s. The British Isles—including Ireland—averaged about 50,000 annually, so that those two areas accounted for some 62 percent of quota immigration. During 1901–10 these nations had provided only 13 percent of European immigration.

TABLE 2.2
IMMIGRATION, 1925–30, BY CATEGORY

Year	Total	Quota	Family	New World	Other
1925	294,314	145,971	7,159	139,389	1,795
1926	304,488	157,432	11,061	134,305	1,690
1927	335,175	158,070	18,361	147,339	11,345
1928	307,225	153,231	25,678	123,534	4,812
1929	279,678	146,918	30,245	97,547	4,967
1930	241,700	141,497	32,105	63,147	4,951
Total	1,762,611	903,119	124,609	705,259	29,560

Source: U.S. Department of Commerce, *Historical Statistics of the United States*, Series C 139–151, Washington: GPO, 1957. There is a seeming discrepancy between the data in this table and that in 2.1. This is because all the "Family" immigration in column four above had some point of origin. From 1925 to 1929 the declared quota was 164,667. For 1930 it was 153,714.

Conversely, Italian and Polish immigration was slashed, as Congress intended: for the entire six years, 1925–30, fewer than 90,000 Italians and 50,000 Poles entered the country. During 1921 alone, the last prequota year, 220,000 Italians and 95,000 Poles had come in. Yet, even under the 1924 law and its regulations, members of these nationalities were learning how to function within the new rules. The annual immigration of each group rose steadily, from 8,000 in 1924 to 22,000 in 1930 for Italians and from 5,000 to 9,000 for Poles in the same period. This increasing sophistication may also be seen in the steady rise in the numbers admitted as family members in Table 2.2.

Migration from the Western Hemisphere increased to 45 percent of all migration, with the bulk of it, more than 60 percent, coming from Canada, and most of the rest, more than 30 percent, coming from Mexico.

In 1925 the Consular Service began to examine and screen prospective immigrants overseas, and shortly thereafter technical advisors from the Immigration Service assisted them. By 1927 twenty-five such advisors were serving in various European cities as were a number of Public Health Service medical examiners. The system of preembarkation examination reduced the percentage of aliens barred at ports of entry only slightly. In fiscal 1925 some 5 percent of all applicants were so barred; in fiscal 1932 the figure was nearly 4 percent.[67]

The planned shift to national origins took place on July 1, 1929, the start of the 1930 immigration year. A committee of experts under the auspices of the American Council of Learned Societies, including the father of immigration history, Marcus Lee Hansen, had complied with the racist notions of the Congress and claimed to have computed the proper ethnic origins of the American people as prescribed by the 1924 law. The result was closer to mysticism than social science. The expert guesstimate was that persons whose ancestors were here before the revolution constituted 43.4 percent of the eligible 1920 population—ignoring blacks, American Indians, and Asians—and that later immigrants and their descendants constituted the rest. The practical results of this were significant: the quota for the United Kingdom went up from 34,007 to 65,721. The quota for the Irish Free State was lowered from 28,567 to 17,853; Germany from 51,227 to 25,957; and those from Sweden, Norway, and Denmark from a combined 18,803 to 6,872. All of this was approved by the secretaries of state, commerce, and labor, and solemnly proclaimed by Herbert Clark Hoover in the first month of his presidency. In an accompanying statement he stated his opposition to national origins—Hoover knew enough statistics to recognize how shaky its empirical base was—but noted that he was "strongly in favor of restricted and selected immigration."[68] Considerable fuss was made about the lowered quotas for Germans, Scandinavians, and Irish—the ethnic leaders of those groups had largely supported restriction, thinking that it was to apply only to the newer immigrant groups—but to no avail. The deed was done.

Just how immigration policy and practice might have evolved in the 1930s had prosperity continued is a fascinating but fruitless speculation. My notion is that there would have been some amelioration of its stringency, especially for Protestants from northwest Europe. But, of course, prosperity did not continue, and the immigration policies and practices of the 1930s were shaped as much by reactions to the Great Depression as they were by the restrictionist assumptions of the 1920s.

CHAPTER THREE

No New Deal for Immigration

The Great Depression, like World War II, which followed it, changed almost every aspect of American life, and immigration was no exception. It is often stated, erroneously, that "in the 1930s the number of people leaving the United States exceeded the number entering."[1] Although, as Table 3.1 shows, there were four consecutive years—1932–35— in which the number of recorded emigrants *did* exceed the number of entrants, the balance for the decade was positive. The average annual immigration for the decade was 6,900; in 1914 more persons than that entered the country every two days. Even though the numbers of immigrants in the 1930s greatly diminished, new "problems" arose that focused on Mexicans, Filipinos, and then refugees from totalitarian regimes in Europe. And, in keeping with the growing concern about numbers of immigrants, the apprehension and deportation of illegal immigrants became increasingly important.

TABLE 3.1
IMMIGRATION AND EMIGRATION,
UNITED STATES, 1931–40

Year	Immigration	Emigration	Net
1931	97,139	61,882	35,257
1932	35,576	103,295	–67,719
1933	23,068	80,081	–57,013

Year	Immigration	Emigration	Net
1934	29,470	39,771	–10,301
1935	34,956	38,834	–3,878
1936	36,329	35,817	512
1937	50,244	26,736	23,508
1938	67,895	25,210	42,685
1939	82,998	26,651	56,347
1940	70,756	21,461	49,295
Total	528,431	459,738	68,639

Source: U.S. Department of Commerce, *Historical Statistics of the United States*, Series C 88-144, Washington: GPO, 1957.

Herbert Hoover had been elected on a platform that hailed immigration restriction but suggested "modification" in cases where "the law works undue hardships by depriving the immigrant of the comfort and society of those bound by close family ties."[2] In December 1929—after the crash but before the Depression—Hoover declared that restriction of immigration had proved "a sound national policy." But, in typical progressive fashion, he still maintained that it ought to be possible to find "a method by which the limited number of immigrants whom we do welcome" suit "our national needs." A year later however, Hoover told Congress: "There is a need for revision of our immigration laws upon a more limited and more selective basis, flexible to the needs of the country." Under the impact of the beginnings of the Great Depression, the president had determined that national needs dictated far fewer immigrants.

> Under conditions of current employment it is obvious that persons coming to the United States seeking work would likely become either direct or indirect public charges. As a temporary measure the officers issuing visas to immigrants have been . . . instructed to refuse visas to applicants likely to fall into this class. As a result the visas issued have decreased from an average of about 24,000 a month prior to restrictions to a rate of about 7,000 during the last month. These are largely preferred persons under the law. Visas from Mexico are about 250 per month compared to about 4,000 previous to restrictions. The whole subject requires exhaustive reconsideration.

Hoover had issued instructions that the "LPC clause" be administered more rigorously. In December 1931 he recommended that these administrative restrictions "be placed upon a more definite basis by law," that deportation laws be strengthened and that all aliens in the country be forced to carry residence certificates, a form of internal passport. These proposals were not acted on. In his final annual message, the defeated president had nothing further to recommend about immigration, but during the 1932 campaign he had taken credit for "rigidly restricted immigration."[3]

Thus, with the kind of creative reinterpretation of the law usually credited to his immediate successor, Hoover completely changed the meaning of the "LPC clause." In 1882 the original phrase had been "paupers or persons likely to become a public charge" and the intent had been to exclude not poor persons, but persons incapable of supporting themselves.[4] Hoover's directive gave consular officials enormous latitude, which some used with murderous effect a few years later. The new interpretation of the old clause was eventually stretched so that many consuls were able to require immigrants to have either substantial assets in their possession or a sponsor in the United States who would file an affidavit attesting a willingness to support the immigrant if necessary and an ability to do so.

But Hoover's claim of credit was misleading. The new administrative interpretation of the "LPC clause" had actually begun at the tail end of the Coolidge administration. As early as September 1928 the State Department instructed American consular officials in Mexico to apply standards more stringently.[5] As historian Robert Divine describes it, visa applicants in Mexico were faced with a "catch-22." The official would ask about their economic status. If an applicant answered that there he had a job waiting, the anti–contract labor clause could be used to deny permission to enter; if the answer was that there was no particular job on the horizon, the "LPC clause" could be used to keep him out. In this way during the 1930 fiscal year immigration from Mexico was cut to fewer than 13,000 from just over 40,000 the year before.[6]

Hoover ordered that this new policy be applied to prospective European immigrants. As a September 1930 State Department press release explained: "If the consular officer believes that the applicant may probably be a public charge at any time, even during a considerable period subsequent to his arrival, he must refuse the visa."[7] Thus, this new interpretation, first used to reduce Mexican immigration, was extended to the rest of the world. Just as Chinese exclusion in 1882 had been the statutory hinge on which the golden door to America began to close, the application of the "LPC clause" to Mexicans in 1928 was the administrative hinge for further narrowing. Once applied successfully to unpopular groups, each method of restriction was then applied to all groups.

Mexican immigration was a question that divided restrictionists for some time. As noted, its numerical incidence grew during World War I when immigrants from Europe were unavailable and continued to grow when Europeans were restricted. Ardent restrictionists, like Congressmen John C. Box (D-TX) and Albert Johnson (R-WA) persistently urged the application of the quota system to the Western Hemisphere, or just to Mexico, which would have resulted in a Mexican quota of 2,900 annually. Box was particularly virulent: he once told a nativist audience that Mexican immigrants were "illiterate, unclean, peonized . . . a mixture of Mediterranean-blooded Spanish peasants with low-grade Indians." But other Texans had different views. John Nance Garner, soon to be Speaker of the House and then FDR's first vice president, insisted that Mexicans in Texas "do not cause any trouble, unless they stay there and become Americanized."[8]

Divine has argued that "the issue of Mexican immigration marks the first permanent defeat the restrictionists had encountered since 1917" since they failed to get either a restricted Western Hemisphere quota or one for Mexico alone.[9] The new interpretation of the "LPC clause" was equally effective in reducing Mexican immigration, although the Depression was probably the more important element in the sharp drop shown in Table 3.2.

TABLE 3.2
RECORDED IMMIGRATION FROM MEXICO, 1901–40

Decade	Immigration	% of U.S. Immigration
1901–1910	49,642	0.5
1911–1920	219,002	3.8
1921–1930	458,287	11.2
1931–1940	22,319	4.2
Total	749,250	3.9

Source: U.S. Department of Commerce, *Historical Statistics of the United States*, Series C 88-144, Washington: GPO, 1957.

Mexicans, of course, were in the Southwest long before the "Anglos" came, and the treaty that sealed the American conquest of the region made special provision for them. According to the terms of the Treaty of Guadalupe-Hidalgo (1848), the 80,000 Mexicans then living on what had

become American soil could either move to what was left of Mexico or remain and automatically become U.S. citizens. A mere 3,000 went to Mexico. Natural increases plus some immigration from Mexico, much of it
informal, produced steady population growth: by 1900, according to one
expert's 1980 "guesstimate" there were somewhere between 381,000 and
562,000 Mexican Americans in the United States, almost all of them in the
Southwest.[10]

While all immigration and census data are somewhat suspect, those for
Mexican Americans are hopelessly confused. Even before the government
began to crack down on Mexican immigration, informal border crossing
in both directions was habitual. The border, which runs some 1,500 miles,
is in fact a collection of binational communities. Its paired cities, from
Matamoros/Brownsville on the Gulf of Mexico to Tijuana/San Diego on
the Pacific, are interdependent economic units within which thousands of
people cross the border daily in each direction to work, shop, and play. The
22,000 visaed Mexican entrants of the 1930s were surely a minor fraction
of the true immigrant traffic.

In 1910 and 1920 the census bureau, counting only immigrants and
their children, recorded some 600,000 and 725,000 "foreign white stock"
Mexicans respectively. "Foreign white stock" was a traditional census term
for immigrants and their children who were neither Asian nor black. But in
the 1930 census—and in that census only—all but 66,000 of 1.3 million
Mexicans were classified as "non-white." That count, like all counts of
peoples of color, covered all generations and is not comparable with previous or later figures. It was probably a substantial undercount. The 1940
census using the rubric "Spanish mother tongue" found almost 1.6 million
persons presumed to be either Mexican nationals or Mexican Americans.

An official California investigatory commission accurately portrayed the
socioeconomic status of most Mexican Americans there in a pre-Depression
report that began:

> The Mexican . . . is today a principal source of farm labor in California . . .
> He does tasks that white workers will not or cannot do. He works under . . .
> conditions that are often too trying for white workers. He will work in gangs.
> He will work under direction, taking orders and suggestions.[11]

But the onset of the Depression changed the needs of California's "factories in
the field," the large agri-business corporations that employed the bulk of the

state's Mexican farm workers. Produce went unharvested and many Mexican workers were displaced by "Anglo" Californians and by internal migrants like John Steinbeck's Joads in *The Grapes of Wrath* who under the stress of the Depression were unemployed and "willing" to do the work. Not surprisingly, many Mexicans tried to get on the growing welfare rolls, such as they were.

The changed conditions caused large numbers of Mexicans and Mexican Americans to leave the United States in the 1930s. Some used their own resources; others were "assisted" by federal, state, and local governments. Although the official statistics indicate that only some 450,000 immigrant aliens departed in the 1930s, most of them Europeans, a number of scholars have reported an extensive program of "repatriation" to Mexico, which included many American-born children. All told, perhaps half a million persons went south across the border. Although most came from the Southwest—largely from Texas and California—perhaps 50,000 came from the Upper Midwest, particularly Michigan, Indiana, Illinois, and Minnesota. Half a century later, an Indiana Harbor resident remembered:

> So they told you, "You are making $7.00 or $8.00 per payday for your family. You can't feed them, you can't do nothing. So we are going to take you off welfare." "Oh, God, what are you going to do, take us off welfare? We'll starve." "No, no, you have an alternative . . . go to Mexico. We have a train available. A train full of Mexican people. A train will stop at the corner of Michigan and Guthrie, on the Pennsylvania Railroad. And they will head for Mexico. In Mexico you will transfer and we'll take you where you come from, close, not actually there, but to the closest town." So actually they weren't forcing you to leave, they gave you a choice, starve or go back to Mexico.[12]

The formal repatriation programs involved the cooperation of the Mexican government. In the best-documented instances, Los Angeles County, with the cooperation of federal immigration officials and Colonel Arthur Woods of the President's Emergency Committee for Employment, expended public funds to charter special trains to send Mexicans and Mexican Americans to Mexico. The rationale was that it would save welfare expenditures. While many of the *repatriados* went gladly, others were deported—with and without warrants—and still others were coerced into going. "I'll never forget as long as I live," a Santa Barbara woman recalled, the way that "they put all the people in boxcars" rather than in passenger coaches.[13] One father later wrote the Los Angeles County Board of Supervisors that all of his children were "born in the U.S. of A.," did not like Mexico and wanted to come back.

I have worked all my life, since I was 19 years of age in the U.S. of A., and that is why I wish to return to the country where I am entitled to live with my children so that they be educated in the schools of your country and not in Mexico.

He listed his children's names and American birthplaces—two in Arizona and four in California. There is no record of any answer, so we do not know whether this man or any of his children—who were American citizens but may not have been able to prove it—were ever able to return.[14] It is clear that many *repatriados* did make their way back, one way or another.

The long-term effects of the deportation/repatriation program on some Mexican American communities are paradoxical. As George J. Sánchez, the premier historian of Mexican American Los Angeles, describes it:

> Ultimately, support for repatriation ended the reign of the Mexican progressives who had been leaders in Los Angeles's Chicano community. The exit of approximately one-third of the city's 150,000 Mexican residents during the repatriation period of the early 1930s ushered in a new type of leadership: American-born Chicano leadership more affiliated with their working-class communities and organized labor backgrounds. After 1935, the Mexican consulate would never again play as crucial a role in organizing local leadership around goals formulated in Mexico City . . .[15]

Early in the century the pioneer historian of California, Hubert Howe Bancroft, had argued that using Mexican laborers to pick California's crops would better serve the state because, unlike Asians, they would go home when the crops were picked. Three decades later, for the first time, large numbers of Mexicans were being sent "home" whether they wanted to go or not.

The administrative restrictions adopted by Herbert Hoover's regime were simply continued by Franklin Roosevelt's. There was nothing even resembling a New Deal for immigration, although Secretary of Labor Frances Perkins was sympathetic to immigrants and did clean up some of the corruption and mismanagement that seems to be endemic in the immigration service.[16] Even before the Depression the Democratic Party's position on immigration was hardly distinguishable from the Republicans'. Although Al Smith, the Democratic candidate in 1928, was rightly regarded as a representative of the immigrant and urban masses, the Democratic platform that year pledged itself to preserving immigration restriction "in full force and effect," though it did favor more lenient provisions for family reunification. Not one of the four platforms on which Franklin Roosevelt ran, 1932 to 1944, contained a word about immigration and there would be no significant changes in immigration law until 1943.[17] Candidate Roosevelt made this clear in his 1932 Turnerian Commonwealth Club address in San Francisco, arguing that:

> Our industrial plant is built . . . Our last frontier has long since been reached . . . There is no safety valve in the form of a Western prairie . . . We are not able to invite the immigration from Europe to share our endless plenty.[18]

That is not to say that had Hoover been reelected immigration policy would have been the same. Hoover wanted immigration restricted even further, while the father of the New Deal was willing to stand pat. As he put it in another 1932 campaign address:

> [The President of the United States] says proudly that he has effectively restricted immigration in order to protect American labor. I favor that; but I might add that in the enforcement of the immigration laws too many abuses . . . have been revealed . . .[19]

It is also clear that Roosevelt did not share Hoover's essentially nativist view of most recent immigrants and their descendants; it is impossible to imagine the Quaker engineer telling the Daughters of the American Revolution, as FDR did, to "remember, remember always that all of us, and you and I especially, are descended from immigrants and revolutionaries."* But for Roosevelt, apparently, immigration was something that had happened in the past. The only other reference to immigration in the indexes of his public papers refers to the colonial period.[20]

The New Deal did, however, treat resident aliens more generously than its predecessor. Instead of repatriation or deportation, the New Deal provided some relief. Deportations, which had risen steadily from 2,762 in 1920 to 19,865 in 1933, dropped to fewer than 9,000 the next year and stayed at about that level for the rest of the decade. Federal relief regulations insisted on the eligibility of resident aliens, although local control of hiring usually discriminated not only against aliens but also against persons of color regardless of citizenship.

---

*A persistent myth holds that FDR began his talk to the DAR "Fellow Immigrants." He did not, but he, himself, may have later claimed that he did.

The first major immigration "problem" addressed by the Roosevelt administration concerned Filipinos. That the Asian Filipinos could enter the United States without significant restriction was, of course, an anomaly, an unintended consequence of American imperialism, which made their homeland an American possession. The federal courts had ruled that Filipinos were "American nationals" and thus not immigrants. On the other hand, since they were neither white nor of African descent they were not eligible for naturalization. A handful of Filipinos had settled in French Louisiana in the eighteenth century, and after the American conquest of the Philippines hundreds of students came to study at American colleges and universities, largely in the Midwest.[21] But the overwhelming majority of Filipino immigrants arrived after the restriction of Japanese labor immigration in 1907–08. In both Hawaii and on the American West Coast Filipinos filled the same low-skill niches in the labor force that Chinese and Japanese had filled before them. Table 3.3 indicates their incidence in Hawaii and on the mainland.

TABLE 3.3
FILIPINOS IN HAWAII AND CONTINENTAL
UNITED STATES, 1910–40

HAWAII

Year	Number	% of Population
1910	2,361	1.23
1920	21,031	8.22
1930	63,052	17.17
1940	52,569	12.42

CONTINENTAL UNITED STATES

Year	Number	California	% in CA
1910	406	5	1.2
1920	5,603	2,674	47.7
1930	45,208	30,470	67.4
1940	45,876	31,408	68.5

Source: U.S. Census data.

Almost 120,000 Filipinos were brought to Hawaii between 1909 and 1934 by the Hawaiian Sugar Planters Association, which had previously been responsible for bringing in Chinese and Japanese. Over 100,000 of the Filipinos were men, nearly 9,000 were women, while 7,000 were children.[22] Some came to the mainland after fulfilling their contracts in the islands; others went back to the Philippines. The California Filipino population was even more overwhelmingly male. In California in 1930, for example, there were more than 28,000 males and fewer than 2,000 females.

A vigorous anti-Filipino movement arose in California in the late 1920s and early 1930s backed by a broad coalition of forces from organized labor to right-wing newspapers and politicians. While the basic cause was economic—during the Depression many whites were eager to get even the "stoop labor" jobs formerly left to assorted "foreigners"—there was also significant cultural conflict. Many middle-class Californians were aroused by what they regarded as the aggressive sexuality of Filipinos, large numbers of whom patronized "dime-a-dance" establishments. One Sunday feature story in the *Los Angeles Times* carried the following headlines:[23]

> "Taxi-Dance Girls Start Filipinos on Wrong Foot"
> "Lonely Islanders' Quest for Woman Companionship Brings Problems of
>   Grave National Moment"
> "Mercenary Women Influence Brown Men's Egos"
> "Minds Made Ripe for Work of Red Organizers"

Similarly, David P. Barrows, president of the University of California, told a congressional committee that the state's "problems" with Filipinos stemmed from the latters' easily aroused sexual passion coupled with their natural propensity for vice and crime, all exacerbated by the deficiencies of modern American society.

> [The Filipino] usually frequents the poorer quarters of our towns and spends the residues of his savings in brothels and dance halls, which in spite of our laws exist to minister to his lower nature. Everything in our rapid, pleasure-seeking life, and the more or less shameless exhibitionism which accompanies it, contributes to overwhelm these young men who come, in most cases, only a few years removed from the even, placid life of a primitive native of a barrio.[24]

This portrayal of Filipinos as persons only a step from savagery was a misconception nurtured in part by the frequent exhibition of Igorots* at Amer-

---

*A name given to several tribal peoples of Luzon who had been largely unaffected by modern civilization.

ican world fairs and even zoos in the decades after the annexation of the Philippines. That the Filipino migrants were not Igorots and that many of them spoke two Western languages (Spanish and English) as well as one of the Philippine languages was irrelevant to the nativists.

A middle-class proponent of Filipino exclusion, Sacramento business-man C. M. Goethe, ignoring the lack of Filipino women in America, warned that the ten million Negroes in the United States were descended from "an original slave nucleus of 750,000" and insisted that "Filipinos do not hesitate to have nine children . . . [which means] 729 great grandchil-dren as against the white parents' twenty-seven."

Then, switching his point of attack, he argued that:[25]

> The Filipino tends to interbreed with near-moron white girls. The resulting hybrid is almost invariably undesirable. The ever increasing brood of Filipino coolie fathers and low-grade white mothers may in time constitute a serious social burden.

As ridiculous as this now sounds, it was heady stuff to a generation that made best-sellers of Oswald Spengler's *Decline of the West* and Lothrop Stoddard's *The Rising Tide of Color Against White World Supremacy*. It was an era in which a leading liberal intellectual, Oliver Wendell Holmes, Jr., could declare, in support of compulsory sterilization, that "three genera-tions of imbeciles are enough."[26]

In addition, many Californians were startled to discover that the state's antimiscegenation laws, which forbade marriage between whites and Ne-groes and between whites and "Mongolians," could not be used to prevent marriages between whites and Filipinos. The legislature quickly passed a law making marriages between whites and "persons of the Malayan race" equally illegal.[27]

There was also the traditional trade union argument. Even before the onset of the Depression the American Federation of Labor's national con-vention resolved in 1928 that:[28]

> Whereas, the desire for cheap labor has acted like a cancer . . . destroying American ideals and preventing the development of a nation based on racial unity; and
>
> Whereas . . . this desire has exploited the Negro, the Chinese, the Japa-nese, the Hindus, as in turn each has been regulated and excluded; and

Whereas, the Malays of the Philippines were in 1924 omitted from the general policy excluding all who cannot become citizens; and

Whereas, there are a sufficient number of Filipinos ready and willing to come to the United States to create a race problem equal to that already here . . . we urge the exclusion of Filipinos . . .

That same year a California congressman introduced the first bill aimed at excluding Filipinos. Within two years hearings were held and there was a congressional debate. The arguments against Filipino immigration were racial and economic. The chief opposition to restriction came from Hawaiian sugar planters, the War Department (which still administered the Philippines), and Filipino leaders. Most notable among the latter was Manual Roxas, speaker of the Philippine legislature, who was in the country as part of a delegation lobbying for independence. Filipino exclusion, according to Roxas,

has no precedent in the annals of colonization since the birth of time. No country, however imperialistic, however commercialistic in its policy in its dealings with its colonies, has ever prohibited the citizens of its colonies from migrating to the mother country.[29]

Other Filipino spokesmen, including Camilio Osias, resident commissioner from the Philippines, suggested that immigration and Philippine independence be tied together, an option that some American lawmakers quickly embraced. When in 1930 the restrictionists failed to get a simple Filipino exclusion clause added to an immigration bill, most of them jumped on the independence bandwagon. It was a nice irony: some of the most pronounced racists in Congress became, in effect anti-imperialists. Hiram W. Johnson (1866–1945), the senior Republican senator from California and a longtime advocate of Asian exclusion, had a provision inserted into a 1932 bill granting independence, which thereafter totally barred Filipinos as "aliens ineligible to citizenship." However, Hoover, who opposed independence, vetoed that bill in January 1933. But in his veto message he stated without qualification that "immigration [of Filipinos] should be restricted at once."[30] Congress overrode the veto but the measure did not go into effect because the necessary approval of the Philippine legislature was not forthcoming.

In 1934, with the support of the Roosevelt administration, a similar bill passed, was signed by the president and accepted by concurrent resolution of the Philippine legislature. The Philippines were to become independent in 1945. The immigration aspects of the law were as follows: instead of exclusion, Filipinos were to receive a quota of fifty spaces per year—half the size of the previous minimum quota. Although Filipinos remained ineligible for naturalization, the law specifically exempted Filipinos from the provisions of paragraph 13 (c) of the 1924 law, the section that excluded "aliens ineligible to citizenship" from immigration, and made it possible for Hawaii to import more Filipino laborers if the Secretary of the Interior thought it advisable.[31]

The basic Filipino "problem" had been solved, but many felt that the solution still left too many Filipinos in the country. In 1933, Samuel Dickstein, a Brooklyn Democrat who became chair of the House Committee on Immigration and Naturalization when his party took over, began to press for ways to get unemployed Filipinos sent back home. He supported legislation, enacted in 1935, to provide any Filipino who applied for it free "transportation and maintenance from his present residence to a port on the west coast of the United States and [subsequent] transportation and maintenance . . . to Manila." In addition, the law forced any Filipino who received a free trip home to foreswear the right of return. In any event only 2,190 persons applied for and received such a trip. Dickstein insisted that his motive was, in part, "humanitarian in behalf of these unfortunate Filipinos." One can imagine what Dickstein, an opponent of the quota system for Europeans, would have said if someone had proposed the same sort of arrangement for unfortunate immigrants from Europe. That an urban Democrat like Dickstein sponsored such a measure shows nicely the attitude that even liberal congressmen had toward Filipinos.[32]

Both the Hoover and Roosevelt administrations confronted the problems caused by Mexican and Filipino immigrants, and, as we have seen, reacted to them in essentially the same way. The "problem" of refugees from Nazi Europe, refugees who were mostly Jewish, arose only as the Roosevelt administration began. Viewed through the horror of the Holocaust, the callous indifference of the United States and the other nations of possible asylum has become a scandal with an extensive literature. But it is not really useful to view the policies of the 1930s, as too many do, through the prism of the Holocaust. Some of the literature can induce one to believe that Franklin Roosevelt and even Rabbi Stephen S. Wise were somehow responsible for the Holocaust. Authors of phrases such as "while six million died" create the false notion that the United States, merely by changing its immigration policies, could have saved all or most of the Jews of Europe, a palpable impossibility.[33] Nor is it accurate to assume that the Holocaust was inherent from the moment the Nazis came to power. By the time Americans learned about what Walter Laqueur has called the "terrible secret" of the Holocaust, the fate of most of the Jews of Europe was sealed. To be sure, even at that late date more could have been done.[34] If one wishes to make a judgment, it is hard to improve on Vice President Walter F. Mondale's, made in 1979: the United States and the other nations of asylum "failed the test of civilization."[35]

Any attempt to understand the pitiful refugee policy of the United States in the Nazi era must confront American traditions about asylum and contemporary political and social pressures. Many share President Jimmy Carter's belief that the United States was and always has been "a nation of refugees," but such a conclusion is unwarranted.[36] It is true, however, that refugees have been received, and sometimes welcomed, from the earliest years of the American experience. The assumption here is that a refugee is, in the common dictionary definition, "a person who flees from one's home or country to seek refuge elsewhere, as in time of war, or political or religious persecution." Protestant religious dissenters, Jews from Brazil, regicides fleeing the Stuart restoration, royalists and republicans, ousted slaveholders and Bonapartists, all found asylum here in the early years of our history. But these refugees were relatively few in number and greatly outnumbered by the 40,000 crown sympathizers, the so-called American Loyalists, who went or were driven into exile during and after the American Revolution. In the waning days of Federalism during the administration of John Adams (1797–1801), there was considerable concern about the subversive activities of some French, Irish, and British resident aliens. This, plus partisan political considerations, resulted in the passage of the short-lived Alien and Sedition Acts, which jailed some aliens for political activity and authorized deportations, but, in the event, deported no one. They surely made potential refugees wary about coming to America.

During most of the nineteenth century, few Americans voiced fears about political refugees, but despite the wide-open American door it was Britain that became the mecca for most European political exiles. The most significant exile activity in the United States was by Latin Americans, particularly Cubans who made a revolution against their Spanish overlords from bases in Tampa and New York.

As noted before, in the early years of the twentieth century, political tests were being applied to immigrants for the first time. But, in the same era, the statutes that were designed to keep criminals out were carefully drafted so that "political offenses" could not be used as grounds for exclusion.[37] In American immigration law there was no distinction between refugees and other immigrants, and the word *refugee* does not appear on the statute books until 1934, although in 1923 a "Near East Refugee Act" did pass the Senate.[38] There was a clause in the literacy provisions of the 1917 immigration act waiving the literacy requirement—but nothing else—for "aliens who shall prove . . . that they are seeking admission to the United States to avoid religious persecution" but it is not clear that even one person gained admission because of that provision.[39]

From the earliest days of his presidency Franklin Roosevelt was aware of the Nazi persecution of Jews, trade unionists, socialists, and others in Germany, and as a humane liberal Democrat he deplored it and spoke out against it. But for years he did little or nothing to change American immigration policy, either to restrict it further or to liberalize it, as many of his closest supporters wished him to do. When, for example, Felix Frankfurter and Raymond Moley urged him to send representatives to a 1936 League of Nations conference on refugees and appoint Rabbi Stephen S. Wise to the delegation, FDR instead took the advice of the State Department and sent only a minor functionary. In an election year he was willing to accept the narrow view of executive power set forth by Secretary of State Cordell Hull (1871–1955). This conservative Tennessee Democrat, whose wife was Jewish, told the president that the law left him "no latitude" even to discuss "questions concerning the legal status of aliens."[40]

Similarly, when his handpicked successor as governor of New York, Herbert H. Lehman (1878–1963), wrote him on two occasions, in 1935 and 1936, about the difficulties German Jews were having in getting visas from some American consulates in Germany, the president sent replies drafted in the State Department. The letters assured Lehman of FDR's "sympathetic interest" and claimed that consular officials abroad were carrying out their duties "in a considerate and humane manner." In addition, the governor was assured that a visa would be issued

> when the preponderance of evidence supports a conclusion that the person promising the applicant's support will be likely to take steps to prevent the applicant from becoming a public charge.[41]

Roosevelt was notoriously distrustful of the State Department, and letting its bureaucrats draft his responses shows that he simply did not want to interfere or even to know what was really going on. Our most activist president could be quite passive when it suited him to be.

There is irrefutable evidence that many State Department officials consistently made it difficult for most refugees in general and Jewish refugees in particular to gain asylum in the United States. One example involving just two individuals reflects a pervasive problem. Hebrew Union College (HUC) had a refugee scholars project, which between 1935 and 1942 brought eleven refugee scholars and some of their families to its Cincinnati campus. Although there was no question of any of these persons becoming a public charge, most were able to enter under a provision of the 1924 act which exempted from quota restriction

> an immigrant who continuously for at least two years immediately preceding [his visa application] has been, and who seeks to enter the United States solely for the purpose of, carrying on the vocation of minister of any religious denomination, or professor of a college, academy, seminary or university, and his wife, and his unmarried children under 18 years age . . .[42]

This provision must have seemed heaven-sent to the scholars that HUC, the premier American institution for training Reform rabbis, was trying to bring out. But, as Michael A. Meyer, the historian of the project, has demonstrated, the State Department, in the person of Avra M. Warren, head of the Visa Division, consistently created difficulties, difficulties that in some cases proved insurmountable.[43]

Despite apparent prima facie qualifications, two German Jewish scholars whom HUC tried to bring out never managed to get to the United States. Albert Spanier had been Hebraica librarian at the Prussian State Library and then a teacher at the Hochschule für die Wissenschaft des Judentums in Berlin until he was sent to a concentration camp after *Kristallnacht** in November 1938. The guaranteed offer of an appointment at HUC got him out of the concentration camp, but it could not get him an American visa. Why? Because Avra Warren's Visa Division determined that the special provision did not cover librarians. Spanier's teaching at the Hochschule did not count either because, in 1934, the Nazis had demoted it—the leading institution for the study of Judaism in the world—from a

---

Kristallnacht, the night of broken glass, November 9, 1938, was a government-organized pogrom that destroyed Jewish stores, synagogues, and community buildings all over Germany, and marked a major escalation of the persecution of the German Jews.

Hochschule to the status of a *Lehranstalt* [institute]. An administrative reg-ulation created by the Visa Division and not found in the statute, held that the grant of a professorial/clerical visa to a scholar coming from a lower-status institution abroad to a higher-status one in the United States was im-permissible.

Spanier and another refugee scholar invited by HUC, Albert Lewkowitz, managed to reach the Netherlands. It was asssumed that Lewkowitz, at least, would get a visa since he had taught Jewish philosophy at the Jewish Theological Seminary in Breslau, an institution whose status the State De-partment did not question. But in May 1940 the Germans bombed Rotter-dam, destroying all of Lewkowitz's documents, and American consular officials insisted that he get a new set from Germany. Five years earlier, in peacetime, FDR had assured Lehman in a letter drafted by the State De-partment that

> consular officials have been instructed that in cases where it is found that an immigrant visa applicant cannot obtain a supporting document normally re-quired by the Immigration Act of 1924 without the peculiar delay and em-barrassment that might attend the request of a political and religious refugee, the requirement of such document may be waived on the basis of its being not "available."[44]

No such waiver was made for Lewkowitz. Both he and Spanier were later rounded up and sent to the Bergen-Belsen concentration camp. Lewkowitz was one of the few concentration camp inmates exchanged and he got to Palestine in 1944. Spanier died in Bergen-Belsen.[45]

As we have seen, actions by three presidents, Coolidge, Hoover, and Roosevelt, granted broad discretionary power to American consuls. Obvi-ously, a wide range of attitudes and performance were represented within the consular corps. One American consul in Germany, Raymond Geist, actually went into concentration camps to help get individuals out; while another, John G. Erhardt, issued as few visas to refugees as possible. No historian has yet made a full-scale investigation of American visa policies, but as early as 1921 American Jewish leaders complained of the overt anti-Semitism of certain State Department officials, particularly, as noted previ-ously, Wilbur J. Carr, the dominant administrator of the consular service from 1909 to 1937, and the small number of Jews who were to get appoint-ments in the foreign and consular services. The published diary of Breckinridge Long (1881–1958), Assistant Secretary of State from January 1940 to January 1944, provides clear evidence of his anti-Semitism. One entry, for example, equated communism with Jewish internationalism and regarded Hitler's *Mein Kampf* "eloquent in opposition to Jewry and to Jews as exponents of Communism and chaos."*[46]

While it is rarely possible to connect a bureaucrat's personal anti-Semitism directly to his or her official decisions, it is not necessary to find the so-called "smoking gun." As far as I am concerned, when one finds a public official, in an era in which anti-Semitism is endemic, making anti-Semitic statements in his private correspondence *and* following policies that effect anti-Semitism, one should assume at least partial anti-Semitic motivation unless there is overwhelming evidence to the contrary.

It is the conjunction that seems to me crucial. Hiram W. Johnson, a governor of California and United States senator from 1917 to his death, is an example of the opposite tendency. There are vile anti-Semitic and anti-black references in his private papers at the Bancroft Library, but Johnson was, if anything, mildly philo-Semitic and pro-black in his public statements and policies.[47]

Late in the 1930s the Roosevelt administration began to move on the refugee question, but its actions can best be characterized by the phrase that describes so much of Western democracy's opposition to fascism—too little and too late. Shortly after the *Anschluss*, the German annexation of Austria in March 1938, FDR created an Advisory Committee on Political Refugees under the chairmanship of James G. McDonald, former High Commissioner for Refugees of the League of Nations, and assigned an interdepartmental committee of government officials to work with it. FDR also instructed Secretary Hull to try to arrange an international conference to "facilitate the emigration from Austria and presumably from Germany of political refugees," adding the caveat, "[N]o country would be expected or asked to receive a greater number of immigrants than is permitted by its existing regulations." He appointed Myron C. Taylor (1874–1959), former chairman of the United States Steel Corporation, to the rank of ambassador and named him to head the American delegation to the conference, which met in Evian, France, in July 1938. Its only accomplishment was to create

---

*David Wyman, who wants not only a smoking gun but to hear the explosion, judges it "not clear" whether Long was an anti-Semite. David S. Wyman, *The Abandonment of the Jews* (New York: Pantheon, 1984), 190–91.

an Intergovernmental Committee on Refugees, headquartered in London, under the chairmanship of George Rublee (1868–1957), an American lawyer. Just before the outbreak of war in September 1939, Rublee did manage to negotiate a sub-rosa agreement looking toward the orderly emigration of 400,000 Jews over a five-year period; the hostilities made it nugatory.[48]

In his note to the appropriate volume of his papers, FDR wrote things he never said to the American people in the crucial years of the refugee crisis, 1938–39.

> For centuries this country has always been the traditional haven of refuge for countless victims of religious and political persecution in other lands. These immigrants have made outstanding contributions to American music, art, literature, business, finance, philanthropy, and many other phases of our cultural, political, industrial and commercial life. It was quite fitting, therefore, that the United States should follow its traditional role and take the lead in calling the Evian meeting . . .
>
> As this is written in June, 1941, it seems so tragically ironical to realize how many citizens of these various countries [which had been overly cautious in their attitude about receiving refugees] either are themselves now refugees, or pray for a chance to leave their native lands and seek some refuge from the cruel hand of the Nazi invader. Even the kings and queens and princes of some of them are now in the same position as these political and religious minorities were in 1938—knocking on the doors of other lands for admittance.[49]

When one compares this account with what the United States actually did and did not do in the months before war broke out in Europe, it is difficult not to believe that a guilty conscience lay behind his remarks, which later would be easy to describe as hypocritical. Of course, Congress and the American people were opposed to any dropping of our immigration barriers, as both Roosevelt and his ambassador, Myron Taylor, knew. The latter assured the American people in a November 1939 radio address:

> Our plans do not involve the "flooding" of this or any other country with aliens of any race or creed. On the contrary, our entire program is based on the existing immigration laws of all the countries concerned, and I am confident that within that framework our problems can be solved.[50]

His confidence, if it really existed, was sadly misplaced.

The American record, as opposed to its rhetoric and post-facto rationalizations, was dismal. Although we do not know how many actual visa applications by would-be German refugees there were—one scholar says more than 300,000 by June 1939—the fact is that between Hitler's coming to power and *Kristallnacht*, emigration from Germany was relatively light; as Table 3.4 indicates, more than half of the German quota spaces for the period 1933–40 went unused. Thus a large portion of the Jews of Germany could have been accepted even within the relatively strict limits of the quota law.

The few attempts by sympathetic congresspersons to admit more refugees were forlorn hopes. The most notable of these was the so-called Wagner-Rogers bill of early 1939, which proposed bringing 20,000 German children to the United States outside of the quota system. Although sponsored

TABLE 3.4

GERMAN QUOTA IMMIGRATION AND
THE GERMAN QUOTA, 1933–40

Year	German Quota Immigration	German Quota Spaces
1933	1,919	25,957
1934	4,392	25,957
1935	5,201	25,957
1936	6,346	25,957
1937	10,895	25,957
1938	17,199	27,370*
1939	33,515†	27,370*
1940	21,520	27,370*
Total	100,987‡	211,895

by the New Deal's most prolific legislator, Senator Robert F. Wagner (D-NY), and a liberal Republican, Representative Edith Nourse Rogers of Massachusetts, the bill never came to the floor for a vote. It had a great deal of support from prominent Americans—including Herbert Hoover—but was

*For 1938–40, Austrian quota of 1,413 added.
†The apparent exceeding of quotas in 1939 resulted from the fact that more than 5,000 persons who received visas under the 1938 quota did not actually enter the United States until the 1939 quota year. This happened every year, but only in 1939 did it result in an apparent excess.
‡David S. Wyman writes that "Had the relevant quotas been completely filled from the *Anschluss* through Pearl Harbor, some 206,000 persons could have entered the United States, only 50,000 more than the approximate number of refugees who did immigrate in those years (*Paper Walls*, p. 209). The

opposed by a sizable majority of ordinary Americans, according to the public opinion polls. We do not know what would have happened had the White House tried to lead public opinion and put pressure on reluctant Democrats. FDR refused to do so. He was willing to allow some administration officials—Secretary of Labor Frances Perkins and Children's Bureau Chief Katherine Lenroot—to testify in its favor. Other officials, such as Secretary of State Hull, took no stand but informed Congress of the numerous administrative difficulties the proposed law would create. Roosevelt even told his wife, in February 1939, that "it is all right for you to support the child refugee bill, but it is best for me to say nothing [now]." Now became never. In June, as the bill was dying, the president annotated a memo asking for his support "File No Action, FDR." In addition, some of his personal and official family viciously opposed the bill: one of his favorite cousins, Laura Delano, wife of Commissioner of Immigration and Naturalization James Houghteling, told people at cocktail parties that the "20,000 charming children would all too soon grow up into 20,000 ugly adults."[51]

One final pre-war episode, that of the German vessel *St. Louis* in May 1939, demonstrates the degree to which American officials' hearts had hardened against admitting any refugees outside of the quota system. The *St. Louis* was a Hamburg-Amerika line vessel bringing 933 passengers, most of them Jewish refugees, to Havana. Many of the refugees were on the American quota list but held numbers that had not yet come up. They and others came to Western Hemisphere ports to wait their turn. There were already some 2,500 refugees in Havana. Seven hundred and forty-three of the passengers had applied for visas and had the necessary affidavits of support. For reasons that are not entirely clear, the Cuban government refused to let the refugees land. Hoping to land those with visa applications in the United States, the vessel proceeded to Miami, but it was refused permission to dock. For a time it was so close to Miami Beach that the passengers could hear dance music being played at the resort's luxury hotels. That was as close as the refugees came to the golden door. The Treasury Department even assigned a Coast Guard cutter to shadow the *St. Louis* to make sure

---

source of his 206,000 figure for quota spaces between November 1938 and December 1941 is a mystery to me. If fiscal 1941 (July 1, 1941–June 30, 1942) were included in the table above, there would be 27,370 more quota spaces but just 4,028 additional immigrants, giving a total of 239,265 quota spaces and 105,015 immigrants. His calculations also ignore the fact that a significant number of refugees—approaching 50,000 persons using his estimate of 150,000 refugees—entered outside of the quota system.

that no one tried to swim ashore. The liner was forced to turn back to Europe, its refugee passengers still aboard. European governmental hearts were a little softer and Great Britain, France, Belgium, and the Netherlands each agreed to take about a fourth of the passengers. Large numbers of them subsequently fell into the hands of the Nazis and perished, but some of the ship's passengers survived to observe the fiftieth anniversary of their rejection at a reunion in Miami.[52]

In late 1938 Franklin Roosevelt did take one effective step by executive action: he "suggested" to Labor Secretary Perkins that the six-month visitor visas of "political" refugees be automatically extended and reextended for successive six-month periods as they ran out. This enabled about 15,000 persons to remain in the United States.[53] Clearly, despite the president's 1941 claim, the vaunted "haven of refuge" did not function very well. But, it is important to note, perhaps 150,000 refugees, the overwhelming majority of them Jews, did manage to reach the United States before Pearl Harbor, a significantly larger number than was admitted by any other nation: many thousands of others could have been saved by a more resolute policy.[54]

CHAPTER FOUR

World War II and After: The Barriers Begin to Drop

Although during World War II immigration from outside the ⊛ Western Hemisphere fell to the lowest levels ever recorded, momentous changes in American immigration policy took place. The initial regulatory changes brought on by the war were restrictive and eventually involved the worst governmental violation of human rights since slavery. But before war's end the first significant rollback of restrictive legislation, the repeal of Chinese exclusion, had occurred, and, by executive action, two token groups of wartime refugees were allowed in without reference to the quota law. In addition, as had been the case during World War I, labor shortages within the United States caused yet another reversal of policy toward Mexican immigration: not only were Mexican laborers again allowed to cross the border with relative impunity, but large numbers were actively recruited by the federal government.

In the five years after the war immigration surpassed the levels of the 1930s but did not reach those of the 1920s, additional bars against some Asian immigrants were removed, and, after a bitter struggle, special legislation—the Displaced Persons Acts of 1948 and 1950—was enacted, which gave the nation its first legislative refugee program. Gross immigration for the decade was roughly twice that of the 1930s, but only in 1950 did the annual level approach that of the later 1920s. Table 4.1 shows immigration in the decade and lists its major sources, but it must be noted that Mexicans brought in under the government-sponsored labor programs were not counted as immigrants because it was assumed that they would all return to Mexico when no longer needed.

TABLE 4.1

IMMIGRATION, 1941–52, BY MAJOR REGIONS

Year	Total	Europe	Americas
1941	51,776	26,541	22,445
1942	28,781	11,153	16,377
1943	23,725	4,920	18,162
1944	28,551	4,509	23,084
1945	38,119	5,943	29,646
1946	108,721	52,852	46,066
1947	147,292	83,535	52,753
1948	170,570	103,544	52,746
1949	188,317	129,592	49,334
1950	249,187	199,115	44,191
1951	205,717	149,545	47,631
1952	265,520	193,626	61,049
Total	1,506,276	964,875	463,484
Percentage	100%	64%	31%

Source: U.S. Department of Commerce, *Historical Statistics of the United States*, Series C-88-144.

The outbreak of war in Europe in September 1939—twenty-seven months before the attack on Pearl Harbor thrust the United States into the war—brought little real change in American immigration policy but, with the fall of France in June 1940, nativists and others feared that Nazi agents, the largely mythical fifth columnists, would be hidden among immigrants or pose as refugees.[1] Great Britain's decision to round up almost all enemy aliens, including Nazi sympathizers and Jewish refugees, and place them in internment camps on the Isle of Man and elsewhere—"collar the lot," said Winston Churchill—was seen by some Americans as an example to emulate, by others as an excess to avoid.[2] The American Jewish community, in particular, was determined to try to prevent the government from interning anti-Nazi German Jewish aliens along with Nazi sympathizers and placing them in the same camps, as the British had done and the Canadians would do. This was largely avoided in the United States but did happen in at least a few instances.[3]

Amidst a flurry of bills aimed at making deportation easier—one of which had been vetoed by the president in April 1940[4]—Congress passed and Roosevelt signed the harsh Alien Registration Act of 1940 at the end of June. Earlier that month a presidential directive transferred the Immigration and Naturalization Service (INS) from the Department of Labor to the Department of Justice, from a department whose functions were essentially protective to one whose functions were essentially prosecutorial. This presidential action greatly pleased congressional nativists and others who were particularly opposed to Labor Secretary Frances Perkins. They felt that she was "soft" on both immigrants and communists. Perkins herself had long wanted to shed the responsibility for immigration, but had suggested that the INS be transferred to the Interior Department, headed by another vigorous liberal, Harold L. Ickes.[5]

The Alien Registration Act, also known as the Smith Act—for Representative Howard W. Smith (1883–1976), a reactionary Virginia congressman who survived an FDR "purge" attempt in 1938—was a complex measure of forty-one sections organized into three largely unrelated titles. Title I was a peacetime sedition act providing criminal penalties for various subversive activities, including interference with the military forces of the United States by anyone, citizen or alien. It was the statutory basis for the conviction of a few Trotskyites in Minneapolis during the war and in the post-war years was used to jail many of the leaders of the American Communist Party. Title II expanded the grounds, most of them involving subversive activities, under which aliens could be deported. Title III required all aliens, regardless of age or gender, to register and be fingerprinted, usually at a post office, and to advise the INS in writing of any change of address.[6] All aliens, even those who lived here for decades, were required to have, but not to carry, a registration card that was tantamount to an internal passport.*

Four months later the nationality laws were completely revised. There were two significant changes. The first clarified the status of Mexicans and others of Amerindian heritage. All Indians born in the United States had been made citizens in 1924; the 1940 statute expanded the rights of naturalization from "white persons and persons of African descent" to include "descendants of races indigenous to the Western Hemisphere." The sec-

---

*Fingerprinting of all American citizens, not just aliens, had long been a goal of J. Edgar Hoover's, a goal Perkins had resisted. Martin, *Madame Secretary*, 441.

ond, echoing the antisubversive provisions of the Alien Registration Act, greatly expanded the existing antiradical provisions barring the naturalization of "persons opposed to government or law."[7]

But the fall of France also triggered Franklin Roosevelt's first of several small gestures toward saving refugees. The president asked his Advisory Committee on Refugees to make lists of eminent refugees and then instructed the State Department to issue temporary visas in the names of those individuals. The State Department's own reports, which are not always reliable, indicate that it issued 3,268 such visas to persons whom it described in flatulent bureaucratic prose as

> those of superior intellectual attainment, of indomitable spirit, experienced in vigorous support of liberal government and who are in danger of persecution or death at the hands of autocracy.

Only about a third of them were used.* The intermediary body, the Emergency Rescue Committee, what we would call today a non-governmental organization, appointed Varian Fry (1907–67) as its representative. Fry, a thirty-two-year-old classicist who had been an editor at New York's Foreign Policy Association, was a most improbable cloak-and-dagger operative, but, as it turned out, a very effective one. He spoke French and German and got credentials as a social worker from the International YMCA, as his "cover" was that he was helping to support refugees in Vichy France. He arrived in Marseilles in early August 1940, planning to stay about three weeks; he left thirteen months later. Working with two American vice-consuls, Hiram Bingham and Miles Standish, Fry helped bring out of occupied Europe a veritable galaxy of cultural superstars including Lion Feuchtwanger, Heinrich Mann, Franz Werfel, Anna Mahler Werfel, Marc Chagall, Jacques Lipchitz, Marcel Duchamp, and Wanda Landowska.[8]

In addition, late in 1940, two administrative measures eased the position of some refugees who had already escaped from Germany and German-occupied Europe. First, American consuls outside of Germany were allowed to issue visas to refugees who had gotten to places like Portugal, French Africa, and China, and charge them to the German quota established in the 1924 immigration act, little used after the war broke out. In fis-

---

*Former Secretary of State Warren Christopher, in a preface to a 1997 edition of Fry's memoir, *Surrender on Demand*, says "almost 4,000," using, I am sure, data supplied by the department.

cal 1941 only 4,028 spaces were used and in fiscal 1942 about half that number. Had this kind of administrative ingenuity been used earlier, many more refugees could have been admitted. Then, in January 1941, an agreement with Canada set up a system whereby a refugee in the United States on a temporary visa would be allowed to enter Canada briefly, apply for a quota number from there, and reenter the United States as a regular immigrant. American law previously forbade a visitor from changing status without leaving the United States.[9]

Nothing further was done to facilitate refugee entry until 1944, although the government did take the lead in providing for refugees in North Africa and then in Europe. Initially this was done under the Office of Foreign Relief and Rehabilitation, put in the State Department in December 1942 following the invasion of North Africa. After the creation of the United Nations Relief and Rehabilitation Administration (UNRRA) in November 1943, it was handled there. Herbert H. Lehman headed both organizations.[10]

Only after Secretary of the Treasury Henry Morgenthau's staff prepared its damning "Report to the Secretary on the Acquiescence of this Government in the Murder of the Jews" and Morgenthau brought it to Roosevelt—under the less jarring title of "Personal Report to the President"—on January 16, 1944, was further action taken to bring refugees to the United States. From its blunt first sentence—"One of the greatest crimes in history, the slaughter of the Jewish people in Europe, is continuing unabated"—to the end it was a damning indictment of American policy in general and of the State Department in particular. The report not only attacked the department's visa policy, which, under the cloak of "national security," had kept immigration well below quota levels, but argued that some of its officials—Breckinridge Long in particular—had deliberately failed to rescue Jews. Prodded by the report, Roosevelt undertook additional actions on behalf of Jewish and other refugees, but was reluctant to believe that Long, an old friend, was the deliberate saboteur of rescue plans.[11] Just six days later FDR issued an executive order creating the War Refugee Board, whose bills were paid by a combination of the President's discretionary funds and money donated by Jewish organizations. Although the language of the executive order stated that

it is the policy of this Government to take all measures within its power to rescue the victims of enemy oppression who are in imminent danger of death and otherwise to afford such victims all possible relief and assistance consistent with the successful prosecution of the war . . .[12]

The truth of the situation had been, was then, and continued to be at variance with the inflated claim. In fact, the War Refugee Board was not authorized to bring even one refugee to the United States. Its overseas representatives were stationed in allied and neutral countries such as Turkey, Sweden, and Switzerland and placed the people it rescued in camps in North and West Africa, the Middle East, Switzerland, and Sweden.[13]

A further step was taken in June 1944. After considerable private and public discussion FDR cabled Ambassador Robert Murphy in Algiers on June 9 that:

> I have decided that approximately 1,000 refugees should be immediately brought from Italy to this country, to be placed in an Emergency Refugee Shelter to be established at Fort Ontario near Oswego, New York, where under appropriate security restrictions they will remain for the duration of the war. These refugees will be brought into the country outside of the regular immigration procedure just as civilian internees* from Latin American countries and prisoners of war have been brought here . . . It is contemplated that at the end of the war they will be returned to their homelands.[14]

Three days later Roosevelt sent a message to inform Congress of the program. He claimed that "notwithstanding this Government's unremitting efforts, which are continuing, the numbers actually rescued from the jaws of death have been small compared with the numbers still facing extinction in German territory."[15]

Sharon R. Lowenstein, the historian of this episode, has rightly called it a "token shipment." It brought 987 refugees, mostly Jewish, from camps in Italy to the United States. They were from eighteen different countries: 369 were Yugoslavs, 238 Austrians, 153 Poles, 95 Germans, and 40 Czechs. All but 69 would remain in America when the camp† was emptied in February 1946, President Truman having issued a directive on December 22, 1945, allowing them to adjust their status. Although the lucky few brought to Os-

---

*These were Germans, Japanese, and Italians from Latin America brought to the United States and interned for "national security." Max Paul Friedman, *Nazis and Good Neighbors: The United States Campaign against the Germans of Latin America in World War II* (New York: Cambridge University Press, 2003).

†The refugee camp at Oswego was run by the War Relocation Authority, originally created to supervise the incarceration of Japanese Americans.

wego were truly a token insofar as the surviving victims of the Holocaust were concerned, the precedent of presidential parole authority would become an important part of American refugee policy during the Cold War and beyond.[16]

Resident enemy aliens encountered serious restrictions as soon as the United States actually went to war. In December 1941 a series of proclamations declared noncitizen Japanese, Germans, and Italians alien enemies and laid down regulations governing their behavior that were later extended to Hungarians, Bulgarians, and Romanians.[17] In mid-January 1942, all alien enemies were required to re-register and receive new identification certificates and carry them at all times.[18] Although the language of these proclamations treated the different enemy nationalities identically, it was clear that the government, from the White House down, had a hierarchical notion about the threat posed by each.

Francis Biddle, Attorney General from 1941 to 1945, tells an anecdote that illustrates this nicely. When he brought the proclamations declaring resident Germans and Italians alien enemies—the one for Japanese had been signed the previous day—to the White House he found the president having his sinuses swabbed out by his physician, Admiral Ross T. McIntyre. Biddle remembered his conversation with Roosevelt as follows:

> "How many Germans are there in the country?" he asked. "Oh, about 600,000," I told him. [Biddle either told him wrong or was confused when he wrote his memoirs. There were about 300,000 Germans, 600,000 Italians, and 90,000 Japanese aliens registered, most of the latter in Hawaii.] "And you're going to intern all of them," he said . . . "Well, not quite all," I answered. "I don't care so much about the Italians," he continued. "They are a lot of opera singers, but the Germans are different, they may be dangerous." "Please, Mr. President," the admiral pleaded, and his patient sank back, as I hastily withdrew. The color had come back to the President's cheeks. The prospect of action always made him feel better. And from his impulsive and absurdly impractical suggestion I knew that his health had improved.[19]

Under Biddle's leadership the Department of Justice was relatively restrained in its arrests and internment of alien enemies. He makes it clear in his memoirs that he wished to avoid the excesses of the British program. According to one FBI document, 16,810 enemy aliens were arrested between December 7, 1941, and June 3, 1945: 7,164 Germans, 6,026 Japanese, 3,596 Italians, and 24 "others."[20] Only about a third of these were interned in INS camps—most of them Japanese—and of the Germans and

Italians some 1,200 were nonresident alien seamen. On Columbus Day 1942 Attorney General Biddle announced that the blanket designation of unnaturalized Italians as enemy aliens was being lifted and called it an "exoneration which [Italian Americans] have so well earned." This was a reasonable move, and one obviously made with an eye on the November congressional elections.[21]

There was nothing reasonable about what happened to the Japanese Americans of the West Coast, more than two-thirds of whom were native-born American citizens. From the very first days after Pearl Harbor the federal government treated all ethnic Japanese as if they were alien enemies. Although what happened to them is usually referred to as "the internment of the Japanese Americans," internment is a misnomer. Internment is a legal process, used since the War of 1812, to move and/or confine persons who are nationals fourteen years of age or older of a nation with whom the United States is at war. What happened to the West Coast Japanese Americans of all ages was simply lawless, although the Supreme Court later ratified, in three awful decisions, what FDR had done by executive order and Congress by statute. The United States Army's Western Defense Command, which was responsible for herding the West Coast Japanese into concentration camps, habitually referred to the citizen Japanese as "non-aliens." All told, more than 120,000 Japanese Americans were incarcerated in ten desolate barbed-wire enclosures with a minimum of physical amenities run by a newly created civilian agency, the War Relocation Authority.[22]

In addition, the government encouraged Peru and fourteen other Latin American nations to deport some members of their German, Japanese, and Italian populations. The American government imported at least 2,264 Japanese, chiefly from Peru, 4,058 Germans, and 288 Italians into the United States, in violation of the immigration laws, and placed them in INS internment camps.[23] In time, some of the Japanese American men interned in the INS camps were allowed to join their families in WRA camps and some Japanese American "troublemakers" were transferred from WRA camps to INS camps. Perhaps the crowning irony came in 1943 when Assistant Secretary of State Breckinridge Long falsely claimed to a congressional committee that the United States had accepted about 580,000 refugees since Hitler had come to power. Apparently one of the ways he inflated the figure was by counting the Japanese Americans in various government concentration camps as if they were refugees; in one sense, of course, that is just what they were.[24]

In addition, after the infamous loyalty questionnaires were distributed in 1943 to all Japanese Americans held by the War Relocation Authority and a minority of understandably "turned off" native-born Japanese Americans spoke of renouncing their citizenship, the Department of Justice drafted a bill that Congress enacted in July 1944 making it simple for them to do so. The purpose was to facilitate the post-war deportation of "disloyal" Japanese Americans. Five thousand seven hundred and sixty-six Japanese American citizens did execute denaturalization declarations, and 1,116 of them were actually sent to Japan right after the war. Eventually, an almost one-person legal crusade by San Francisco attorney Wayne Collins stopped the process as the federal courts eventually ruled that acts of renunciation made behind barbed wire were, in essence, made under duress and were therefore null and void.[25]

While wartime fears about national security caused a tightening of both immigration regulations and those governing resident aliens, wartime demand for labor caused a relaxation of such regulations. The World War II program to bring "temporary" Mexican workers to the United States was not unique: during World War I the United States had also actively recruited Mexicans. The earlier program was possible because of the so-called ninth proviso of Section 3 of the 1917 immigration act. This allowed the INS Commissioner, with the permission of the Secretary of Labor, "to control and regulate the admission and return of otherwise inadmissible aliens for temporary admission."[26]

Among those who had then pressed for even further relaxation of the regulations was Herbert Hoover in his role as food administrator. He wrote to Felix Frankfurter, then an official in the Labor Department, that "we need every bit of this labor we can get and need it badly." Among the regulations he wanted lifted was one that called for two photographs of each immigrant: part of Hoover's rationale for this request was that "the Mexican has a primitive suspicion of the camera."[27]

Authorized on May 23, 1917, the program lasted until March 1921. Perhaps 500,000 Mexicans came, most of them after the Armistice, and about half of those were actually registered under the program. Whether legal or illegal they worked not only on farms, but also on railroads, in mining, and in manufacturing establishments. Arrangements were left largely to employers and the role of the government, once the program was authorized, was all but invisible.[28]

When in 1942 Southwestern employers again looked south of the border to ease wartime labor shortages, relations between the two countries had so evolved that Washington felt that it had to gain prior approval from Mexico City. The Mexican government, remembering not only the World War I program but also the "voluntary" repatriations and deportations of the 1920s and 1930s, insisted on having a say about where its citizens worked and what their wages and working and living conditions would be. Thus there were complex binational negotiations before an agreement was reached that "guaranteed" workers minimum wages, decent working and living conditions, and round-trip transportation. The American labor movement also received guarantees that "prevailing wages" would be paid. The program initially focused on agricultural workers, usually called *braceros* from the Spanish *braccar* (to wave one's arms), from Mexico to the United States. First established by an executive agreement between the United States and Mexico in July 1942 and revised in April 1943, it was legalized by Congress in 1943 and extended to cover West Indian and Bahamian workers who toiled largely in eastern agriculture, as did some Canadians and Newfoundlanders. Government data report just over 225,000 agricultural workers imported during the war years, nearly three-quarters of them from Mexico.[29] To be sure, other workers came informally. A separate wartime bracero program provided about 50,000 maintenance workers for western railroads.[30] Congress continued importing foreign agricultural workers on a much larger scale into the mid-1960s, and executive branch waivers were issued sometime after that.

Because of notorious anti-Mexican discrimination in Texas, the Mexican government refused to allow any braceros to be sent there, but large numbers of Mexican workers went to Texas—and elsewhere—on their own as they had been doing for decades, without being sanctioned by the program. As we shall see, the wartime program would be evoked again during the Korean War and in a different way in the Immigration Reform Act of 1986.

As part of the original agreements, Mexico and the United States jointly instituted a forced "Savings Fund"—a kind of social security—into which 10 percent of the wages of the perhaps 400,000 braceros who worked between 1943 and 1949 was withheld, transmitted to Mexico, and was supposed to be paid to them when they went back to Mexico. Given the notorious corruption endemic in Mexican institutions it is not surprising that many—perhaps most—of the braceros never got the money that was rightly due them. There were some attempts to get payment from Mexican banks in the late 1940s, but they got nowhere and were largely ignored on both sides of the border.[31]

The manipulation of the bracero program by organized American agriculture and its political allies was one legislative result of pressure group politics in wartime; the repeal of the once sacrosanct Chinese Exclusion Act was another. Its key instrument was the awkwardly named Citizens Committee to Repeal Chinese Exclusion and Place Immigration on a Quota Basis. Formed on May 25, 1943, the committee conducted a whirlwind campaign of persuasion focused on opinion makers.[32] The repeal was enacted that December. The key person on the committee was Richard J. Walsh, a New York publisher and husband of the novelist Pearl S. Buck, whose books—and the films made from them—had helped create in the minds of many Americans a favorable if essentially false image of China and the Chinese. The more than 150 persons on the committee's letterhead represented a broad spectrum of the American economic and intellectual elite, from Roger Baldwin of the ACLU and academic socialist Broadus Mitchell on the left to magazine publisher Henry R. Luce and retired Admiral Henry R. Yarnell on the right. Even before the committee was organized, six separate bills to repeal Chinese exclusion had been dropped into the congressional hoppers and hearings had begun on two of them.

The campaign for repeal is instructive. It treated repeal as a good behavior prize for a wartime ally, China, and studiously ignored the American Chinese and deliberately minimized the effect that repeal might have. Writing to a longtime anti-Asian publicist Walsh stressed that:[33]

> [The committee supports] only the broad policy of removing the discrimination against the Chinese . . . that is putting them under the quota law. As you know the Chinese quota would be very small, and very much less than the number of Chinese who now get in illegally. No one, as far as I know would advocate any change in the quota system, or letting down the general immigration bars.

Relatively conservative mass media echoed the Committee's line. The *Saturday Evening Post*, for example, editorialized that:[34]

> The Chinese quota would work out to about 107 a year. Small as the number is, however, it would have a great moral effect on the Chinese. It isn't the in-

ability to get into America that annoys them, but the insult implied in total exclusion.

Similarly, when Franklin Roosevelt sent a special message to Congress urging passage of the repeal bill, he spoke as commander in chief, who regarded the legislation as important in "winning the war" and establishing "a just peace." Since China's resistance to Japan depended in part on "the spirit of her people and her faith in her allies" the president argued that:

> We owe it to the Chinese to strengthen that faith. One step in this direction is to wipe from the statute books those anachronisms in our laws which forbid the immigration of Chinese people into this country and which bar Chinese residents from American citizenship. Nations, like individuals, make mistakes. We must be big enough to acknowledge our mistakes of the past and correct them.

In addition FDR insisted that repeal would counter Japanese propaganda, and that the small number of Chinese entrants would not be a significant factor in the domestic economy. Anticipating the logical argument that repealing the exclusion just of Chinese but not other Asians was discriminatory, the president admitted that:

> [although repeal] would give the Chinese a preferred status over certain other Oriental people, their great contribution to the cause of decency and freedom entitles them to such preference.

And, finally and prophetically, he noted that the bill's passage would "be an earnest of our purpose to apply the policy of the good neighbor to our relations with other peoples."[35]

The bill Congress acted on, introduced into the House by Warren Magnuson (D-WA), was a relatively simple three-part measure. The first part repealed some or all of fifteen statutes enacted between 1882 and 1913 which had enforced Chinese exclusion. The second gave a quota to "persons of the Chinese race," set at 105 annually, with a preference of up to 75 percent given to persons "born and resident in China." This meant that a Chinese born anywhere in the world—say Canada—had to be charged to the tiny Chinese quota, a stipulation that applied to no other group. The third part amended the nationality acts so that "Chinese persons or persons of Chinese descent" were eligible for naturalization on the same terms as other eligible aliens. The bill was supported by the congressional leaders of both parties and it passed both Houses of Congress without recorded votes.

Both in and out of Congress traditional nativists offered some opposition. John B. Trevor, an important spokesperson for anti-immigrant pressure groups for decades, told a House committee that while his supporters wanted "the practical suspension of all immigration" they particularly opposed Chinese "who are, morally, the most debased people on the face of the earth." And he accurately predicted that their admission would soon be followed by the admission of other Asians.[36] The general population seemed more evenly divided than the Congress. A November 1943 Gallup poll showed that 42 percent of a national sample approved repeal, 40 percent opposed, and 18 percent were undecided, with the West Coast, tradtional home of anti-Asian feeling and the region that the Citizens Committee propagandized the hardest, more strongly favoring repeal than the nation at large.[37]

When the president signed the bill in December he issued a special statement expressing his "particular pride and pleasure" in so doing and his conviction that "the Chinese people" would regard it as "a manifestation on the part of the American people of their affection and regard."[38] Although it was only a small step toward an ethnically egalitarian immigration and naturalization policy, it can now be seen that the repeal of Chinese exclusion was the hinge on which the nearly closed golden door of immigration began to swing open again. And, as both FDR and John B. Trevor had predicted, the door soon opened a bit wider as the same process was applied first to Filipinos and "persons of races indigenous to India" and then to all Asian peoples.

In addition the government also made it possible for educated Chinese to study in the United States. Beginning in 1942 the Cultural Division of the State Department provided grants to enable many Chinese to study at American universities; in 1949, when Chinese Communists led by Mao Tse-tung had driven the Chinese Nationalists off the mainland to Taiwan and began the People's Republic of China, there were some 5,000 Chinese, many of them students, in the United States on nonimmigrant visas. Many, perhaps most, of these "stranded Chinese" received immigrant visas and eventually became U.S. citizens.[39]

The 1943 legislation, however, ignored the major immigration problem of Chinese Americans, the reunification of Chinese American families. Although that question had been addressed by two of the bills introduced in

1943, neither was given serious consideration. After all, China, and not Chinese Americans, was the focal point. But in 1945 and 1946 three statutes, only one of which specifically mentioned Chinese, transformed the demographic structure of Chinese America. The first, the December 1945 War Brides Act, allowed the admission of "alien spouses and alien minor children" of citizen members or veterans of the armed forces as nonquota immigrants.[40] Six months later the privilege was extended to "alien fiancées and fiancés."[41] Very large numbers of the 16,000 Chinese Americans who served in United States forces during World War II, many of whom were able to gain the expedited citizenship offered to service personnel, took advantage of these provisions to bring in wives and children, while others went to China to find wives or had fiancées sent to them. The third statute, a brief 1946 amendment to the act repaling Chinese exclusion, allowed Chinese wives of nonveteran American citizens to enter as nonquota immigrants.[42]

The combined effects of these laws made possible a relatively sizeable immigration of Chinese women in the immediate post-war years, as Table 4.2 indicates. As small as the numbers were, the migration of nearly 10,000 Chinese women had a major demographic impact on the structure of the Chinese American community, which contained, as late as 1950, only 28,000 females fourteen years of age and older. The Chinese quota for the years covered in Table 4.1 allowed for a maximum of 840 immigrants, less than a twelfth of those lawfully admitted.[43]

TABLE 4.2

IMMIGRATION OF CHINESE BY GENDER, 1945–52

Year	Total	Male	Female	% Female
1945	109	45	64	59
1946	233	71	162	69
1947	1,128	142	986	87
1948	3,574	257	3,317	93
1949	2,490	242	2,248	90
1950	1,289	110	1,179	91
1951	1,083	126	957	88
1952	1,152	118	1,034	90
Total	11,058	1,111	9,947	90

Source: INS, *Annual Reports*, 1945–53.

As noted, the rights of naturalization and full-quota immigration were extended in 1946 to include two additional Asian groups, Filipinos and "persons of races indigenous to India." The congressional favor to Filipinos had its own logic: it was a prize for "good behavior" during the war and a ❦ kind of present for the war-delayed grant of independence to the Philippines, which took place on July 4, 1946. Two days previously Congress had added Filipinos to the list of those entitled to be naturalized and on the now joint Independence Day a presidential proclamation upped the annual Philippine quota from 50 to 100.[44] While these numbers may seem small, this increased immigration plus citizenship for Filipinos would provide a base for the large expansion of Filipino immigration after 1965. As the geographer D. W. Meinig has pointed out, post–World War II Filipino migration to the United States provides "an excellent illustration of the fact that imperialism on any major scale may continue to alter the internal geography of the imperial state long after the formal geographical relationship has ended."[45]

Similar provisions were made in 1946 for "persons of races indigenous to India," who received an annual quota of 100 and the right of naturalization.[46] This special treatment for Indians—and after 1947 for Pakistanis— requires more detailed explanation. Although perhaps 70 Asian Indians, mostly merchants and professionals, had been naturalized by various United States courts in the early twentieth century, the government eventually decided that Indians were aliens ineligible to citizenship, a view upheld by the Supreme Court in *Thind v. U.S.* (1923). Thus began a two-decade-long fight by members of the Indian American community to regain the right of naturalization. Their victory in 1946 cannot be attributed, as can that for Chinese or Filipinos, as a kind of price for good wartime behavior: Indian nationalists had sat out the war and India was still part of the British Empire. Nor was it a matter of letting in any who were proposed: in the same year bills calling for admitting Koreans and Thais failed to pass, and, of course, in 1946 few spoke of doing anything positive for Japanese. The extension of rights to Asian Indians was a triumph of American anticolonial ideology and of Indian lobbying.

The key figure in the Indian victory was the New York import merchant, "J. J." Singh. Born into an elite Rawalpindi family in 1897, Singh came to the United States in 1926. In a 1951 *New Yorker* profile, Robert Shaplen wrote:

Sirdar Jagjit Singh, the president of the India League of America, a privately sponsored nonprofit organization that seeks to interpret India to, and to further Indian causes in, this country, is, at 53, a handsome, six-foot Sikh who by means of persistent salesmanship, urbane manners, and undeviating enthusiasm, has established himself as the principal link between numberless Americans and the vast mysterious Eastern subcontinent where he was born.[47]

Singh's tactics were those of the tireless lobbyist; he cultivated members of Congress, influential opinion molders, and the press. His eventual triumph was a bipartisan bill, first introduced in 1944 by Emanuel Celler (D-NY) and Clare Booth Luce (R-CT). Others who supported his cause ranged from Roger Baldwin of the ACLU to press baron William Randolph Hearst. Reintroduced in July 1945, it became law a year later. The crucial fight was in the House, where opposition to it was frankly racial. As one opponent put it:

> Advocates of the policy that we should let down our immigration barriers to those people who cannot be assimilated into our population are traveling with the same crowd of no-good do-gooders and down fallen uplifters who think this country should be run as a free-lunch counter for the whole world.

As often happens there was no recorded House vote on final passage. The crucial vote was on a motion to recommit—in other words kill the bill—which failed 207 to 83.[48]

The new law caused more stir in India than in the United States. Just four days after President Harry S. Truman signed the bill, Mohandas K. Gandhi penned a congratulatory note to Singh, calling him "solely responsible" for the act's passage. That is surely an exaggeration. But it is not too much to say that it is all but impossible to imagine the passage of such an act in 1946 without the labors of Singh or someone like him. On the other hand, the lopsided vote of support surely presaged the total disappearance of racial bars that was soon to come.[49] Nor did many persons take advantage of the new law. Between its passage and 1965 some 7,000 persons immigrated under its provisions, the overwhelming majority of them nonquota relatives of persons who were or became American citizens. Dalip Singh Saund (1899–1973), who had come to study at Berkeley just after WW I and remained as an Imperial Valley farmer, was naturalized and then elected to Congress as a Democrat from California in 1956, thus becoming the first Asian American congressperson.[50]

Despite these not inconsiderable liberalizations, American immigration law continued to be blatantly racist and discriminatory. The quota system was wounded, but it survived. The same Congress that gave naturalization rights to Filipinos and Indians and put Chinese wives of American citizens on a nonquota basis also, in the so-called War Brides Act of 1946, retained the "aliens ineligible to citizenship bar" which affected chiefly Korean and Japanese women, but also barred all non-Chinese Southeast Asians. And, in the very statute admitting Asian Indians to citizenship, some racist pedant put in language to determine to what quota a probably nonexistent immigrant "of one-half Chinese blood and one half the blood of a race indigenous to India" should be charged.

These piecemeal wartime and post-war changes created very little public stir. But later in the Truman administration battle would again be joined over European refugee admissions as Congress struggled over the question of what to do about those still in the displaced persons camps.

CHAPTER FIVE

Admitting Displaced Persons: 1946–1950

As we have seen, the United States went all through World War II without developing any kind of comprehensive refugee policy, although a number of ad hoc arrangements were made. When the war with Hitler came to an end in May 1945 there were anywhere from seven to eleven million displaced persons (DPs) in Europe; large numbers of them were soon repatriated to their own countries, but many literally no longer had a country. This was true not only for the survivors of the Holocaust but also for persons who fled west before the advance of the Red Army and those whose nations had either been absorbed—like the Baltic states—or forced into socialism under Soviet tutelage. By early fall 1945, there were something fewer than two million persons in Western Europe still officially classified as DPs while others continued to arrive from the east.

Late that winter the International Refugee Organization (IRO) adopted official definitions of "refugees" and "displaced persons" that were accepted by the American Congress in mid-1946 when it formally joined the organization, the newly created United Nations arm of UNRRA.[1] Congress qualified American membership with provisos stating that no persons would be "admitted to or settled or resettled" in the United States without congressional approval and that membership would not change any American immigration laws.[2]

Under the IRO definitions a refugee was:

1. . . . a person who has left, or who is outside of, his country of nationality or of former habitual residence, and who, whether or not he retained his nationality, belongs to one of the following categories:

    (a) victims of the Nazi or fascist regimes or regimes which took part on their side in the second world war, or of the quisling or similar regimes which assisted them against the United Nations . . . ;

    (b) Spanish Republicans and other victims of the Falangist regime in Spain . . . ;

    (c) persons who were considered refugees before the outbreak of the second world war, for reasons of race, religion, nationality or political opinion.

2. . . . a person, other than a displaced person . . . who is outside of his country of habitual residence, and who, as a result of events subsequent to the outbreak of the second world war, is unable or unwilling to avail himself of the protection of the Government of his country of nationality or former nationality.

3. . . . persons who, having resided in Germany or Austria, and being of Jewish origin or foreigners or stateless persons, were victims of Nazi persecution and were detained in, or were obliged to flee from, and were subsequently returned to, one of those countries as a result of war circumstances, and have not yet been firmly settled therein.

4. . . . unaccompanied children who are war orphans or whose parents have disappeared and who are outside their countries of origin.

    A displaced person was defined as a refugee who: "has been deported from, or has been obliged to leave his country of nationality or of former habitual residence, such as persons who were compelled to undertake forced labor or who were deported for racial, religious or political reasons. . . . If the reasons for their displacement have ceased to exist they should be repatriated as soon as possible."[3]

Official policy could not overcome ingrained prejudice. General George S. Patton, Jr., one of the senior American commanders in Germany, defined DPs differently in his diary: some persons, he wrote, "believe that the Displaced Person is a human being, which he is not, and this applies particularly to the Jews who are lower than animals." Leonard Dinnerstein, the historian of America's reactions to and treatment of Holocaust survivors, quotes Patton as believing that the "Jewish type of DP is, in the majority of cases, a sub-human species without any of the cultural or social refinements of our time."[4]

While Patton's views were extreme, it was notorious at the time that many in charge of United States occupation policy were less than friendly to the often disorderly DPs and seemed more partial to the orderly German civilian population. We now know that U.S. Army intelligence and counter-intelligence officials in Europe, already fighting the Cold War, gave succor to major war criminals, such as Klaus Barbie, and helped them to flee abroad in exchange for information about and assistance against the Soviet Union. At the top of the American chain of command in Germany, General Lucius D. Clay, soon to be appointed High Commissioner for Germany, argued as early as mid-October 1945, that DPs "must obey German laws, and that it is only through aid of an efficient German police force that the small occupation Army can control Germany."[5] While it is not possible to work out a calculus of motives, an endemic anti-Semitism, a desire for order and efficiency, plus the notion that German help might soon be needed against the Russians, all combined to produce among Army officers and other American officials unfeeling if not downright callous actions and reactions toward the DPs.

It is instructive to compare the treatment of DPs, Hitler's victims, with the treatment meted out to some of his supporters. Most overtly, there were the rocket scientists, of whom Wernher von Braun (1912–77) was only the most prominent. Those whom the United States government got its hands on, and who were willing to come to America and work on the American rocket program—which became the American space program—were welcomed, their naturalization facilitated, and, contrary to law, their Nazi past ignored. Altogether according to Clarence Lasby, at least 642 such persons and their families were brought to the United States.[6]

As the imperatives of the Cold War grew, Congress quietly regularized what we now know American intelligence agencies had been doing anyway. The 1949 statute creating the Central Intelligence Agency gave the agency a "quota" equal to that of many small nations. Under the law, whenever the CIA director, with the approval of the Attorney General and the Commissioner of Immigration determined that:[7]

> the entry of a particular alien . . . is in the interest of national security or essential to the furtherance of the national mission, such alien and his immediate family shall [be admitted to the country] without regard to their admissibility under the immigration or any other laws and regulations [up to the number of] one hundred persons in any one fiscal year.

It is not yet possible to determine how often this lawless provision of the law was used, nor whether the CIA brought in war and/or other criminals, or facilitated the illegal naturalization of any persons it brought into the United States under this provision.

Despite the hostility shown to DPs by U.S. government officials in Europe—and indifference was probably more prevalent than outright hostility—at the top in Washington and in Europe policy was different. Both President Truman and General Dwight D. Eisenhower, the Supreme Commander in Europe, wanted humane treatment but neither had any real understanding of either the forces at work or the special problems involved. The first high-ranking American official to express concern about the Army's treatment of the liberated Jews and others was Treasury Secretary Henry Morgenthau, who suggested to Truman that a cabinet committee be created to deal with the DP problem, but the president rejected the notion in June 1945. Morgenthau, who was about to leave the cabinet, persisted and approached Acting Secretary of State Joseph C. Grew, suggesting that Earl G. Harrison, a former commissioner of immigration and dean of the University of Pennsylvania Law School, be sent to Europe to investigate and report on the problems of displaced persons. When Grew brought this suggestion to Truman, the president agreed and signed a letter of instruction to Harrison that had been drafted in the State Department.[8]

Harrison's report went directly to the president at the end of August and appeared in the Department of State *Bulletin* at the end of September 1945. It was a bombshell. Harrison described between 50,000 and 100,000 Jews living under guard behind barbed-wire fences, in camps of

> several descriptions, (built by Germans for slave-laborers and Jews) including some of the most notorious of the concentration camps, amidst crowded conditions, in complete idleness, with no opportunity, except surreptitiously, to communicate with the outside world . . .

In terms of solutions, the report was clear: most Jews in the camps wanted to go to Palestine, but some, "the number is not large, wish to emigrate to the United States where they have relatives, others to England, the British Dominions, or to South America." The former commissioner of immigration had nothing to say about the difficulties DPs—clearly persons likely to become a public charge—might have in getting American visas. Harrison's conclusion was unambiguous:

> the main solution, in many ways the only real solution, of the problem lies in the quick evacuation of all nonrepatriatable Jews in Germany and Austria, who wish it, to Palestine.[9]

This was, of course, a solution beyond the capability of American policy to execute; the British were increasingly reluctant to allow more Jews into their Palestine mandate.[10] Harrison also pointed out that the majority of repatriatables in the camps were not Jews.

Despite some emigration, legal and illegal, to Palestine, the number of Jewish DPs continued to grow as persons from Soviet-occupied areas moved west. This movement was spurred by a revival of anti-Semitism in Poland which resulted in a July 1946 pogrom in which some forty Jews were killed. Neither the Catholic Church in Poland nor the communist government there took any appropriate action and each, essentially, resorted to blaming the Jewish victims and excusing the Polish perpetrators.

How many Jewish DPs were there? At the end of 1945 the United States Army calculated that there were some 207,000 Jewish DPs in the western-occupied zones of Germany and Austria, and in Italy. Two months later the American Jewish refugee organization, the Joint Distribution Committee, estimated that there were 231,000 Jewish DPs in those areas. The United Nations estimated that there were some 1,171,000 DPs in the western-controlled territory at the end of 1946 and 963,000 in November 1947. Thus Jews were fewer than one-fifth of all DPs at the end of 1946; after that their incidence grew somewhat as the total number of DPs shrank. It is impossible to be more specific. Part of the numbers problem is that most authorities registered DPs by nationality rather than by religion; another important factor is the general chaos and confusion that reigned in postwar Europe.[11]

As a result of the Harrison report a number of improvements were made in the conditions under which DPs lived, their food ration was increased, and General Eisenhower acquired an advisor on Jewish affairs, Simon H. Rifkind, a Russian-born federal district judge and American Jewish community leader. But DPs continued to be abused in some subordinate commands and the living conditions of many remained deplorable. In some places German police—often the very same ordinary policemen who had enforced anti-Jewish laws during the Third Reich—were given supervisory power over Jewish and other DPs. During a March 1946 raid on a DP camp in Stuttgart in search of black market goods, police killed a concentration camp survivor. As late as mid-June 1946, Ira A. Hirschmann, an American IRO official, reported to UNRRA Director Fiorello La Guardia about one Munich "camp": "1800 Jewish DPs most former concentration camp inhabitants were massed in a parking garage. Only three repeat three toilets for all men, women and children."[12] Robert W. Ross did not exaggerate when he wrote that: "The last chapter in the Nazi persecution of the Jews was written in the displaced-person camps and in the emigration of survivors during the years after the war in Europe."[13]

The military always insisted that it was doing the best that it could under the circumstances, but when one remembers what this same military was able to accomplish in 1948 during the Berlin airlift it is clear that what was really lacking was the will and a sense of urgency. Had the nation seen the feeding of DPs in 1945–47 as important as the feeding of Berliners in 1948 the story would have been different. But Jewish DPs, and DPs in general, were not a high priority for the military, the American government, or, for that matter, the American people.

A Gallup poll in December 1945 asked Americans whether more European immigrants should be admitted than before the war, or the same number, or fewer. Five percent said more, 32 percent said the same, 37 percent said fewer, 14 percent said none at all, and 12 percent had no opinion.[14]

Under those circumstances it can be argued that President Truman showed some courage when, at the end of December 1945, he issued a formal directive reserving half of the quotas of European countries for DPs which, he hoped, would bring some 40,000 DPs a year to the United States. The president's public statement insisted that "any effort to bring relief to these displaced persons and refugees must and will be strictly within the limits of the present quotas as imposed by law." While that may have been technically true insofar as the total number of European quota immigrants was concerned, Truman's directive actually contemplated exactly the kinds of switching of quota slots between countries that the law forbade. In addition, the directive made an important change in the way the "likely to become a public charge" clause was administered. As we have seen, affidavits of support had to be filed by financially competent individuals; the Truman directive allowed blanket guarantees for large numbers of persons to be issued by competent agencies, such as the National Refugee Service. This began the practice of having voluntary social service agencies, later known as VOLAGS, play a role in refugee and other immigrant settlement, a role that they still perform today.* Had such a policy been in effect during the Nazi era, greater numbers of western European Jews would have found asy-

---

*Many of these were organizations run by religious denominations, what George W. Bush would call "faith-based." Thus the essence of his 2001 proposal was not new: what was new was the public stress on "faith"—as opposed to nonsectarian social service—which was, of course, a patent attempt to appeal to a particular political constituency.

lum in the United States. That Truman could do this is evidence of the greater power that had accrued to the American presidency during World War II.[15] No significant public notice was taken of the directive and, despite the president's wishes, only about 5,000 DPs—not all of them Jews—entered the United States in the first nine months of 1946. These DPs represented fewer than 10 percent of European immigration in that period.

Disappointed, Truman told reporters early in October 1946 that he would ask Congress to admit Jews *outside* the quotas. Almost immediately the DP issue became a public concern. Later that month a poll question asking specifically whether respondents favored "allowing more Jewish and other European refugees to come to the United States to live than are allowed under the law now" drew a 72 percent negative response. Only 16 percent of the responses were positive, while 12 percent of those who responded had no opinion.[16]

Many American Jewish organizations and leaders felt strongly that any discussion of bringing large numbers of DPs to the United States would involve weakening the commitment of the American government, such as it was, to a Jewish homeland in Palestine.*[17] Others, however, applauded Truman's suggestion, which drew verbal attacks not only from leaders of traditional nativist forces but also from many who simply wanted immigration policy left alone. Truman's 1946 announcement triggered six years of intense discussion and debate over immigration policy, which led, in the final analysis, not only to special laws for refugee admissions but also to the first major revision in American immigration law since 1924, the McCarran-Walter Act of 1952.

Unlike the breakthrough made for some Asian groups in 1943–46, the passage of DP legislation involved a long and bitter fight, a fight that was continued in the struggle over general immigration legislation that culminated in the McCarran-Walter Act of 1952. Contemporary liberals and most historians of immigration since then have treated the immigration legislation of 1948–52 as a further triumph of the forces of American nativism,

---

*There is no way here to explicate fully the seemingly paradoxical situation in which many American Jewish leaders, especially those with strong Zionist commitments, were, at best, lukewarm to the admission of more Jewish DPs into the United States. It was paralleled by a situation in the 1980s when the Shamir government in Israel tried to deflect the flow of Soviet Jews from the United States and some figures in that government indicated that if Jews didn't want to come to Israel they didn't care whether they got out of the USSR or not. In each case, reasons of state were more important than the rights of individuals.

and essentially a continuation of the policies and practices of the early 1920s. Yet it now seems clear that the nativist forces suffered a qualified defeat. The leading nativist in Congress, Nevada's Democratic Senator Patrick A. McCarran, admitted as much in a private letter to his daughter, "I met the enemy and he took me on the DP bill."[18]

Toward the end of 1946 leaders of two American Jewish organizations, the American Jewish Committee and the American Committee for Judaism, created a broadly based group of noted Americans, the Citizens Committee on Displaced Persons, which spearheaded a drive for special legislation to bring DPs to the United States. As had been the case with the Citizens Committee to Repeal Chinese Exclusion, the new committee did not concern itself with basic immigration law but merely lobbied for special legislation to admit the group it was interested in, in this case displaced persons. Although Irving Engel of the American Jewish Committee managed the committee and Lessing Rosenwald and members of his family provided most of the financing, the new Citizens Committee's letterhead had a distinctly non-Jewish appearance. Earl Harrison agreed to chair its board.[19] The day-to-day management of the committee and eventually its lobbying operation in Washington were run by William S. Bernard, a Yale-trained sociologist.*

President Truman, in his January 1947 State of the Union message, proposed to the first Congress since 1930 to have Republican majorities that it "turn its attention to this world problem, in an effort to find ways whereby we can fulfill our responsibilities to these thousands of homeless and suffering refugees of all faiths."[20] At the end of January the Citizens Committee publicly announced its goal: the admission of 400,000 European refugees over a four-year period. Although we now know that the Citizens Committee worked closely with David K. Niles, President Truman's special assistant on minority affairs, for tactical reasons it managed to get a conservative, midwestern, Protestant Republican, Congressman William G. Stratton (1914–2001) of Illinois, to introduce the bill its staff had drafted.

---

*In his valuable essay, "Refugee Asylum in the United States: How the Law Was Changed to Admit Displaced Persons," *International Migration Review* 13 (1975): 3–20, Bernard ignores Rosenwald's financial support, saying only that: "Financing . . . which eventually reached a total expenditure of something over $1,000,000, came from both large and small contributions. What was particularly heartwarming was that many of the contributions were from small donors" (p. 7), and argues that the elite committee was a "People's Lobby" (p. 16).

Stratton, a former member of the America First Committee, startled some of his supporters by his sponsorship, and his biographer, writing more than four decades later, is unable totally to explain it. He does show how the move gained him support in heavily ethnic Cook County but cost him support downstate. One of Stratton's support team, an Illinois Republican committeeman, warned him that, while it would gain him support "among certain foreign element groups . . . nobody in Illinois, outside of the Jews, wants any more Jews in this country."[21]

The bill, introduced on April 1, 1947, was a relatively straightforward one. It called for the admission of 100,000 displaced persons over and above the quotas in each of four years. The bill insisted that the immigrants meet all of the other requirements of American immigration law and gave preference to close relatives of American citizens and allied war veterans. In its final form the Displaced Persons Act of 1948 incorporated the IRO's definition of a refugee cited above, but added to it a number of categories of persons reflecting the new Cold War imperatives: persons of German ethnic origin who were born in Czechoslovakia, Estonia, Hungary, Latvia, Lithuania, Poland, Rumania, Russia, or Yugoslavia (called "German expellees" in the law, but many were not expelled), Polish veterans in exile, Greek displaced persons, European refugees from China, Italian refugees from the Venezia-Giulia, and post-1948 refugees from Czechoslovakia. The act also provided its own political litmus test by forbidding the issuance of a visa

> to any person who is or has been a member of, or participated in, any movement which is or has been hostile to the United States or the form of government of the United States.

The federal commission set up to administer the DP program later estimated that "more than 100,000 refugees were adversely effected [sic]" by this clause and the Internal Security Act of 1950, which listed specific organizations whose members were barred. Other provisions placed in the bill by immigration restrictionists included requirements that 30 percent of those admitted be farmers and insisted on job and housing guarantees by sponsors.

A large number of restrictions, many of them specifically designed to reduce the number of Jews admitted, were placed in the bill and many of its original supporters were sadly disappointed by the result. But the old aphorism about administration being more important than legislation clearly applied to the DP bill. Much more important than the restrictions, in the long run, were the establishment of the United States Displaced Persons Commission and provisions in the law that enabled "private or public agenc[ies] approved by the Commission" to act as sponsors. Truman appointed three liberal, "pro-refugee" commissioners to run the DP agency, a Protestant, a Catholic, and a Jew. Each had wide experience in immigrant and refugee resettlement. The Protestant chair, Ugo Carusi, was a former U.S. commissioner of immigration (1945–47); Edward M. O'Connor, a fifteen-year veteran of welfare work, had directed War Relief Services for the National Catholic Welfare Conference; and Harry H. Rosenfield had been a delegate to UNESCO and an official of the Federal Security Administration. Dinnerstein describes their effect on the DP program well:[22]

> the Commissioners established a system which reflected their liberal biases and undercut the letter and spirit of the law passed by the Congress.

Perhaps the most innovative aspects of the DP law were the provisions that allowed various voluntary agencies to issue assurances to guarantee that the displaced persons actually admitted to the United States would not become "public charges" and to oversee refugee resettlement on a case-by-case basis. These VOLAGS, and the religious and ethnic groups that created them, have become, in David Reimers's words, "the major non-governmental groups influencing American immigration policy"—not just refugee policy—throughout the years since World War II.[23]

The federal government, through the DP Commission, even loaned various VOLAGS more than $1.5 million to finance their activities.* Almost 90 percent of the more than 300,000 "assurances" of support filed with the DP Commission came from VOLAGS rather than from individuals.[24] Although nineteen separate agencies were eventually accredited by the DP Commission, more than two-thirds of those persons brought in under the DP program were resettled by just four agencies: the National Catholic Welfare Council settled 151,694; the Church World Service, an umbrella Protestant group, took responsibility for 51,010; the National Lutheran Council sponsored about 42,000; and the United Service for New Americans, a Jewish group, placed 38,524.[25]

The recognition of and financial support given to the VOLAGS by the federal government represented a sea change in the process by which

---

*Only nine of the nineteen agencies accredited to the Commission received loans and almost two-thirds of the total went to one agency, the National Catholic Welfare Council.

American immigration policy was executed. Although interest groups had long had an effect on the enactment of immigration law, the introduction of VOLAGS in the 1948 statute was the first time that Congress had authorized a role for private groups in the administration and implementation of immigration policy.

To be sure, as is often the case, practice had preceded the statute. A number of private agencies, particularly Jewish agencies such as the American Joint Distribution Committee (est. 1914) and the National Refugee Service (est. 1939), had long been involved in refugee resettlement, and, as noted above, the Truman directive of December 1945 had authorized corporate affidavits of support, but the DP act gave congressional sanction to that practice. The most comparable and immediate administrative precedent was the collaboration of the National Refugee Service with the War Relocation Authority in resettling the 1944 Oswego "token shipment" of refugees, which, in turn, had been preceded by the WRA's collaboration with a number of Christian agencies—most notably the American Friends Service Committee—in resettling internal refugees, the west coast Japanese Americans.[26] Similar kinds of arrangements had long been made between the government and religious groups in administering the affairs of American Indian reservations.

As opposed to the patently pro-immigrant DP Commission, the State Department and Immigration and Naturalization Service personnel continued to regard themselves as gatekeepers whose function was to "protect" America from foreign contagion and it was these two agencies that administered and supervised the admission process. After being selected for admission to the United States by the refugee bureaucracy, DPs still had to undergo agonizingly protracted State Department and INS procedures before they could board the ships the IRO had chartered for them. A recent historian of the DPs relates the following anecdote.[27]

> One DP was asked whether he would be willing to join the U.S. Army. He said he would. Then the Immigration officer asked, "If, while in the Army, you had a chance to capture Stalin, what would be the worst punishment you could give him?" The DP shot back: "I'd bring him here to [this DP camp] and make him go through processing for emigration to the States!"

More prosaically, a refugee official actually laid all of the papers in one case file end-to-end and found that they measured fifty-one feet.[28]

Rather than the 400,000 refugees over four years, the 1948 law authorized the issuance of 202,000 visas over and above the quota system over two years. In a face-saving measure that maintained the illusion that the old quota system remained intact, each displaced person admitted had to be assigned to some existing quota. But, for the first time, quotas could be mortgaged and Congress pretended that these mortgages would be paid off. It is difficult to believe that any but the most naive members of Congress thought that this would occur. To take an extreme case, within four years the tiny Latvian annual quota of 286 persons had been mortgaged to the year 2274. Thus the quota system was technically maintained as a wall to keep immigrants out, but the DP acts and other refugee measures created wide gates in the wall.

During the next session of Congress the struggle over DP admissions resumed, and in June 1950 the DP Act was extended to run for two more years and the authorized total was raised to just over 415,000 persons, slightly more than the original goal.

But, due in part to increased immigration to the newly created state of Israel (May 14, 1948), which, as the Harrison report had noted in 1945, was the goal of most of the remaining Jewish DPs, and to the increasing Cold War orientation of the act, only a minority of those admitted over the four-year life of the law (1948–52) were Hitler's victims. A larger number were members of groups that had supported the Third Reich or benefited from it, and, despite explicit provisions in the 1950 act prohibiting the entry of

> any person who advocated or assisted in the persecution of any person because of race, religion or national origin, or to any person who has voluntarily borne arms against the United States,

a significant but indeterminable number of persons who had actually been part of the Nazi apparatus got into the United States as displaced persons, as a number of sensational deportation procedures of persons who worked as guards in concentration camps have demonstrated.[29] In theory each potential immigrant underwent ten separate security checks, but clearly many of the checks were matters of going through the motions; in practice, of course, investigators were much more concerned about communists than about former fascists or their collaborators.[30]

Nevertheless the overwhelming number of those admitted were the kinds of persons the law had been framed to assist. All told, just over 400,000 persons were admitted under the authority of the two DP acts.[31] The DP Commission reported that the various federal agencies spent about $19 million of appropriated funds, which works out to a cost of less than $46 a head. To be sure, other funds were expended by international organizations such as the IRO, which were provided by the American taxpayers and by VOLAGS, but by any computation the total cost was relatively modest.

It is not possible to categorize, with precision, what kinds of persons came. In terms of nationality and ethnicity, for example, the Commission's statistics treated all Ukrainians as if they were Poles and many individuals listed as "German" were children of DPs who happened to be born in German camps. More than 70 percent of those admitted under the DP program were refugees from the USSR and Eastern Europe.[32] About three out of four were in some kind of family group and about 56 percent were males. Despite the perception that the program was largely for Jews, only about 16 percent, or 63,000 persons, were recorded as Jewish; about 47 percent, or 187,000 persons, were listed as Roman Catholic; about 34 percent, or 136,000 persons, were lumped together as "of Protestant and Orthodox faith"; and 2 percent, or 8,000 persons, were classified as "other."

As has been true of most immigrant groups, younger persons predominated: 52 percent were under thirty years of age and only 12.4 percent were over forty-nine years of age. Unlike the pre-war refugees, those admitted under the DP acts were not well educated. The median of school years completed of those in the labor force—i.e., adults but not housewives—in December 1951 was 8.2 years. Data for May 1952, covering almost the entire program, show that just over a quarter (28.1 percent) had more than eight years of schooling and only about one in fourteen of those twenty-five and older reported four years or more of higher education.

In the actual task of resettlement the U.S. DP Commission and the VOLAGS were greatly assisted by state DP commissions and committees that were eventually established in thirty-six of the then forty-eight states. Some of the state commissions were formed to help lobby for passage of the 1948 law, but most were created after the statute was enacted. In thirty-four states, commissions or committees were established by the governors, but in Rhode Island and Maine they were created by acts of the legislature. Only twenty-two of the state commissions had funds made available to them, and none had budgets of more than $12,000 annually. Like the U.S. Commission, the state bodies drew much of their support from VOLAGS; most of the funds for the Michigan Commission, for example, came from the Community Chest of Metropolitan Detroit.

"Without the State commissions," the national commission reported, "the Displaced Persons Commission could never have performed its necessary functions in the field." The Minnesota Displaced Persons Committee, established by Governor Luther W. Youngdahl (R) in November 1947, worked out a division of responsibility with the federal body that served as a model for the whole program. Under the "Minnesota Plan," the state agency:

1. Coordinated the work of VOLAGS within the state, but the agencies retained responsibility for their own operations.
2. Served as a central agency for information within the state.
3. Provided information and assistance for individuals not associated with VOLAGS who wished to sponsor DPs.
4. Coordinated social planning for DPs in individual communities and facilitated the utilization of state social service agencies.

Although held up as a model, Minnesota attracted only 2 percent of the DPs, about equal to its portion of the total population.

Conversely 70 percent of those admitted under the DP acts initially settled in either the Middle Atlantic states (44.5 percent) or the East North Central states (25.5 percent), which each contained 20 percent of the nation's population. New York, which got 31.3 percent of the DPs, and Illinois, which got 11 percent, attracted the lion's share. The patterns of settlement resembled, fairly closely, those followed by nineteenth- and early-twentieth-century immigrants from the same areas of Europe. The DPs went where their countrymen had gone before them. Thus California, soon to be a mecca for immigrants, attracted only 4.1 percent of the immigrants under the DP acts, although it contained 7 percent of the national population.

This propensity to cluster continued despite attempts to spread the DPs more evenly throughout the country. In December 1950 for example, 42 percent of the 19,000 persons initially settled in the South had left that region, mostly for the East North Central states, a pattern that continued to be reflected by later reports. And, despite the goal of the restrictionist framers of the law to admit farmers and farm laborers, the December 1950 reports showed an increase of more than 25 percent in the number of those DPs living in the nation's ten largest cities. Similarly, although just over 30 percent of those who reported their prior occupations said that they were "farmers or farm laborers," by December 1950 not quite 6 percent were working in agriculture. The Commission's published statistics on post-settlement migration end in 1951, but there is every reason to believe that the tendency to cluster and to move to metropolitan centers continued.

The overwhelming majority of the displaced persons in the labor force were unskilled or semiskilled workers. The Commission's data reported that fewer than 6 percent of DPs and 1 percent of German expellees were employed as "professional, technical and kindred workers" and no more than 12 percent and 16 percent of the two groups in the skilled "craftsmen, foremen and kindred workers" category.[33]

The Commission and most subsequent commentators have judged that the resettlement of more than 400,000 displaced persons was a qualified success and there is no reason to challenge that assessment here. However, one does not have to agree with all of the Commission's claims: for example, the law was not "non-discriminatory" although those who administered it tried with some success to mitigate some of the law's discriminations. But the Commission never challenged the exclusion of Asian refugees, although some 3,300 Europeans stranded in Asia, most notably members of the Jewish refugee community in Shanghai, were admitted under the terms of the act. Nor does one have to accept its Cold War platitudes—the Commission bragged that its program assisted "in the mutual defense of the free world."[34]

In addition we can now see that, from the point of view of immigration policy, the DP program established important precedents and pioneered certain procedures that would be utilized time and again in the decades to come. Under the DP acts, for the first time, refugee immigration became a major factor in American immigration. The 400,000 immigrants admitted as refugees during fiscal years 1949 through 1952 represent nearly half of the 900,000 legal immigrants of those years. Because of the convictions of its leaders and as a loyal element of the Truman administration, the DP Commission as it went out of existence called for a broad liberalization of immigration law, but that liberalization would not come for many years. Instead, Congress enacted, over Truman's veto, the 1952 McCarran-Walter Act, which seemed to represent another triumph for the restrictionist spirit established under the National Origins Act.

CHAPTER SIX

The Cold War and Immigration

$\mathbf{A}$n analysis of the McCarran-Walter Immigration Act of 1952 reveals a paradox. It is part and parcel of the second Red Scare, a scare that began long before Senator Joseph R. McCarthy gave his name to that disreputable enterprise in February 1950. Many historians have written the act off as "just nativism," perpetuating a sometimes unconscious parallel: the first Red Scare during and after WW I produced the nativist National Origins Act of 1924, the second Red Scare at the end of WW II produced the nativist McCarran-Walter Act of 1952. The parallel is not totally false: the 1924 act was essentially nativist and there were strong nativist elements in its 1952 successor. But there were also liberalizing elements in the 1952 act, part of the Cold War transformation of American immigration policy that helped lay the demographic basis for the multiculturalism that emerged in the United States at the end of the twentieth century. This paradoxical combining of nativist and liberalizing elements reflected the subordination of immigration policy to foreign policy. From the 1920s to the 1950s American foreign policy had turned almost 180 degrees. The 1924 act was partly a product of the post–WW I isolationism and disillusionment with Wilsonian universalism, while the 1952 act was partly a product of the Cold War with its thrust for American hegemony and leadership of the "free world."*

Roughly the same forces were engaged in the legislative struggle over

---

*There was sometimes a similar relationship between foreign policy and civil rights. The refusal of service in Maryland roadside eating places to African ambassadors, who often doubled as UN representatives and habitually drove between New York and the capital, caused distress in the State De-

the 1952 act as in the fight on the displaced persons bills. As WW II was ending, a subcommittee of the House Committee on Immigration held hearings on immigration policy in six cities. Despite conflicting testimony calling for both loosening and tightening restriction, the subcommittee reported in late 1945 that "no widespread popular demand exists for immediate, drastic changes in the existing law, and that, in fact, no such changes are necessary." It also recommended a major "impartial and complete" study of American immigration by "experts," perhaps envisioning a latter-day Immigration Commission.[1]

Early in 1946 nativists on the House committee led the last major initiative of the old restrictionist forces. Representative Ed L. Gossett (D-TX) proposed to slash every quota in half for five years, reducing total quota spaces to about 75,000 annually. He was voted down, 10–7. From 1946 through 1965 the real thrust of immigration legislation was toward liberalization. In 1946 Congress further weakened "oriental exclusion" by providing quotas and citizenship for both Filipinos and "natives of India." The next session of Congress passed the first DP bill and for the first time in more than two decades, immigration was again becoming a major political issue. Far from routed, the extreme restrictionist forces fought a rear-guard action to protect the limits established in 1924.

A key difference in the post–WW II battles over immigration was the defection of organized labor, an almost reflexive foe of immigrations since the post–Civil War era, which now supported increased European immigration. In the 1946 hearings, for example, the CIO representative testified that continued liberalization was needed to avoid "national isolationism" and the AFL spokesman insisted that: "We need people. We cannot get enough of them." Neither mentioned two factors that influenced their changed positions: New Deal changes that had set minimum wages and brought collective bargaining into the American consensus, and the fact

---

partment, which needed their support at the UN. As Kennedy aide Harris Wofford tells the story, after a campaign of many months by the State Department Office of Protocol was having some effect, a particularly blatant incident—an ambassador refused service—made Washington headlines. President Kennedy called the Protocol Officer and asked, "Can't you tell these African ambassadors not to drive on Route 40? It's a hell of a road—I used to drive it years ago, but why would anyone want to drive it today when you can fly? . . . Tell them to fly!" *Of Kennedys and Kings: Making Sense of the Sixties* (New York: Farrar, Straus & Giroux, 1980), 127. For other examples see Mary L. Dudziak, *Cold War Civil Rights: Race and the Image of American Democracy* (Princeton: Princeton University Press, 2000).

that so many of their members were sons or daughters of the kinds of immigrants nativists had striven to keep out."*

During the period in which Congress passed the two DP bills it also passed the Internal Security Act of 1950 over Truman's veto. Enacted at one of the high points of the Cold War, shortly after the beginning of the Korean War (1950–53), the law was largely aimed at domestic enemies of the republic, real and imagined. But it also attempted to protect the United States from foreign contagion by barring the admission of any communist or fascist.[2]

Although the Internal Security Act changed immigration law very little—numerous bars against "subversives" of all varieties were already on the books—it seemed at the time and to some historians since to mark a significant shift in the formulation of immigration policy. For example, in 1957 Robert A. Divine argued that:[3]

> The decisive turning point in the postwar debate on American immigration policy came in 1950 [when the bill that became the 1952 act was introduced.] . . . The long controversy over the re-evaluation of American immigration policy, sterile and unfruitful during the 1940s, swiftly reached a climax during the first two years of the next decade.

Stemming in part from a reluctance on the part of many liberal historians to see any "good" news emerging from the "bad" Cold War, such views ignore the very important breakthroughs made in the 1940s. Those breakthroughs ended exclusion of several Asian groups and seriously damaged the quota system by setting up two tracks, one dealing with "immigrants," the other with "refugees." To be sure, the quota system would not fall until 1965, but by then it was more like a colander than a shield. In addition, along with the clearly "bad news" of the restrictionist aspects of the 1952 act, there was also distinctly "good news": in that the new law abolished all racial and ethnic bars to immigration and naturalization.

In 1947 the Senate Judiciary Committee authorized a study of immigration that in 1950 resulted in a 900-page report and recommendations. Produced by a staff appointed by the committee's restrictionist chair, Senator Patrick A. McCarran (D-NV), the report recommended only minor

---

*Of course not all trade unionists and their supporters changed. As the twenty-first century began, Vernon M. Briggs published *Immigration and American Unionism* (Ithaca, NY: ILR Press, 2001), in which successive chapters were titled "Mass Immigration Ceases, Unionism Takes Off (1921–65)" and "Mass Immigration Returns, Unionism Declines (1965–2000)."

modifications in the national origins system. While explicitly repudiating "any theory of Nordic superiority"—after all that was what Hitler had preached—the report nevertheless recommended adherence to the old system, for, essentially, the old restrictionist reasons. It rejected distributing unused quota numbers on the basis of demand, arguing that such an action "would shift more quota numbers to the countries of southern and eastern Europe." And it engaged in thinly veiled anti-Semitism, pointing out that the America's Jewish population had increased "twenty-one-fold" since 1877 while the total population had increased only "threefold" in the same period.

The staff report did recommend some changes. It accepted the concept of an "Asia-Pacific Triangle." This concept had been advocated since 1947 by Representative Walter Judd (R-MN), a former missionary who wanted to end all aspects of "oriental exclusion." The Asia-Pacific concept granted each Asian nation east of Iran without a quota—and only China, the Philippines, India, and Pakistan had quotas in 1950—an annual quota of one hundred, plus an additional one hundred for the entire triangle covering persons of mixed ancestry and residents of colonies. The quotas were racial as well as national: a Chinese citizen of Great Britain who entered as a quota immigrant would still be charged to the tiny and oversubscribed Chinese quota and not the large and undersubscribed British quota.

The Judd proposals gained widespread support and passed the House in early 1949. There had been principled objections from the American Legion and the nativist American Coalition, which opposed any weakening of the 1924 formula, and from the American Jewish Committee, which found all "racial" quotas objectionable, eerily predictive of that group's eventual stand on affirmative action decades later. In advocating his cause, the Minnesota congressman stressed what we can call Cold War arguments. He believed that the adoption of his proposals would "influence greatly the battle for men's minds and hearts that is going on between the two philosophies of life and government that are locked in mortal struggle in our world." He assured his colleagues that the small size of the quotas meant "that there will not be any flooding of America with people of lower economic standards or other cultural patterns." Most senators favored the Judd formula but the Judiciary Committee had agreed to make no revision of immigration law until its report was available to provide guidelines for an omnibus immigration bill.

Liberals also had an immigration agenda. Two successive New Deal commissioners of immigration and naturalization, Earl Harrison and Ugo Carusi, had advocated abandonment of the quota system in 1944 and 1945. Without making specific recommendations, each based his argument on changed international conditions. In the latter year liberals formed the National Committee on Immigration Policy to recommend and lobby for reforms. Many of its key figures, including staff director William S. Bernard and committee chair Earl Harrison, also figured in the successful fight for DP legislation. Bernard's 1950 book, *American Immigration Policy: A Reappraisal*, was, in essence, the committee's agenda.[4] He argued that the national origins system implied "the doctrine of racialism," but, rather than scrap it, Bernard urged increasing, perhaps by 100 percent, the existing quota of just over 150,000 annually and allowing unused quota spaces to be used by persons from nations with oversubscribed quotas.

Not surprisingly, similar recommendations came from the U.S. Displaced Persons Commission. Its final report, written before but published shortly after the final passage of the 1952 McCarran-Walter Act, made seven general policy recommendations:[5]

1. "Liberalize" the immigration laws and "adjust" the national origins system to make it consistent with the United States' "present role as the leading nation of the free world."
2. Admit, on a nonquota basis, "300,000 refugees from communism, and victims of overpopulation in Europe, over a three-year period."
3. "Complete the unfinished business of the DP program."
4. "Provide reception facilities and leadership education and training for refugees from communism in Europe."
5. "Cooperate with other free nations in an international effort to enable people from overpopulated lands in Europe to migrate to underdeveloped" nations or to other countries whose economies can be strengthened by immigration.*
6. Create a special U.S. agency to administer "programs for refugees from communism and overpopulation."
7. The U.S. should "continue to be the arsenal of hope for the free world" by helping to solve the problems of refugees and victims of overpopulation.

Congress, after going through the unusual procedure of having joint House-Senate hearings during 1951, had two distinct measures before it in

---

*The notion that immigration should flow from overcrowded, developed Europe to underdeveloped countries—a notion that FDR had toyed with on a number of occasions—evinced a total misunderstanding of what the migration pressures of the second half of the twentieth century would be.

1952: an avowedly restrictionist measure sponsored by Senator McCarran and Representative Francis E. Walter (D-PA) and a more liberal—or better, less restrictive—substitute put forth by Senators Herbert Lehman (D-NY) and Hubert H. Humphrey (D-MN).[6]

The doomed substitute strongly resembled the McCarran-Walter bill. It accepted the national origins principle but modified it in two major ways:

1. The basis for national origins was switched from the 1920 to the 1950 census, and would have expanded the 154,000 annual ceiling by more than a third, to about 214,000.
2. At the end of each year unused quota numbers would be redistributed to European refugees, relatives, skilled laborers, and hardship cases without regard to national origins.

The Lehman-Humphrey bill accepted that part of the Judd bill that gave quotas of one hundred to Asian nations, but made two significant modifications: Asians would be charged to the quotas of the country of their birth, so that a person of Chinese ethnicity born in Britain, for example, would be charged to the British quota and the designation of an Asia-Pacific Triangle was dropped. The liberals' measure also barred subversives, but called for more rigorous standards of proof of subversion and would have created an independent board to review the decisions of consular officers, who had been all but sovereign since the institution of the visa system in 1924.

The long and complicated restrictionist bill, with some amendments, eventually became the 1952 Immigration and Nationality Act (INA). It recodified immigration and naturalization law and made important changes in both. The major changes in immigration law were in four areas: the quota systems for Europe and for Asia, deportation, and subversion.

For Europe, it continued the national origins system, maintained 1920 as the base year, raised the annual quota numbers slightly (from 154,000 to 158,000) to accommodate nations newly entitled to quotas, and allocated some 85 percent of the slots to northwestern Europe. More than two-thirds of them went to just three nations: Great Britain (including Northern Ireland) got 65,000, Germany almost 26,000, and the Republic of Ireland nearly 18,000. It gave priority within those quotas to those with skills in demand in the United States and to relatives of citizens and resident aliens. For Asia it accepted the basic provisions of the Judd bill, giving one hundred spaces to each previously excluded Asian nation. But persons of Asian ethnicity, no matter where they were born or had citizenship, had to be charged to the quotas of the nation of their ancestry. If two persons born in France but of colonial ancestry, one Senegalese and the other a Chinese from Vietnam, applied for American visas, the Senegalese would be charged to the large French quota, while the Chinese from Vietnam would be charged to the small Chinese quota. While adopting an "Asia-Pacific Triangle" formula that included all Asian nations, it set a regional cap of 2,000 such visas annually. Thus, in any given year, some Asian nations did not even use their supposed one hundred visas. Finally, in a move too little noted by most commentators then and now, the remaining bar to the naturalization of most Asians was removed. No longer was there a category of "aliens ineligible to citizenship" because of ethnicity. A racist restriction that had persisted from the earliest days of the republic had been removed and Charles Sumner's goal of a color-blind naturalization statute had finally been realized.

In practice the act was not as restrictive as it seemed. Many members of Congress and commentators failed to grasp that there continued to be two classes of immigrants who could enter without reference to quotas: immigrants from the Western Hemisphere and spouses and minor children of United States citizens.

The fact that Asians who immigrated could now become naturalized and then bring in some family members "without numerical restriction" meant that Asian immigration would increase more rapidly than the quota numbers indicated. The continuation of nonquota immigration from the New World presaged the eventual domination of immigration by Latin Americans, chiefly from Mexico. The act did narrow the hemispheric gate by placing the inhabitants of European colonies in the New World under the quota system. Almost all of these colonies were in the circum-Caribbean and the universe of potential immigrants was almost totally black. Such immigration had increased, partly because of patterns developed during WW II and partly because of the availability of inexpensive air transportation after WW II. The 1952 act not only charged such immigrants to the quotas of the mother country, but also, more significantly, placed a limit of one hundred on the number who could enter annually from any one colony. Thus, Jamaicans or Barbadians, who had previously been able to enter without numerical restriction, were now largely shut out. Some British scholars have argued that this change in American law greatly increased the number of post-1952 Caribbean migrants to Britain. Colin Holmes, the dean of scholars of British immigration, writes that:[7]

> Before 1952 a convenient safety-valve for Jamaicans, among whom there was a particularly long tradition of work-migration, had been available in the United States. However, entry into the U.S. was severely curtailed by the 1952 McCarran-Walter Act which limited the number of immigrants from the British West Indies to 800 per year, of whom only 100 could be Jamaicans. This restrictive legislation encouraged Jamaicans to turn towards Britain.

The admission without regard to numerical limitation of other persons from the Western Hemisphere and of spouses and children of United States citizens was not new—similar provisions existed in the 1924 act—but the growth of immigration from Latin America, the overseas residence in Asia of millions of American citizens, and the fact that no ethnic groups were barred from naturalization meant that there would be many Asians entered as family members in the so-called second, third, and fourth preferences listed below. This would not become a "flood," to use Judd's metaphor, but those populations would grow significantly during the period before 1965.

The McCarran-Walter Act (INA) preferences were as follows:

1. Highly skilled immigrants with skills urgently needed in the United States and the spouses and children of such immigrants. Up to 50 percent of quotas.
2. Parents of U.S. citizens over age twenty-one and unmarried adult children of U.S. citizens. Up to 30 percent of quotas, plus unused visas from number 1.
3. Spouses and unmarried adult children of permanent resident aliens. Up to 20 percent of quotas, plus any unused visas from 1 and 2.
4. Brothers, sisters, and married children and accompanying spouses and children. 50 percent of numbers not required for first three preferences.
5. Nonpreference: Applicant not entitled to any of the above preferences. Fifty percent of numbers not required for the first three preferences, plus any not required for fourth preference.

The bill also made deportation easier and incorporated provisions of the so-called "Wetback Bill" passed earlier that year, which extended the range of the Border Patrol on the Mexican border from a "reasonable distance" to "twenty-five miles" and empowered its agents to conduct warrantless searches of "any railway car, aircraft, conveyance or vehicle" and "to have access to private lands, but not dwellings."[8] In another seemingly "tough" anti–illegal immigrant section, the act made "harboring" an illegal alien a felony punishable by as much as five years' imprisonment and a $2,000 fine. But this was followed by the infamous "Texas proviso," which stipulated that employment of illegal aliens, "including the usual and normal practices incident to employment," did not constitute "harboring."[9] Thus a rancher in the Rio Grande Valley who drove his pickup truck across the border, loaded it with Mexicans who wanted to work, and brought them back, committed a sanctioned illegal act. If apprehended, the Mexicans were merely sent back across the border, usually without any formal procedure.

The act also adopted many of the antisubversive provisions of the 1950 Internal Security Act with a special exception. Immigrants from totalitarian nations who demonstrated that they had been unwilling members of subversive organizations and/or had opposed totalitarianism (for all intents and purposes this meant communism) for at least five years were exempt. One of the most resented aspects of the law were provisions that barred the granting of even temporary visitor visas to "subversives," which meant that some intellectuals, such as Jean-Paul Sartre, were never able to lecture in the United States.[10]

The congressional debates over the INA in many respects reprised those of the 1920s, and with the same general result. But this time the liberal attack was more pointed and had better support, and in some restrictionist responses, an embattled, defensive note could be heard. Senator Walter F. George (D-GA), for example, hoped that "the time has not come when one must apologize for being a hateful Anglo-Saxon."[11] Just a few years earlier such a remark would have been unthinkable. But despite the change in tone the crucial votes were not even close. It was no surprise that the bill not only passed, but that at the end of June 1952, the restrictionists overrode President Truman's veto by two votes, 57 to 26, in the Senate and more comfortably, 278 to 113, in the House. In his veto message Truman, too, was fighting the old battle. Denouncing the INA as "an arrogant, brazen instrument of discrimination," he went on to argue that:

> The basis of this quota system was false and unworthy in 1924. It is even worse now. At the present time, this quota system keeps out the very people we want to bring in. It is incredible to me that, in this year of 1952, we should again be enacting into law such a slur on the patriotism, the capacity, and the decency of a large part of our citizenry.[12]

The president also made explicit his notion of the primacy of foreign policy in matters of immigration:

Our immigration policy is . . . important to the conduct of our foreign relations and to our responsibilities of moral leadership in the struggle for world peace.

In early September 1952, just as the presidential election was heating up, Truman established, by executive order, a special Commission on Immigration and Naturalization composed of former federal officials and representatives of VOLAGS.[13] Its report, *Whom We Shall Welcome*, published as the Truman administration was ending, made seven general recommendations that went well beyond those contained in the alternative bill that Lehman and Humphrey had proposed.[14]

1. Abolish the national origins system.
2. Establish a unified quota system that would allocate visas without regard to national origin, race, color, or creed.
3. Set maximum annual quota immigration at one-sixth of one percent of the total population at the most recent census. (For the 1950s this would have meant an annual quota of 251,000 as opposed to the 158,000 then authorized.)
4. Transfer immigration and naturalization regulatory functions, then divided between the Department of Justice and the Department of State, to a new agency, a Commission on Immigration and Naturalization, whose members were to be appointed by the president and confirmed by the Senate.
5. The new commission would allocate visas, not on national lines but on the basis of: the right of asylum, reunion of families, needs in the U.S., special needs in the "Free World," and general immigration.
6. Reserve for "the next three years" 100,000 quota spaces annually for refugees, expellees, escapees, and displaced persons. (This echoed a Truman message of March 24, 1952.)[15]
7. Reallocation of visas within the quota by the Commission every three years "subject to review by the President and Congress."

The report was all but ignored by the congressional leadership. Neither house of the Republican-controlled 83rd Congress (1953–55) even held hearings on it, although nearly fifty separate futile bills were introduced to put some or all of its provisions into effect. However, Senator McCarran did issue a press release condemning the report as following the "communist line" and arguing that it was a

tragic fact that the out-and-out Reds have ready colleagues . . . the "pinks," the well-meaning but misguided "liberals" and the demagogues who would auction the rights of America for alleged minority-bloc votes.[16]

Yet *Whom We Shall Welcome* did become a liberal icon. The Truman commission's report provided a national agenda largely realized in 1965, with a final element accepted in 1980 when Congress recognized the right of asylum.

Despite the great emphasis by both sides in the debate on maintaining the quota system, an examination of what happened during the thirteen years that the 1952 act was in effect shows how irrelevant its apparent restrictions were to much of the actual immigration flow. Because of the bifurcated nature of the act, which provided for both quota and nonquota immigration, the number of legal immigrants proved much larger than envisaged. The bill provided 158,000 quota spaces annually. Over thirteen years this should have yielded a total of just over 2 million immigrants; in actuality, 3.5 million came. Of those 3.5 million only about a third—35.5 percent—were quota immigrants. Indeed nonquota immigrants outnumbered quota immigrants in every year of the act's life. In other words, as some put it, "the tail was wagging the dog." And, although the debate in Congress and in the media continued to focus on Europe, immigrants from Europe were in the majority in only two of the thirteen years. Table 6.1 shows the volume and sources of immigration during the INA years.

TABLE 6.1
IMMIGRATION, 1953–65, BY MAJOR REGIONS
(IN THOUSANDS)

Year	Total	Europe	%	Americas	%	Asia	%
1953	170	82	48	78	46	8	5
1954	208	92	44	96	46	10	5
1955	238	111	47	110	45	11	5
1956	322	157	49	145	45	17	5
1957	327	170	52	134	41	20	6
1958	253	115	45	113	45	21	8
1959	261	138	53	93	36	25	10
1960	265	120	45	120	45	21	8
1961	271	109	40	140	52	19	7
1962	284	104	37	156	55	20	7
1963	306	109	36	170	56	23	8
1964	292	108	37	159	54	21	7
1965	297	101	34	171	58	20	7
Total	3,494	1,516	43	1,685	48	236	7

Source: U.S. Department of Commerce, *Historical Statistics of the United States*, Series C 89–119, Washington: GPO, 1976.

Although the incidence of Europeans had been declining steadily since World War I, the years 1953–65 constitute the first peacetime period in American history in which Europeans did not compose an absolute majority of all immigrants. In the years before WW I, more than nine immigrants in ten had been Europeans; between the end of WW I and 1952 the ratio was about two in three. Before 1952 immigration from the Americas had been dominated by Canadians, most of whom were either Europeans or their descendants; during the McCarran-Walter years Latin Americans and Caribbeans comprised two-thirds of New World immigrants. Less prominent, but a harbinger of things to come, was the entry of almost a quarter of a million Asians.

In the 1970s and 1980s, immigration and what we have learned to call multiculturalism began to be noticed by large numbers of journalists and scholars. Unfortunately, almost all of the former and far too many of the latter traced the cause to the 1965 immigration act, ignoring the similar if less-pronounced effects stemming from the 1952 statute. Part of the reason was inattention, but one of the reasons for that inattention was a refusal on the part of liberal journalists and scholars to believe that anything "good" could come from a "bad" Cold War act. For example, in 1989 a Rand/Urban study was prefaced by the statement: "After a lull lasting more than 40 years, immigration to the United States began to increase considerably in the late 1960s after the passage of the 1965 [immigration act]."[17]

Changes in the volume of immigration were extreme in the twentieth century, dropping steadily from the first decade's peak of almost 9 million to just over half a million in the 1930s, and then, as we have seen, rising steadily to a million in the 1940s and two and a half million in the 1950s.

But even while the volume of immigration grew, the percentage of foreigners in the American population continued to shrink. As previously noted, this had run in a 13–14 percent range from before the Civil War until after WW I. Then, as we saw in Table 1.1, it dropped steadily until it fell below 5 percent in the 1970 census. Thus, although its chief framers intended to maintain the status quo, the McCarran-Walter Act of 1952 was a vehicle for significant change in both the number of immigrants and in the sources of immigration.

To be sure, not all of the growing volume of immigration could be attributed to the 1952 law: throughout the life of the statute both Congress and Presidents Eisenhower, Kennedy, and Johnson earmarked certain groups, mostly refugees from communism, for special treatment. The more generous treatment of refugees was facilitated in part by the McCarran-Walter Act itself, even though the word *refugee*—anathema to the extreme restrictionists—appears nowhere in it. An obscure provision—Section 212 (d) (5)—gave the Executive Branch, specifically the attorney general, discretionary parole power to grant temporary admission to unlimited numbers of aliens "for emergency reasons or for reasons deemed strictly in the public interest."[18] This came to mean, in practice, that the executive branch would admit select groups of aliens—Hungarians, Cubans, Tibetans, and Vietnamese—and Congress would later pass legislation regularizing that action. A conservative Congress was thus sanctioning, whether it realized it nor not, the precedent set by FDR in 1944. But, instead of the single boatload of fewer than a thousand refugees, the new parole authority eventually brought in more than a million immigrants. No longer could a cabinet officer counsel a president, as Cordell Hull had counseled FDR in 1936, that the law left "no latitude" for executive action.[19]

Despite formally ignoring the recommendations of Truman's special commission as such, the very next Congress enacted a refugee law quite similar to its sixth recommendation. The Refugee Relief Act of 1953, which Dwight Eisenhower had urged Congress to adopt, authorized the issuance of 214,000 visas over and above the quota system, as opposed to the 300,000 Truman and his commission had recommended.[20] Nearly 190,000 persons actually entered under its provisions. Congress thus not only continued in the "liberal" policy of superimposing refugee immigration on top of "restrictionist" regular immigration quotas, but it also made an important breakthrough: for the first time it included Asians as refugees. Of course, the stranded Chinese students who had been allowed to stay after the establishment of the People's Republic of China in 1949 were really Asian refugees, but Congress chose not to call them that. Under the 1953 law visas were provided for 2,000 Palestinians, for 3,000 refugees "indigenous to the Far East," and for 2,000 "refugees of Chinese ethnic origin" as long as the latter were vouched for by the Nationalist Chinese government of Taiwan. The majority of the visas went to three groups: 55,000 for "German expellees" residing in West Germany, West Berlin, and Austria; 45,000 to refugees of Italian ethnic origin; and 35,000 to "escapees" residing in West Germany.

The very language of the law showed its Cold War origins: it was to apply to "refugees," "escapees," and "German expellees." A refugee was defined as

> any person in a country which is either communist or communist-dominated, who because of persecution, fear of persecution, natural calamity or military operation is out of his usual place of abode and unable to return thereto, who has not been firmly resettled, and who is in urgent need of assistance for the essentials of life or for transportation.

Similarly an "escapee" was one who had "fled from the [USSR] or other communist, communist-dominated, or communist-occupied area of Europe including those parts of Germany occupied by the" USSR, and a "German expellee" was

> any refugee of German ethnic origin . . . who was born in and was forcibly removed from or forced to flee from Albania, Bulgaria, Czechoslovakia, Estonia, Hungary, Latvia, Lithuania, Poland, Rumania, Union of Soviet Socialist Republics, Yugoslavia, or areas provisionally under the administration or control or domination of any such countries.

In 1957, as the United States became more heavily involved in the Middle East, Congress passed a Refugee-Escapee Act that broadened the definition of a "refugee/escapee." It now included persons "from any country within the general area of the Middle East"—which congressional geography defined as stretching from Libya to Pakistan, from Turkey to Ethiopia and Saudi Arabia—"who cannot return . . . on account of race, religion, or political opinion." It also quietly ended and forgave the quota mortgages allowed by the DP acts, expanded the power of the attorney general to admit otherwise inadmissible aliens, and liberalized admission policies for stepchildren, "illegitimate" children, and adopted children of U.S. citizens and permanent residents.[21]

Although on three separate occasions (1953, 1955, and 1960) President Eisenhower sent messages to Congress calling for further liberalization of the immigration laws, none of the ten significant public laws on immigration passed during the Eisenhower years did that. Since the Democrats controlled both Houses of Congress during the last six years of the Eisenhower era, there was, in effect, a bipartisan majority against any further restructuring of immigration law. Eisenhower's final proposal, in a presidential election year, was similar in many ways to Truman's proposal at the end of his term. Eisenhower urged:[22]

1. Doubling the annual immigration quota to 316,000.
2. Removing the ceiling of 2,000 on the Asia-Pacific Triangle.
3. Changing the base year for the quota system from 1920 to 1960.
4. Basing the quotas on actual immigration between 1924 and 1959.
5. Reallocating each year's unused quota slots according to need.

Despite ignoring these sweeping presidential recommendations, the Congresses of the Eisenhower era did pass six supplemental refugee acts, which, all told, admitted more than 90,000 persons, resulting in a total of nearly three-quarters of a million refugees admitted under various statutes between 1945 and 1965.

In addition the Eisenhower administration used its parole power, most notably on behalf of Hungarian "freedom fighters" after the failed revolt of November 1956. About 200,000 Hungarians fled their homeland and more than 35,000 eventually came to the United States. As the Hungarian quota was a mere 865 annually, almost all were admitted on parole. The administration, using discretionary funds, set up a special refugee processing center at Camp Kilmer, New Jersey, while assorted VOLAGS were instrumental in getting most of the Hungarians out of the camp and resettled. In July 1958 Congress passed a law enabling Hungarian parolees to become permanent residents, which placed them on the path to citizenship, a status most of them soon attained. The next month a separate statute authorized the attorney general to make that change of status administratively, which meant that the executive branch could admit refugees on parole and then give the resident alien status without needing congressional sanction.[23] Thus the parole procedure, begun so modestly by FDR but ignored by Truman, would be used extensively by Eisenhower and his successors.

A final law passed during the Eisenhower administration in July 1960 was labeled the "Fair Share Refugee Act," but did little to increase the allocation of refugee slots. While it did slightly extend the expiration dates of two existing refugee statutes, its most significant innovation was adding the possession of marijuana to the growing list of offenses that could bar admission.[24]

Yet it is clear that Eisenhower was not much interested in immigration and saw it, essentially, as an instrument of foreign policy. John F. Kennedy, on the other hand, was identified with immigrants and immigration policy. He had voted to sustain Truman's veto of the McCarran-Walter Act and as a senator was an active sponsor of immigration legislation, including several unsuccessful attempts to broaden the McCarran-Walter Act. His only success with a public law had been one which admitted 4,811 "refugees" from an earthquake in the Azores.[25] Even more important, he had written—or at least signed his name to—a panegyric called A Nation of Immigrants (1958). While Robert Kennedy's posthumous notion that his brother had championed "no cause . . . more warmly than the improvement of our immigration policies" is clearly hyperbole, the long frustrated immigration reformers were understandably expectant when JFK entered the White House in January 1961.[26]

CHAPTER SEVEN

Lyndon Johnson and
the End of the Quota System

Even before the election of 1960 the stage seemed to be set for significant immigration reforms, reforms that would expand normal admissions and change the basic law rather than nibble around its edges, as had been the case since 1943. For the first time the Democratic platform attacked the national origins system as "a policy of deliberate discrimination" that "contradicts the founding principles of this nation" and is "inconsistent with our beliefs in the rights of man." The Republicans, returning to a theme not voiced by them since the Taft administration, recognized that immigration "has been a great factor" in American growth, and that it "had been reduced to the point that it does not provide the [appropriate] stimulus to growth." In addition, their platform proclaimed that "Republican conscience and Republican policy" required that "the annual number of immigrants we accept be at least doubled," and "obsolete immigration laws be amended by abandoning the outdated 1920 census data and substituting the 1960 census." It also insisted that admission "be based upon judgment of the individual merit of each applicant."[1]

While John F. Kennedy's razor-thin victory gave heart to those, like William Bernard, who had long struggled for a liberalization of immigration policy, a Nixon victory might well, in the short run at least, have provided a more immediate change. JFK's influence in Congress was modest, and immigration matters were controlled by reactionary and racist Democratic committee chairs: Francis E. Walter, a Pennsylvanian who entered the House in 1933 at the outset of the New Deal, and James O. Eastland, who represented Mississippi in the Senate from 1943 to 1978. Both men opposed any significant change in the immigration system.

The Kennedy administration did not even attempt to do anything about immigration in its first months. Late in 1961 the White House sent over a draft bill authorizing special assistance to Cuban refugees from the newly installed Castro regime, a version of which was passed almost a year later as the Migration and Refugee Assistance Act of 1962. This act included persons who had "fled from an area of the Western Hemisphere" in its definition of refugees and recognized, finally, that refugee problems were going to be continuous. It was the first refugee statute not to have an expiration date. The legislation delegated broad executive powers to the president—not, as in the past, to the attorney general—and authorized the expenditure of up to $10 million annually for the emergency use of refugees.[2] The eventually massive Cuban refugee program, begun by executive order in 1961, was regularized by the act, which also became the basis for a smaller Chinese program.

An act originating in Congress, rather than the White House, made further piecemeal adjustments. It authorized automatic minimum quotas of one hundred for newly independent nations, scrapped the 2,000 annual ceiling on the aggregate quota for the Asia-Pacific Triangle so that each nation in that area would have one hundred annual spaces, and made a few even more minor changes.[3]

During the 87th Congress (1961–63) a number of bills intended to liberalize the McCarran-Walter Act were introduced but none proved successful. Late in the session, on the tenth anniversary of the 1952 act's passage, Chairman Walter announced that the staff of the House immigration subcommittee would make an "in-depth" study of immigration and refugee problems. Those in favor of major changes saw this, correctly, as a delaying tactic. The study never materialized.

Shortly after the next session of Congress began, Kennedy said in a press conference that a liberalization of immigration had a high place on the administration's agenda.* His chief advisor in immigration matters was Abba Schwartz, appointed in 1962 as Assistant Secretary of State to run the Bu-

---

*Immigration figured not at all in the early accounts of the Kennedy years. It is neither in the skimpy index of Theodore C. Sorensen, *Kennedy* (New York: Harper & Row, 1965), nor in the extensive one in Arthur M. Schlesinger, *A Thousand Days: John F. Kennedy in the White House* (Boston: Houghton Mifflin, 1965). The former does not mention Abba Schwartz; the latter discusses only Schwartz's role in mitigating the ban on "subversive" immigrant visitors, pp. 699–700.

reau of Security and Consular Affairs, a fief of McCarthyites left over from the Dulles era.[4]

Six months later, in July 1963, a presidential message to Congress recommended a comprehensive series of amendments to the 1952 act concentrating "primarily upon revision of our quota system." The message emphasized the "elimination of past discrimination"—specifically citing Italians and Greeks—and focused on European immigration. Kennedy envisaged phasing out the quota system over a five-year period and replacing it with a formula taking into account:[5]

1. "The skills of the immigrant and their relationship to our need";
2. "the reuniting of families";
3. "the priority of registration." [First come, first served.]

Specifically the president proposed:

1. To reduce existing quotas gradually at the rate of 20 percent a year. The quota slots released each year would be placed in a "quota reserve pool" to be distributed according to the principles of Kennedy's formula.
2. That natives of no country receive more than 10 percent of the total quota in any one year.
3. To empower the president to allocate up to 50 percent of the unallocated quota numbers "to persons disadvantaged by the change in the quota system" and up to 20 percent to refugees.

The president was to receive advice, but not instruction, from a newly created "seven-man Immigration Board," with the Speaker of the House and the president pro tem of the Senate each appointing two members while the president named three.

Kennedy also called for utilization of the 60,000 quota numbers "wasted each year," and abolition of the Asia-Pacific Triangle. He proposed two changes in the family-reunification provisions: parents of American citizens, who were currently given preference, would be accorded nonquota status; and preference would be extended to parents of resident aliens. Kennedy asserted that "these changes will have little effect on the number of immigrants admitted," which was patently false.

The president also called for three other significant changes:

1. To make it unnecessary for "highly trained or skilled persons" to have employment before being admitted and to create a "special preference" for workers with lesser skills who could fill specific needs in short supply.

2. To grant nonquota status, as was granted to other Western Hemisphere nations, to natives of Jamaica and Trinidad and Tobago as both were now independent nations. Natives of remaining New World colonies would continue to get only limited numbers of visas from the quotas of their mother countries.

3. To admit persons with mental health problems, long totally barred from entry, if the attorney general was persuaded that they would not become public charges. (This provision, one of the most detailed in the message, perhaps reflects the sensitivity of a man with a mentally retarded sister.)

Despite this presidential leadership, a strong push from inside Congress for bills incorporating the Kennedy-Schwartz proposals introduced by Philip A. Hart (D-MI) in the Senate and Emanuel Celler (R-NY) in the House, and the death in May 1963 of Francis E. Walter, chief stumbling block to immigration reform, no legislation had resulted by the time of Kennedy's assassination.[6] What would have happened had Kennedy lived, no one can say, but the proposal was, it seems to me, too clever by far. There is no reason to believe that Congress would give up so much of its power over immigration to any president.

Some supporters of immigration reform feared that it would be buried with the martyred president; his successor, Lyndon Johnson, unlike Kennedy, had voted in 1952 to override Truman's veto of the McCarran-Walter Act. Few, if any, of those doubters were aware that Congressman Johnson had been an advocate and a fixer for some Jewish refugees in the late 1930s and early 1940s. As historian Robert Dallek has reported, beginning in early 1938, Johnson was instrumental in helping "hundreds" of European Jews, most of them friends or relatives of some of his constituents, gain entry to the United States. He even arranged for some of them to be sheltered, illegally, in National Youth Administration camps in Texas.[7]

In any event, President Johnson was not Senator Johnson. In 1964 he unequivocally announced his support for immigration reform in his first state of the union address. The Democratic platform later that year essentially reiterated its 1960 immigration plank while the Republicans, about to nominate Barry Goldwater, backed away from their 1960 pledge and merely supported family unification and a continuation of what it called the "Fair Share" refugee program. Immigration was not a major issue in the 1964 campaign, which resulted in a landslide victory for Johnson.

No significant legislation resulted in the remainder of the 88th Congress

(1963–65), but in 1965 Congress, at Johnson's urging, took up the immigration measure, which was on the triumphant president's "must" list. The key congressman, Representative Michael A. Feighan (D-OH), a Cleveland conservative who had been in Congress since 1942 and headed the key House subcommittee, received Johnson's fabled "treatment." Called to frequent Oval Office consultations, White House dinners, and flights on Air Force One, Feighan obediently and unexpectedly shepherded the bill through the House. In the Senate, Mississippi's Eastland, half of a 2–14 minority that opposed the Senate version of Feighan's bill in the Senate Judiciary Committee, allowed Senator Edward M. Kennedy (D-MA) to manage it.[8]

Although the cast of characters had changed, the same old arguments from 1952 and earlier were trotted out during the debates. The chief advocate for the status quo was now Senator Sam J. Ervin (D-NC). He insisted that the McCarran-Walter Act was not discriminatory but was rather

> like a mirror reflecting the United States, allowing the admission of immigrants according to a national and uniform mathematical formula recognizing the obvious and natural fact that those immigrants can best be assimilated into our society who have relatives, friends, or others of similar background already here.[9]

Ervin never admitted that the "mirror," like those at amusement parks, was badly distorted. It reflected, not the population of the 1960s but the one recorded in the 1920 census.*

The legislative history of the 1965 act is complex. The meaningful debates were not about *whether* to change the old system, but by what degree and how. The major modification introduced as a result of the congressional debate was the first imposition of a cap on immigration from the Western Hemisphere. Pushed by Ervin and others, it was one of the few restrictionist victories. The most extreme restrictionist proposal, by Senator Allen J. Ellender (D-LA), was for a five-year halt to all immigration. The often flatulent congressional debate warrants little attention. Rather the act itself, the largely mis-

---

*Ervin became a folk hero to the myriad foes of Richard Nixon for his bravura role in the televised Watergate hearings in 1973. Most viewers were unaware of his reactionary role in civil rights and labor legislation. He denounced most civil rights legislation as "steal[ing] freedom from one man to confer it on another."

taken assumptions on which it was based, and, above all, on the way that it has transformed the very nature of American immigration deserve our attention.[10]

The passage in 1965 of the landmark Immigration Act along with the Voting Rights Act and the laws creating Medicare/Medicaid, make that year the legislative high point of late-twentieth-century liberalism. One of the curiosities of the historiography of that liberalism is that most of its historians have ignored immigration reform. It is treated briefly, if at all, in most survey texts, and is, for example, mentioned only in passing in Allen J. Matusow's volume on the 1960s in the *New American Nation* series.[11]

The 1965 law* retained many of the provisions that had characterized legislative immigration restriction from its very beginnings before WW I and bore a distinct family relationship to the two statutes that were its direct ancestors, the 1924 and 1952 immigration acts. While it resembled Kennedy's 1963 proposal, there were three major differences:

1. Instead of modifying the quota system, the new law abolished it.
2. The new law, as noted, placed a cap on Western Hemisphere immigration.
3. The attempt to shift the locus of immigration change from congressional committees to a board of experts was abandoned.

The basic thrust of the 1965 law was to scrap completely the concept of national quotas and origins and to substitute overall hemispheric limits on visas issued: 170,000 for persons from the Eastern Hemisphere, 120,000 for those from the Western Hemisphere. No country in the Eastern Hemisphere was to have more than 20,000 visas in any one year. (In a 1976 statute hemispheric limits were abandoned and replaced by a global ceiling of 290,000 visas, with the 20,000 per nation caps applying everywhere.) These provisions seemed to establish an annual limit of 290,000 immigrants, slightly below the mid-1960s level. Under both the original and the 1976 version the 290,000 visas were to be distributed according to a system of preferences similar to those guiding the 1952 act. As had been the case during the life of the McCarran-Walter act, two parallel systems were also adopted. The first, essentially a continuation from the 1924 and 1952 acts, exempted certain close relatives from both preference requirement and numerical limits. The second added refugees of all kinds, who, as it turned out, came in unprecedented numbers, even though the 1965 act had set

---

*Technically, the new law, sometimes called the Hart-Celler Act, was a series of amendments to the 1952 INA act.

aside 6 percent of preference visas (17,400 annually) for refugees. Nothing better demonstrates the illusory nature of the limits placed on refugee immigration than the fact that, on the very day he signed the 1965 immigration act, Lyndon Johnson also issued an open invitation to Cubans fleeing Castro—"I declare this afternoon to the people of Cuba that those who seek refuge here in America will find it"—which soon brought many more than 17,400 Cubans to the United States in almost every year since then.

Lyndon Johnson signed the bill into law in a ceremony on Liberty Island in New York Harbor with the then-dilapidated and unused buildings on Ellis Island in the background. For once he understated the importance of one of his bills.

> This bill that we sign today is not a revolutionary bill. It does not affect the lives of millions. It will not reshape the structure of our daily lives, or really add importantly to our wealth or our power.[12]

LBJ was not indulging in uncharacteristic modesty. He was saying what his experts had told him. He and they saw the 1965 act as redressing the wrongs done to those "from Southern and Eastern Europe" in 1924 and 1952. Members of his administration had testified before Congress that few Asians would enter under the new law.* This misperception was also held by the leading Asian American organization, the Japanese American Citizens League, which complained that for the foreseeable future Asians would continue to be discriminated against, even though post-1965 discrimination would be de facto rather than de jure.

What did the new law do? On its face, not very much. It did abolish the Asia-Pacific Triangle but it retained most of the nonethnic barriers that Congress had been erecting to limit entry to the country since the 1880s. The LPC clause, the requirements for mental and physical health, and the various ideological and moral tests all remained. Since the new law so resembled its predecessors, it is not surprising that few observers, if any, expected major changes to result.

---

*Schwartz relates an illuminating anecdote about official testimony. The evening before he was to testify on the merits of what became the 1965 act, Secretary of State Dean Rusk telephoned Schwartz, who was managing the bill, to say that he was inclined not to testify as he was against letting in "people like the . . ." [ellipsis in original] and that, "After all we are an Anglo-Saxon country." Schwartz told him, essentially, that LBJ wouldn't like it. An hour later Rusk called him back with some questions about details that showed that he had been studying the briefing book Schwartz had provided. The next day, according to Schwartz, Rush was "the Administration's most articulate and effective witness." Schwartz, *The Open Society*, pp.119–20.

The greatest apparent difference, apart from dropping the hated quota system, was that the 1965 law placed a much heavier emphasis on family re-unification, as the following chart comparing their preference provisions demonstrates.

CHART 7.1

PREFERENCE SYSTEMS: 1952 AND 1965
IMMIGRATION ACTS

IMMIGRATION AND NATIONALITY ACT, 1952

Exempt from preference requirements and numerical quotas:
Spouses and unmarried minor children of U.S. citizens.

1. Highly skilled immigrants whose services are urgently needed in the
   U.S. and their spouses and children.   50%
2. Parents of U.S. citizens over age twenty-one and unmarried adult
   children of U.S. citizens.   30%
3. Spouses and unmarried adult children of permanent resident aliens.   20%

Any visas not allocated above distributed as follows:

4. Brothers, sisters, and married children of U.S. citizens and accompanying
   spouses and children.   50%

Nonpreference applicants: Any remaining visas.

IMMIGRATION ACT OF 1965

Exempt from preference and numerical requirements:
Spouses, unmarried minor children, and parents of U.S. citizens.

1. Unmarried adult children of U.S. citizens.   20%
2. Spouses and unmarried adult children of permanent resident aliens.   20%
3. Members of the professions and scientists and artists of exceptional ability.
   [Requires U.S. Dept. of Labor certification.]   10%
4. Married children of U.S. citizens.   10%
5. Brothers and sisters of U.S. citizens over age twenty-one.   24%
6. Skilled and unskilled workers in occupations for which labor is in short
   supply. [Requires U.S. Dept. of Labor certification.]   10%
7. Refugees from communist or communist-dominated countries, or the
   Middle East.   6%
8. Nonpreference: any remaining visas. [Since there have been more preference
   applicants than can be accommodated, this has never been used.]

In practice the law worked quite differently than its sponsors had anticipated. Expecting the future to resemble the past, they ignored evidence available to them. As we have seen, even under the restrictive 1952 act the incidence of European immigration to the United States steadily dropped while the volume of total immigration rose. Yet the experts continued to believe the great fallacy that large numbers of European immigrants were ready, qualified, and able to come to America. Twenty thousand annual arrivals from many European countries, expert opinion held, would absorb most of the Eastern Hemisphere preference visa slots. Had the 1965 act, or something very much like it, been passed in 1952 when Truman recommended a full-scale revision of immigration law, such a result might well have been obtained. But by 1965 Europe was economically prosperous and most of those Western Europeans who wished to come were unable to meet LPC and other restrictions and, of course, Eastern Europeans, under Soviet-sponsored controls, were not then free to emigrate.

Growing numbers of Latin Americans and Asians came to the United States in the years after World War II and once they achieved permanent resident status a whole cohort of relatives became eligible to enter the country as second-preference immigrants. And, as historian Elliott Barkan has shown, unprecedented percentages of these immigrants became naturalized citizens as soon as the five-year waiting period expired. When that happened cohorts of their relatives became eligible as first-, fourth- and fifth-preference immigrants, while others could enter exempt from numerical preference.[13] Of course, those who followed could initiate the same process. Since the 1965 act went into effect this kind of migration, in which related immigrants follow one another as links in a chain, has accounted for a preponderance of all nonrefugee migration. Such chain migration is likely to continue as long as the law and conditions in most of Asia and Latin America remain essentially unchanged.

Although the law speaks of a global ceiling of 290,000, that applies *only* to immigrants subject to numerical limitation. Legal immigration, which averaged a quarter of a million annually in the 1950s, expanded to nearly a third of a million in the 1960s, nearly 450,000 in the 1970s, more than 600,000 in the 1980s, and more than 970,000 in the 1990s. Increasingly this was immigration from Asia and Latin America. Table 7.1 analyzes immigration in 1971 and 1978—the lowest and highest years for legal immigration in the 1970s—and shows the pattern of admissions by type and by region.

TABLE 7.1
NUMBERS AND CATEGORIES OF IMMIGRANTS
ADMITTED, 1971 AND 1978

Category	1971	1978
Subject to numerical limitation	280,626	341,104
Exempt from numerical limitation	89,852	260,338
Relatives	(83,486)	(125,819)
Others	(6,366)	(134,519)
INS Total	370,478	601,442

REGIONAL SOURCES OF LEGAL IMMIGRATION,
1971 AND 1978 (IN THOUSANDS)

Year	Total	Europe	%	Amer.	%	Asia	%
1971	370	97	26	161	44	103	28
1978	601	73	12	263	44	250	42

Source: INS *Annual Report* 1971, Table 6; and INS *Statistical Yearbook*, 1978, Tables 4 and 6.

Even in 1971, the low year, immigrants subject to numerical limitation were only 76 percent of legal immigration, a figure below the experts' expectations. In the high year, 1978, they were only 57 percent. The number of those entering "subject to numerical limitation" steadily ran at a level slightly below the maximum. The numbers of those entering under other categories fluctuated erratically. Although the 1965 act devoted a fifth of its preference visas to persons with special skills—individuals who fell under categories 3 and 6—they accounted for fewer than 4 percent of immigration in the years under consideration. Most of the many professionals and other skilled persons who came entered under other provisions of the law. Part of the reason for the low utilization of the third and sixth preferences was the relatively slow growth of the American economy, but, in addition, getting a visa in those categories required securing an additional certification from the U.S. Department of Labor. Given a choice, immigrants generally chose the simpler way.

Perhaps the most misleading aspect of the law is the presumed 20,000 cap on entries from any one nation. That cap applies only to those entering subject to "numerical limitation." In 1985, for example, there were 61,000 legal entries by Mexicans, 48,000 by Filipinos, and 35,000 by Koreans, to list only the three largest national groups. The 20,000 cap has been illusory.

Clearly, the 1965 law has not worked in the way that either its proponents or its opponents expected. Although there was in 1965 the usual oratory about opening the floodgates, not even the most consistent restrictionist in Congress predicted that during the 1980s more than six million legal immigrants would enter the United States. Nor did anyone even hint that Latins and Asians would so completely dominate American immigration. By the 1980s more than four-fifths of all legal immigrants came from either Asia or Latin America: if we could accurately include illegal immigrants in our calculations, the figure would undoubtedly exceed nine-tenths. The 1965 act, intended to redress the grievances of European ethnic groups and to give more than token representation to Asians has, in one sense, turned traditional immigration patterns to the United States upside down.

In another sense, however, the patterns of immigration have remained consistent. People tend to immigrate to the United States when there is a clear economic and/or social advantage. In the years after 1965 the average Briton, or German, or Scandinavian could see no such advantage in emigration; neither could the average Japanese. Eastern Europe was filled with people who wanted desperately to come, but they could not get out. Large numbers of qualified persons from much of Asia, the Caribbean, and from the northern parts of Latin America, however, did believe they could improve their lives by emigrating and they came to North America in unprecedented numbers.

Paradoxically, but not surprisingly, the steady rise in legal immigration stimulated and was accompanied by a rise in illegal immigration.* Any discussion of illegal immigration is problematic because it is all but impossible to describe it accurately. As opposed to the numbers used for legal immigrants, which are generally accurate if not precise, the numbers used to describe illegal immigrants are all fictive. One authority has used the phrase "counting the uncountable," but that only applies to honest attempts to discover the approximate size of the problem. Others, such as the INS and advocates for and against the immigrants in question, simply invent numbers that suit their purposes. For example, the INS, in one of its

---

*Many persons find the term "illegal immigrants" offensive and prefer such "politically correct" locutions as "undocumented persons." That term is nonsense: most have "documents," many of them forged. I use the term illegal immigrants to describe any and all persons who enter the United States in violation of statute law, or having entered legally for a limited time, stay on illegally.

more moderate treatments of the subject, states in large, boldface type, that "An estimated 5 million undocumented immigrants were residing in the United States in October 1996." Four pages later, in normal unemphasized type, it admits that its estimates "must be used with caution because of the inherent limitations of the data." "Data" is a pretty fancy term for some of the inputs it used. A footnote to the same section reveals that for two years it had been counting 25,000 estimated illegals from the Dominican Republic as if they were from tiny Dominica! And elsewhere in normal type at the very end of the section it admits that it had dropped a formerly used table about the numbers of aliens and citizens crossing the land borders because "survey data" indicated that the procedures previously used had resulted "in an overstatement of the total number of entries into the United States. The methodology used to derive estimates of the number of passengers per vehicle and the proportion of aliens and U.S. citizens is being evaluated and revised."[14] In other words, the INS had a good count on the cars, trucks, and buses that crossed the border but not of the people who were in them!

Rather than methodology, I would call it BOPSAT—the acronym for "a bunch of people sitting around a table"—which is what happens when a group of "experts" discuss a problem and give an answer that is essentially the average of their educated—or some cases uneducated—guesses.*

With that as prologue I will discuss briefly—and tentatively—what were almost certainly the two largest national groups involved in illegal immigration in the period from the 1960s into the 1980s: the Irish and the Mexicans. The latter, of course, are the archetypical late-twentieth-century illegal immigrants, while the Irish are a special case. The two groups have very different histories, but each became the major beneficiary of different immigration programs in 1986.

The one place in Western Europe from which large numbers of qualified persons wished to emigrate to the United States was the Republic of Ireland, which had many more qualified would-be immigrants than quota spaces. Since few Irish had come in previous decades, the would-be immigrants had few eligible relatives to get them included in a high preference

---

*I have some experience with the process. In 1983 the Presidential Commission on the Wartime Relocation and Internment of Civilians (CWRIC), in preparing to advise Congress how much its proposed award of $20,000 to each Japanese American survivor of the 1942–46 camps would cost, convoked a panel of several social scientists and one historian (me) to tell it how many of the 120,000 Japanese Americans incarcerated by the War Relocation Authority between 1942 and 1946 were still alive. With caveats, our estimate was some 20,000 persons too low, or, as budgets go, $400 million too low.

category. Ireland, of course, had been one of the prime suppliers of immigrants in the era of relatively unrestricted immigration in the century before 1924; about 4.5 million Irish came in that period. In 1900 the census counted nearly 10 million foreign-born persons in the United States: almost one in six—15.7 percent—was Irish.[15]

But in the three decades after 1930 only about 80,000 Irish immigrated to the United States—fewer than 3,000 a year—so that, when the 1965 act went into effect, there were relatively few persons in Ireland with relatives in the United States who could qualify them for a preference slot. Like the rest of western Europe, Ireland in the 1960s and early 1970s enjoyed prosperity and underwent a great deal of modernization, but by the 1980s economic conditions deteriorated and pressures increased. As a result many thousands of Irish immigrated to the United States in the 1970s and 1980s, self-described as "New Irish."

Unlike almost all of their Irish predecessors, most of them were illegal immigrants who entered the United States on visitor's visas and simply stayed on. Also unlike most of their predecessors, they were relatively well-educated and took jobs well above the entry level. The INS data show that 43,000 nonimmigrant Irish entered in 1978, 34,000 of them on tourist visas. In 1987, with unemployment in Ireland at 19 percent, 105,000 Irish nonimmigrants entered the United States legally, 81,000 of them as tourists. In contrast, 3,060 Irish entered as immigrants in that year. By the mid-1980s, the presence of large numbers of illegal Irish—estimates ran from 40,000 to 250,000—was an open secret, largely ignored by the mainstream press but a regular feature of such ethnic papers as the *Irish Echo* and the *Irish Voice*. Eventually, the Irish Immigration Reform Movement, a pressure group for legalization, was created and by the later 1980s its green-and-white stickers—"Legalize the Irish"—could be seen in shop windows in ethnic neighborhoods, in ethnic bars, and as an extra adornment on rapid transit ads from Boston to Washington. The movement gained mainstream support from politicians and such community leaders as New York's Cardinal John J. O'Connor.[16] Despite all this publicity, the INS, notorious for its policies of selective enforcement, which "located" more than 1.5 million deportable aliens in 1997, could find only forty-six Irish! It could have found more than that in a Saturday night surveillance of one of the more popular Irish bars in New York or Boston, or at an Irish or Irish American soccer game.

In the late 1980s an informant took me to such a bar in Boston's South End. An illegal immigrant I interviewed—a university graduate in accounting—told me that, unable to find a job in Ireland, he flew to Boston at a friend's urging, entered legally on a six-month tourist visa, and was still there, years later, working illegally. He worked as a relief bartender in several Boston bars and did the books for two of them. He was paid in cash. He hoped to marry an American citizen, leave the country, and come in legally as her husband. Were he legal, he thought that he could get a job with a future in an American corporation, but what he was making illegally in Boston was more than he could make legally in Ireland.*

Illegals, even relatively secure ones as most of the Irish were, cannot behave normally. A woman calling herself Rosie Kiernan told a *New York Times* reporter that despite a recent family death in Ireland she "couldn't risk going back home." The expired tourist visa in her passport might have been spotted by immigration officials. They would not have detained her, but would have recorded her name and passport number, which might have precluded her return.[17]

Illegal Mexican immigration is more familiar and more rooted in history. Much of what is now the western United States once belonged to Mexico, and the 1848 treaty that ended the United States' war of expansion against Mexico gave the perhaps 60,000 Mexican citizens who chose to remain in the newly conquered territory full rights as United States citizens, another case of naturalization by conquest. Both natural increase and immigration, much of it informal, enlarged the Mexican American population substantially but not massively in the decades before WW II. Then, as noted previously, the bracero program, adopted as a wartime expedient in 1942, survived in one form or another until December 31, 1964. All told, nearly 5 million foreign agricultural workers were imported, some 4.6 million of them Mexicans. Many, to be sure, entered more than once. Southwestern agriculturalists in general, and particularly those in California, became addicted to Mexican labor. It is also obvious that a side effect of that addiction was an exacerbation of the recurring illegal alien crises of the later twentieth century and beyond.

Although the bracero program is thought of as a wartime expedient, the vast majority of such workers came later, as table 7.2 shows. In no year before 1949 were as many as 100,000 foreign workers admitted for temporary

---

*In the 1990s economic conditions in Ireland changed and, as I write in early 2003, many Irish immigrants, legal and illegal, are returning to their native land.

employment in American agriculture; in no year between 1951 and 1964 were fewer than 200,000 admitted. The program peaked between 1955 and 1959; in each of those years more than 400,000 braceros were admitted.[18]*

TABLE 7.2
IMPORTED AGRICULTURAL WORKERS, BY DECADE AND
COUNTRY, 1940s–60s (IN THOUSANDS)

Period	Number	Mexico	B.W.I.	Bahamas	Canada	% Mexican
1942–49	437	332	59	18	29	76
1950–59	3,253	3,119	48	26	60	96
1960–64	1,271	1,170	54	5	42	92
Total	4,961	4,621	161	49	131	93

Source: Congressional Research Service, *U.S. Immigration Law and Policy*, Washington, D.C.: GPO, 1979, Table 3, p. 40.

By the end of the 1950s the foreign worker agricultural program was coming under increasing attack from groups interested in labor and welfare. These opponents gained support from the Department of Labor in both the Eisenhower and Kennedy administrations, but the agricultural interests continued to hold sway in Congress. President Kennedy signed a bill extending the bracero program in October 1961, but stated that he did so reluctantly. In 1963 his administration proposed a one-year extension, and an attempt by agricultural interests to extend it for two years was defeated in the House by sixteen votes. In December 1963 the last congressional extension—for one year—was signed by President Johnson. In the course of the legislative process, the Senate Agriculture Committee chair, Allen J. Ellender, who opposed all immigration but had consistently supported temporary agricultural workers, promised that he would not seek a further extension in 1964. He and others who represented agricultural employers assumed that they would be able to bring in workers under the provisions of the 1952 Immigration and Nationality Act, but shortly after the 1964 elections Labor Secretary W. Willard Wirtz announced that he would not approve such admissions. The last stand of the "pro-forces" in Congress came in September when a proposal to switch authority over such admissions from the Labor Department to the Department of Agriculture was defeated

*Between 1956 and 1964 tiny experiments were made in importing Asian agricultural workers. Several thousand were brought across the Pacific, including 3,387 Japanese and 162 Filipinos.

in the Senate by one vote—that of Vice President Hubert H. Humphrey, who broke a 45–45 tie.

The legislative death of the program did not mean the end of all legally imported agricultural workers. It was still possible for growers to get ad hoc approval for specific situations. The famous Delano, California, grape strike was triggered by one such exception. Just before that strike, an earlier, smaller, and shorter strike in the Cochella Valley occurred after growers there got an exemption for their grape harvest early in 1965. This resulted in their having to pay, because of Labor Department insistence, $1.40 an hour to the braceros, although they were then paying Filipino American workers only $1.25 and Mexican American workers $1.10. This led to a support strike at Delano. The Cochella Valley strike was quickly won with wage equity at the higher level, but the Delano strike and the ensuing grape boycott went on for years.[19]

Not surprisingly, illegal immigration increased greatly after the end of the importation program. As the INS noted in its 1970 annual report:

For the 6-year period [after the expiration of the program] 71 percent of the 1,251,406 total deportable aliens located were of Mexican ancestry. Year by year [that percentage] has risen from 50 percent in 1965 to 80 percent this year.[20]

In 1965 the golden door had been pushed open much wider, but, as the examples of the illegal immigrants show us, not for everyone. An entirely different mix of peoples was lining up to come in. To understand fully the impact of the 1965 law it is necessary to switch our focus from the law and its administration to the immigrants themselves and the regions from which they came.

PART II

Changing Patterns in
a Changing World, 1965–2001

CHAPTER EIGHT

Immigrants from Other Worlds: Asians

Asians and Latinos, until recent decades minor if controversial components of migration to the United States, are now its dominant elements. In the not very heavy immigration year 1999, almost 650,000 legal immigrants were enumerated by the INS. More than 450,000 of them, 70 percent, were from these two broad groups, with the larger portion, some 260,000 from what we call Ibero-America. These figures ignore, of course, the sizeable but unknown number of illegal immigrants in 1999, the preponderance of whom were surely Asian and Latino.*

As we have seen, Asian immigrants, except for Filipinos, were all but barred from entry to the United States between 1924 and 1943. Between 1920 and 1960 the total number of Asian Americans recorded in the census grew from 332,000 to 878,000, but more than half of that increase came from the addition of more than 275,000 Asian Americans in Hawaii, who were included in U.S. data only after statehood in 1959. Even including these Hawaiians, and natural increase, the incidence of Asian Americans in the population remained marginal in the first six decades of the twentieth century: a quarter of one percent in 1900 and a half of one percent in 1960.[1]

In the 1980s, after the census reported a total Asian American population of nearly 3.5 million—a 2 million increase in just ten years—students

---

*This enumeration ignores 8,771 legal immigrants in 1999 whose origin was unknown. Since 1820 there have been, according to the INS, almost 300,000 such persons admitted, the population of a medium-sized city.

of population began to take notice, but, like their predecessors, they continued to underestimate future growth.[2] By the year 2000, the census recorded 10.2 million Asian Americans, who accounted for about 3.6 percent of the American population. If one uses the data for persons of mixed ancestry, 11.9 million persons, or 4.2 percent of the population, reported some Asian ancestry in 2000.[3] Thus the incidence of Asians or part Asians in the population rose from about one person in 300 in 1920 to one person in twenty-five in 2000. In addition, the census showed significant changes within the Asian American community. When the 1965 immigration act was passed more than 90 percent of all Asian Americans were members of just three ethnic groups: Japanese, Chinese, and Filipino. In 2000 those three groups composed not quite half—49.6 percent—of the Asian American population. (Table 8.1 shows the growth of Asian American population in the twentieth century.)

TABLE 8.1
ASIAN AMERICAN POPULATION BY MAJOR ETHNIC
GROUP, 1960–2000 (IN THOUSANDS)

Group	1960	1970	1980	1990	2000
Chinese	237	436	812	1,645	2,433
Filipino	182	337	775	1,420	1,850
Asian Indian	—	76	387	815	1,679
Vietnamese	—	—	245	615	1,123
Korean	—	70	367	799	1,077
Japanese	459	591	701	848	797
Other Asian	—	—	180	767	1,284
Total	878	1,430	3,467	6,909	10,243

Source: Census Bureau data.

As had been the case since Asians were first enumerated in 1860, the Asian American population in the year 2000 was highly concentrated. Although Hawaii was, by far, the most heavily Asian American state, only a little more than two Hawaiians in five were Asian Americans, some half a million persons. Twice as many Asians—just over a million—lived in New York, and almost 3.7 million lived in California. Those two states contained 18.7 percent of the nation's population, but 43.6 percent of its Asians. Thus more than half the nation's Asian population—51.2 percent—lived in those three states.

The cause of the rapid and sustained growth in the Asian American population has not been a high birthrate but immigration. From 1930 to 1960 Asians were 5 percent of all legal immigrants.* In the 1960s that rose to 12 percent, in the 1970s it was 34 percent, in the 1980s it was 37 percent, and in the period 1991–99 it was 30.8 percent. In addition, Asians, once thought to be unassimilable, were naturalizing much more rapidly than most immigrants. In the 1960s Asians were 12.9 percent of all naturalizations. In the 1970s that figure was 33.5 percent, in the 1980s and 1990s it averaged around 37 percent. (That percentage is likely to decline because, in reaction to the punitive legislation affecting legal resident aliens enacted in the early 1990s, Latino Americans, as will be shown, began naturalizing at a much higher rate.)[4]

To be sure, the whole notion of "Asian Americans" was originally a government construct, and a racist one at that.[5] Bangladeshi and Chinese, say, have as much—or as little—in common as do Belgians and Bulgarians. But, however contrived, this blanket category has become "real" in American ethnic identity politics.[6] Since the 1960s, campus groups and others have worked to set up coalitions of all Asian Americans or sometimes for "all persons of color," and in an emulation of the push for African American studies programs, agitating for Asian American courses, programs, and, in a few institutions, departments.

Most Asian American intellectuals seem to support such programs. Lisa Lowe, for example, a postmodern literary critic, identifies a persistent cultural concept that Asian Americans are "perpetual immigrants" or "foreigners within."[7] Less common are those who reject all such notions. Eric Liu, a second-generation Chinese American and former speechwriter for Bill Clinton, insists that he is an "accidental Asian," and sneers at those whom he calls "Professional Asian Americans."[8] Perhaps the most common attitude among U.S.–born Asian American graduates is an awareness of identity politics but not much involvement in them.

Most western states and the federal government have long given at least lip service to the notion of a distinct Asian American community. One of the first national manifestations of this was that presidents, beginning with Jimmy Carter in 1978, proclaimed "Asian American weeks." In 1992, Public Law 102–450 expanded the celebration to a month. Similarly the

---

*Asia by INS definition includes all of what geographers regard as Asia except for Russia, the former Soviet Union, and former republics of the Soviet Union. Thus Uzbekistan, for example, is, according to INS geography, in Europe.

United States Commission on Civil Rights publishes studies such as *The Economic Status of Americans of Asian Descent: An Exploratory Investigation* (1989) and *Civil Rights Issues Facing Asian Americans in the 1990s* (1992),* while the Census Bureau has produced large volumes like the 1990 Census of Population volume, *Asians and Pacific Islanders in the United States.* The comparable volume from the 1960 census was *Nonwhite Population by Race.*[9] Starting in the 1960s some activists went beyond talking about Asian American groups and began to talk about coalitions of all people of color, or, at the extreme margins, of Asian Americans as a part of a Third World Liberation Front.

On the other hand, more conservative members of the long-established Asian ethnic-heritage groups attempt to separate themselves from these catch-all ethnic concepts, especially when such concepts place them in coalitions with low-status groups. In Los Angeles, for example, in the post–World War II era, large numbers of Japanese Americans participated in "white flight" from an expanding African American presence in central Los Angeles, and, decades later, conflicts between Korean American shopkeepers and their black customers on both coasts erupted into sometimes fatal violence.[10] Thus, rather than attempting to generalize further about Asian Americans en bloc, it makes more sense to treat the major Asian ethnic groups as discrete entities, acknowledging their different origins, histories, and aspirations.

Chinese Americans were not only the earliest Asian group to come to the United States in appreciable numbers, but they are now the most numerous. The fact that China and the United States were allies during World War II resulted in the wartime statute repealing the Chinese Exclusion Act and granting the right of naturalization. Despite the fact that the proclamation of the People's Republic of China in October 1949 made the United States and China Cold War enemies who engaged in a bloody, undeclared war in Korea from the end of 1950 until mid-1953, the newly legal Chinese immigration continued and set off a series of demographic changes that transformed the Chinese American community. The 78,000 Chinese Americans of 1940 had become nearly 2.5 million in 2000.

In 1940 Chinese Americans were overwhelmingly male (74 percent),

---

*Most of the Commission's studies focus on African Americans, and on schooling, but occasionally look at such issues as the civil rights of "women," of the "handicapped," and at least once, examined, awkwardly, *Civil Rights Issues of Euro-ethnic Americans in the United States* (1980).

largely big-city urban (71 percent), and, for the first time, citizens (52 percent) outnumbered aliens. Almost two Chinese Americans in five lived in just two cities, San Francisco and New York. Beginning with the institution of the draft in October 1940, some 16,000 Chinese American men and a few Chinese American women served in the American armed forces.[11] As noted in Chapter Four, the servicemen, many of whom became citizens through special Army naturalization programs, were among the first Chinese Americans in the post-war era who were able to bring their wives to America. And, in the immediate post-war years it was these and other women who dominated the immigration of Chinese to America. Between 1945 and 1960 some 40,000 Chinese immigrated to the United States: 63 percent were female. For the years through 1952 females represented roughly 90 percent of close to 12,000 immigrants. Since the Chinese quota was just 105 persons a year through 1952,* the vast majority came in as nonquota immigrants authorized by a variety of statutes. In addition to the family-reunification provisions that existed in both the 1924 and 1952 immigration acts, Chinese men took advantage of the War Brides Act of 1945, the Alien Fiancées and Fiancés Act of 1946, and, as will be discussed in Chapter Ten, the Refugee Relief Act of 1953.[12]

Although most accounts of the post-war migration of Chinese women stress its positive effects, the transformations in the Chinese community triggered by the arrival of these women also created serious problems. The traditional picture of these brides, painted by the sociologist Rose Hum Lee in 1956, was of young women wooed and won by young Chinese American veterans who rushed to China to marry them in 1946. This has been challenged by the closest student of post-war Chinese American family life, Xiaojian Zhao.[13] She shows that large numbers of the "brides" were women who had been married for years and existing in China as "living widows." Zhao shows that both the median and the average age of these "brides" was about thirty-three years—the range was sixteen to sixty-six years—the vast majority had been married for more than five years at their time of entry into the United States, and, not surprisingly, about eight out of ten had already borne children. As had been true throughout the exclusion era an improbable proportion of these children, almost 80 percent, were boys.

*From 1952 until 1965 there was, in effect, a double Chinese quota. One hundred quota slots were allocated to "China"—really Taiwan—and 105 for "Chinese," who could be of any nationality.

Zhao's analysis of the social stress in these marriages is also very different from Lee's: she cites high incidences of divorce, spousal abuse, and even suicide.[14] Zhao documents these stresses by quoting letters from husbands to Chinese-language newspapers that are, to Western notions, incredibly blunt.[15] One man, using a pseudonym, wrote to a San Francisco journal in October 1950 about his marriage, which had been arranged and consummated in China and followed by a ten-year separation.

> My ugly Chinese wife [*huanglian bo*] knows nothing. We have nothing in common. What I like, she doesn't. Where she likes to go, I don't. We often fight over things like that. Imagine a man like me, working from morning till night for a living and suffering from such a wife at home. How can I face the world? I have thought many times of divorcing her, but my son is still young. All sorts of feelings well up in my heart and I suffer so much. Please give me guidance.

The editor, almost certainly male, admonished him, arguing that "the issue is not how to westernize her or how to accommodate her, but to find a common ground to reconcile your differences." Applying community mores, the editor told the husband that "forsaking his wife was unacceptable."[16]

Mao Tse-tung's triumph in 1949 and the creation of what the American media and politicians almost always called "Red China" soon made direct immigration from the People's Republic of China impossible, but much nonquota Chinese immigration continued from Hong Kong, still a British enclave. While the Cold War in Asia would create nightmares for many Chinese Americans, for one group it was a blessing in disguise.

About 5,000 nonresident citizens of what had been the Chinese Republic were in the United States when that government fled the mainland to Taiwan.[17] Most of them were students at elite colleges and universities who had come to the United States in the four years after WW II. Others had been sent on various goodwill missions or were Chinese Nationalist officials who did not go back. Many of these "stranded Chinese," as they came to be called, were able to remain with the assistance of the State Department.[18]

Most of these government-sponsored Chinese were at the other end of the cultural and social hierarchies of mid-twentieth-century China from the country wives who were the bulk of the "war brides," or, for that matter, from the vast majority of Chinese who had previously come to the United States. The differences were not only of class and education, but also of geography and culture. Almost all of the early Chinese immigrants to the United States were from South China and spoke what is usually described as Cantonese. The students and officials were chiefly northerners and spoke Mandarin. Many of the post-war careers of "stranded Chinese" produced the kinds of immigrant success stories that Americans love to read about.

The elite students were, in one sense, a continuation of the tradition begun by Yung Wing, whose B.A. (Yale, 1854) was the first earned by a Chinese at an American college.[19] Prior to the wartime and post-war increments, some 40,000 Chinese nationals had won degrees from American institutions of higher education.[20] In previous eras all but a few handfuls of them had returned to China, while most of the students marooned by the Cold War remained in America.*

One of those students who remained, Donald Tsai, who had come to the United States to attend college in 1941, told interviewers in 1979 that[21]

> Many students came from China on scholarships from the Chinese government, although I myself did not come as a scholarship student. Those were very difficult scholarships to obtain, through competitive examinations . . . Some of us had to work . . . I did various kinds of jobs, library, binding room, tutor. We were paid thirty-five cents an hour. So after a whole month of work . . . we would get a check for about twenty to twenty-five dollars. China Institute helped a little bit by giving us tuition scholarships . . . I went to M.I.T. for graduate school. M.I.T. was my father's school also . . . There was no thought of staying.

Tsai believed that his cohort of students "was the reason why you see so many Chinese people in the United States who are eminent professionals, teachers, and so forth . . ."

By far the most spectacular economic success story from the "stranded" group was achieved by Shanghai-born An Wang (1920–90), a 1940 graduate in electrical engineering from Chiao-t'ung University in his natal city.

---

*The best-known person to return was the physicist Hsue-shen Ts'ien, considered to be the "father" of the first Chinese satellite. One of the reasons he returned is said to be his harassment by American security officials. As the infamous Wen Ho Lee affair of the late 1990s demonstrated, such harassment and suspicion of foreign-born Chinese is a continuing feature of their lives. Ironically, the only spy for the PRC we know about, Larry Wu-tai Chin, who committed suicide after his apprehension in 1985, had been brought into the country by the American Central Intelligence Agency.

The Chinese government sent him to Harvard for graduate work in a technical program in 1945. He got an M.S. in Physics in 1946, and then worked briefly for the Chinese government in Canada, returning to Harvard, which awarded him a Ph.D. in 1948. Like so many previous Chinese immigrants, he had left a wife in China who divorced him at an unknown date. He married a fellow stranded Chinese, Lorraine Chiu, who was studying at Wellesley College; both became naturalized in 1955.

While working as a research fellow at the Harvard Computation Laboratory he was asked to develop a nonmechanical way to store information inside a computer. He succeeded by sending "flows of electrical current through arrays of magnetic cores consisting of tiny, doughnut-shaped memory cores of ferrite material" and secured a 1955 patent on a device for doing so. His method became the basis of almost all computer memory until the invention of the microchip in the 1970s. He founded Wang Laboratories in 1961 and became, for a time, one of America's richest men, and a major philanthropist. His company eventually had some spectacular failures caused by bad management and nepotism.[22]

But for large numbers of Chinese Americans the Cold War was a nightmare. The second Red Scare was well under way even before Joseph R. McCarthy began his demagoguery in February 1950, which has given the phenomenon its most popular name. Much of the literature on "McCarthyism" focuses on its baneful effects on American intellectuals, but its greatest impact, I would argue, was upon radicals in the labor movement and immigrant groups, particularly those who had come from nations that were within the so-called Communist Bloc.* No immigrant group in America was more vulnerable than Chinese Americans because so many of them had either gained admission by fraud—chiefly by varieties of the "paper sons" device—or by illegal entry.

In addition, the Chinese American community, which had traditionally presented a united front in opposition to the INS efforts to keep Chinese out or to deport them, was rent by rivalries that focused on politics in China. The most important political organizations in Chinese America were the various local branches of the Kuomintang, the party of Sun Yat

---

*The minor idiocies of those years are legion. When I entered the U.S. Army in 1952, the classification and assignment folks initially earmarked me for intelligence because of high scores and the fact that I could read two foreign languages. When they discovered that my mother had been born in Hungary, from whence she departed in 1900 as an infant, I was automatically ineligible.

Sen now taken over by Chiang Kai-shek. As Him Mark Lai, the doyen of the historians of Chinese America, has shown, by the 1940s the Kuomintang was allied with the most conservative forces in Chinatowns.[23] Many in the community believed that Kuomintang agents regularly gave the INS the names of leftists allegedly in the United States illegally.

Although the Communist Party was not particularly strong in the Chinese American community, support for the PRC grew steadily after October 1949. Unlike their Cold War counterparts from Europe and the Caribbean, some Chinese exiles and refugees had at least grudging admiration for the modernization that the new regime accomplished and the international respect that this commanded not only for China but for Chinese. After relations between the PRC and the United States normalized in the late 1970s, many of them returned for visits. In addition, the old Chinese tradition of accepting "The Mandate of Heaven" when a new regime became securely established took effect, so that many who were not at all leftists drifted away from the Kuomintang and reconciled themselves to the Beijing regime even while not embracing all aspects of Maoist policy.

This kind of political tolerance was inexplicable to most American Cold War exponents. The FBI investigated and for a time harassed some of the most traditional organizations of Chinese Americans, the family associations, which are based on the fictive assumption that all persons with the same or similar last names are related, because these organizations communicated regularly with their opposite numbers in the PRC. As late as 1969 FBI chief J. Edgar Hoover testified that "up to 20,000 Chinese immigrants can come into the United States each year" which "provides a means to send illegal immigrants into our nation [who could] aid in operations against the United States."[24] As was often the case, Hoover didn't know what he was talking about: his figure reflected only Chinese from Taiwan and Hong Kong.

But the INS, abetted by the State Department, continued to be Chinese Americans' greatest antagonist during the 1950s. In December 1955 a great furor was raised by Everett F. Drumright, then consul general in Hong Kong. Jokingly referred to as Rightdrum by foreign service colleagues because of his politics, Drumright reported massive passport and visa fraud aimed at getting Chinese from Hong Kong into the U.S.[25] While fraud clearly existed, it was not to the degree that Drumright charged, and he went on to claim, without evidence, that the Chinese communists were using the system to infiltrate agents into the United States. He was later rewarded by the Eisenhower administration with a promotion as Ambassador to "free China" on Taiwan.

There followed a series of raids, primarily in San Francisco and New York, on both left-wing Chinese organizations and the conservative family associations. It was in this atmosphere that the "Chinese Confession Program" was born.[26] Taking advantage of the political turbulence in American Chinatowns in the 1950s, the INS instituted the program, which acted as a kind of amnesty, but an amnesty that often involved a forced exposure of the confessor's relatives and friends. According to historian Mae M. Ngai, the program evolved from an investigation in Hong Kong of thirty-four persons who claimed to be descendants of a Lew Bok Yin who had established himself as a native-born United States citizen in a 1902 court proceeding. The investigators concluded that Yin had obtained his citizenship fraudulently. Seventeen of the thirty-four were already in the United States and the INS eventually deported three of them. Ten of those remaining were either former or current members of the armed forces and the INS persuaded them to confess so that they could become citizens under their real names. To do so, however, they had to expose the whole family. Other confessions were pursued in the San Francisco Bay Area and in early 1957 the program was extended to the whole country.

The confession program, like so many of the INS prosecutorial activities, involved the ethically dubious principle of selective enforcement. Judging from whom it deported and tried to deport, the INS targeted Chinese American leftists. Some of the stories that have emerged are heartrending. One of the best known is that of Maurice Chuck, a radical San Francisco journalist. Trapped by the confession and later courtroom testimony of his own father, he was convicted, stripped of his fraudulent citizenship, and sent to prison. After serving his time he was supposed to be deported, but his attorneys successfully demonstrated that his life would be in jeopardy were he sent to Taiwan. (Deportation to the PRC was not then an option.) In the late 1970s Chuck went public about the whole "paper-son" scam and his case seems to have been the first to be discussed in English-language publications of general circulation.[27] Ngai, who interviewed him in 1993, elicited further details: Chuck told her that although his father's confession had exposed him, they had shared a hotel room during the trial and that his father wept every night. The father, of course, as a confessor was not subject to legal penalties.[28]

The extent of the confession program and how it should be evaluated is somewhat conflicted, and there are discrepancies and variations between the two major accounts in the scholarly literature. Using INS annual reports between 1957 and 1965 Ngai wrote in 1998 that "at least 25 percent of the Chinese American population in 1950 was illegal" and constructed a table showing that 11,336 persons had made confessions implicating 19,124 other illegal persons.[29] Zhao in 2002 cited larger figures for the same years from a 1972 INS press release: 13,895 confessions implicating 22,083 persons.[30] She makes no attempt to estimate the percentage of the whole community that was illegal.

Probably neither set of figures is "correct." INS coup-counting has been notoriously inaccurate as the "data" are often used to justify expanded budgets. In addition INS and Census Bureau data often conflict. Regardless, determining how many illegal immigrants there are has been characterized as a matter of "counting the uncountable" and I am convinced that any attempt to do so with any kind of specificity is a case of misplaced concreteness. What the scholarship makes clear is that a large minor fraction of the Chinese American population before 1965 was the result of both fraud and surreptitious entry.

More significant are the varying interpretations that the two scholars place on the program. Ngai argues that despite its unfairness, the "Confession Program enabled Chinese immigrants to take a step out of the shadow of exclusion [and] served as a means of renegotiating the terms of Chinese Americans' membership in the nation." Zhao, who avoids an explicit evaluation, clearly has a less positive view. She finds most significant the fact that the confession program and other investigations of past immigration fraud "compelled the Chinese American community to find new ways to deal with discriminatory government policies" and argues that, beginning in 1957, the community began to play traditional American ethnic group politics, lobbying in Washington, and forming alliances with other ethnic groups.[31]

The INS, on the other hand, viewed the confession program as one of its great victories. Long after the confession program ended it continued to brag about the numbers of confessions, of illegal immigrants exposed, of slots cancelled. But, as had been the case with the judicial victory validating the Geary Act in 1893, it was a very limited triumph. Few Chinese were deported. In the same 1972 press release that gave the Confession Program its maximum body count, the INS acknowledged that "no special treatment is to be given to aliens of [Chinese] nationality not accorded to all others." Because of the Immigration Act of 1965, Chinese were no longer treated as a separate race, and Chinese were admitted according to their country of nationality rather than as a "race."

By the time the Confession Program ended, the immigration act of 1965, plus the ability of Chinese aliens to become naturalized, made further use of the paper-son strategy unnecessary. The influx of Chinese was growing and the growth by natural increase was considerable. In addition to those who came from Hong Kong, Taiwan, and the PRC, very large numbers of persons who considered themselves Chinese emigrated from Southeast Asia, as did smaller numbers from such places as British Guiana, Peru, and Canada. After 1965 such immigrants no longer appear in the INS data as Chinese, but once they are settled in the United States and the census taker comes around—or when the census form arrives in the mail—almost all will check the Chinese square—or have someone check it—in filling out the form.

As shown in Table 8.1, the steady increase in Chinese American population meant that persons of Chinese birth or ancestry, who in 1940 had consisted of about six of every 10,000 Americans, represented almost one American in a hundred by the year 2000. And although its rate of growth slowed perceptibly in the 1990s, that rate of growth was more than four times that of the American population as a whole. Still highly concentrated in two states, California and New York, where almost three out of five (58 percent) of all Chinese Americans lived, the socioeconomic profile of Chinese Americans began to change in the second half of the century and by 1982 their public image had undergone some significant changes as well. At the end of that year *Newsweek* magazine labeled all Asian Americans as "A Model Minority," but clearly placed the emphasis on Chinese, who had become the largest single Asian American group.* The sociologist Peter I. Rose has put it quite nicely, describing the change in image as one from "pariahs to paragons."[32]

The "model minority" stereotype, like all successful stereotypes, has some basis in reality. Large numbers of Chinese Americans had distinguished themselves, particularly in the professions and as entrepreneurs.

---

*As will be shown in a few pages the Model Minority concept was invented in 1965 and originally referred only to Japanese Americans.

But it ignores the fact that large numbers of Chinese Americans, most of them recent immigrants, live in poverty and are poorly educated. And these negative social indicators not only exist in almost all Asian American groups, but predominate in some of them.

The empirical data showing income and education for Chinese Americans in the latter decades of the twentieth century take on what statisticians call a bipolar shape. That is, when compared to general American norms, relatively large numbers of Chinese Americans are clustered at the high and low ends of the scale with relatively fewer in the middle ranges. Of the 1.65 million Chinese Americans enumerated in the 1990 census, nearly seven out of ten were foreign-born and nearly half a million of them had arrived in the previous ten years.*

At the top end, 3.4 percent of all Chinese Americans over twenty-five years of age in 1990 had doctorates, as did 2.2 percent of all Asian Americans, 1.5 percent of all Americans of foreign birth, and only 0.8 percent of all Americans.[33] At the bottom end, 11 percent of foreign-born Chinese over twenty-five years of age had less than a fifth-grade education as did 14 percent of the women in that group. Some 43 percent of all Chinese Americans, wherever born, had not gone beyond high school. The traditional notion among students of immigration, going all the way back to E. G. Ravenstein, who wrote in 1889, was that immigrants had social characteristics roughly midway between the averages for the countries they left and the countries they went to.[34] Contemporary Chinese, among others, do not fit this pattern.

We can also expect this pattern of high educational achievement surpassing national norms to continue for some time for large numbers of Asian Americans: their "overrepresentation" on elite American college campuses is proverbial and the showings of some younger Asian Americans in such things as the Westinghouse Science Talent Search are remarkable. In 1983, for example, the national winner was Paul Ning, a sixteen-year-old Taiwan-born student at the Bronx High School of Science. And that was no fluke. Of the forty finalists in that year's contest, twelve—30 percent—were Asian Americans, nine of them immigrants. There are members of all immigrant groups who do not do particularly well in school. Culture is also important. Those of us who teach and are reasonably accessible have office

---

*The detailed data from the 2000 Census were not yet available when I wrote in early 2003.

visits from Asian American students, particularly from those in the sciences, to protest perfectly respectable grades. As one young Chinese American student—American-born of immigrant parents—explained to me after I told her why I would not change her B+ to at least an A–, "If I come home with a 'B' my mother will kill me."

These achievements should not cause us to ignore the fact that large numbers of Chinese, mostly immigrants, have little formal education and live in poverty. The poverty figures are particularly striking. According to the 1990 census, 9.5 percent of all native-born families were below the government's poverty line, as were 14.9 percent of immigrant families and 23.4 percent of immigrant families who arrived in the 1980s. For the same categories of Chinese Americans the percentages were 3.1 percent, 12.6 percent, and 20.2 percent.

When we look at the lower end of the socioeconomic spectrum for Chinese Americans we see relatively large numbers of immigrants who have arrived since the early 1970s, and are poor and grossly exploited, largely by fellow Chinese Americans, in restaurants and in the garment industry. Many of them entered the United States illegally or came on nonimmigrant visas and stayed on after their documents expired. Some of the illegals paid $30,000 or more to smugglers—referred to in the ethnic community as "snakeheads"*—to get them into the country. Some who cannot pay the full amount are held in bondage by their exploiters until the debt, which often accrues interest, is paid off.[35]

In recent decades Chinese women workers in New York City's garment industry played out a new chapter in a classic immigrant story. At the beginning of the twentieth century Jewish and Italian women garment workers, largely exploited by Jewish entrepreneurs, struggled to form a union, the International Ladies Garment Workers Union (ILGWU). The climactic event was the 1911 fire at the Triangle Shirtwaist Company, which cost the lives of 146 persons, 125 of them young immigrant women, 62 of whom leaped to their deaths while horrified crowds watched.[36]

In a brilliant book, Xiaolan Bao has told the story of immigrant Chinese

---

*Most American readers will be more familiar with the Mexican smuggler, the "coyote." The latter collect much smaller fees, in advance, and often abandon their charges just across the border. The snakeheads, who have to charter ships, etc., have a much greater capital investment, which necessitates a long-term interest in the workers. The rise in price—it was said to be $3,000 in the 1950s—also reflects the greater prosperity in China.

women, struggling against Chinese shop owners and the union that represents them, the same ILGWU, later renamed Unite!. There was no single great tragedy but the crucial event was a brief 1982 strike—the women got some of what they wanted after one demonstration, which shocked Chinese traditionalists who expected women to be obedient—that was as much against the union as against the bosses.[37]

Each Asian American group has a differently complex history, though the stories of the other Asian immigrant groups treated in this chapter— Japanese Americans, Filipino Americans, Korean Americans, and what we now call Asian Indian Americans—are less legally complex than the Chinese American story and can be treated more briefly here, while Southwest Asian Americans will be examined in a subsequent chapter with other refugees.

The post-war Japanese American community was to a very large degree shaped by its harrowing World War II ordeal and by the transforming changes occurring in its ancestral homeland. For much of the second half of the twentieth century, attempts to come to grips with its recent past energized the Japanese American community, and, even as the new century began, the wartime incarceration remained the central event of Japanese American history. To be sure, the long and eventually successful campaign for redress resulted in 1988 legislation requiring a formal governmental apology for the wartime incarceration, and a $20,000 tax-free payment to each of the 80,000 surviving victims did provide a kind of closure for many.[38]

Earlier, the long-delayed admission of Hawaii as a state in 1959 gave Japanese Americans not only increased numbers but disproportionate political representation in Washington. The Hawaiian delegation has been dominated by Japanese Americans, particularly by two veterans of the WW II 442nd Regimental Combat Team. Daniel K. Inouye (b. 1924) was elected to the first Hawaiian delegation to the House of Representatives in 1959; he served there until 1963, when he moved to the Senate where, as of 2003, he was still serving. For a third of those thirty-nine Senate years he was paired with Spark M. Matsunaga, who, after seven terms in the House, filled the other Hawaiian Senate seat between 1977 and his death in 1990. Both men, along with a clutch of younger Japanese American House members from California and Hawaii, provided crucial leadership in the struggle for redress.

Outsiders, too, focused on wartime events. Before it was applied, willy-nilly, to all Asian American groups, the phrase "model minority" was coined in 1966 by the conservative social scientist William Petersen, who referred only to Japanese Americans. The phrase has infuriated two generations of Asian American activists, who have created a fairly large polemical literature denouncing it.[39]

Petersen's original use of the phrase was two-edged. On the one hand he gave unstinted praise to the recuperative powers of the battered Japanese American community, which, he argued, was a minority group of a different and more admirable kind than most of America's downtrodden. On the other hand, he used Japanese American success to set off what he saw as the failures of other minority groups and the federal government. As Petersen put it:

> The history of Japanese Americans, however, challenges every such generalization about ethnic minorities . . . Barely more than 20 years after the end of the wartime camps, this is a minority that has risen above even prejudiced criticism. By any criterion of good citizenship we choose, the Japanese Americans are better than any other group in our society, including native-born whites. They have established this remarkable record, moreover, by their own almost totally unaided effort. Every attempt to hamper their progress resulted only in enhancing their determination to succeed. Even in a country whose patron saint is Horatio Alger, there is no parallel to this success story.[40]

In contrast Petersen argued that "For all the well-meaning programs and countless scholarly studies now focused on the Negro, we hardly know how to repair the damage that the slave traders started." Although Petersen, I am sure, would not agree, it seems to me that his argument could be used to justify the current pressure for some kind of reparations for slavery.

Alone of the major Asian American communities, Japanese Americans did not experience particularly high levels of population growth in the second half of the century. But Japanese immigration to the United States, which had been cut off in 1924, was not allowed to resume until after the 1952 McCarran-Walter Act ended racial bars to both naturalization and immigration.

As Table 8.2 demonstrates, Japanese immigration after 1952 was never very large: fewer than a quarter million since mid-century, or about 5,000 per year. Because of this relatively low level of immigration, Japanese Americans, from being the most numerous Asian American group between 1910 and 1970, had fallen to sixth by the 2000 Census. That census recorded an 8 percent decline in the number of Japanese—from 866,160 to 796,700.* This was the first time that a decrease in the size of an Asian American group had been recorded since the forty-year decline of the Chinese American population ended in 1930. Even in Hawaii, where Japanese had once dominated the population, only one person in six was Japanese in 2000.

TABLE 8.2
IMMIGRATION FROM SELECTED ASIAN NATIONS,
BY DECADE, 1961–99

Nation	1961–70	1971–80	1981–90	1991–99	Total
China	109,771	237,793	444,962	431,410	1,233,936
India	27,189	164,134	250,786	323,988	766,097
Japan	39,988	49,775	47,085	60,212	197,060
Korea	34,526	267,638	354,987	135,261	792,412
Philippines	98,376	354,987	548,764	463,355	1,465,482
Vietnam	4,340	172,820	280,782	260,805	718,747

Source: INS data. These figures, for nations, significantly understate the immigration of ethnic Chinese as persons immigrating from Hong Kong—as long as it was separated from China—and other nations are not included although they appear in census data.

The initial post-1952 immigration from Japan was predominantly of women: large numbers of them were "occupation brides." Unlike the Chinese "war brides" all but a handful of the Japanese women were married to military and civilian occupation personnel who were Caucasian or African American, mostly the former.[41] In addition significant numbers of post-war immigrants were siblings and parents of newly naturalized pre-1924 immigrants, and thus had little long-term demographic impact. In short, Japanese American population growth was even smaller than one would expect given the gross immigration numbers.

If it had been possible for Japanese to emigrate to the United States immediately after the war, undoubtedly a large number of young adults would have done so, but by the time that emigration was possible, after 1952, the

---

*A change in basic census rules in 2000 makes all such comparisons problematic. For the first time persons were able to choose more than one ancestry. I am here comparing the number who said they were Japanese in 1990 with those who said that they were "Japanese" and "Japanese plus some other group" in 2000.

Japanese "economic miracle" had begun to transform Japan. Post–WW II Japan, especially since the 1970s, has been a nation that exports automobiles, high-tech gadgets, and capital instead of its people. But by the latter decades of the twentieth century the Japanese economy was losing headway. With an aging population and a shrinking labor force, Japan has become trapped between its need to import workers and its deeply felt desire to keep its population homogeneous.

In some ways, Japanese America resembles Japan. Its rapid recovery from its wartime ordeal was viewed by some as a kind of miracle, and its aging population is somewhat similar to that of the former homeland. But Japan's population is relatively homogeneous while third and subsequent generation Japanese Americans have practiced exogamous marriage to a greater degree than any other Asian American ethnic group. According to the problematic figures in the 2000 census, three Japanese Americans in ten reported some non-Japanese ancestry. By the twentieth century's end one of the burning issues among Japanese Americans concerned with their ethnic perpetuation was how to treat "hapa," or persons of part-Japanese heritage. The problem is not new, but the open discussion of it is.[42]

The 1990 census snapshot of Japanese Americans reveals an aging, largely middle-class community, just over two-thirds of whom were native-born. The median age for the whole community was 36.5 years. This contrasted with the national average of 33 years for all persons, 30.4 years for all persons of Asian ancestry, and 32.3, 31.3, 29.4, and 29.1 for all Chinese, Filipino, Asian Indian, and Korean Americans respectively. Fewer than 1.5 percent of those over twenty-five had fewer than five years of schooling and a similar percentage had doctorates, while more than three-fifths—62 percent—had progressed beyond high school. The lack of substantial immigration in the past forty-plus years is one of the factors that make the Japanese American demographic profile not unlike that in Japan.

A very different scenario was played out by immigrants from the Philippines and Korea. The first large increments of Filipinos, as we have seen, came in as American nationals in the decades between the American conquest and the Great Depression. They were given a mini-quota in the mid-1930s and granted the right of naturalization in 1946, although a 1943 statute for military personnel enabled some 10,000 to be naturalized as soldiers if they entered the military while in the United States.[43] Others, who entered the

U.S. forces in the Philippines during 1939–42 were specifically denied citizenship on that basis shortly after the war but were granted it by Congress in the Immigration Act of 1990.

The 1940 census listed almost 100,000 Filipinos, a small majority of them in Hawaii. Immigration resumed in the 1950s when about 20,000 came, followed by almost a hundred thousand in the 1960s, and, as indicated in Table 8.2, some 1.4 million immigrated to the U.S. between 1971 and the end of the century, more than recorded for any other Asian ethnic group.[44] From the beginning of the post-war immigration a majority of immigrants from the Philippines were women, reducing the badly skewed gender ratios of the first half of the century to something much closer to parity. By 1970 almost 46 percent of the 336,000 Filipino Americans were female, up from 37 percent in 1960, and less than 10 percent before the war. By 1980 there was a bare female majority and in 1990 Filipina Americans were almost 54 percent of the community's population.

The earliest increment of these immigrant women was war brides, few of whom were married to Filipino men. In the Philippines, as was the case everywhere the American Army served, many wives were abandoned by their husbands: in the Philippines such women were derided as "*gang pier lamang,*" or "wives up to the pier only." More numerous were Filipinas who married middle-aged Filipino men, long resident in the United States, who returned briefly to their homeland after naturalization to find a wife. These wives were usually significantly younger than their husbands.

Eventually the most numerous group of Filipino immigrants were nurses. There had been no significant number of Filipina nurses in the United States prior to 1948. In that year Congress passed the Information and Education Exchange Act, which authorized the State Department to create an Exchange Visitor Program (EVP). The notion was that nursing graduates would combine postgraduate study with practical clinical experience in U.S. hospitals and then return home to bolster the health care system in the Philippines. By 1973 more than 12,000 nurses from the Philippines had come to the U.S. under the EVP but large numbers of them did not return home. Instead, with the support of staff-short American hospitals, particularly public ones, they were able to obtain green cards and remain in the United States as employees. Many eventually became citizens.

Nurses from the Philippines had distinct advantages over most foreign nurses. English was the language of instruction in Philippine nursing schools and, probably even more important, thanks to the long American occupation and initiatives in the 1920s by the International Health Board of the Rockefeller Foundation, Philippine nursing education was created on an American model.

Many women in the Philippines viewed a nursing career as a ticket to a better life abroad, and nursing education boomed. Fueled by a worldwide nursing shortage and consequently higher salaries, the number of graduate nurses in the Philippines soared from 7,000 in 1948 to 57,000 in 1953. These nurses went not only to the United States, but to the United Kingdom, Canada, Australia, New Zealand, and to the oil-rich nations of the Middle East. An end-of-century report by the Philippine Nurses Association estimated that more than 150,000 Filipina nurses were employed overseas. Those with jobs at home earned 9,000 to 15,000 pesos a month, compared to 80,000 to 150,000 overseas.[45] By mid-2002, persistent recruiting to fill overseas vacancies created a severe shortage of nurses in the Philippines. Filipino nurses and administrators told of hospitals that had lost 75 percent of their nurses in two years.[46]

As bad as that seems for the Philippines—if not for the emigrating nurses—it has to be pointed out that as is true for many other contemporary countries of emigration, the remittances that overseas workers send back are crucial for the national economy. The official 2002 estimate was that remittances to the Philippines amounted to $6 billion annually, some 8 percent of the gross national product. On the eve of her departure for a state visit to the United States, President Gloria Macapagal-Arroyo spoke of thanking the Filipino community in the United States for "boosting the Philippine economy and for shoring up our national stability through their foreign exchange remittances to Manila."[47]

It is not only nurses, but also other medical professionals and paraprofessionals from the Philippines and other overseas sources who keep American hospitals going. Filipino immigrants, mostly female, have created a remarkable niche for themselves in the United States: of 150,000 Filipino workers identified in the 1990 census, some 20 percent were in the health care sector. Nineteen-ninety census data show the degree of specialization: it divides all employment into sixteen sectors and subsectors, one of which is "health services." That sector employed nearly 9.7 million workers, or 8.4 percent of all workers. One hundred fifty thousand of those workers were identified as Filipinos, 20 percent of all Filipino workers in the United States.

The 1990 census profile of the Filipino American community reveals that the foreign-born majority—64 percent of the 1990 population—had less poverty and more education than the native-born minority, the opposite of the usual situation. It is not, however, surprising. Many of the foreign-born are daughters and sons of the Philippine middle class, while most of the native-born are the children of plantation laborers and farm workers.

In terms of poverty the differences were substantial: 8.3 percent of the native-born Filipino families were below the federal poverty line as opposed to only 4.6 percent of all Philippine-born families. However it should be noted that for all American families poverty levels were higher—10 percent—and that 14.5 percent of all foreign-born families were below the line.

The difference in education is relatively slight if we simply compare Filipinos born in the Philippines with those born in the United States: 26 percent of the foreign-born over twenty-five years of age have bachelor's degrees as opposed to 22 percent of the native-born. But if one looks at only those immigrants who arrived between 1980 and 1990, twice as many—45 percent—have bachelor's degrees, reflecting the increasingly middle-class character of recent Filipino immigration to the United States.

Korean Americans, unlike the Asian American groups discussed above, had no substantial community in the United States until after the Korean War. Except for a few scattered individuals, mostly students, the major increment of pre-1950s immigrants, some 7,000 in number, came to Hawaii under the auspices of the Hawaiian Sugar Planters Association during a brief window of opportunity between 1903 and 1905, a window that Korea's Japanese overlords quickly slammed shut, although in the years after 1910 they did allow some 800 "picture brides" to immigrate to Hawaii under the umbrella of the Gentlemen's Agreement. Korean immigration had three characteristics that differentiated it from the other East Asian migrants of that era. Many of the first group of Koreans came in family units; large numbers of them had been converted to Christianity by American and Canadian missionaries in Korea; and almost all came to consider themselves exiles.[48]

Many in the tiny Korean American community were staunch nationalists who rejected any notion that they were Japanese subjects. For example, in 1913 when a group of Korean laborers was assaulted by a mob in Hemet, California, and the Japanese consul general in Los Angeles intervened to get them compensation, the laborers refused to have anything to do with him. A more extreme—and isolated—example of exile nationalism had occurred five years earlier in San Francisco.

Durham W. Stevens, a minor onetime American diplomat who had been employed as an advisor to the Japanese foreign office since 1875, was sent to the United States on a lecture tour to advance Japanese interests. In a San Francisco lecture praising Japan's actions in Korea he made derogatory statements about the country and its inhabitants, inflaming the local Korean community: one of its members, a thirty-three-year-old immigrant, shot him twice on March 23, 1908. Stevens died two days later. Arrested and tried for the assassination—his lawyer called it "patriotic passion"—Chang In-hawn was convicted only of second-degree murder and sentenced to twenty-five years, but was released in 1919. Long in ill-health, he committed suicide in 1930. In 1975 his body was exhumed, taken to Korea, and reburied, with honors, in the national cemetery in Seoul.[49]

The most famous and eventually influential of those exiles was Syngman Rhee (1874–1965). Imprisoned from 1897 to 1904 for political activities in Korea, Rhee came to the United States after he got out of jail and made vain attempts to get Theodore Roosevelt to use American power to protect Korean independence, as an 1882 treaty required. (Roosevelt noted privately to his Secretary of State that the Koreans "couldn't strike one blow in their own defense.")[50]

A scholar, Rhee earned three American degrees—a B.A. from Georgetown, an M.A. from Harvard, and a Ph.D from Princeton (1910)—and remained in the United States, except for one brief visit to Korea in 1912, until 1945, when the American government installed him as the head of a provisional government in Seoul. He was later elected the first president of the Republic of Korea (South Korea). His tenure lasted until 1960, when he was again forced into exile—this time by his own people. He died in Honolulu in 1965.[51]

The numbers of Korean Americans on the mainland, most of whom remigrated from Hawaii, were even smaller than those in the islands: on the eve of World War II there were perhaps no more than ten thousand persons of Korean birth or ancestry in both places combined.[52] In the aftermath of Pearl Harbor, Rhee and other Korean American leaders prevailed upon the American government not to declare Koreans "enemy aliens," as it might well have done. A few Koreans assisted the government with interned Japanese nationals as guards, censors, and interpreters at INS detention camps.[53]

Before and during the war, Kilsoo Haan, founder, leader, and perhaps only member of the Sino-Korean Peoples League, not only propagandized, profitably, about a coming Japanese attack on the United States but insisted that Japanese Americans, in general, were disloyal.[54]

When the war ended Koreans were still ineligible for either naturalization or immigration: like Japanese, they would not be eligible until the 1952 immigration act ended formal racial discrimination, although a number of students came in the immediate post-war years. Only some 6,000 immigrated in the 1950s, after which, as Table 8.2 indicates, the rate picked up rapidly. From 1961 through 1990 nearly 800,000 Koreans immigrated, establishing thriving and varied communities in the United States.

Most of the earliest post–Korean War immigrants were "war brides," almost all of whom married non-Koreans. Since large American military forces have been stationed in Korea continuously since 1950, Korean brides have continued to come to the United States with their American husbands. The most detailed study, by Ji-Teon Yuh, argues that the term "military brides" is a more appropriate way to describe the nearly 100,000 women who have come since the 1953 armistice stopped the fighting. As was true earlier in Japan, the American military authorities pressured soldiers not to bring home Asian wives, a policy continued in Korea long after it had been abandoned in Japan. Many of the Korean women who married American soldiers had been sex workers in what Yuh calls "militarized prostitution," which encouraged many in the growing Korean American community to assume that all military brides were former prostitutes. First called "women in shadows" by Bok-Lim Kim in 1977, military brides have been largely ignored if not shunned by the rest of the Korean American community.[55]

Looking at the statistical profile of the Korean American population in 1990, the single most striking fact is the high proportion of its workers who are employed in retail trade: better than three Korean American workers in ten—31 percent—are so classified by the census, a much higher figure than for any other Asian American group. (For the entire American labor force the figure is one worker in six.)

Although it does not show up in the census summary, the particular economic niche Koreans have carved out for themselves is much narrower. The vast majority of those 108,000 retail workers are employed in small Korean-owned family businesses, some 6,000 of whom were what the census calls "unpaid family members." (The census does not count those under sixteen years of age.)

In California the largest concentration of those businesses is convenience stores in poor neighborhoods,* while in New York and other East Coast cities Korean greengrocers have established a more upscale specialty. In the bustling Koreatown centered on that portion of Olympic Boulevard adjacent to downtown Los Angeles there is an amazing variety of retail establishments of almost every type: no Angeleno Korean need ever shop anywhere else.

Other aspects of the community profile are what one would expect for an increasingly middle-class and entrepreneurial population: relatively high education and low poverty. In 1990 more than a third of all Korean Americans over twenty-four years of age—34.5 percent—had bachelor's degrees or better.

Because of the military brides, Korean Americans have the most skewed contemporary gender ratio of any of the Asian American groups studied here: 56.1 percent of all Korean Americans in 1990 were female. All the Asian groups discussed so far have a female majority, as does the United States. The incidence of women in the Asian American population—51.2 percent—varied only insignificantly from either that in the entire American population—51.3 percent—or that for all immigrants—51.1 percent. This contrasts with the nineteenth and early twentieth centuries, when there was a heavy male preponderance in immigration. The current situation reflects both the family-immigration dominance mandated by the 1965 immigration act and its successors and the greater variety of employment opportunities available to recent female immigrants.

One special aspect of recent Korean immigration has been the extent of adoptions of Korean children by Caucasian American parents. Adoption of foreign children, which, in American immigration statistics, was insignificant until after the Korean War of 1950–53, boomed in the 1990s. In the first year of the decade 7,093 adopted children entered; for 1999 the number had grown to 16,369. Of the 12,596 adopted immigrants in 1997, 97 percent were under ten years of age and nearly half—46.6 percent—were less than one year old. Only about a little more than a third—36.5 per-

---

*A fatal encounter in one such convenience store triggered the 1992 riots in Los Angeles. See Nancy Ablemann and John Lie, *Blue Dreams: Korean Americans and the Los Angeles Riots* (Cambridge, Mass.: Harvard University Press, 1995).

cent—of these adopted children were boys. The imbalance was due to the great preponderance of girls in Asian adoptions: 77.3 percent of the nearly 6,000 adoptions from Asia involved girls. For the rest of the world the numbers were nearly equal. In 1997 adopted children comprised 1.6 percent of all American immigrants.

Until very recently the majority of adopted Asian children have been from Korea, but at century's end China was providing the largest number. In 1997, for example, 3,295 adopted Chinese children were brought to the United States. Only 70 of them were boys. A relatively balanced group came from Korea in 1997: of 1,506 adopted children, 800 were boys. Between them, China and Korea accounted for almost two out of five—38.1 percent—of the world total. Only Russia, which provided American parents 3,626 children, 1,843 of them girls, allows foreign adoption on a large scale.[56]

The final large Asian immigrant group to be considered here has been labeled "Asian Indians" by the census bureau since 1980, at the request of leaders of that community who were distressed by the confusion with American Indians. The earliest census term was "East Indians" and the 1946 statute that granted them the rights of naturalization and independence spoke of "natives of India," which became inappropriate when independence from Britain and partition into India and Pakistan took place the following year. (Until 1952, when it became redundant, the statute enabled Pakistanis as well.)

Before the twentieth century only scattered numbers of persons from the subcontinent had come to North America, most of them seamen and merchants. The first Indian to have public impact was the Hindu missionary, Swami Vivekananda, who came to the United States to participate in the World Parliament of Religions at the 1893 Chicago World's Fair and remained for the better part of the next three years lecturing, teaching, and proselytizing. Before returning to India he established the Vedanta Society in New York, the first Hindu institution in North America. For the next half-century Hinduism in America was essentially the preserve of Caucasians, largely upper-middle-class women, often devoted to yoga and similar practices.[57]

Labor immigration from India began early in the twentieth century. The majority of these immigrants landed in Victoria or Vancouver, British

Columbia, and worked their way south. (There was no regular steamship service between India and North America then: the Canadian ports were more convenient.) They worked in lumber mills, on railroads, and in agriculture. Most were turbaned Sikhs who were ignorantly described as Hindus or "Hindoos" in the press, and called "rag heads" by racist agitators. Immigration records for the 1901–10 decade showed almost 5,800 immigrants, just 109 of them female. H. A. Millis, the sociologist who investigated Asian immigrants for the U.S. Immigration Commission, believed that in 1909–10 there were about "5,000 East Indians of the working class in the United States," most arriving after 1905. By the time Millis wrote, most immigration from India had been cut off, not by statute but by a selective use of the existing regulations. The Commission's report showed that in the years 1907–11 some 1,600 immigrants from India were kept out both on various medical grounds, chiefly trachoma, and by a creative use of the "likely to become a public charge" clause. In 1917 the so-called barred-zone provisions kept out all South Asian immigrants until the 1946 act that made Indians eligible for naturalization and thus immigration.

Neither that act nor the 1952 act enabled large numbers of Asian Indians to immigrate to the United States. A considerable portion of the West Coast workingmen had married exogamously, mainly with Mexican American women, and did not have families to bring.[58] Only in the 1970s, as Table 8.2 shows, did Asian Indian immigration exceed 10,000 a year; in the 1980s 25,000 came annually and in the 1990s more than 30,000.

The 1990 census shows a distinctly upscale Asian Indian community profile. Among its foreign-born only a little over a quarter reported to the 1990 census that they did not speak English "very well," the lowest percentage of any Asian immigrant group. Foreign-born members of the other groups treated here gave that answer much more readily: every third Filipino and more than three out of five Koreans were so recorded. In terms of formal education, fewer than 4 percent of the Asian Indian population over twenty-five reported having less than a fifth-grade education, while nearly six out of ten—58.1 percent—had bachelor's degrees or better. Consequently the poverty levels were quite low: only 7.2 percent of all Asian Indian families.

Alone of the Asian groups treated here, a majority of the 1990 Asian Indian population—54.9 percent—was male, and its geographical distribution was different, too. Largely because there was no appreciable Asian Indian community in Hawaii, its population in the East was larger than that in the West. New York and New Jersey combined had more of the 2000 population of Asian Indians—24.5 percent—than did California and Hawaii combined—18.8 percent—although California had more Asian Indians than any other state. (Many were technicians and entrepreneurs in Silicon Valley, a group that will be discussed in Chapter 12.) Along with California, New York, and New Jersey, two other states—Texas and Michigan—had more than 100,000 Asian Indians, and the five combined had almost three of five of the nation's Asian Indians, 59 percent. In New Jersey, and a number of midwestern states including Illinois and Michigan, Asian Indians were the largest single Asian minority.*

The most curious employment niche that Asian Indians in America have moved into is the motel business. In addition, that business is dominated by one large clan named Patel, most of whom come from Gujarat, a region of western India. One community joke speaks of "hotel, motel, Patel." The Asian Indian dominance is not just folklore. A survey of the motels along Interstate 75, which connects Detroit and Atlanta, a few years ago showed that 40 percent of the motels were owned by Asian Indians—most of them named Patel.

While the census breakdown does not isolate motel workers, it is apparent from the 1990 data that a high percentage of Indian workers are concentrated in a variety of white-collar occupations. A third of all Asian Indian workers are in "professional and related services," a category in which a quarter of all Asian workers and some 23 percent of all American workers are found. Almost a tenth of all Asian Indians are in finance and related industries, and, as observing rush-hour passengers at any of the lower Manhattan mass transit venues will demonstrate, very large numbers of them work on Wall Street. Perhaps because of the age-old Indian cultivation of mathematics, a large percentage work as number crunchers in brokerage houses and other branches of the securities industry.

This impressionistic profile of the larger Asian American groups underscores that few, if any, meaningful generalizations can be made that apply to all of them. Second, as groups they are among the more successful of recent immigrants to the United States, although surely there are many individuals who wish that they had never come. One of the few measurable

---

*As Americans are becoming increasingly aware, Michigan has long been home to the largest concentration of Arab Americans, but they are not "Asians" in Census Bureau geography.

characteristics that all of the groups, save the Japanese Americans, share— that a majority of their populations are relatively recent immigrants—will not long continue.

There are, of course, certain characteristics that cannot be measured easily and some that cannot be measured at all. In the twentieth century, despite an almost total reversal of their legal disabilities, persons of color, even those who were highly successful, could rarely completely transcend certain limits placed upon them. If that was true even of the more successful immigrant groups—and these Asian American groups were certainly that—the limits placed upon their less successful fellow immigrants were even more difficult to overcome.

CHAPTER NINE

Immigrants from Other Worlds: Latinos

Of the three most prominent groups of Spanish-speaking mi-grants to the United States—Mexicans, Puerto Ricans, and Cubans—only two are immigrant groups. Puerto Ricans (as noted earlier) are American citizens and thus will not be treated extensively here. But because of how the census counts what it now classifies as "Hispanic or Latino" Ameri-cans,* it is necessary for us to glance at the Puerto Rican population living on the mainland. When the census gives data about the Hispanic/Latino population it almost always adds the note that these persons "may be of any race." This is necessary because Hispanics and Latinos have already been included in the total population under one of the "racial" categories, al-most all as either "black or white." Table 9.1 shows the census tabulation.

---

*The way that the government treats racial/ethnic aggregates is problematic. Like "Asian American" and "Asian and Pacific Islander" the "Hispanic/Latino" designation has evolved. For a long time the government spoke of "Spanish-surnamed persons." That "Hispanic" is also used to cover Brazilians, who speak Portuguese, and "Latinos" is very confusing. Former Vice President Dan Quayle once as-sumed, to great glee among Democrats, that "Latinos" spoke Latin. Many recent immigrants from Mexico have only a limited grasp of Spanish as their native tongues are various Amerindian lan-guages.

TABLE 9.1
HISPANIC OR LATINO POPULATION, 2000

Group	Number	% of U.S.	% of H/L
Hispanic or Latino (any race)	35,305,818	12.5	100
Mexican	20,640,711	7.3	58.5
Puerto Rican	3,406,178	1.2	9.6
Cuban	1,241,685	0.4	3.5
Other Hispanic or Latino	10,017,244	3.6	28.4
Central American	1,686,937		4.8
Salvadoran	655,165		1.9
South American	1,353,562		3.8
Dominican Republic	764,945		2.2
Unspecified other*	6,111,665		17.3

Source: Census 2000 PHC-T-10.

The 2000 census was the first time that the Hispanic/Latino population exceeded that of the African American or black population, which the census tabulated at 34,658,190 persons, or 12.3 percent of the population. However, since the census included in that tabulation 710,353 persons who said that they were Hispanics, the non-Hispanic African American population can be reckoned at 33,947,837, or 12.1 percent.

The general perception that most Hispanics are foreigners is false. The March 2000 Current Population Survey, which had slightly smaller total numbers than the census, reported that only two of five Hispanics (39.1 percent) were foreign-born, and that a quarter of those were naturalized citizens. In short, only about 30 percent were not U.S. citizens. The same survey reported that more than three out of five Asians and Pacific Islanders were foreign-born and that not quite half of them had become naturalized citizens.[1]

Although Hispanic people can now be found throughout the nation, in 2000 almost half were in just two southwestern states, California and Texas, but the major segments were concentrated in three distinct regions: Mexican Americans and Central Americans in the Southwest, Puerto Ricans and Dominicans in the Northeast, and Cubans in the Southeast. The broader diffusion is epitomized by the high ranking of Illinois, far from any

*These are persons who either checked "other Hispanic" and did not specify, or wrote in "Spanish," "Hispanic," or "Latino," or are "Not elsewhere classified." In other words, the census doesn't have a clue in what category more than a sixth of this population belongs. And I find it difficult to believe that no one wrote in "Chicano," which the Bureau apparently doesn't record.

of the traditional focal points of Hispanic population. Every eighth Illinois resident in 2000 was Hispanic, a total of 1.5 million persons. Most— 1.1 million—were Mexican Americans, but almost 400,000 other Hispanics were enumerated. The diffusion of the Hispanic population throughout the nation will almost certainly continue in the coming decades.

In the 2000 census seven states recorded more than a million Hispanics, as shown in Table 9.2. Those seven states contained 76.8 percent of the nation's total. No other state recorded as many as 800,000 Hispanics.

TABLE 9.2
STATES WITH MORE THAN A MILLION HISPANICS, 2000

State	Hispanics	% Hispanics	% State Pop. 2000	1990
California	10,966,556	30.7	32.4	25.8
Texas	6,669,666	18.9	32.0	25.5
New York	2,867,583	8.1	15.1	12.3
Florida	2,682,715	7.6	16.8	12.2
Illinois	1,530,262	4.3	12.3	7.9
Arizona	1,295,617	3.7	25.3	18.8
New Jersey	1,117,191	3.1	13.3	9.6
Total	27,129,590	76.8		

Source: Census 2000 PHC-T-10.

New Mexico is not represented in Table 9.2 because of its small population, but its 756,386 Hispanics constitute 42.1 percent of the total population, making it, as it has always been, the most Hispanic state or territory in the nation. Before relatively large amounts of non-Hispanic migration to New Mexico during and after World War II it had been overwhelmingly Hispanic, and is the only state with two official languages, English and Spanish.

California is not only a core area for Mexicans, but is also the home to 2.5 million other Hispanics: the 2000 census recorded almost 600,000 Central Americans, 160,000 South Americans, 140,000 Puerto Ricans, 72,000 Cubans, and 1.5 million Hispanic persons whose answers could not be subdivided into more precise national or ethnic categories.

Mexicans, of course, had been in what we think of as the American Southwest long before it was American. The perhaps 100,000 Mexicans who lived in the territory torn from Mexico as a result of the Mexican-

American War were granted, by the 1848 Treaty of Guadalupe Hidalgo, the right to become American citizens merely by taking an oath of allegiance without having to undergo naturalization. In the course of the next few decades these native sons and daughters of the region found themselves outnumbered by much larger groups of Euro-American migrants and immigrants, becoming, as some have put it, strangers in their own land. To be sure, some members of the upper classes retained economic and social power: the career of California's Romulado Pacheco (1831–99) is a case in point.

Born in Santa Barbara, Pacheco was a successful rancher and businessman when he took the required oath of allegiance in 1850. He was appointed a county judge three years later and in 1857 was elected to the state legislature as a Democrat. After the outbreak of the Civil War, Pacheco switched first to the Union Party, under whose banner he was reelected, and then to the Republican Party, which appointed him state treasurer in 1863, an office he subsequently retained by election. In 1867 he lost that office to another Californio, as many former Mexican citizens styled themselves. In 1871 he was nominated and elected lieutenant governor, and when the governor was appointed to the United States Senate, Pacheco served the last nine months of his term, becoming the first state governor of Mexican ancestry. He later won three elections to the U.S. House of Representatives,* and after leaving the House was appointed minister to Central America in 1890, a post he held until shortly after the Democrats took over the White House in 1893.[2]

Many of the daughters—but rarely the sons—of the old Mexican elite married "gringo" settlers, as Pacheco's widowed mother had done long before the American conquest. But Pacheco was an exception, if a notable one. Albert Camarillo has eloquently described more common kinds of adjustment:

---

*When the son of Italian immigrants Anthony Caminetti (1854–1923) made the first of his two successful campaigns for Congress in 1890, he had the gall to advertise that, if elected, he would be the first "native son" to be elected to Congress from California. To add to the irony, during his service as Woodrow Wilson's Commissioner General of Immigration, he presided over the introduction of more stringent admission regulations for Mexicans. He was the second Italian American congressman; the first was Francis Barretto Spinola (1821–1891), American-born, who was elected as a Democrat from a Brooklyn district in 1886, and twice reelected.

. . . most Mexicans, be they members of the elite or of the working class, chose neither co-optation nor violent resistance but instead managed to accommodate themselves to different circumstances resulting from Americanization. Beneath the glamour and romanticization of the escapades of the legendary Joaquín Murieta in California, or the 1859 revolt led by Juan Cortinas in South Texas, or the night-riding, fence-cutting, resistance activities of the hooded Gorras Blancas (White Caps) of New Mexico (1889–91), the social and cultural changes among the great majority of Mexican Americans took place largely unnoticed. By the end of the nineteenth century Mexican Americans had developed a bicultural and biracial accommodation which for most resulted in separation from the majority of whites. With the exception of contact between European Americans and Mexican Americans in the arena of employment, the social lives of most Mexican Americans occurred within their rural colonias (colonies or small settlements) and urban barrios (neighborhoods).[3]

Immigration data show only 13,315 Mexican immigrants in the fifty years after 1850, but, as the footnote to these "data" in the INS reports points out, "land arrivals [were] not completely enumerated until 1908." Some of the "data" are simply ridiculous—for example, immigration for the decade of the 1890s is 971, a little more than one immigrant every two weeks. This is absurd, given that the 1890s were a time when there was constant informal long- and short-term border-crossing and changes of residence all along the southern border. While Americans commonly regard the border as a barrier, it is also something that unites people on either side.* There is general agreement among scholars that the net population changes of either Mexicans or Mexican Americans due to immigration or emigration were not large in the years before 1910. Even then farsighted Anglo Californians had clear ideas about the proper place for workers from Mexico.

Hubert Howe Bancroft (1832–1918), the pioneer historian of California and an extreme racist, welcomed both Asian and Mexican labor under certain conditions:

we want [them] for our low-grade work, and when it is finished we want [them] to go home and stay there until we want [them] again.[4]

---

*As noted previously this is especially the case between the twinned cities that extend along the border from Matamoras/Brownsville on the Gulf of Mexico to Tijuana/San Diego on the Pacific.

Employers of Mexican migrant labor in California and, to a lesser degree, in Texas echoed these words for decades, but as we now know, in the years after Bancroft wrote, large numbers of the migrants did not return home. Instead they made new homes north of the border.

Around 1910 events on each side of the border pushed and pulled larger and larger numbers of Mexicans into the United States. The beginnings of the Mexican Revolution set off almost two decades of warfare and extreme political instability that both loosened the country's social fabric and expedited modernization and emigration. On the American side, continuing irrigation of semiarid land,[5] the invention of the refrigerator car, and the evolution of a nationwide distribution system for produce all facilitated the development of large-scale capitalist agriculture, creating what Carey McWilliams dubbed "factories in the field." After World War I that agribusiness created the single greatest "pull" factor affecting twentieth-century Mexican immigration.[6] But even before that the California citrus industry had grown largely dependent on Mexican and Mexican American workers, who often resided in what Gilbert C. Gonzalez has called "citrus villages."[7] These developments all rested on a base of migrant labor, which was, as the twentieth century progressed, heavily Mexican in the Southwest. Even in the depths of the Great Depression most migrant labor in California was Mexican despite the influx of dust bowl refugees immortalized in John Steinbeck's *The Grapes of Wrath*.

These permanent factors, reinforced first by the temporary labor shortages of World War I and then by the restrictive immigration legislation of the early 1920s, created a boom in recorded immigration from Mexico. Immigration from Mexico, legal and illegal, transitory and permanent, continued except for the worst years of the Great Depression. The several extensions of the wartime bracero program cemented the mutually dependent reciprocal relationships between southwestern growers and Mexican and Mexican American workers, and influential southwestern legislators, including Lyndon Johnson, who thwarted efforts to put effective legal measures in place to halt and/or reverse the flow of migrants.

Legal immigration from Mexico—which does not include the wartime or post-war braceros—grew steadily from some 60,000 in the 1940s (one in twenty of the nation's immigrants) to 1.6 million in the 1980s (22.6 percent of all immigrants and more than twice as many as came from all of Europe). In each of the three decades after 1960 more immigrants came from

Mexico than from any other nation, and, for the entire period one immigrant in six came from Mexico. (See Table 9.3.)

TABLE 9.3
IMMIGRATION FROM MEXICO, BY DECADE, 1941–90

Decade	Number	% of All Immigrants
1941–50	60,589	5.9
1951–60	299,811	11.9
1961–70	453,937	13.7
1971–80	640,294	14.2
1981–90	1,655,843	22.6
Total	3,110,474	16.6

Source: INS data.

Mexicans, whether foreign- or native-born, present a distinctly different profile from the Asian groups examined in the previous chapter. Using the 1990 census data, only 44.2 percent of Mexican Americans over twenty-five years of age were high school graduates, and only one in sixteen had a bachelor's degree or higher. Most other Hispanic groups had more educational accomplishment. South Americans and those who recorded themselves as Spaniards led the way: 70.7 percent of the former and 76.7 percent of the latter were high school graduates while a fifth of each group had bachelor's degrees or better. Cuban Americans and Puerto Ricans also received more education than the Mexican group.

As one would expect, their low educational achievement meant that relatively few Mexicans held managerial jobs: more than a quarter of all non-Hispanic males over sixteen years of age held such jobs as opposed to less than an eighth of all Mexican American males. Lower on the job ladder, about three of ten Mexican males were factory workers and laborers as opposed to less than one in five non-Hispanic males. Women's jobs were similarly distributed: Mexican women were more than twice as likely to be laborers and operatives than their non-Hispanic sisters: about one in six for the former and one in twelve for the latter.

Income figures are even more revealing. More than two of ten Hispanic families in 1990 lived in poverty, as compared to fewer than one in ten for non-Hispanic families. Within the Hispanic group, family poverty rates ranged from 33 percent for Puerto Ricans and 30 percent for Dominicans at the bottom to 23 percent for Mexicans and 20 percent for Central Americans in the middle, and 11 percent for Cuban families and 10 percent for "Spaniard" families at the top.

These numbers clearly reflect working-class populations whose native cultures have not placed great emphasis on education. Yet the three censuses between 1970 and 1990, despite the continuing massive migration of Mexicans and others, show decided improvement. In 1970 the high school and college completion proportions for all Hispanics were three in ten and one in twenty respectively; by 1980 it was four in ten and one in thirteen; and, to repeat, in 1990 almost half had completed high school and one in eleven was a college graduate. Using the March 2000 Current Population Survey, which estimated that 6.9 percent of the Mexican American population of nearly 21.7 million persons were college graduates, one can calculate that about one and a half million Mexican Americans were in that category. The figures indicate a growing Mexican American middle class.

Cuban Americans are at the top end of the socioeconomic spectrum of Hispanics. All but a tiny fraction of the one and a quarter million Cuban Americans counted in the 2000 Census can be attributed to their continuing exodus from Castro's Cuba and the American-born generations these immigrants have produced. Even in the first year of the twenty-first century some 25,000 Cubans came, which made the island the seventh largest provider of immigrants to the United States. However it must not be forgotten that Cubans came to North America before the United States was born and that the United States and Cuba have had a long and complicated historical relationship.

The first Cuban American whose biography we know is Félix Francisco Varela y Morelos (1788–1853) who became an important figure in the history of Catholicism in New York City.* Born in Havana, he was orphaned by age six and spent most of the rest of his childhood in the custody of his grandfather, commander of the garrison at St. Augustine, Florida. Destined for the priesthood, he was sent back to Havana from whose university he received a baccalaureate degree in 1806; five years later he was ordained. Teaching at the San Carlos Seminary, by 1822 he became Cuba's leading philosopher and teacher. Elected in 1821 as Cuba's spokesman to the Spanish Cortes (parliament), he made three liberal proposals—for Cuban autonomy,

---

*Fourteen other persons of Cuban birth, three of them nineteenth-century figures, are in the *American National Biography*.

the abolition of slavery, and support for Latin American revolutions. The restoration in Spain of the reactionary Bourbon regime of Ferdinand VII, who dissolved the liberal Cortes, made it impossible for Varela to return to Cuba. In 1823 he arrived in New York, a refugee without ecclesiastical sanction. The Irish Bishop of New York, nervous about his politics, refused to grant him clerical status, so the Cuban refugee moved to Philadelphia, where he published a Spanish-language political magazine advocating Cuban independence. In 1825 the New York clerical authorities accepted him and for the next twenty-five years he was a key figure in New York City's Catholic life, largely ministering to Irish immigrants and their families. In 1850 he retired to his boyhood home in St. Augustine, where he died.[8]

In the nineteenth century two different groups dominated immigration from Cuba to the United States. One consisted of political exiles who, in the second half of the century, set up revolutionary juntas in New York and Tampa that worked to overthrow Spanish rule. Among them was the greatest figure of nineteenth-century Cuban history, José Martí (1853–95). Based in New York, he worked to spark a Cuban revolution for more than a decade before he was killed in an early battle of the island's War for Independence. The other group was made up of cigar workers and their families concentrated in Key West and Tampa.[9]

American immigration authorities did not report Cuban immigration separately until 1925: in the next twenty-five years only some 50,000 Cuban entrants were tallied. The 1950 census found only 30,000 foreign-born Cubans in the whole country, of whom 13,000 were in New York, 8,000 in Florida, and 1,000 in California. During the 1950s Cuba was in a state of political and economic turmoil. In the decade *before* Castro came to power, about as many Cubans came to the United States as had come in all previous history. The 1960 census reported 80,000 foreign-born Cubans plus 40,000 of the second generation. This migration made Miami the capital of Cuban America. The immigrants of the 1950s were largely members of the elite who saw the handwriting on the wall, and persons looking for work.

The Fidel Castro era of Cuban history began with his seizure of power on January 1, 1959; immediately a flurry of persons close to the old regime fled into what they thought would be a short exile. Only in the following year, when it became clear that a real social revolution was taking place, did large numbers of Cubans begin to leave. Although the Eisenhower administration broke off diplomatic relations with Cuba at the start of 1961 and the new Kennedy administration launched the ill-conceived and miserably executed Bay of Pigs invasion in April of that year, more or less regular air-line service between Havana and Miami continued uninterrupted until the Cuban Missile Crisis of October 1962.

During those months more than 150,000 Cubans came to the United States. For three years after the missile crisis there were no direct flights be-tween Cuba and the U.S., but those with money could come to the United States via third countries, most often Spain or Mexico. Some 30,000 came that way until the Johnson administration signed a "memorandum of un-derstanding" with Cuba reinstating direct flights between Cuba and Mi-ami, usually one or two a day. That arrangement, which lasted until 1973, brought about 250,000 more Cubans. From then until the chaos of the Mariel boatlift of 1980—to be discussed in the next chapter—very few came. All told, 894,992 Cubans arrived in the U.S. since 1950, and the 1.25 million Cuban Americans of the 2000 census would increase the island's population by more than 10 percent if they were to return, or in the case of those born in the U.S., to migrate.

That, of course, is not going to happen. María Cristina García, the finest historian of the community, has described how Cuban exiles have become, over time, Cuban Americans.[10] Although the rhetoric of return continues, often beginning with the phrase "When Castro falls . . ." the original exile generation, whose coming was compelled largely by ideology, is passing from the scene. Were the regime to change tomorrow, many Cuban Amer-icans would return for a visit, as some have been able to do since the 1990s, but their roots are now in the United States. Perhaps nothing symbolizes that more than the fact that one of two Cuban Americans in the House of Representatives, Lincoln Diaz-Balart, is Fidel Castro's nephew.* Had a regime change occurred in the 1960s, or even the 1970s, a substantial "re-turn" might have been expected. Most of the immigrants from Cuba of the last three decades, including what they call *balseros*—raft people—are much more economic than political refugees, no matter what they tell the INS. In the next chapter the complex ways in which Cubans were accepted into the United States will be examined as one aspect of the politics of

---

*Diaz-Balart's life course illustrates aspects of the Cuban American story. Born in Havana in 1954, he graduated from the American School in Madrid (1972), took a 1976 B.A. from the University of South Florida and a 1979 law degree from Case Western Reserve, was elected to the Florida House of Representatives in 1986, to its Senate in 1988, and to the U.S. House of Representatives in 1992 as a Republican, and was reelected five times.

refugee policy. Here an end-of-century snapshot of what is now a multigenerational community will be analyzed.

The million and a quarter Cuban Americans of the 2000 census were heavily concentrated in Florida, where two out of three Cuban Americans lived. What is often overlooked is that Florida's 833,120 Cubans represent less than a third of the state's nearly 2.7 million Hispanics. That the Cubans dominate public consciousness both outside and, to a lesser extent, inside Florida, is due to their organization and to imbalanced media coverage. Within the state, Miami-Dade County was the most heavily Hispanic large county in the nation: its 1.3 million Hispanics were almost three-fifths of the county's population and almost half of the state's Hispanics although Miami-Dade contained only a seventh of the state's total population. The concentration of Cubans was even more extreme: of the state's 883,000 Cubans, 650,000—a whopping 73.6 percent—lived in Miami-Dade, while an additional 51,000 Cubans, 5.7 percent of the state total, lived in Broward County, one county north of Miami-Dade. Yet despite this preponderance, Cubans were a bare majority, 50.4 percent, of Miami-Dade's Hispanics and just over a quarter of the county's total population.

The latest census data suggest that, rather than diffusing from its original South Florida base, as had been the case, the Cuban American population is increasing its concentration in Florida. The 2000 census showed a total population gain for Cuban Americans of 19 percent over 1990, but the gain in Florida was 23 percent. For the same period, New Jersey, which had attracted a steady 15 percent of Cuban Americans, actually had a decline, from 85,000 to 77,000. A local paper quoted a thirty-three-year-old Cuban American who had lived in New Jersey since the 1980s but was packing his new Nissan Altima for a move to Florida: "You ask 'What happened to so-and-so?' and you hear 'He left, she left.' In Miami there are more job opportunities, and it's cheaper. The Cuban community is all around, I feel like I'm in Cuba there, like I'm home."[11] Even Cuban Americans who live elsewhere look at Miami as home base.[12]

Although no place can compare with South Florida as a home for displaced Cubans, there is a mini-diaspora of Cubans that has taken some as far away as Australia. Although there are more Cubans in Mexico and several South American nations than in all of Europe, perhaps the largest single group of exile/immigrant Cubans is in Spain, where, in the late 1990s, Spanish officials estimated there were 10,000 Cubans but community activists claimed triple that number.

The sustained impact of decades of high-profile Cuban migration has transformed Miami. Until the post-Castro exodus began, the city had during its relatively short history lived on winter tourism, which became an industry there only in 1896 after the Rockefeller partner, Henry M. Flagler, pushed his Florida East Coast Railroad into Miami.[13] The impetus of Cuban entrepreneurs has made Miami a banking center whose face turns south to Latin America, and this has attracted American branches of major South American banks.

The historian David Reimers used the story of Carlos Arboleya to epitomize Cuban success. The former chief auditor of Cuba's largest bank, Arboleya fled with his family and $40 after Castro nationalized the banks. No Miami bank would hire him—he was called "overqualified." After a brief successful career in a shoe factory—quickly rising to controller and vice president—he was able to reenter banking and after eight years in the U.S. was a citizen and president of a local bank. This was not an isolated case. By the late 1970s perhaps one in three employees of Miami's commercial banks were Cubans, including 16 of 62 bank presidents, 250 vice presidents, and more than 500 other banking officials.[14]

The Horatio Algeresque nature of the Arboleya story should not obscure the fact that many Cuban professionals who fled were never able to recover their former success. Downward mobility is a recurring aspect of exile life, especially for older and less supple persons who do not relate well to their new environment. Some lawyers, unable to pass the Florida bar, could only function as "advisors" and some physicians, who remained unlicensed, could not practice openly.

For a socioeconomic profile of the Cuban American community I use the Current Population Survey for March 2000, which gives results similar to those of the 2000 census, which were not yet available for Hispanic subgroups. Cubans were a settled, well-established group, significantly older than most other Hispanics. They were largely middle class, as the discussion of those in Miami's banks suggested, but with a larger number of poor persons than one would expect to find in such a population. Cuban household sizes were more comparable to those of the group whom the census classifies as "non-Hispanic whites." Only one Cuban household in seven had five or more members as opposed to one in eight for "non-Hispanic whites." The numbers for other Hispanic groups were a little less than one in five for Puerto Ricans, and a little more than one in three for Mexicans.

Similar results were reported for education. While 88.4 percent of "non-Hispanic whites" twenty-five years of age or older were high school graduates, the percentages for the Hispanic groups were significantly lower, but with the Cubans clearly at the top: nearly three in four Cubans, almost two of three Puerto Ricans, and just over half the Mexicans reported having high school diplomas.

The poverty data clearly show Cubans to be closer to the other Hispanic groups than to the "non-Hispanic whites." Only about one person in twelve from that latter group was in poverty, compared to one Cuban in six (17.7 percent), and one person in four for Mexicans and Puerto Ricans.

So far this discussion of Hispanic/Latino population in 2000 has ignored the important "other" category, a category into which the census placed nearly three of ten Hispanic/Latinos, slightly more than 10 million persons. The Census Bureau cannot categorize properly more than 6 million persons who constitute better than one in six (17.3 percent) of the entire Hispanic/Latino group because they gave answers that cannot be further analyzed. These answers included 1.7 million persons who checked the "other Hispanic" box but did not write in which "other" they were, while almost 4.4 million others checked that box but wrote in unclassifiable answers including "Hispanic," "Spanish," and "Latino."

Of the nearly 4 million persons who wrote in useful answers under the "other Hispanic" box, the largest number—almost 1.7 million—were Central Americans who will be discussed in the next chapter. The rest were either 1.35 million South Americans—a very recent and largely unstudied addition to the immigrant mix who by the late 1990s were regularly contributing almost 7 percent of the nation's legal immigrants—or just over three-quarters of a million Dominicans. Before a discussion of the latter group it is appropriate to note one of the larger effects of emigration upon most of the Western Hemisphere nations to the south of the United States.

One of the important but little remarked aspects of this variegated Hispanic migration is the impact that it has on the nations from which the migrants come. Students of migration often speak of it as a kind of safety valve to drain off excess population, but more and more of them are becoming aware of the importance of remittances sent back home. The Multilateral Investment Fund, created in 1993 to encourage private-sector development in Latin America, reported that in 2000 immigrant remittances, mostly from persons in the United States, to the Caribbean and Latin America exceeded $20 billion for the first time and have long contributed substantial portions of the economies of many of those nations. The fund estimated that those remittances were increasing at annual rates of 7 to 10 percent. These remittances exceed U.S. and other humanitarian aid sent to the region and are equal to almost a third of the region's foreign direct investment. In six countries, remittances exceeded 10 percent of gross domestic product, ranging from a high of 17 percent for Haiti, followed by lesser amounts for Nicaragua, El Salvador, and Jamaica, with the Dominican Republic and Ecuador trailing at 10 percent. Even for much larger and more prosperous/less impoverished Mexico, the amount of remittances exceeded farm exports by 60 percent, were equal to tourism revenues, and equivalent to two-thirds of oil revenues.[15]

Unlike the South American groups, we know a great deal about Dominican immigrants. They are highly concentrated in the New York City metropolitan area, where nearly three-quarters of them live: some 450,000 in New York, three-fifths of the nation's total, while about 100,000 live across the river in New Jersey. Most are foreign-born and one census estimate for 1998 showed 412,000 Dominicans as the most numerous group of foreign-born in New York City, far exceeding the second-ranked group, 235,000 former Soviet citizens.[16]

It was estimated in the mid-1990s that 700,000 Dominicans—almost 10 percent of the 7.5 million population of the Dominican Republic—had emigrated since 1985, and that about 400,000 of them were admitted as legal immigrants to the United States. More Dominicans receive public assistance than any other nonrefugee group of immigrants: about 28 percent of the Dominican immigrants who arrived since 1980 have received public assistance for some period of time. Only Vietnamese, at 38 percent, and persons from the former USSR, at 33 percent, have higher rates of dependence on public assistance.

Very large numbers of Dominican immigrants regard themselves as sojourners who will end their days back in the Caribbean, and their home government shares that view.

In a remarkably frank public statement, Dominican President Leonel Fernández Reyna, who took office in August 1996, acknowledged in September 1996 that "many Dominican families residing in the United States . . . have benefited from welfare and food stamps." As the United States Congress had enacted laws that discriminated against resident aliens in the matter of public assistance, Reyna, who had attended elementary and high school in New York City, urged Dominicans in the United States to become U.S. citizens to get or regain eligibility for benefits.

> If you . . . feel the need to adopt the nationality of the United States in order to confront the vicissitudes of that society stemming from the end of the welfare era, do not feel tormented by this . . . Do it with a peaceful conscience, for you will continue being Dominicans,* and we will welcome you as such when you set foot on the soil of our republic.[17]

The distinction, made here and in the next chapter, between immigrants and refugees, is, in one sense, a distinction without a difference. In a legal sense, however, it can be crucially important to the individual immigrant if she or he is recognized as an "official refugee," and thus entitled to all sorts of benefits and legal protections that are denied to legally admitted resident aliens. How this dichotomy developed within American immigration policy will be traced and analyzed in the next chapter.

---

*The Dominican Republic had recognized dual citizenship only in 1994.

CHAPTER TEN

Refugees and Human Rights: Cubans, Southeast Asians, and Others

The admission of refugees has been the wild card in the immigration policy of the United States ever since the end of World War II. Begun timorously by Franklin Roosevelt and expanded significantly by Harry Truman, America's refugee policy received statutory status only with the ad hoc Displaced Persons Acts of 1948 and 1950. The McCarran-Walter Act of 1952, the Refugee Relief Act of 1953, the Immigration Act of 1965, and the Refugee Act of 1980, to name only the major pieces of legislation with refugee provisions, all provided specific limits and/or numerical caps on refugees, and, after 1980, asylees. None proved effective, as, time and time again, America's fluctuating foreign policy created new demands that overrode the prescribed limits. In addition, American membership in the United Nations made it difficult for the United States to ignore mutually agreed-upon policies of the UN and its refugee organizations.

Refugee policies have brought some 4 million persons to the United States since 1945 and the relative incidence of refugees has grown in recent years. In fiscal 2001 the INS reported that 108,508 "refugees and asylees" amounted to 10.2 percent of the 1,064,318 "immigrants admitted" that year. Those numbers, however, are legal fictions. Much more than half of those the INS recorded as immigrants in 2001—650,000 persons—had been in the United States for varying lengths of time but were only able to adjust their immigration status during the year. Partly because of the often incredible backlogs at the INS, the numbers of persons whose admission fell into the "adjustment" category in the years since 1990 or thereabouts have been much larger than previously.

The refugee/asylee numbers are distorted in another way. Some persons who are clearly refugees are admitted under other immigration statutes or regulations. In addition, the government has created a variety of special categories that describe and tabulate refugees as something else. For 2001 this special nomenclature did not make much difference,* but for a number of years the INS refused to call the 140,000 Cuban and Haitian boat people admitted without legislative sanction in 1980 refugees. It listed them for many years as "Cuban-Haitian entrants, status pending." Table 10.1 shows refugee/asylee admissions since World War II by decade and Chart 10.1 shows the number of refugees and asylees graphically and lists all of the programs under whch they entered.

TABLE 10.1
REFUGEE/ASYLEE ADMISSIONS SINCE WORLD WAR II,
BY DECADE

Years	Number
1946–50	213,347
1951–60	492,371
1961–70	212,843
1971–80	539,447
1981–90	1,013,620
1991–00	1,021,266
Total	3,492,112

Source: INS *Statistical Yearbooks*, 1997, Table 31, and 2000, Table 29.

---

*For 2001 there were two such categories of persons: 376 "Amerasians," children fathered by American military personnel overseas and brought to the United States, and 5,468 Soviet and Indochinese "parolees."

CHART 10.1
REFUGEE AND ASYLEE INITIAL ADMISSIONS AND
ADJUSTMENTS TO LAWFUL PERMANENT RESIDENT
STATUS: FISCAL YEARS 1946–2001

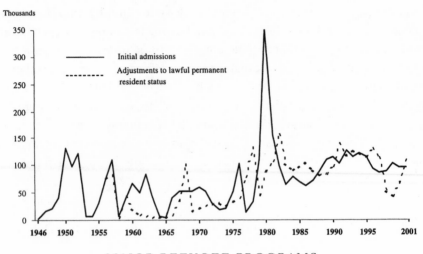

MAJOR REFUGEE PROGRAMS

1949–53	Displaced Persons Act	1978–84	Indochinese Refugee Adjustment Act	3/75–3/80	Indochinese refugees paroled
1954–57	Refugee Relief Act			1980	Refugee-Parolee adjustments began
11/56–7/58	Hungarians paroled	2/70–3/80	Refugee-Parolees admitted	4/80	Refugee Act admissions began
1959	Hungarian adjustments began	1/59–3/80	Cubans paroled	1981	Refugee Act adjustments began
1966–80	Refugee conditional entrants	1967	Cuban adjustments began	4/80–10/80	Mariel boatlift
				1985–87	Mariel adjustments

Source: INS *Statistical Yearbook,* 2001, p. 83.

The post–World War II refugee story is a complex one; each refugee has a story, and the experiences of refugees from dozens of countries merit historical attention. In this chapter I will focus on the two largest refugee programs—those for Cubans and Southeast Asians, while discussing the broader refugee experiences.

Although usually the government decides who is or is not a refugee, some actual refugees are able to enter in other categories. For example, a

Bosnian refugee who had a qualifying relative in the United States might come in as a family member.

This was particularly true of Cubans, who, as citizens of an independent nation in the Western Hemisphere, could, until late 1965, enter without numerical restriction. Thus, close to 150,000 Cubans who were refugees were not so designated by the INS. In the early years those immigrants were largely members of the upper and upper-middle classes; after 1965 most have been family members of U.S. citizens or resident aliens.

The various Cuban refugee programs are the longest lasting in American history and the most generous in terms of support. The post-Castro emigration of Cubans occurred primarily during three brief spurts in the forty-plus years since 1958. The first period began before the revolution and continued until the Cuban Missile Crisis of October 1962; the second period, characterized by chartered flights from the Varadero airport outside Havana, lasted from 1965 to 1973; and the third was the chaotic months of the Mariel boatlift during 1980. By 2000 some 900,000 Cubans had been admitted.

One of the myths of the Cuban refugee story is that it began on January 1, 1959—the very day that Fidel Castro's forces took over. In fact, some of those closely associated with the old order were already deserting the sinking regime of Fulgencio Batista, the right-wing dictator whose control steadily diminished throughout 1958. During 1959 perhaps 4,000 rich and well-to-do Cubans had come to Miami while others had gone to Mexico, Venezuela, France, and Spain. Throughout 1960 thousands more came to the U.S., many of them on tourist visas, despite the INS data reporting only six Cuban refugees for the 1951–60 decade. People simply got on airplanes and came: the flight took less than an hour and cost $25. In mid-1960, as Cuba began to nationalize large corporate assets, many of them American-owned, it also limited severely what money and possessions refugees could bring out and usually confiscated the remainder. For a while refugees were able to take only five American dollars. Eventually it became illegal to take any real cash, so many Cuban refugees arrived penniless.

In November 1960 the Eisenhower administration appointed Tracy S. Voorhees, who had headed the President's Committee for Hungarian Relief, to look into the situation of Cubans in Miami. He was allocated $1 million in emergency relief from funds appropriated for foreign aid, a sure sign that the Cold War had come to the Caribbean.[1] It was natural for planners to think that the Hungarian refugee arrangements would serve as a model—governments, like historians, usually expect the future to resemble the past—but the two situations would turn out to be fundamentally different in almost every respect.

In the Hungarian case a finite number of refugees—some 38,000, of whom nearly 31,000 eventually received resident alien status—were able to leave Hungary during a very brief window of opportunity measured in the days and hours of the tragic Hungarian revolt of October 1956, which Soviet forces, spearheaded by tanks, brutally suppressed. Usually called "Freedom Fighters," although many were simply escapees, the 38,000 came to the United States under U.S. government auspices, with the government firmly in control. They were screened in Europe, transported by ship to the United States, and housed, rescreened, and processed at Camp Kilmer, New Jersey. Then they were sent to sponsors and jobs throughout the country, with the placement managed by VOLAGS. Legally, they came in under the attorney general's parole authority—which meant that they could openly seek employment—and the opportunity for them to become resident aliens was regularized by a statute enacted almost two years after their arrival.[2]

The misconceptions of the federal authorities about the Cubans were matched by those of many of the refugees, who insisted that they were not immigrants, but exiles. They would have agreed with the Nazi-era refugee, Bertolt Brecht (1898–1956), who wrote:

> I always found the name false which they gave us: Emigrants.
> That means those who leave their country. But we
> Did not leave, of our own free will
> Choosing another land. Nor did we enter
> Into a land, to stay there, if possible for ever.
> Merely we fled. We are driven out, banned.
> Not a house but an exile shall the land be that took us in.[3]

Most Cubans nurtured the illusion that they would return to their island "when Castro falls." To be sure, had Castro been overthrown or otherwise disposed of in the early 1960s, large numbers of the recently arrived Cubans would have returned, but as years turned into decades, as young Cuban-born children became Americanized, and American-born children and grandchildren refused to be Cubanized—although most retained, like other immigrants and children of immigrants, some aspects of the culture of the homeland—the notion of return gradually evaporated except in the minds of all but a few die-hards. María Cristina García, the historian of the Miami Cuban community, distinguishes between "Cuban exiles" and "Cuban Americans," but makes it clear that these are states of mind, which, in many cases, refer to the same individuals at different stages of their life experience.

More than four decades after Castro seized power, Cuban refugees are still coming. Almost all arrived under their own impetus by air or sea and were quickly enveloped by the existing Cuban American community of perhaps 30,000 in South Florida as the exodus began, a community that the newcomers soon came to dominate. The government never had control of the Cuban refugees, but, rather, collaborated with them and the organizations that supported them, first long-established Catholic charities and then newly formed community organizations with a rightist political orientation: the most important of these latter groups is the Cuban American National Foundation, founded in 1981, the first year of Ronald Reagan's presidency. Cuban refugees have been special burdens on local government, a constant bone of contention between Cuban Americans and other South Floridians.

As relations between the United States and Cuba deteriorated, the tempo of the exodus increased. Crucial tension-increasing elements included Cuban seizure of American-owned property in Cuba, chiefly oil refineries and sugar mills, the growing incidence of Cuban government actions seen as violating human rights, its growing alignment with the Soviet Union, and increasing American attempts to isolate Cuba. Shortly after Voorhees arrived the Dade County Welfare Planning Council called upon the federal government to assume the cost of Cuban refugees. On December 7, 1960, a federal Cuban Refugee Center was opened in Miami. In a little over a year its staff grew from fourteen to more than three hundred. The Eisenhower administration, which we now know had developed a plan to invade Cuba, broke off diplomatic relations with Cuba on January 3, 1961, two years and two days after the Castro regime began and seventeen days before power passed to the Kennedy administration.

Just before that break took place an extraordinary quasi-clandestine operation began, which would continue until the Cuban Missile Crisis ended normal airline service between the two nations in October 1962.* Eventually given the name "Operation Pedro Pan,"[4] it enabled desperate Cuban parents to send some 14,000 of their children, alone or in small groups, to

---

*Curiously, the fiasco invasion at the Bay of Pigs on April 17, 1961, hardly caused a blip in the regular airline service between Havana and Miami.

the United States.[5] There were a number of precedents in recent history for such a drastic action. Americans are most likely to think of the *kinder transports* that took some 10,000 Jewish children out of Nazi Germany shortly before the outbreak of war in 1939 or of the thousand British children sent to safe homes in the U.S. before and during the "blitz," but the middle-class Cuban parents were more likely to have been aware of the thousands of Spanish children who had been sent to Western Europe, the Soviet Union, and Mexico during the Spanish Civil War of 1936–39. (We now know that at the end of that Civil War the Franco government secretly seized an unknown number of children of its left-wing opponents and gave them to Franco's supporters or sent them to be brought up in convents or monasteries.)[6]

The Cuban parents took this extreme step because they believed one or more false rumors, perhaps propagated by the American Central Intelligence Agency. One false rumor was that Castro was about to nationalize their children and indoctrinate them with the communist ideology; another, less common, was that the children were going to be sent to the Soviet Union or one of the eastern European nations. Some rumors were printed as fact in American media.[7] A real danger was compulsory military service: the refugee children were overwhelmingly teenaged boys, some of whom would have almost certainly wound up in Castro's military misadventures in Angola.

An Irish-born Catholic priest, Bryan O. Walsh (1920–2001), administrator of Catholic charities in Miami, ran the program and described its origins and history.[8] According to interviews conducted by María Cristina García employees of Pan American and KLM Airlines assisted the operation and staffs of various Havana embassies, particularly the British and Dutch, smuggled documents into the country. Most of the Cubans who ran the network were eventually arrested and imprisoned by the Cuban authorities, some of them for many years.[9]

Operation Pedro Pan—but not the problem of unaccompanied refugee children—was terminated during the Cuban Missile Crisis of 1962 when regular airline flights between Havana's José Martí Airport and the United States ended. Although there were some toddlers, usually accompanied by an older sibling, about 60 percent of the 14,000 Pedro Pans were teenaged boys and only about 3,000 were girls.*

---

*The one U.S. government publication on the topic, the Children's Bureau's *Cuba's Children in Exile*, has five pictures of children, four of them girls. This stress on females is typical of immigrant/refugee iconography.

About half of the children were cared for by relatives who were already in the United States; the rest, cared for by various welfare organizations, have been the focus of most of the Pedro Pan literature. The children who needed foster care were overwhelmingly from Catholic families, although a minority were Protestant or Jewish. As had been the case during the DP and Hungarian programs, most were resettled by agencies of the appropriate faith. Federal data for the period up to April 30, 1967, show that 85 percent of 8,331 children who were federally funded were served by the Catholic Welfare Bureau; about 10 percent were in the care of the Florida State Department of Welfare, and the rest were served by Protestant and Jewish agencies. The Children's Bureau calculated that the cost of this in federal funds was $28.5 million, almost all of it to pay for foster care. Although most of the literature speaks of foster care with families, almost twice as much federal funding went to institutional or group homes. Of those settled in foster homes outside of South Florida, most were placed with middle-class Catholic families. Few of these families spoke Spanish, as was the case of the staffs of the various institutions. In addition to the agencies listed above, 137 children's agencies in 110 cities, 40 states, the District of Columbia, and Puerto Rico were involved in the foster care of unaccompanied Cuban children.[10]

The legacy of the Pedro Pan operation is mixed. Joan Didion, one of the few writers who even mentioned it in the 1980s, quotes writings critical of Pedro Pan by former alumni published in the dissident exile journal *Areito*, and treats the operation as, essentially, Cold War hysteria.* Of the two English-language books devoted to Pedro Pan, that by Víctor Andrés Triay (b. 1966) is essentially apologetic and finds the questions raised by Didion and others incomprehensible.[11] But Yvonne M. Conde (b. ca. 1951), herself a Pedro Pan child who was reunited with her mother after less than a year and was never in a camp or a group home, writes that:

> In 1990 I read *Miami* by Joan Didion. The words on page 122 glared back, defiant, daring me to believe them: "14,156 children, each of whom was sent alone, by parents or guardians still living in Cuba." . . . How could there have been such a mammoth exodus of Cuban children, and I had never heard of it?

---

*Didion's book, although about Cuban exiles, has, as its subtext, a critique of Reagan-era Central American policies.

I knew that at the age of ten, I too was sent out of Cuba alone by my parents to the United States. Did that mean that I was part of this exodus? Joan Didion's words changed my life, becoming my mind's unyielding stalker for the next several years.[12]

Conde distributed some 800 questionnaires in the 1990s and got 442 responses from an unscientific sample of her fellow Pedro Pan alumni. Asked "Do you think your parents did the right thing by sending you out alone," they overwhelmingly agreed: 85.31 percent yes, 9.56 percent no, with 5.13 percent unsure. But when asked "Would you do what your parents did under the same circumstances," only 45.94 percent said yes, 32.5 percent said no, and 21.56 percent answered that they were unsure. More than a quarter of those who answered the first question failed to respond to the second, suggesting an even greater amount of ambiguity.

After Pedro Pan ended in October 1962, few unaccompanied children came during the next three years. But in that period some 56,000 more Cubans came to the U.S., mostly by air via third countries, mainly Spain and Mexico. Many were parents or siblings of children who had preceded them: such people, in accordance with the family-unification motif of U.S. immigration policy, were given special preference for visas. Another 5,000 came on the return trips of ships and planes that delivered the ransom for Bay of Pigs prisoners, while some 4,000 left Cuba by unsanctioned departures on small boats. The 90-to-120-mile passage from north central Cuba to the Florida Keys can be simple or hazardous depending on weather conditions, and no one can calculate how many Cubans have drowned attempting it.

Then, on September 28, 1965, Fidel Castro announced that any Cuban with relatives in the United States who wanted to leave Cuba could do so after October 10. President Lyndon Johnson used the signing of the epochal 1965 immigration act on Liberty Island four days later to announce, as a kind of answer, that "I declare this afternoon to the people of Cuba that those who seek refuge here in America will find it . . . Our tradition as an asylum for the oppressed is going to be upheld."[13] That tradition, although political rhetoric almost never admits it, was and is highly flexible, depending upon who was being oppressed by whom, and where it happened.*

---

*Congress, too, often claims the same tradition: the beginning paragraph of the Refugee Act of 1980, for example, claimed that "it is the historic policy of the United States to respond to the urgent needs of persons subject to persecution in their homelands . . ."

In October Castro announced that all who wished to leave must do so through the small port of Camarioca, a little east of Havana. While some left Camarioca on Cuban vessels, most were picked up by Cuban exiles who sailed from South Florida to get them. While some of both sets of vessels were seaworthy and safe, many, perhaps most Cubans, embarked on small craft unsuited to crossing the Gulf Stream. The U.S. Coast Guard, which had been rescuing distressed refugees since late 1962, established a veritable picket line of vessels between Camarioca, and the Florida Keys to try to ensure the safety of the refugees during the few weeks that the 1965 exodus took place.

After complex negotiations—carried on not face-to-face but through Swiss diplomats in Washington and Havana—the United States and Cuba each signed a Memorandum of Understanding made public on November 6, 1965. It established ground rules that tried to combine Cuba's desire to be in control of those who left Cuba and the United States' wish to know, in advance, who was coming. The agreement provided for immigration of "immediate relatives" of persons already in the U.S.* Cuba, rather consistently, refused to release political prisoners, whom the U.S. asked for, young men of military age (fifteen to twenty-six), and individuals it deemed necessary for Cuba's economy. In what it styled "Operation Sealift," the U.S. government sent three good-sized ships to Camarioca which brought back 4,598 refugees over a ten-day period in mid-November.

Then, as provided in the Memorandum and further strengthening the control that both sides wanted, Castro "closed" Camarioca but allowed two chartered planes a day to pick up refugees at Varadero, a secondary airport outside of Havana: these planes brought out between three and four thousand Cubans a month. Such flights continued regularly until August 1971: during that time, when weather conditions or mechanical problems cancelled a flight or flights, every effort was made to make them up. After August 1971 the flights were often canceled and/or suspended for long periods of time by the Cuban government. The last large group of refugees— what Castro liked to call *gusanos* (worms) were some 3,400 old, ill, and disabled people. The passenger lists were closely monitored by both sides so that when the Varadero airlift ended on April 6, 1973, each side could say with confidence that 3,048 flights over a period of more than seven years had carried 297,318 refugees to the United States.

---

*American press releases spoke of such persons having "first priority" but there was no "second priority."

These and other Cuban refugees were given very special status by the federal government, special treatment that caused many in South Florida to resent their presence. Florida's existing poor were relatively disadvantaged; Florida, although not one of the poorest states, competed with Mississippi in providing the least adequate provision for its poor. The 1959 data showed Florida thirtieth in per capita income and forty-seventh in per capita welfare expenditures. The new Kennedy administration, with Health, Education, and Welfare (HEW) Secretary Abraham J. Ribicoff (1910–92) taking personal charge, quickly established a relatively high level of benefits for needy refugees and encouraged a wide variety of often-imaginative programs for the growing refugee community.

In terms of public assistance, needy refugee Cubans, who were thought to be temporary visitors, got larger allowances than did poor American citizens in Florida. The maximum amounts other Floridians could receive were $66 monthly for a single person, while families with dependent children had to get by on a maximum of $81 monthly. The rates for the recently arrived refugees were $71 for a single person and $100 for a family, with or without children. In addition Ribicoff and his staff were creative in getting other resources funneled to the Cubans.* And, remarkably, these benefits were extended not just to refugees who entered on parole status, but also those who entered as regular resident aliens.[14]

And while middle-class Americans often fantasize that poor minority populations have it better than they do, in the 1960s South Floridians had ample evidence that their government was providing newly arrived foreigners with more benefits than poor local American citizens could qualify for.

Typical nativistic complaints arose as the burgeoning Cuban American population began to predominate in certain Miami neighborhoods. A Little Havana soon emerged in which the use of English was no longer necessary and in some parts of it was all but useless. Some apartment houses began to sprout signs saying "No Cubans Allowed"† and Cuban driving—with some reason—was widely criticized: Cubans "use horns for brakes" was a common complaint.

---

*The 1969 film *Popi* satirized the favored treatment given Cubans by having a Puerto Rican New Yorker, played by Alan Arkin, move his family to Miami and register as Cubans to improve their standard of living.
†When I was a boy in Miami, living in what is now part of Little Havana, the polite apartment house signs said "Gentiles Only," while others said "No Dogs, Cats, or Jews."

In addition to direct financial aid, the government made extraordinary efforts to accommodate the skills and talents of the refugee Cubans, who, in the early years of the migration, were largely drawn from the Cuban middle classes: for example, by 1961 it was estimated that two-thirds of the pre-Castro faculty of the University of Havana was living in Dade County. The University of Miami, with federal help, established research projects and fellowships to utilize some of the newly available talent which, in time, helped a previously academically undistinguished institution become a significant center for research on Latin America. HEW also supported an intensive sixteen-week Spanish-language Post-Graduate Medical Program for Cuban refugee physicians at the University of Miami through which some 2,500 Cubans passed. The federal government also financed and otherwise facilitated the training and retraining of many Cuban refugee professionals, a service it had not provided to previous refugee professionals.

Congress and the INS also made special rules for the Cubans, who, for a while at least, were the favored refugees of the American government. In 1966, for example, Congress passed the Cuban Refugee Adjustment Act, later denounced by Cuba's National Assembly as a "legislative abomination." In it, by statute, Cubans admitted or paroled into the U.S. after January 1, 1959, and physically present in the U.S. for one year could be given permanent resident status at the discretion of the attorney general. This overrode existing law and transformed what was a complicated procedure for other parolees, who had to leave the country and return to get their status changed, into a routine procedure for Cubans.* A memorandum issued by INS Commissioner Doris Meissner in April 1999 made it clear that this policy still applied to Cubans and only to them.[15]

These privileges continued despite the fact that those who came before the first interruption of immigration in 1962 had a very different socioeconomic profile than did those who came later. In the early 1960s almost a third of the Cubans arriving in the U.S. were professionals, managers, and

---

*This kind of idiocy—having to leave the country to get one's status changed—is not limited to American law. In 1996, when I held the Fulbright Chair of North American Studies at the University of Calgary, Canadian immigration personnel erroneously admitted me on the wrong form. Although the mistake was admittedly theirs and not mine, I was required to go to the border and reenter. The procedure at the border took perhaps five minutes—the university made sure that the paperwork had been done in advance. The drive to the border and back took the whole of a working day for me and a university official. It was an instructive experience for a historian of immigration. Like so many Canadian procedures, it was mimetic of American practice.

owners of small businesses; at the end of that decade such persons represented about an eighth. Further the agreed restrictions of the Memorandum of Understanding resulted in much higher percentages of women and older persons gaining entry. What had begun as an elite migration became more and more representative of the white Cuban population.

By the end of those flights a substantial percentage of the small but significant populations of Cuban Chinese and Jews had come to the United States. The 1953 Cuban census reported some 16,000 residents of Chinese ethnicity; by 1973 more than half of Cuba's Chinese had migrated to the United States, many of them to the greater New York area. About the same number of Jews as Chinese had lived in pre-Castro Cuba, most of them members of families who had emigrated there from central and eastern Europe in the 1920s and 1930s. Like the Chinese, most had become small-scale entrepreneurs: by 1973 a substantial majority had emigrated to the U.S., Israel, or elsewhere in Latin America. In 1990 a Miami journalist estimated that there were some 10,000 Cuban Jews in the metropolitan area and that they dominated four local congregations.[16]

If Chinese and Jews were overrepresented in the Cuban exodus, black Cubans were distinctly underrepresented. Although race is recorded differently in the censuses of the two nations, there can be no doubt about this underrepresentation. The 1953 Cuban census put the black and mulatto population at 27 percent, while an American count in 1970 recorded just 3 percent of Cuban Americans as black. As in the United States, blacks in Cuba tended to be at or near the bottom of the socioeconomic pyramid, but since in Cuba amelioration of their condition was one of the stated aims of Castro's revolution, they had more reasons to stay. This, plus their well-founded fears about American racism, easily explain initial black underrepresentation among the exiles. The American policy of reunifying families during the Varadero period further limited opportunities for the "regular" migration of blacks.

During the quiet years between the end of the Varadero flights in 1973 and the spring of 1980 there were few dramatic events, but, one way or another, 185,000 Cuban refugees arrived according to American immigration statistics during those "quiet" years, an average of more than 30,000 annually, almost a hundred a day, every day, for six years.

At decade's end, the administration of Jimmy Carter (1977–81), the first in American history to attempt to make human rights an essential part of

American foreign policy, sent a statute through Congress that was an attempt to regularize refugee policy and to place numerical limits on refugees admitted.[17] The Refugee Act of 1980 was the last major American immigration statute of the twentieth century that could properly be called a "reform" measure in the traditional meaning of that word: to liberalize.

The impetus for reform in the Carter administration stemmed from problems with the refugees who came in the wake of the United States' misbegotten war in Vietnam. As will be spelled out later in this chapter, between 1975 and 1979 a patchwork of ten separate refugee programs brought 400,000 "unexpected" Southeast Asians to the United States between 1975 and 1980. The 1980 statute provided, in the words of the INS summary, "the first permanent and systematic procedure for the admission and effective resettlement of refugees."[18] The 1965 law anticipated admitting 17,400 refugees a year, though a president could promise, as LBJ promised the Cubans, to take all comers.

The 1980 law, less unrealistically than that of 1965, set the refugee figure at 50,000, and reduced the numbers to be admitted as regular immigrants by 20,000 annually. This, presumably, would produce annual immigration of 320,000 (270,000 regular immigrants + 50,000 refugees) plus however many came in "without numerical limitation." With a trace of realism, the law did provide that, although 50,000 would be the normal number of refugees, the president might raise that number after annual consultation with Congress. In practice, however, those annual presidential predictions have been wishful thinking.

The 1980 law defined a refugee in language conforming to the criteria adopted by the United Nations in 1967:

> any person who is outside any country of his nationality or in the case of any person having no nationality, is outside of any country in which he last habitually resided, and who is unable or unwilling to avail himself of the protection of that country because of persecution, or a well-founded fear of persecution, on account of race, religion, nationality, membership of a particular social group or political opinion.

This was broader than the previous definitions on the American statute books, but as the Senate had "advised and consented" to the UN protocol for refugees in 1968 it could not be regarded as a real departure from stated American policy. What did break new ground was the 1980 statute's recognition, for the first time, of the right of asylum; it created a new legal category of refugee, an "asylee." Asylees are refugees, who, if they are to be successful in their quest for legal residence in the United States, must meet, eventually, all of the criteria for refugees or be expelled. But unlike a refugee, who is a person attempting to gain admission to the United States, an asylee is a person who applies for refugee status while already present on American soil. This can be a person legally in the United States on some kind of a nonimmigrant visa—for example, a student, a tourist, a visiting athlete or cultural performer—or according to the statute as interpreted by the courts, a person who, one way or another, is on American soil illegally. The law capped asylees at 5,000. Both refugees and asylees may adjust their status to resident alien a year after arrival for refugees and a year after gaining refugee status for asylees. Resident aliens are eligible to begin the five-year process for American citizenship.*

Congress also attempted to limit the parole power of the attorney general. The new provision stipulated that the attorney general "may not parole into the United States an alien who is a refugee" and then added the weasel words "unless the attorney general determines that compelling reasons in the public interest with respect to that particular alien require" it. Although Congress obviously envisaged parole being granted in only a few individual cases, the Carter administration granted parole status to more than 100,000 Cubans within weeks of the passage of the 1980 law.

The new law was a reform measure tinged with realism as it attempted to make practice and theory congruent. Surprisingly, it was spectacularly uncontroversial. The original bill sailed through the Senate by a vote of 85–0, cosponsored by that ideological odd couple, the liberal Massachusetts Democrat Edward M. Kennedy (b. 1932) and the right-wing South Carolina Republican Strom Thurmond (1902–2003). This represented a polar change of attitude toward refugees from that which had existed before, during and after World War II. Even after the "discovery" of the Holocaust, the modest provisions of the Displaced Persons acts of 1948 and 1950 had been bitterly disputed. Some thirty years later the notion that the United States was obligated to take in refugees of all kinds and have a relatively generous policy toward them had become part of a general consensus.

*There are different ways of counting refugees and asylees. The former are counted in INS statistics in the year of their arrival, but asylees are only counted in the year in which their applications are approved.

The Refugee Act of 1980 was signed on March 17. A little over a month later, on April 21, the so-called Mariel crisis demonstrated just how useless the limits laid down in the act were. At issue, initially, were about 3,500 dissident Cubans, who were part of a group of more than 10,000 who, claiming asylum, occupied the grounds of the Peruvian Embassy in Havana on March 28.

Well into April the increasingly unsanitary situation on the embassy grounds was unresolved. Nine nations agreed to take some 7,000 of the asylum seekers, with the U.S. agreeing to take 3,500. This left nearly 4,000 unaccounted for, but Costa Rica agreed to take them temporarily if the U.S. and Peru guaranteed that they would not have to stay in Costa Rica.

The agreement provided that all would first be flown to Costa Rica and then to their ultimate destinations. The flights began on April 16, but four days later—after about 7,500 had departed—Castro suspended the flights to Costa Rica, saying that the refugee flights could continue only if they went directly to the United States. The U.S. refused to accede to this demand. Why the Carter administration refused to agree to what would have been, in essence, a reversion to a Varadero-type arrangement of supervised direct chartered flights is not clear, but one suspects that in a presidential election year it did not want to give more ammunition to those who said that the Democrats were "soft on Castro."

Then, on April 21, Castro announced that anyone who wanted to leave Cuba could do so, but that they could leave only through the small fishing port of Mariel, a little west of Havana, and he invited Cuban exiles to come and get their relatives. This set off a chaotic exodus which, at its height, brought some 13,000 refugees a week from Cuba to South Florida. The United States Coast Guard, which again did picket duty, enumerated 124,776 persons—60 percent men, 22 percent women, and 18 percent minors—who crossed the Straits of Florida safely and recorded 27 refugees lost at sea, but it missed many of both the living and the dead. It assisted 1,387 vessels and estimated that the Mariel patrol cost an average of $650,000 a week for the services of the Coast Guard alone.[19]

Some of the exiles who set out from Florida for Cuba took all comers once they got to Mariel. Others came and got only their relatives and friends, while still others were forced by the Cuban authorities to take certain refugees. Castro released a number of individuals—perhaps 10,000—from jails and mental institutions, and the reputation of this minority gave all the "Marielitos," as the boatlift refugees came to be called, a bad name. The media treatment was scandalous.* At a time when the INS was still able to exclude homosexuals from entering the country, a relatively responsible paper like *The Washington Post* reported that "up to 20,000" of the Mariel Cubans were homosexuals. (García says that the actual number was closer to 1,000.)[20]

The Mariel exodus left the well-intentioned refugee-control strategy of the administration in ruins. It also created a dilemma for Carter and his policy makers. Cold War anticommunist imperatives plus humanitarian ideals called for accepting all who fled communism and made such a policy seem a way to embarrass America's great hemispheric enemy in Havana. But the administration's desire to control refugee flows and a bureaucratic respect for law and order rather than justice suggested that the exodus be interdicted. The result was strenuous vacillation. First there were stern admonitions from the INS and others and a few fines were actually imposed on the owners of returning boats, but the Cubans on them were allowed to disembark. Then, when public reactions to such moves seemed hostile, President Carter, echoing Lyndon Johnson in 1965, announced two weeks into the crisis that the United States would welcome all Cubans "with an open heart and open arms."[21] Then after stories about Castro opening up the jails were overemphasized by the American media, the administration again got tough: it had the Internal Revenue Service impose fines on boat owners who brought back Cubans and the Customs Service seized more than a thousand vessels. The number of arrivals fell from a high of 13,000 a week to fewer than 700. Finally, on September 25 the Cuban government stopped the exodus; the Mariel episode lasted 162 days.

In a purely bureaucratic move in May, the INS had ruled that the Marielitos were not refugees, or asylees, but "Entrants (Status Pending)" and applied that tag to Haitians as well. The term had no status in statute law and a friendly Congress soon gave most Marielitos the same status as other Cubans. In October 1980, just before the presidential election, a successful amendment to the Refugee Education Assistance Act, which gave persons classified as Cuban and Haitian entrants—once they were released

---

*Hollywood, which has largely ignored the refugee, joined in with *Scarface* (1983), a gory Brian De Palma film that was a "remake" of Howard Hughes's *Scarface* (1932). In the original, supposedly based on the life of Al Capone, a Jewish American actor, Paul Muni, played the Italian American criminal; in the remake, based on nothing, Italian American actor Al Pacino played a Marielito refugee criminal who becomes a kingpin drug dealer.

from confinement—all the rights of refugees under the 1980 act, making them eligible for a panoply of social services and benefits.[22]

The Cubans in the Mariel exodus differed from their predecessors. About 70 percent were male, many of them men unable to leave earlier because of their military eligibility, and at least 15 percent and perhaps as many as 40 percent were blacks and mulattoes.[23] A little over four-fifths of the 125,000 Marielitos were quickly released by the INS on the parole authority of the attorney general. Some 22,000 were detained. More than 20,000 of those, persons who had either committed crimes in Cuba that would not be crimes in the United States, such as criticizing the government, or charged with minor offenses, were soon also paroled. This left a residue of about 1,800: 1,200 suspected criminals, and 600 serious mental cases. In time, 1,590 of these were released; 210 were never released by the INS but turned over directly to federal prison authorities.

Not everyone paroled by the INS was quickly resettled and many of these remained in federal facilities. Most of those were moved to military bases in Arkansas, Pennsylvania, and Wisconsin, from which piecemeal resettlement continued.* Conditions in these camps resulted in riots. The worst of these occurred at Fort Chaffee, Arkansas, where perhaps a thousand of the 18,000 Cubans there rioted, setting fire to two buildings in the process. There were no fatalities, but forty detainees and fifteen police were injured. By mid-October 1980, the number awaiting resettlement was down to some 8,500, all at Fort Chaffee, and resettlement was complete early in 1981.[24]

Thus, when all was said and done, about 94 percent of the Mariel migrants were, more or less successfully, absorbed into the general population, although clearly a stigma attaches to them as a class, a stigma that is perhaps more observed by other Cubans than by the general population.

In the decades after Mariel, Cuban refugee immigration continued at a steady but not spectacular pace. From 1981 through 2000, more than 300,000 Cubans came, an average of more than 15,000 a year. During most of that time an agreement was in place between the two countries to allow up to 20,000 immigrants annually, with an emphasis on family reunification.

There continued to be irregular immigration as well, as more boat people came, often in less and less seaworthy craft, culminating in what the

---

*It is instructive to note that the human rights–oriented Carter administration considered incarcerating Marielitos on its Guantánamo base in Cuba, but it never did so. (García, *Havana USA*, 74.)

Cubans call *balseros*, or rafters, who put to sea confident—sometimes falsely so—that if they got into difficulties at sea they would be rescued by the American Coast Guard. In the first seven and a half months of 1994 more than 6,000 *balseros* were rescued, brought to Miami, and in most cases quickly paroled and able to gain the now-traditional benefits. Amidst domestic turmoil in Cuba, due partly to the fall of the Berlin Wall, the growing independence of eastern European nations, the disintegration of the Soviet Union, and the ensuing reduction of its economic support for Cuba, Castro publicly threatened, in mid-August 1994, to permit another mass emigration. The Clinton administration announced that it would not permit another boatlift and promised a naval blockade of Cuba if one was attempted. It also got the cooperation of the leadership of the Miami Cuban community, which discouraged exiles from sending boats to Cuba.

On August 18, 1994, the Clinton administration reversed more than thirty years of American policy by announcing that any Cuban boat people or rafters who were picked up at sea would no longer be taken to the United States, as formerly, but sent to the base at Guantánamo, where parole was not possible and the long arm of federal courts could not reach.* The only options such detainees had were acceptance by some third country or a re-turn to Cuba. Fairly large numbers of *balseros* and others continued to get through, and, unlike Haitian boat people, if they did get to the United States, continued to be released quickly and given parole status. Castro's aim in all of this was for a relaxation or elimination of the American eco-nomic embargo, but the Clinton administration would not budge. Such a relaxation against a communist enemy, only ninety miles away, would have been politically disastrous.

The Case of Elián Gonzales

Although by no means central to U.S. refugee policy, the case of one tiny Cuban, Elián Gonzales, which was a media event for months in 1999–2000, cannot be ignored. In November 1999 Gonzales was the sole—and

---

*This doctrine dated back to *Johnson v. Eisentrager* 339 U.S. 763 (1950). The "aliens" concerned were German nationals who were confined in the custody of the United States Army in Germany fol-lowing their conviction by a military commission of having engaged in military activity against the United States in China after the surrender of Germany.

to many Miami Cubans, miraculous—survivor of a *balsero* attempt that cost the lives of his mother, her lover, and a number of others. Brought to Miami, he was paroled routinely by the INS to a cousin. However, his father, who was still in Cuba and had not given his permission for the boy's departure, wanted him back, which was anathema to many in the exile community. Lawyers were hired who filed for amnesty in Elián's name. In terms of normal family law the case was a no-brainer: the father had custodial rights and six-year-olds are not competent to make legal decisions. But there was one Cold War precedent that gave the exile community hope.

In 1980 twelve-year-old Walter Polovchak and two other children had been brought to Chicago by their Soviet parents on immigrant visas. Five months later the parents decided to return to the USSR. Walter and an older sister did not want to go, and ran away to the home of a cousin who was an established Chicago resident. The police, called by the parents, took the children into custody, but on the advice of the INS and the State Department, did not take the normal step of returning them to their parents' custody. The government arranged for them to file for asylum under the new 1980 law. The parents got a lawyer and filed suit for Walter's custody, but not his sister's, and left, as planned, for the USSR. The Illinois court frustrated the suit by making Walter a ward of the court. An Illinois appellate court quickly ruled for the parents, but the State Department issued a "departure control order" that declared, absurdly, that it was against the national interest for Walter to go home with his parents. The parents' lawyer filed suit in federal court and the government stalled, apparently aiming for a target date of October 3, 1985, some five years away, when Walter would turn 18, and become, in both American and Soviet law, capable of making his own decision. The stall was almost successful, but the case did come to trial. On July 17, 1985, a federal district court found for the parents. The government, naturally, appealed. The Seventh Circuit Court of Appeals heard the case on September 9, and ruled the next day that the government had violated the parents' rights, but, because of Walter's imminent maturity, revoked the order of the lower court returning Walter to his parents in the USSR. At that stage of the Cold War communist parents could not expect justice from American courts: for them the old maxim, justice delayed is justice denied, held true. (*Polovchak v. Meese* 774 F. 2d 731 [1985]).

In a different political climate almost a decade after the collapse of the USSR and a different administration of justice, Elián's case was another matter. But before the courts could rule, there was turmoil in Miami. After some weeks of dawdling Attorney General Janet Reno told the INS to resume its custody of the boy. The cousin refused to give him back. Elements of the Miami Cuban community vowed to "defend" the boy and crowds surrounded the small house where the boy was living with his cousin. A predawn surprise raid by heavily armed federal officers got physical possession of Elián, and a press photographer on good terms with the protestors, waiting inside the house, got pictures of the heavily armed intrusion and the frightened child that became front-page news all over America. Elián's father was given a special visa to come from Cuba to the United States—many in the exile community hoped, in vain, that once here he would defect—and both the federal district court and the Sixth Circuit Court of Appeals upheld the INS decision. In late June 2000 the Supreme Court refused to interfere. Elián and his father returned to Cuba, national heroes. The six months of turmoil over the boy further separated the Miami community from the Democratic Party—some Republicans had gone through the motions of introducing a bill to make the boy a United States citizen—and could have been a factor in Al Gore's crucial loss of Florida and the presidency less than five months later.

The subsequent administration of George W. Bush continued the most-favored refugee treatment of Cubans. In a presidential press conference just after the midterm elections in 2002, Bush was asked to comment on the situation of 200 Haitian boat people, who on October 29, 2002, had successfully eluded the supposedly rigorous homeland defense protection and gotten their vessel into Miami's Biscayne Bay and scrambled ashore on the Rickenbacker Causeway, sat down, claimed asylum, and got their picture on the front pages of most American newspapers. The president stated that "the immigration laws ought to be the same for Haitians and everybody else—except for Cubans," and claimed that his administration was "in the process of making sure that happens."[25]

President Bush's remarks stirred hope in the hearts and minds of Haitian advocates that policy would soon change. But the next day, like a good cop, bad cop routine, the Department of Justice announced that it would extend the same strict detention and deportation rules that it had only been applying to Haitians to all other undocumented, sea-arriving migrants except Cubans. And, five days after that, the obligatory notice of the new policy appeared in the Federal Register. The policy, which calls for indefinite detention and quickened deportation, dealt yet another blow to immigrant advocates who, days before, had hoped public pressure would persuade the Bush administration to ease the rules.[26]

The president's remarks nicely encapsulate decades of distinction between the two Caribbean nations, each of which is filled with people who would rather be in the United States. It is tempting to label Haitians as the "least-favored immigrants" but that would be inappropriate. Although their treatment vis-à-vis Cubans is clearly second class, to say the least, would-be Haitian and Cuban refugees share one advantage: proximity to the United States. The vast majority of the world's 20 million refugees are in nations of first asylum, mostly developing nations in Asia and Africa. The United States can pick and choose which of the tens of thousands of refugees it admits annually. In 2000, for example, it admitted 72,143 refugees, broken down as follows:

TABLE 10.2
REFUGEES ADMITTED TO THE U.S., 2000

Region/Nation	Number	Percentage
Europe	37,664	52.2
Bosnia-Herzegovina	19,033	
Ukraine	7,334	
Russia	3,723	
Croatia	2,995	
21 others	4,579	
Asia	13,622	18.9
Iran	5,145	
Iraq	3,158	
Vietnam	2,841	
Afghanistan	1,709	
12 others	769	
Africa	17,624	24.4
Somalia	6,026	
Sudan	3,833	
Liberia	2,620	
23 others	3,406	
North America	3,233	4.5
Cuba	3,184	
Haiti	49	
Total	71,143	

Source: INS, *2000 Statistical Yearbook*, Table 24.

There are three striking things about those 2000 numbers. The unprecedentedly large numbers for Africa are a direct result of American peacekeeping in Somalia; the fact that no refugees were admitted from Central America reflected a continuing fear of what Ronald Reagan called "feet people" swamping America; and the very large number of countries—thirty—from which refugees had been admitted in one or more years between 1994 and 1999 but were not represented on the 2000 list. Nine nations were represented by just one refugee, including the People's Republic of China!

Most asylum seekers come from nearby nations in the circum-Caribbean. Of 358,255 asylum cases pending at the beginning of fiscal 1999, for example, 320,419 (94.4 percent) were from Caribbean and Central American nations: El Salvador and Guatemala, with 180,000 and 104,000 respectively, head the list, which contains 14,823 Haitians.[27]

Haitians have been coming to the United States since before it was a nation. Haitian troops were a part of the French forces that helped defeat the British in the American revolution, and shortly before the adoption of the Constitution, Jean Baptiste Point du Sable, the Haitian son of a slave woman, became the first non-Indian resident of Chicago.* We know that after the success of the Haitian revolution in 1804 many Haitian slaveholders fled to the United States bringing slaves with them, but we have no reliable estimate of their number. During the Reconstruction era after the Civil War two Haitian Americans served in Congress, six in the legislatures of four states, and two as lieutenant governors. A largely Haitian American organization in New Orleans, the *Comité des Citoyens* (Citizens' Committee) was responsible for bringing the ill-fated Supreme Court case of *Plessy v. Ferguson* (1896), which unsuccessfully challenged racial segregation, and the litigant himself, Homer Plessy (1858?–1925), was a Haitian American. Three nineteenth-century Haitian American Roman Catholic nuns—Sisters Marie Elizabeth Lange, Thérèse Maxis Duchemin, and Juliette Gaudin—were founders or cofounders of orders that ministered to black Americans.[28] Although the INS did not begin counting Haitian immigrants separately before 1932, we know that there was an established immigrant community of some 500 middle-class Haitians in New York City before 1925.[29]

---

*One 1856 Chicago memoirist put it: "the first white man who settled here was a Negro" (Richard C. Lindberg, "du Sable, Jean Baptiste Point"; http://www.anb.org/articles/20/20-00302.html; *American National Biography Online*, February 2000.

Between 1932 and 1960 INS records show 7,000 Haitian immigrants, many of them exiles from the increasingly authoritarian Haitian regimes. The Haitian American community remained predominantly middle class. Between 1961 and 1980 some 90,000 came, most of them lower class, less skilled and less educated than their predecessors. The 1980 census recorded 92,000 Haitian-born persons: almost 90 percent of them told the census that they had arrived since 1965. During that period Miami superseded New York as the major concentration of Haitian Americans. Miami's Little Haiti, home to more than 50,000, was very different from that city's thriving Little Havana. The Northeast Miami section where the enclave has developed is one of the most dilapidated in the city.

The 1980 refugee act further stimulated an already existing pattern of illegal migration, encouraging Haitians to apply for asylum. In almost all instances the United States rejected Haitian asylum requests, arguing that Haitians were economic refugees and thus ineligible. Unfortunately for the asylum seekers they were fleeing from right-wing tyrants. If the notorious Duvaliers—Papa Doc and his son Baby Doc—had been communists, surely the American government would have been more sympathetic.

Although, as we have seen, some Haitians got in during the chaos of the Mariel crisis, not one Haitian refugee or asylee was accepted by the INS for permanent refugee status during the decade 1981–90. A total of eighty-six had been admitted during the previous decade.

Charges of racism based on the differential treatment meted out to Cubans, largely middle class and white, and to Haitians, 100 percent black by American standards, were picked up in 1989 by Bruce Morison (D-CT), then chair of the House subcommittee on immigration, who echoed those remarks, telling a reporter that the INS did not treat Haitians fairly. "There's been a lot of discrimination [against them] . . . They're black, they are from a nation close to ours, and their country isn't communist." INS officials, no longer able to discriminate openly, went to great lengths to deny the deliberate discrimination against Haitians. The district director of the INS in Miami, Perry Rivkind, even fantasized that "I've always said I wish a boatload of blue-eyed Anglo-Saxon Protestants tried to enter the U.S. illegally. They too would be subject to exclusion."

In 1981 the INS opened the now notorious Krome Avenue detention center in Miami for Haitians. It was supposed to hold 400 detainees in fifty-inmate pods, each with bunk beds, chairs, one TV, showers, toilets, and pay telephones, but was overcrowded from the start. In June 1995, when a visiting congressional delegation found that the local INS attempted to conceal overcrowding, several employees were disciplined—but not dismissed. In August 2000, U.S. Attorney General Janet Reno ordered another investigation of the Krome center after detainees alleged that female inmates were promised freedom and other favors in exchange for sex. The government had so little confidence in the discipline of its Florida custodial personnel that three female inmates who had complained about sexual contact were released because Washington feared for their safety.[30]

It is instructive to note that, despite the ideological differences between the Carter, Reagan, Bush I, Clinton, and Bush II administrations, each has persistently discriminated against Haitian entrants as opposed to Cubans. The Reagan administration began the practice of towing Haitian, but not Cuban, vessels back to where they came from, the first Bush administration initiated the use of the naval base at Guantánamo for detained Haitians, and the Clinton administration expanded the use of the Cuban base, out of the federal judiciary's reach, as a warehouse for Haitians.

Well into the 1970s refugee flows into the United States were dominated by Europeans and Caribbeans, but very few Asians were able to enter as refugees before the mid-1970s.[31] Most of these were Chinese, who, if adults, had been vouched for by the government on Taiwan; most of the rest were orphans, many from Korea, who had been adopted by U.S. citizens, largely Caucasian Americans. Others were representatives of the dying European empires in Asia, such as the 16,000 Indonesians listed as refugees in the 1950s and 1960s, who were chiefly if not entirely persons of Dutch or part-Dutch ethnicity displaced by the liberation movement there. There were also, of course, small but significant numbers of regular Asian immigrants after 1952 and even larger numbers after 1965.

In the first five post–WW II years, persons of European nationality composed more than 99 percent of all refugees (211,938 of 213,347) and most of the 1,403 others were persons of European birth who had acquired Latin American nationalities. In the 1950s Europeans represented 93 percent of refugees (456,146 of 492,371), with 81,000 Poles, 62,000 Germans, 60,000 Italians, and 58,000 Hungarians constituting more than half of the total. In the 1960s, Cubans composed 62 percent of the total (131,557 of 212,843) while Europeans took up 26 percent (55,235) with 18,000 Yugoslavs accounting for the largest single European nationality.

The onset of the refugee programs stemming from the American defeat in the Vietnam War in 1975 meant that the 680,000 refugees of the 1970s, including the 140,000 Cubans and Haitians the INS called "entrants," were dominated by more than 350,000 Cubans and over 180,000 Southeast Asians (150,000 Vietnamese, 22,000 Laotians, and 8,000 Cambodians). The European component was just over 70,000, a little over 10 percent of the decade's total refugee intake, with nearly half, 31,000 from the Soviet Union, most of them Jews.

The 1980s was the first decade in which as many as a million refugees arrived. More than 70 percent were from Asia. These 712,000 Asians were dominated by 581,000 refugees from the war in Vietnam—324,000 from Vietnam, 143,000 from Laos, and 114,000 from Cambodia. Included in these numbers are an indeterminate number of persons other than Vietnamese, Cambodians, and Laotians. There were large numbers of relatively small ethnic minorities, the most numerous of whom were Hmong, and significant numbers of Chinese.[32] The total number of European refugees more than doubled to 155,000, reflecting increased Eastern European instability. Almost half, 72,000, were from the USSR; 34,000 came from Poland and 30,000 from Romania.

In the 1990s, the continuing turmoil in Eastern Europe plus the dissolution of the Soviet Union shifted the emphasis in refugee admissions back to Europe. More than half of the nearly one million refugees admitted in the decade were Europeans, and just over three-fifths of the European refugees were from the USSR and some of its former component parts. Almost a third of the decade's refugees came from Asia, with 86 percent of them attributable to the war in Vietnam and its aftermath. One-eleventh, some 88,000 individuals, came from the New World, more than two-thirds of them Cubans.

The mechanics of the Vietnam War refugee migration were, in many ways, quite similar to those of the Hungarian refugee program in the 1950s, but the Southeast Asian exodus was much larger and lasted longer. Again, the United States chose who was to come, often screening them not only in camps in nations of first asylum, such as Thailand, but also in American military bases in such places as the Philippines and Guam. In the early years of the programs, once refugees arrived in the United States, they were sorted out and resettled from military bases.

Unlike the Hungarians and most other twentieth-century refugees coming to the United States, there was no significant immigrant population in the United States with whom most Southeast Asians could identify. (Ethnic Chinese were, of course, an exception.) Few Vietnamese, even fewer Cambodians and Laotians, and almost no Hmong had ever migrated anywhere outside of Southeast Asia before the 1970s. Most of the few who had, traveled to France, the colonial overlord. (Included in the latter group was the man known to history as Ho Chi Minh.)[33] Only after the United States assumed in 1954 the full responsibility for the defense of what became known as South Vietnam was there any noticeable number of Vietnamese, mostly students and government officials, in the United States.

As late as 1970 there were probably not even 10,000 Southeast Asians in the United States and most of those did not have immigrant status. After the United States' ignominious withdrawal from Vietnam in 1975, the administrations of Gerald Ford and Jimmy Carter cobbled together ten distinct programs for Southeast Asian refugees that brought some 400,000 people, mostly Vietnamese, to the United States within four years. Other refugee programs for Southeast Asians followed and, after many refugees began to become citizens in the 1980s, regular migration from Southeast Asia outside of Vietnam continued to grow with what were, in reality if not in law, largely refugees from what its foremost American scholar, George Herring, has called "the war that would not end."[34] By 2000, according to the United States census, there were more than 1.6 million Americans whose presence was a direct or indirect result of the Vietnam War (1.1 million Vietnamese, and about 170,000 each of Cambodians, Laotians, and Hmong).[35] And the growth of these communities continues by both immigration and natural increase. In 2001, for example, Vietnam was the fifth largest source of legal immigrants apart from refugees: more than 35,000 were recorded, 3.3 percent of regular immigration in that year.

The government and the volunteer organizations (VOLAGS) that worked with them wanted very much to spread these refugees throughout the country, but these efforts at ethnic dispersion have largely failed. As of 1975, for example, only a fifth of all Vietnamese refugees were in California: in both 1990 and 2000 the figure was just a hair under two-fifths.[36] Demographically, those who came from Southeast Asia constituted a population quite different from most other refugee groups. The refugees from the war in Vietnam were predominantly women and children. Their cultural levels ranged from Vietnamese, Cambodian, and Laotian elites who had acquired French culture as well as their own, larger numbers who were practicing Catholics, and a majority who were monocultural and Buddhist. Almost all of the Hmong were from a preliterate society. The transition of the refugee generation to American society was not an outstanding success: poverty levels were extremely high.[37] In 1990, 63 percent of the Hmong population in the United States lived below the poverty level, as did 42 percent of the Cambodians, 32 percent of the Laotians, and 24 percent of the Vietnamese.[38]

As for European refugees, both the Carter and the Reagan administrations constantly pressured the Soviet leaders, with some success, to allow Jewish refugees, sometimes called refuseniks, to leave. Nothing better demonstrates the relaxation of tensions between the United States and the People's Republic of China than a story Jimmy Carter tells in his memoirs. In early 1979 when Deng Xiaoping became the first leader of the People's Republic of China to visit the United States, Carter reports, Deng, noting the problems the United States was having with the USSR over its restrictive emigration policies, volunteered:

> If you want me to release ten million Chinese to come to the United States, I'd be glad to do that.

To be sure Deng was pulling Carter's chain—Carter responded by offering him "ten thousand journalists"—but it is still a remarkable anecdote for two reasons. First, it presaged the relatively good relations that would prevail between the two formerly hostile powers despite setbacks, and second, it shows that the issue of immigration, once a matter of humiliation for China, was no longer a bar to good relations.[39]

The pressures on the Soviet Union had become pronounced in the early 1970s, and emanated more from Congress than from the White House. The adoption in 1972 of the so-called Jackson Amendment—for Henry M. Jackson (1912–83), a senior Democratic senator from Washington—tried the carrot-and-stick approach by linking favorable trading privileges for the USSR to a more liberal Soviet emigration policy. Both of these would have been unheard-of notions in the most fervid years of the Cold War, and, to be sure, the amount of trade and emigration fluctuated with the varying temperature of the Cold War. When détente and later *glasnost* prevailed, both grew: when relations become strained they shrank, but the trend was toward greater growth. Few things better illustrate the changing attitudes toward Jews in the second half of the twentieth century than the contrast in attitudes about Jewish immigration. In the 1930s and 1940s Congress and public opinion resisted even the slightest efforts at easing restrictions that inhibited Jewish flight. By the 1970s, Congress, with relatively conservative leadership, successfully pressured both the executive branch and the Soviet Union to let more Jews out and into the United States.

Clearly, the 1980 refugee act cemented a refugee segment firmly into the legislative structure of American immigration, even though there were continuing problems with various aspects of the program. These troubling aspects helped to exacerbate the backlash against immigration that punctuated the politics of immigration during the administrations of Ronald Reagan, George Bush the elder, and Bill Clinton.

CHAPTER ELEVEN

Immigration Reform: Myths and Realities

Twenty-one years after Congress changed the course of immigration with the epochal 1965 act, it passed the Immigration Reform and Control Act (IRCA). Both were regarded as "reform" measures but they pushed immigration policy in opposite directions. In 1965, and for many years before that, reform meant loosening the restraints placed on immigration in the tribal twenties, what Lyndon Johnson called righting the wrong done to those "from southern or eastern Europe."[1] By 1986 immigration reform meant undoing, *somehow*, much of the unintended consequences of the 1965 act: the domination of contemporary American immigration by persons from Latin America and Asia and a greatly increased volume. From that time those claiming to be reformers can be slotted along a broad ideological spectrum running from extreme, old-style nativists, spewing hate, through the "white collar" nativists of the Federation for American Immigration Reform, to the mainstream multiculturalists who chaired two national commissions to reform immigration: Father Theodore M. Hesburgh (b. 1917), the former president of Notre Dame,* who led the Select Commission on Immigration and Refugee Policy

---

*Hesburgh's brief account of his Commission's work in his autobiography shows him not to have a firm grip on the facts of American immigration history. He thought, among other misconceptions, that the Progressive Era immigration commission was the "Pendleton Commission" and that Leland Stanford was responsible for Chinese immigration. (Hesburgh, *God, Country, Notre Dame* [New York: Doubleday, 1990], pp. 274–79.)

(SCIRP, 1979–81), and former congresswoman from Texas, Barbara Jordan (1936–96), who headed the United States Commission on Immigration Reform (USCIR, 1991–97). Both commissions advocated reducing the number of immigrants and providing a more "balanced" mix of those coming to America.

In the late 1970s and the early 1980s a wide variety of factors pushed immigration policy to the fore. The Mariel boatlift, the government's apparent inability to cope with sudden immigration crises, and larger societal issues contributed to an increasing climate of fear, which in the past often bred anti-immigrant attitudes, violence, and legislation. The Marielitos—and, by association, all immigrants—were quickly identified with crime and the new scourge of AIDS. The traditional fear that immigrants would "steal" jobs from "Americans" was heightened by the severe "stagflation" and recession that bedeviled the American economy between 1975 and 1983, producing double-digit inflation, soaring interest rates, and the highest unemployment figures since the Great Depression. Public officials had also contributed to growing fears about "too much" immigration in general, and illegal immigration in particular. Leonard F. Chapman, Richard Nixon's Commissioner of Immigration and Naturalization between 1973 and 1977, heightened public anxieties with scare stories about a largely nonexistent illegal immigrant crisis.

Reflecting the nation's mood, in 1978 Congress created SCIRP, with instructions to report in 1981. (How little Congress cared what SCIRP might recommend is indicated by its passing of the landmark 1980 Refugee Act, a year before the Commission was to report.) This was the first such body created by Congress since the Dillingham Commission reported in 1911. Like the Dillingham Commission—and unlike Truman's 1953 Commission on Immigration and Naturalization—SCIRP suggested reducing immigration. Its 1981 report, claiming that undocumented migration was the country's number one immigration problem, was an important influence in the passage of the Immigration Reform and Control Act of 1986 (IRCA), five years later.[2] Its proposals were mixed. On the one hand, it supported most of the reforms enacted by the 1965 law and, in a seemingly unprecedented suggestion, proposed a broad amnesty for long-resident illegal immigrants in the country to regularize their status; on the other hand, it proposed tighter border controls, which were easier to propose than to effect, and in a typically American act of faith in technology, urged research to develop a forgery-proof identity card. Hesburgh argued in his memoir that many immigration problems could be solved by a "law requiring all American citizens and legal residents to carry an upgraded social security card with a microchip carrying essential information,"[3] a proposal his colleagues did not accept.

Father Hesburgh, unlike many Catholic clergy who stressed humanitarian factors and natural law, insisted that the economic well-being of those already in America was the most important factor to be considered and did so in a way that embraced the notion of limited opportunities, which echoed the national mood. Writing on the "op-ed" page of *The New York Times* as part of the campaign for the passage of IRCA in early 1986, he argued that

> during the next 15 years, assuming a persistently strong economy, the United States will create about 30 million new jobs. Can we afford to set aside more than 20 percent of them for foreign workers? No. It would be a disservice to our own poor and unfortunate.[4]

When Hesburgh wrote, in 1986, employment stood at 109.6 million persons with an unemployment rate of 4.0 percent; fifteen years later there were 135.9 million employed, more than 13 percent fewer than he had predicted, with an unemployment rate of 4.2 percent. During those fifteen years legal immigration hovered near a million annually, with substantial illegal immigration.

Hesburgh's argument, that cheap immigrant labor reduces the standard of living of all workers, is an old one. It was first used against Chinese and blacks migrating north during and after the Civil War, and has since been used against Irish, Germans, French Canadians, Italians, Jews, and other so-called "new immigrants," Japanese, Filipinos, and almost every conceivable immigrant group. Today it is most commonly applied to Hispanics. Many take its doctrine for gospel, but it fails to explain why, during the century and a half since the Civil War, the South, the region of least immigration, has had a lower standard of living than areas of high immigrant concentration elsewhere. To point this out is not to argue that immigrants are responsible for prosperity, but to note that immigrants go where the jobs and the better wages are. Would wages be higher if there were no immigrants? Perhaps. It is an argument without end and more complex than sketched here. What these nativists see as "job stealing" others describe as economic growth. In the 1980s economists as different as John Kenneth Galbraith and the members of Ronald Reagan's Council of Economic Advisors took the position that immigration was necessary for economic growth.

Other opponents of immigration used the same economic arguments but added a divisive, nativistic twist, often combined with a lopsided view of American history. Columnist Carl Rowan, for example, in 1981 claimed that

> The United States is a nation without meaningful control of its borders. So many Mexicans are crossing U.S. borders illegally that Mexicans are reclaiming Texas, California, and other territories they have long claimed the Gringos stole from them.

Less specific but equally nativist were the comments of Alan K. Simpson, who represented Wyoming in the Senate between 1979 and 1997 and was one of the most persistent and consistent new-style immigration reformers in the Republican Party. A member of the Hesburgh Commission, he regularly set forth what is usually called the cultural argument, namely that some immigrants were simply unable to assimilate into American culture. Defending the SCIRP report in 1981 he insisted that

> A substantial proportion of these new persons and their descendants do not assimilate satisfactorily into our society . . . [They] may well create in America some of the same social, political, and economic problems that exist in the countries from which they have chosen to depart. Furthermore, if language and cultural separation rise above a certain level, the unity and political stability of our nation will—in time—be seriously eroded.[5]

Shortly thereafter the new president, Ronald W. Reagan, who later contributed significantly to the nation's fears about being flooded by what he called "feet people" from Central America, began his administration by establishing a President's Task Force on Immigration and Refugee Policy, much to Hesburgh's annoyance,[6] which recommended a moderate version of immigration reform.* After the usual platitudes about tradition, national values, and the Constitution, Reagan articulated the issue that divided him

---

*The difference between a commission and a task force is more than semantic. A commission is appointed jointly by the president and the congressional leadership while a task force is usually composed of just executive branch officials.

and many Republicans from the most intense immigration reformers. In his June 30, 1981, policy statement, Reagan stated:

> We must also recognize that both the United States and Mexico have histori-
> cally benefited from Mexicans obtaining employment in the United States. A
> number of our States have special labor needs, and we should take these into
> account. Illegal immigrants in considerable numbers have become produc-
> tive members of our society and are a basic part of our work force. Those who
> have established equities in the United States should be recognized and
> accorded legal status. At the same time, in so doing, we must not encourage
> illegal immigration.

In other words, he was supporting an amnesty. Insofar as refugee policy was concerned, the adminstration's proposals were essentially the same kinds of attempts at ethnic distribution as every administration since FDR's had espoused, with the same largely negative results. "We shall strive to distribute fairly," the Reagan policy statement continued, "among the various localities of this country, the impacts of our national immigration and refugee policy, and we shall improve the capability of those agencies of the Federal Government which deal with these matters."

And, in a typical Reagan peroration, the president insisted that his policies would solve all problems and do so justly: "With the help of the Congress and the American people, we will work towards a new and realistic immigration policy, a policy that will be fair to our own citizens while it opens the door of opportunity for those who seek a new life in America."[7]

The heated five-year congressional debate over immigration "reform" that followed initially focused on proposals sponsored by Alan Simpson in the Senate and Romano Mazzoli, a Democrat from Louisville, Kentucky, in the House. Both men were intelligent and articulate and the measures they supported, usually called the Mazzoli-Simpson bills, were more restrictive than either the SCIRP proposals or the legislation that finally passed in 1986. Those failed bills would have raised slightly the stated limits on immigration, but by placing all family immigration within the numerical caps, would have decreased significantly the actual number of immigrants admitted. In addition, the bills would have abolished the fifth preference—adult brothers and sisters of United States citizens—and thus eliminated important links in the existing pattern of chain migration that had characterized American immigration since 1952. Simpson justified his attack on family reunification—a cornerstone of American immigration policy since 1921—with his typical cultural argument: "I do feel that family preference categories should be based on the U.S. concept of the nuclear family and not on the definition of such a family as expressed in other nations."[8]

After five years of debate, during which the House and Senate both were for immigration reform but could not agree on all provisions, a compromise measure sponsored by Simpson and Peter W. Rodino, a New Jersey Democrat who served in the House between 1949 and 1989, was enacted in 1986. Crucial to its passage was the maintenance of the family-reunification provisions.

The Immigration Reform and Control Act of 1986 (IRCA) was hyped by many of its backers, the INS, and much of the media as a solution to most immigration problems. At the bill-signing ceremony, Ronald Reagan, conveniently ignoring the epochal 1965 act, called it "the most comprehensive reform of our immigration laws since 1952," and went on to predict that

> future generations of Americans will be thankful for our efforts to humanely regain control of our borders and thereby preserve the value of one of the most sacred possessions of our people—American citizenship.[9]

IRCA was, essentially, a schizoid measure reflecting the deep divisions in Congress over immigration policy. Despite the anti-immigrant rhetoric in Congress and the media, the law, on balance, actually expanded immigration rather than restricting it. There were, to be sure, provisions that were intended to "get tough with" immigrants. Ironically, these "get tough" provisions, especially the ones that Reagan claimed would enable Americans to "regain control of our borders," failed as most authorities—but not the INS—quickly recognized.

The two major restrictive provisions, as summarized by the INS:

1. Created sanctions prohibiting employers from knowingly hiring, recruiting, or referring for a fee aliens not authorized to work in the United States.
2. Increased enforcement at U.S. borders.

Since most immigrants, legal or illegal, come to the United States to work, an effective system of employer sanctions would, sooner or later, all but eliminate illegal immigration. Enforcing such sanctions, especially in regions where the use of illegal workers was a way of life, would be difficult under any circumstances. But Congress had no intention of passing a statute that would put large numbers of respectable and often wealthy citizens in legal jeopardy. The word *knowingly* in the statute is a clear indication of this. Criminal statutes—and hiring an illegal alien is a crime—do not normally absolve perpetrators who claim that they did not know what they were doing.

And, if the *knowingly* were not enough, Congress—at the behest of southwestern and western legislators—deliberately impeded effective enforcement. Perhaps the best single example of this is Section 116 of Title I of IRCA, entitled "Restricting warrantless entry in the case of outdoor agricultural operations."[10] The relevant clause of that section of the law reads:

> . . . an officer or employee of the [INS] may not enter without the consent of the owner (or agent thereof) or a properly executed warrant onto the premises of a farm or other outdoor agricultural operation for the purpose of interrogating a person believed to be an alien as to the person's right to be or to remain in the United States.

Note that the limitation is on outdoor premises. Nothing in the law prevented warrantless INS raids on indoor places of employment, and, in fact, most of the successful INS/Department of Labor raids have been on immigrant-owned, sweatshop-type employment: the owner-operators of these relatively small businesses have little clout with politicians. The notorious selective enforcement policies of the INS, added to the statutory inhibitions on the efficiency of its agents, have a clear consequence: once agricultural workers get away from the border zone, their risk of arrest is minimal.

To be sure, the INS catches lots of illegal immigrants. In every year since 1977 it has reported close to a million or more apprehensions. Most of those are at or near the border and include large numbers of multiple apprehensions of the same individuals, many of whom, eventually, manage to get across. If we look at 1988, the first full fiscal year after IRCA went into effect, we find that the INS reported 1,008,145 "apprehensions" of whom 937,080—or 93 percent—were "expelled." Only 22,848—2.4 percent of those expelled—were actually deported, while 914,232—97.6 percent—were merely "required to depart."[11] Of the total number of apprehensions, 949,722—94.2 percent—were recorded as having Mexican nationality, and an even larger number, 985,479—97.8 percent—were persons who had entered illegally, what the INS called "entry without inspection."

The remaining 22,666—2.2 percent—who made up the bulk of the deportees, were classified according to their mode of entry, as follows:

Visitor visas	13,060
Immigrant visas	4,509
Students	1,289
Crewmen	512
Stowaways	385
Temporary workers	267
Transits without visa	64
"Other"	2,580
Total	22,666[12]

The reason that so few are actually deported is simple. Deportation can be a slow, expensive legal process. No one in his right mind wants to put many illegal immigrants in jail—full federal incarceration in the 1980s was estimated to cost about $35,000 per person per year, more than the cost of an Ivy League education. Those caught right at the border are often turned back without written formalities, but those apprehended farther inland are asked to sign a voluntary departure form. The advantages for the immigrants are twofold: the INS will usually transport them to the border at government expense, and aliens who agree to "voluntarily depart" remain eligible to enter the United States legally.

Congress has made sure that the law does not interfere with the Southwest's supply of agricultural laborers. In the 1980s many of those who "voluntarily departed" were migrant agricultural workers who were going home after a stint of harvesting American crops, and would after a time return and go through the process all over again. This can be viewed as an arrangement that benefits almost all concerned. Farmers have gotten their crops picked, consumers can buy produce at lower prices, the workers, while exploited, have earned money for their families, and the INS has compiled statistics to show how good it is at catching people. Of course, the law has been violated, but this was one of the instances, as Charles Dickens's Mr. Bumble put it, in which "the law is a ass, a idiot."[13]

IRCA, and a spate of later statutes, called for "enhanced border security" and authorized ever-larger INS budgets for equipment and personnel so that it could, as the phrase went, "regain control of our borders." Thus, the Border Patrol, a component part of the INS since 1924, had been putting on shows regularly, going back to the Eisenhower administration, to please its congressional masters although its leaders understood that these would, in the long run, have little effect on immigration flows. In late 2002 the INS Web site touted the efficacy of "Operation Hold the Line" (El Paso, 1993), "Operation Gatekeeper" (San Diego, 1994), and BORSTAR, an anti-smuggling unit and search-and-rescue teams.[14]

The notion that these procedures actually had the desired result can only be called wishful thinking, which the INS indulged in regularly.[15] The fact of the matter is that the land borders of the United States, just counting the lower forty-eight, measure 5,525 miles and have never been controlled. British and Canadian troops, hostile Indians, Mexican revolutionaries, bootleggers during prohibition, drug smugglers today, and, of course, immigrants since 1882, have violated American borders with relative impunity. The publicized Border Patrol operations concentrating on specific points are able to curtail unauthorized border crossings in a given area, but the immigrants who really want to get in, simply go somewhere else. The scholar Frank Bean, who examined "Operation Hold the Line," found four distinct types of illegal border crossers in El Paso. The two types most troublesome to the citizens of El Paso—street vendors and teenagers crossing to party—were stopped, but long-distance migrants headed for the interior U.S. and daily commuters were only inconvenienced by the massing of agents at the border.[16]

And, although little noticed at the time, a separate section of IRCA made it much easier to enter the United States. Against the advice of the INS, Congress created an experimental Visa Waiver pilot program allowing certain tourists and certain other nonimmigrant aliens to enter the United States without applying for a nonimmigrant visa. The program caught on, and, fifteen years later became notorious when it became known that some of the terrorists who executed the mass murder on September 11, 2001, had entered under this program, which in the meantime had become greatly expanded.[17] In the aftermath of 9/11 the blame fell not on Congress but on the hapless INS.

More significant than the "get tough" provisions of the 1986 IRCA legislation were parts of the law that expanded legal immigration. The three major ones were:

1. Authorized legalization (i.e., temporary and then permanent resident status) for aliens who had resided in the United States in an unlawful status since January 1, 1982. This is what everyone calls "amnesty," but the word does not appear in the statute, which speaks of "legalization of status," and is not normally used by the INS.

2. Created a new classification of seasonal agricultural workers [SAW] and the provision for the legalization of such workers.
3. Allocated 5,000 preference visas in each of fiscal years 1987 and 1988 for aliens born in countries from which immigration was adversely affected by the 1965 act. Everyone but the INS calls it "The Lottery."

The Amnesty Program was the much debated major innovation of IRCA, although a kind of amnesty, called "registry," had been on the statute books since 1929.[18] The law originally provided that any alien who had been in the U.S. continuously since before the passage of the 1921 immigration act, was of "good moral character" and eligible, could adjust to legal permanent-resident status. The time limit had been periodically moved forward. A minor provision of IRCA advanced it to 1972, where it remained at the beginning of 2003. Thousands of persons have been legalized through "registry."[19]

In addition the Chinese Confession program was yet another way in which immigration law had previously legalized persons who were, admittedly, in the country illegally. But the total prior legalizations were only a tiny fraction of those legalized by IRCA in 1986.

There were two separate amnesty programs under IRCA: the general program and the one for "Seasonal Agricultural Workers" (SAW). The general amnesty program, while using the registry concepts of a specific cutoff date and continuous residence, gave those applying only a one-year period, May 5, 1987–May 4, 1988, in which to register, and made the eventual granting of legal permanent-resident status dependent on future behavior.* By the close of the one-year window 1.7 million aliens had successfully applied under this part of IRCA legalization.

The SAW program was added to the bill very late in its consideration by California Republican Senator Pete Wilson with the backing of the Reagan administration.[20] It was, in essence, another version of the bracero program, except that it contained provisions for eventual legalization of the workers. There were no hearings and little detailed analysis. Providing such workers was a necessary element to get the votes of southwestern senators and representatives, which was crucial in securing a congressional majority. The

---

*Temporary residence could be revoked if "it appears to the Attorney General that the alien was in fact not eligible for such status"; or if the alien became ineligible for admission or had been convicted of a felony or three misdemeanors; or failed to apply for permanent status within thirty-one months after temporary status had been granted, or had applied and had that application rejected.

deal was brokered by the then Democratic Representative Charles E. Schumer, whose Brooklyn district was home to many immigrants and very little agriculture. Its two major provisions were the above-mentioned bracero-type program and a much less restrictive amnesty program that enabled illegal immigrants who had worked in agriculture for at least ninety days between May 1985 and May 1986 to regularize their status and begin the process that could result in citizenship.

While there had been studies of how many illegal immigrants might qualify for citizenship in the original program, no one had the slightest idea of how many SAWs might apply for legalization. The Congressional Budget Office guessed 250,000, and this convenient figure was used in the congressional debate by SAW proponents. In the event, more than 1.3 million SAW applications were accepted, as were more than 1.7 million applications for "regular" amnesty. Thus, the "minor add-on" eventually amounted to more than two-fifths of the total number of persons accepted into the amnesty program, some 43 percent. All told, some 3.1 million illegal aliens began the process of legalization under IRCA: those who became permanent residents and citizens would be able to sponsor relatives who could enter—in some cases, without numerical limit—so the potential number of immigrants added to the population was considerably higher.

By 1998 some 2.68 million illegal immigrants, 88 percent of the accepted applicants, had achieved permanent resident status and several thousand more have achieved it since then. A large percentage of the amnestied immigrants have taken the further step of becoming American citizens, but there is no way of determining how many.

Who got into the amnesty program? The data show what one would expect. Almost 70 percent were Mexicans and more than 20 percent of the rest were from the New World, largely Central America. More than two-thirds, 68 percent, were male. Most applicants of both genders were young—59 percent were under thirty years of age and only 10 percent were over forty-four. They were highly concentrated within the United States: more than two-thirds applied from just two states, 54 percent from California and 14 percent from Texas.

Although political rhetoric and INS propaganda made amnesty seem a simple choice, for many its terms created intense personal dilemmas. The cutoff dates often split families. For example, if a parent crossed the border in 1980 with a child, both would be eligible to apply, but if another child and a spouse had come in 1983, they would not be. In 1990, long after the time for applying had run out, Congress made it possible for family members of legalized immigrants to stay and work or go to school until they, too, could become legalized. And, although a much discussed and expected "second amnesty" had not, as of the beginning of 2003, taken place, Congress and the various subsequent administrations have become quite inventive in finding ways for illegal immigrants to remain and work on a temporary basis.

Amnesty also created problems for American foreign policy. The "get tough" provisions of IRCA and the accompanying political rhetoric created understandable fears in many of the nations of the circum-Caribbean that large numbers of their citizens who were illegal immigrants in the United States would be sent home. This would diminish the immigrant remittances that were an important part of their national income. For example, in 1987, El Salvador's President José Napoleón Duarte, who was an important supporter of American anticommunist policies in Central America, unsuccessfully appealed to President Reagan, asking that Salvadorans illegally in the United States be given "extended voluntary departure" (EVD) status, which would enable them to remain and continue to work legally and presumably send remittances that he estimated ran between $350 million to $600 million annually, a sum larger than annual United States aid."[21]

The remaining expansion of immigration under IRCA began as a very small program that was, in reality, a kind of affirmative action for certain white persons, but no sponsor called it that. In 1986 a Democratic Congressman from greater Boston, Brian J. Donnelly, moved a successful amendment to IRCA that allocated 5,000 nonpreference visas in each of the two subsequent years for aliens born in countries from which immigration was adversely affected by the 1965 immigration act. This meant, in effect, European countries. The words "born in" were crucial to the purpose of the amendment. Normally immigration statutes and records refer to nationality rather than place of birth, but in this case "born in" was designed to bar natives of third-world nations, mostly former colonials, who had European citizenship. Successful applicants were chosen through a lottery conducted by the State Department.

Donnelly and his colleagues in the Massachusetts delegation— including, most importantly, Senator Edward M. Kennedy, a power in immigration matters—assumed correctly that natives of Ireland would get a disproportionate share of these visas: they got more than 40 percent for the first two years of the program. Congress later, in what was called "diversity transition," expanded the program to 40,000 visas annually for 1992–94, with a minimum of 40 percent—that is 16,000 visas annually for three years—reserved for "natives of Ireland," but provided a fair formula for diversity later that had 55,000 visas allocated to it annually.

In the final analysis, IRCA was not "reform legislation" in either the original or the contemporary meaning of the term. Nor was it, as had been claimed, a measure that would reduce immigration. It was clearly a failure administratively, but, in human terms, it gave some 3 million human beings a better chance for a successful life.

Wholly apart from IRCA legalizations, the numbers of legal immigrants continued to grow through the 1980s and into the 1990s, and in all probability the numbers of illegal immigrants were not significantly slowed by IRCA's "get tough" provisions. As these facts became all but universally acknowledged, calls for even more stringent immigration legislation were made and new struggles over immigration policy became even more intense in the years immediately after IRCA began to take effect.

CHAPTER TWELVE

"Controlling Our Borders": Struggles over Immigration Policy

What the historian David Reimers called "the turn against immigration" began in earnest in the aftermath of the 1986 Immigration Reform and Control Act (IRCA), and in an atmosphere of national dissatisfaction with many aspects of American life.[1] Yet, by the time Reimers's book appeared, in 1998, the turn against immigration seemed to have reversed its course. Before examining the struggles over immigration policy in the 1990s, however, it is appropriate to summarize the changes—or apparent changes—in the national climate of opinion about immigration during the decade.

In 1990, just four years after passing IRCA, Congress passed yet another immigration act, which the INS summarized as "a major overhaul of immigration law." By the middle of the 1990s public dissatisfaction with immigration probably reached a post-1924 peak. Barbara Jordan, chair of the United States Commission on Immigration Reform (USCIR) which had been created by the 1990 act, caught the national mood when she reported to Congress in May 1994, that, instead of a discussion about immigration, there was a "furor."[2] At that time there were 150 separate immigration bills in Congress, some calling for a "moratorium" on all immigration, reminiscent of the House's action in 1921.

Public opinion polls had long shown majority hostility to immigration. Chart 12.1 shows Gallup poll responses to the same question—"In your view should immigration be kept at the present level, increased or decreased?"—since the beginning of 1965. Just before the passage of the 1965 immigration act, 7 percent of Americans thought that immigration ought to be increased, while 33 percent thought that it should be decreased. Twenty-one years later, on the eve of the 1986 IRCA legislation, 49 percent thought that immigration should be decreased, while 7 percent continued to think it should be increased. Polls taken in July 1993 and January 1995 reflect the peak of anti-immigrant feeling: in each, nearly two-thirds—65 percent—favored decreasing immigration while in the 1993 poll the small minority favoring an increase remained right at 7 percent; in 1995 this figure inched down to 6 percent. Indicative of immigration's greater relevance, the percentage answering "don't know" or not answering dropped steadily from 21 percent of all respondents in 1965 to only 2 percent in 1993, and remained under 10 percent in the four polls since then. But opinions shifted sharply after Congress began passing the punitive anti-immigrant legislation of the mid-1990s. In three successive polls over a period of twenty-one months, between February 1999 and January 2001, the percentages of those favoring less immigration and those who thought that the current level was about right were at about two-fifths each, while the percentage of those who thought that immigration should be increased, which had remained remarkably constant for thirty years at about 7 percent, doubled in the six years after June 1995 to reach 14 percent in mid-2001. Thus, in mid-1995 fewer than a third of Americans—31 percent—reported a favorable view of immigration levels; just six years later more than half—56 percent—did so.

CHART 12.1
AMERICAN ATTITUDES TOWARD THE VOLUME OF
IMMIGRATION, 1965–2001

"IN YOUR VIEW SHOULD IMMIGRATION BE KEPT AT THE
PRESENT LEVEL, INCREASED OR DECREASED?"

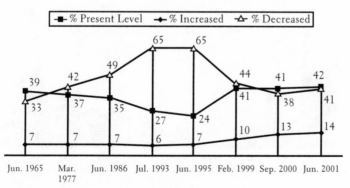

Source: Gallup Poll News Service, Poll Analysis, July 18, 2001.

This series of Gallup polls is particularly valuable because the questions are neutral and the same question was asked over relatively long periods of time. Conversely, some polls taken when the anti-immigrant furor was boiling seemed designed to magnify nativist attitudes. In 1993, for example, an often-cited *New York Times*–CBS News poll posited a patently false option—"most of the people who have moved to the United States in the last few years are here illegally"—and found that 68 percent of those who responded agreed. But none of the polls discussed here measured the intensity of respondents' beliefs. Even at times when immigration was a "hot-button" issue, it generally ranked low among the topics that Americans say they cared most about, except in areas where immigration is of special concern, such as South Florida or much of California. And, it must be noted, throughout history, Americans—no matter how they feel about contemporary immigration—are overwhelmingly positive about past immigration.

Despite fluctuations in attitudes, the actual course of immigration remained relatively constant. Apart from the great spike caused by IRCA shown in Chart 12.2, the volume of immigration showed a persistent increase from the post–World War II era to the end of the century, as Table 12.1 shows.

CHART 12.2
IMMIGRANTS ADMITTED: FISCAL YEARS 1900-2000

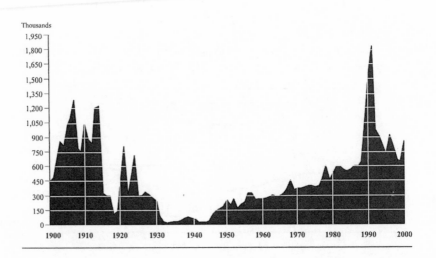

Source: INS, *Statistical Yearbook*, 2000.

TABLE 12.1
IMMIGRATION BY DECADE, 1941–2000

Years	Immigration (in millions)
1941–50	1.0
1951–60	2.5
1961–70	3.2
1971–80	4.5
1981–90	7.3
1991–00	9.1
Total	27.6

Source: INS, *Statistical Yearbook*, 2001, Table 1.

Note that almost three-fifths of the legal immigrants of those sixty years came in the final two decades.

The INS recorded the more than 3 million aliens legalized by IRCA as if the persons being legalized had entered the country in the year that they were legalized, even though 1.7 million of them presumably entered before 1982, and the 1.3 million Seasonal Agriculture Workers before 1986. The previous number of such adjustments in any period had never been large enough to cause a major distortion. Thus Chart 12.2—versions of which were widely disseminated in the media—shows some 5.4 million immigrants entering the country between 1989 and 1992, when, in fact, more than 3 million of them had been present for some time. This misleading "data" only served to heighten the existing fears.* Including those legalizations, the aggregate number of legal migrants reported for the period of 1981–2000 was 16.4 million. Since large numbers of those legalized came in the earlier 1980s, we cannot say what the "real" as opposed to the statistical legal immigration actually was—they all came at some time—but a responsible recording of that data would have eliminated those ominous spikes showing just over a million, a million and a half, and almost two million, and almost one million in the 1989, 1990, 1991, and 1992 fiscal years, respectively.

*This is not to suggest that showing the data in that way was malign: it was simply a bureaucratic practice instituted when legislations and other adjustments of status were a tiny fraction of the total and did not significantly distort the data. A similar misconception has been created by the way that the census reported Hispanic "race" data, as noted previously. Of course, if the media were both sophisticated and responsible, such things would not be a problem. But since they are not, releasing data in misleading formats is misfeasance on the part of the statistical officials; misinterpreting it is malfeasance by the media.

The INS's misleading numbers enabled the media to speak, incessantly, of immigration in those years as the heaviest in our history. That was not true. In five of the years between 1905 and 1914, immigration exceeded one million persons—the 1,285,000 of fiscal 1907 remains the peak year—and the 10.1 million immigrants of those ten years still represent the numerical high-water mark of American immigration. When one considers that in 1914 the population of the United States was about 99 million and in 2000 it was 281 million, it is clear that the relative incidence of immigrants was significantly higher in the earlier period. The false widely shared perception that the country was being flooded with an unprecedented number of immigrants was a significant aspect of the "furor" Jordan complained about.

Congress, which helped to create the furor, also responded to it. In the twelve years after IRCA—that is, from 1986 to 1998—twenty-one significant pieces of immigration legislation were enacted. Not all of these were acts designed to lessen immigration, and some actually increased it.[3]

For example, two statutes, the Chinese Student Protection Act and the Soviet Scientists Immigration Act, passed in late 1992, were residual Cold War statutes.[4] The first provided permanent resident status to nationals—mostly students or former students—of the People's Republic of China who were in the United States after June 4, 1989, and before April 11, 1990. The intent was to protect students who had participated in or shown sympathy with the pro-democracy demonstrations halted by Beijing's Tiananmen Square massacre. The second enabled American industry to employ scientists from the former Soviet Union in the biological, chemical, and nuclear sciences.

Several other pieces of legislation, such as the Immigration Nursing Relief Act of 1990, provided for adjustment from temporary to permanent resident status for foreign nurses who had been employed in the United States for at least three years and met established professional standards. It also created a new, "nonimmigrant" category for the temporary admission of qualified registered nurses.[5] To describe persons being allowed into the country as "nonimmigrants" sounds like an oxymoron. What it means is that they are supposed to be temporary, not permanent, immigrants: the first large group of these were the World War II braceros. As we have seen, considerable numbers of these "nonimmigrants" have simply stayed and many of them eventually became permanent residents. In the 1990s "nonimmigrant" immigrants, as opposed to visitors, became an increasingly important component of the American labor force: they may work, legally, for specified periods of time.* Many of the other immigration statutes of the 1990s were designed to place limits on immigration or to make life more difficult for unnaturalized legal immigrants already present in the United States.

The first major statute, the Immigration Act of 1990,[6] was the last statute in the twentieth century to attempt a general overhaul and it has a generic relationship with the 1921, 1924, 1952, and 1965 acts. It was another composite amalgam of provisions, some of which "got tough" while others significantly expanded employment-based immigration. In addition it:

1. mitigated significantly the ideological litmus tests for visitors, which dated back to the McCarran-Walter Act of 1952. While the ban continued on anyone still a Communist Party member, most communists who had left the party as recently as two years before applying for a visa were no longer excludable.
2. evinced the increasing concerns about crime. Among other things the law made anyone who had engaged in prostitution or commercialized vice excludable for ten years. It can be argued that the lessened concern about communism was "balanced" by a heightened concern about crime and vice, although the latter was seen as five times as reprehensible as Marxism.
3. transformed the pro-Irish diversity program created in IRCA, by stages, into a real diversity program.
4. created the United States Commission on Immigration Reform (USCIR, 1991–97), initially headed by Barbara Jordan.

The 1990 law raised the number of immigrants to be admitted according to a fixed cap to an annual level of 700,000 for the years 1992–94, and dropping to 675,000 after that. It broke down the 675,000 into 480,000 "family-sponsored," 140,000 "employment-based," and 55,000 "diversity" immigrants, a.k.a. "lottery visas." Spouses and unmarried minor children of U.S. citizens were not subject to numerical limitation. Under the new law the refugee cap remained at 50,000 annually (a number exceeded in almost every year since its establishment in 1980) and the number for asylees doubled to 10,000 (another cap often exceeded). Rather than a liberalization of policy, these numerical changes were an attempt to bring the law into alignment with reality.

---

*Many visitors work, but they do so illegally. Students are a third category of nonimmigrant immigrants: they may work at jobs that have some presumed connection with their education but they must maintain their student status.

The real expansion produced by the 1990 law was in employment-related immigration, both permanent and allegedly temporary. In addition to the 140,000 annual employment-based permanent immigrants, the 1990 law provided for larger annual numbers of temporary employment-based immigrants. It authorized 131,000 H category visas, and created four new categories of temporary visas: O, P, Q, and R.* There are also temporary immigrants admitted as Exchange Visitors, Intracompany Transfers, and, of growing significance, persons admitted under the U.S.-Canada Free-Trade Agreement of 1988 and its successor, the North American Free-Trade Agreement (NAFTA) of 1993.[7]

The 1990 act also created Temporary Protected Status (TPS), which enabled the attorney general to exempt from deportation illegal alien nationals of countries that were suffering from armed conflict or natural disasters. This permits them to work and, presumably, to continue to send home remittances to their ravaged countries. TPS is not a permanent exemption from deportation, or a change in status, but a temporary reprieve issued for a fixed period of not less than six or more than eighteen months, but renewable. Congress itself granted TPS to illegal Salvadorans in the United States for eighteen months starting on July 1, 1992,[8] which the Clinton administration later extended to December 31, 1994. Both the Bush I and Clinton administrations granted TPS to hundreds of thousands of Latin Americans and a smaller number of Africans.

The final and most unusual aspect of the 1990 act was its transformation of the diversity option. Despite justified charges of favoritism, the 1990 statute continued to provide 40,000 visas annually during fiscal years 1992–94 for nationals of "certain countries" identified as having been "adversely affected" by the 1965 act and arranged it so that at least 40 percent of those slots—16,000 visas a year for three years—were reserved for Irish. The statute treated natives of Northern Ireland as if that part of Great Britain were a separate country. But after a "diversity transition" period (1992–94), diversity was made an honest program. Beginning in 1995, as many as 55,000 diversity immigrants were admissible annually. Eligible applicants had to be from nations that did *not* have a cumulative total of 50,000 immigrants in the previous five years, and no more than 3,850 "winners" could come from an eligible nation in any year.[9]

---

*For a listing of each kind of visa see Table 12.4, p. 257.

Not all lottery winners qualify for visas. In 1998, for example, only 45,499 of the 55,000 "winners" actually became immigrants. Of the winners Europe got the largest number—21,765 (44.1 percent)—more than three-quarters of them from former Eastern Bloc nations. The next largest group was from Africa: 15,025 (30 percent), a particularly significant figure since there were "only" 44,668 immigrants from Africa including every category. Diversity increased legal immigration from Africa by more than 50 percent in that year. The other quarter of 1998 diversity admissions was distributed as follows: Asia, 8,631; North America, 2,014; South America, 1,044; and Oceania, 2,014.*

The election of centrist Democrat Bill Clinton in 1992 did not seem to presage a negative turn against immigration. Immigration had not been a major campaign issue and the new president's promise to put together an administration "that looked like America"—that is, one with more women, African Americans, Hispanics, and other underrepresented groups—seemed to presage an immigrant-friendly administration. This was not to be the case. When public opinion turned strongly against immigrants, Clinton made sure that he could not be seen as "soft" on immigration, especially illegal immigration. Why public opinion changed when it did is not clear and probably reflects political opportunism more than any real or perceived difficulties with immigration. Objectively, the middle years of the 1990s have none of the characteristics generally associated with turns against immigration: the economy was expanding, unemployment was declining, and there was no widely perceived external threat.

But public opinion clearly did change. Persistent anti-immigrant propaganda from responsible and irresponsible critics had an effect. Public opinion was surely affected by the media's largely hostile accounts of what was wrong with immigration, and the results, I suspect, were cumulative. The association of immigrants with crime, heightened by the Mariel boatlift from Cuba, and Hollywood's often glamorized and overemphasized treatment of not only the Italian "mafia," but also of alleged Russian and Chinese "mafias," surely had its effects. Most of what was shown on news

---

*In no year of the 1970s and 1980s prior to 1987 did as many as 2,000 citizens of Ireland qualify for admission. For the years 1987 through 1994, largely due to the special diversity rules, there was a total of some 65,000—an average of about 8,000 a year, with a peak of 17,000 in 1994. In 1998, with its "affirmative action" status gone, there were 907 Irish immigrants. These numbers do not include citizens of Northern Ireland.

programs was even more negative than stories in the print media. There were dozens of negative and sensational stories about border crossers, including one oft-repeated clip of supposed illegal immigrants dashing across freeway traffic to safety near the San Diego–Tijuana border, apparently staged and scripted by a West German television crew. Even serious television journalism consistently sent a negative and misleading message: immigrants are economic basket cases.

Perhaps almost as effective in creating a negative image of immigrants and immigration policy was the constant depiction of the federal immigration apparatus as inept, or corrupt, or both. The phrase "a broken system" became one of two mantras for critics and reformers of every shade of opinion. (The other was "controlling our borders.") Reflecting public perceptions, the Jordan Commission's first interim report, issued shortly before the midterm elections in 1994, was titled *U.S. Immigration Policy: Restoring Credibility*.

The general perception of INS inefficiency was correct. Of the twenty government agencies that the Clinton administration identified as having a "high impact" on the American public, the INS received the lowest overall grade—"C–"—from Syracuse University's well-respected Maxwell School of Government, and was the only one of the twenty agencies that did not get a grade of better than "C" in any of the five judged categories. The school's crisp summary of the agency's problems was: "Infusion of resources doesn't solve mission conflicts, system deficiencies."[10]

And, if one looks carefully, evidence of INS incompetence can be found in its own reports. For example, the only record the government had for many of the millions of foreign visitors and other kinds of nonimmigrants is the I-94 card, the form handed out by airline personnel on flights from foreign countries to the United States, which are collected by immigration officials when alien passengers are admitted. The INS seems to have lost or misplaced all of the millions of cards for 1997; the INS has also reported the "unavailability" of these and related records for two or three months of 1979, all of 1980, and most of the data of 1981 and 1982.

INS backlogs and bottlenecks are of almost mythic proportions. Insiders routinely advise friends that, if a form is lost or misplaced, don't count on it ever being found; it is more prudent to start the paperwork over again. Doris Meissner, Commissioner of Immigration and Naturalization from October 1993 to November 2001, and clearly the best occupant of that office in decades, admitted to a *Los Angeles Times* reporter that historically the INS, "despite the thousands of committed and hardworking employees, has never had a culture that truly emphasizes the importance of service and rewards it."[11]

However well deserved the brickbats were, few were tossed at one of the major causes of the INS's ongoing problems. Neither the Maxwell School nor the Jordan Commission indicated that Congress habitually overtasked and underfunded the beleaguered agency. To be sure, in recent years Congress threw lots of money at the problem. During Meissner's seven years, for example, generally a time of a shrinking federal workforce, the number of INS employees increased 89 percent, from 18,000 to 32,000, while its budget more than doubled from $1.58 billion to $4.3 billion.[12] The vast majority of the new personnel were designated for the Border Patrol, which in the 1990s became the largest and least professional federal law enforcement agency. Congress designated much of the increased budgets for gadgetry: reinforced fences, electronic sensors, and other technological devices to be installed at heavy border-crossing points. On occasion, Congress mandated the use of complex electronic systems that had not yet been invented. Consequently, service to immigrants seeking naturalization and other legitimate requests were neglected.

The Jordan Commission's reports told Congress what it wanted to hear. An effort at balance did not disguise an emphasis on illegal immigrants and the border. Its 1994 report insisted that "The credibility of immigration policy can be measured by a simple yardstick: people who should get in, do get in; people who should not get in, are kept out; and people who are judged deportable are required to leave." And it added that "far more can and should be done to meet the twin goals of border management: preventing illegal entries while facilitating legal ones." Embracing the simplistic faith of the new-style immigration reformers, that report concluded that money, technology, reorganization, and better management could fix everything. Thus its recommendations included "a simpler, more fraud-resistant system for verifying work authorization," a "computerized registry" using everyone's social security number, and such old-fashioned remedies as more Border Patrol agents and fences, and denying many public benefits to illegal immigrants. If these "reforms" didn't work, it threatened to break up the INS.

Even before the midterm elections of 1994, Congress passed the first of four statutes in a two-year period designed to show that it could "get tough" with immigrants. The Violent Crime Control and Law Enforcement Act of

September 13, 1994, authorized the establishment of a criminal alien center to keep tabs on immigrant crime, made it easier to deport criminals and reject asylum seekers, strengthened the penalties for passport and visa offenses, and provided more money for the Border Patrol and other aspects of "border management." It also created a new type of nonimmigrant visa, the "S" visa, which allowed the attorney general to bring in alien witnesses who could provide information about terrorism, some of them probably former terrorists. Such persons became sources for the "secret evidence" used in deportation proceedings against presumed terrorists. As has been the case with those brought in under the authority of the director of the Central Intelligence Agency since the Truman administration, there is no separate public record of such immigration and it is not clear that such persons are included in the published statistical data.

The midterm election of 1994 was notable for shifting control of the House of Representatives to the Republicans who campaigned on a "contract with America," which did not mention immigration. It brought to power the Georgia Congressman Newton L. (Newt) Gingrich. Elected to Congress in 1978 he became minority whip in 1989, and Speaker of the House in 1995. Although now largely forgotten, he was, briefly, one of the most dominant figures in American politics.*

The 1994 election produced the even shorter-lived triumph of an anti-immigrant ballot measure in California, Proposition 187, "Prop 187" in common parlance. Although it was patently unconstitutional, its overwhelming adoption by the voters of the country's most populous state was a national political event. A key to its significance was its central place in the 1994 reelection campaign of Republican Governor Pete Wilson. After polls showed him trailing his Democratic opponent by 17 percentage points, he made Prop 187, created by zealous immigration reformers including Alan C. Nelson, Reagan's INS Commissioner and other former INS officials, a centerpiece of his campaign, calling it the "save our state" initiative.

Even though as a U.S. Senator Wilson had sponsored the amendment to IRCA that made it all but impossible for the INS to apprehend illegal agricultural workers on the job, his backing of Prop 187 was successful;

---

*Gingrich had a 1971 Ph.D. in history from Tulane and taught for eight years at West Georgia College without publishing significantly. He resigned from Congress, in disgrace, never taking his seat after being reelected in 1998.

Wilson was reelected governor with 55 percent of the vote while Prop 187 garnered nearly 60 percent voter approval. According to exit polls, the initiative was favored by 64 percent of white voters, 57 percent of Asian American voters, 56 percent of African Americans, and even 31 percent of Hispanic voters. It was not a straight Republican vs. Democrat battle: some California Democrats, like U.S. Senator Dianne Feinstein, backed the proposal. President Bill Clinton, who had earlier endorsed the Jordan Commission recommendations, opposed Prop 187.[13]

The triumph of Prop 187 rekindled the vigilante spirit of the old Wild West. Numerous citizens or legal residents were wrongly suspected of being illegal. Some reported being turned away from emergency rooms and pharmacies, and being harassed by police, for not having immigration documents. "A customer at a Santa Paula restaurant demanded to see the cook's green card, declaring that it was every citizen's duty to report illegals."[14]

They did not have that duty very long. Within days of the election U.S. District Judge Mariana R. Pfaelzer issued a preliminary injunction barring enforcement of most of the new statute. In 1997 she made that injunction permanent, noting, for example, that the education ban conflicted with a 1982 Supreme Court ruling and that the core of the initiative conflicted with the federal government's exclusive authority to regulate immigration. Finally, in September 1999, almost five years after it was approved by the electorate and after Wilson's successor, Gray Davis, a Democrat, had dropped the state's appeal to the U.S. Supreme Court, Judge Pfaelzer is-

---

OFFICIAL 1994 CALIFORNIA VOTER INFORMATION
PROPOSITION 187 • ILLEGAL ALIENS

Makes illegal immigrants ineligible for public social services, public health care services (unless emergency under federal law), and public school education at elementary, secondary, and post secondary levels.

Requires various state and local agencies to report persons who are suspected illegal aliens to the California Attorney General and the Immigration and Naturalization Service. Mandates California Attorney General to transmit reports to the Immigration and Naturalization Service and maintain records of such reports.

Makes it a felony to manufacture, sell or use false citizenship or residence documents.

sued a final order. All that remained of Prop 187 were two laws that criminalized the manufacture and use of false documents to conceal illegal immigration status, acts that had long been illegal under federal law.[15]

In the short run, however, the naked nativism demonstrated by Prop 187 seemed to be a key to electoral success. Nationally, most Republican politicians and many Democrats, including Bill Clinton, scrambled to align themselves with the anti-immigrant forces. But there were notable exceptions among the Republicans, none more significant, as it turned out, than then Texas Governor George W. Bush, who publicly denounced Prop 187 and similar measures. As the British magazine *The Economist* put it in 1996, Texas and California represented "two states of mind" on the immigration issue. Texas not only had a more powerful Hispanic vote but its trade relations with Mexico were much more important, relatively, than California's.[16] In Congress, a newly elected Republican senator, Michigan's Spencer Abraham, became one of his party's most effective voices for immigrants' rights.

The fallout from Prop 187 can be seen in three federal statutes passed in the months before the 1996 presidential election. Their very names indicate their intent: Antiterrorism and Effective Death Penalty Act (April 24); Personal Responsibility and Work Opportunity Reconciliation Act (August 22); and Illegal Immigration Reform and Immigrant Responsibility Act of September 30 (IIRIRA).[17] Like 1994's Violent Crime Control Act, none of the three significantly affected the numbers of persons legally permitted to enter the United States. Despite the incessant intoning about "controlling our borders," Congress, unable to agree to making effective changes in the immigration laws, "got tough" with unnaturalized legal immigrants instead. One of the unintended consequences of making border crossings more difficult was to persuade many illegal Mexican immigrants to end their long-established circular patterns of annual rotation between Mexico and the United States. Instead, they stayed in the United States, hoping for another amnesty and an opportunity to get their families north of the border.

The Antiterrorism/Death Penalty Act was in part a response to the 1990s' two major terrorist atrocities on American soil. The first, executed by immigrant Muslim terrorists, blew up part of New York City's World Trade Center in February 1993, killing six people. The second, done by a native-born Christian terrorist with U.S. Army training, destroyed the Alfred P. Murrah Federal Building in Oklahoma City, killing 168 people. We now know, all too well, how ineffective those antiterrorist provisions were. Other aspects of the law, utterly unrelated to either terrorism or the death penalty, did strip certain legal protections from unnaturalized legal immigrants in what the INS summary called "procedural improvements."

Believing that Prop 187 reflected the national mood, both parties in 1996 adopted platform planks that spoke sternly about immigration, although each used the phrase "a nation of immigrants" in the beginning of its plank. The Democrats, traditionally the party of immigrants, insisted that "we must remain a nation of laws. We cannot tolerate illegal immigration and we must stop it." And in a fantasy version of recent history the party claimed that the Clinton administration had gained control of the border. More convincingly and reflecting the party's many immigrant advocates, the platform chastised the GOP for going too far. The Democrats upbraided "the mean-spirited and short-sighted effort of Republicans in Congress to bar the children of illegal immigrants from schools" and found deplorable "those who use the need to stop illegal immigration as a pretext for discrimination."

The 1996 Republican platform was less ambiguous. Calling for "a sensible immigration policy," it attacked Bill Clinton for not being tough enough on border control and for opposing "Proposition 187 in California, which 60 percent of Californians supported." It went on to propose specific and drastic measures against legal immigrants and American-born children of illegal immigrants:

> Illegal aliens should not receive public benefits other than emergency aid, and those who become parents while illegally in the United States should not be qualified to claim benefits for their offspring. Legal immigrants should depend for assistance on their financial well-being, not the American taxpayers. Just as we require "deadbeat dads" to provide for the children they bring into the world, we should require "deadbeat sponsors" to provide for the immigrants they bring into the country. We support a constitutional amendment or constitutionally-valid legislation declaring that children born in the United States of parents who are not legally present in the United States or who are not long-term residents are not automatically citizens.[18]

In the weeks before the election Congress passed all but the most extreme immigration proposals of the Republican platform.* The August

---

* In the early 1920s California nativists of both parties advocated a constitutional amendment making the American-born children of "aliens ineligible to citizenship" [i.e., Asians] also ineligible to citizenship. The 1990s proposals would make the American-born children of illegal immigrants ineligible. Same idea, different target.

Personal Responsibility and Work Opportunity Reconciliation Act was one of the most mean-spirited acts passed by a modern American Congress. Its major provisions established restrictions on the eligibility of legal but not yet naturalized immigrants receiving "means tested" public assistance, specifically barring them from food stamps and the program of Supplemental Security Income (SSI), and established a five-year period after entry during which future legal immigrants would be similarly barred. It also enabled and encouraged states to place similar restrictions on state-run programs. These provisions affected not only unnaturalized immigrants but also their American-born—and it therefore American citizen—minor children. Further harassment was contained in the Illegal Immigration Reform and Immigrant Responsibility Act passed—like its predecessor with much Democratic support—and signed into law by Bill Clinton just days before the 1996 election. It increased border personnel, authorized construction of further barriers on the Mexican border, and stiffened penalties for various immigration law violations. Finally, in a classic example of legislative futility, it instituted three- and ten-year bars to admissibility for aliens seeking to reenter the United States after having been unlawfully present. In the overwhelming majority of cases the border authorities could not possibly identify such persons. The same statute added more than a dozen further restrictions on both legal and illegal aliens. Despite protests that focused on the restrictions of the rights of legal immigrants, candidate Clinton not only refused to apply his veto but also hailed it as "landmark reform legislation."[19]

For those who thought that emulating Prop 187 was a key to electoral success, the 1996 election provided a rude awakening. Not only did Bill Clinton—who was less hostile to immigrants—win a smashing victory, despite well-founded doubts about his sexual behavior and veracity, but a mobilized swell of Hispanic voters boded ill for supporters of draconian immigration legislation. Perhaps the most salient single result was the defeat of nine-term right-wing Republican congressman Robert K. Dornan, whose district was in the heart of "Reagan country," Southern California's Orange County, by a Hispanic Democrat, Loretta Sanchez. Although Sanchez, American-born with an MBA, won the hotly disputed election by only 984 votes, the demographic realities her victory represented set off alarm bells in Washington. By 2002 Sanchez would get 60 percent of the vote in her fourth successful campaign.

In four separate statutes passed in 1997 and 1998, Congress retreated from some of the more extreme provisions of the immigration statutes it had passed in 1996. In the August Balanced Budget Act of 1997 it restored many of the benefits legal aliens were denied in 1996.[20] Under that law "qualified aliens," a newly minted term defined as including legal permanent residents, aliens granted asylum or similar relief, aliens paroled into the United States for at least one year, certain battered family members, Cuban/Haitian entrants, Amerasians, veterans or certain active-duty personnel,* members of Indian tribes and certain Native Americans born in Canada, and those who had worked in the United States for ten years, were exempt from many of the punitive provisions of the Personal Responsibility/Work Opportunity Act passed a little less than a year previously. In November 1997, Congress continued its retreat by passing the Nicaraguan and Central American Relief Act (NACARA), which undid the negative effects of the IIRIRA Act of 1996 by allowing some 400,000 long-term "illegal residents" (another newly minted term) to gain previously denied benefits.[21] Those affected were approximately 200,000 Salvadorans, 150,000 Nicaraguans, 50,000 Guatemalans, and 5,000 Cubans.

Two more rescisions of preexisting benefits came in 1998. The first was inserted into the Agricultural Research Reform Act in February and restored eligibility for food stamps to "qualified aliens" of the same groups benefited by NACARA who were over sixty-five, under eighteen, or disabled.[22] The second was the Non-Citizen Benefit Clarification Act, passed in October,[23] which essentially restated provisions that had been enacted in the three preceding statutes. It minted yet another term, "nonqualified aliens," establishing that such persons were ineligible for food stamps, but eligible for SSI if aged and/or disabled, and withdrew from the states the right to make such aliens ineligible for Medicaid.

These rescisions signified that the turn against immigration was over, at least for a time. Part of the reason for the relatively rapid reversals was a sense, in the minds of many swing segments of the voting population, that the key provisions of the immigration statutes of the mid-1990s were simply unfair.

---

*Many alien members of the armed forces with large families earn so little that they qualify for SSI. The federal government, which barred non-citizens from airport security jobs in the aftermath of the terrorist attacks of September 11, 2001, accepts aliens in the military. Go figure.

Nowhere was this more apparent than in California. In the 1998 elections the Republicans lost all major and most minor statewide offices by near landslide proportions: the Democrat Gray Davis got 58 percent of the vote while his Republican opponent, Dan Lungren, who as state attorney general had led the defense of Prop 187, got just 38.4 percent. The Hispanic Democratic candidate for lieutenant governor, Cruz M. Bustamante, won with 52.7 percent of the vote. Even more telling, not one initiative on immigration was among the twelve that qualified for the ballot.[24]

For the rest of the Clinton years immigration was further expanded by a number of relatively minor statutes affecting immigration positively. The most significant of these was the American Competitiveness in the Twenty-first Century Act of 2000, which increased the number of H1-B visas for "specialty occupation" workers to 195,000 for fiscal years 2001 through 2003 and increased allowable visas in that category by an indeterminate amount for 1999 and 2000.

The pro-immigration forces were greatly bolstered in early 2000 when the Executive Council of the American Federation of Labor/Congress of Industrial Organizations (AFL/CIO) announced its support for a blanket amnesty for illegal immigrants and an end to most sanctions against employers who hired them. This reversed labor's traditional anti-immigrant policies.

Reactions from labor's enemies and friends of long standing demonstrated that it had turned an important policy corner. A representative of the United States Chamber of Commerce praised the council's action. "It's certainly a departure from organized labor's traditional position, which was that an increased number of immigrant workers is bad for domestic workers . . . This is an area where the business community and organized labor can work together." Conversely, Vernon M. Briggs, Jr., a senior professor at the Cornell University School of Labor and Industrial Relations and who worked hand-in-glove with the anti-immigration Washington think tank, the Center for Immigration Studies, argued that "the unions have made a terrible mistake in putting the interests of immigrant workers first."[25]

It seemed clear as the century came to an end that the relatively heavy immigration levels of the previous decades would continue and that, with labor now supporting immigration, it would be immigration business as usual. Perhaps the simplest way to show what "business as usual" entailed is to examine, in detail, the total number of foreign persons—or, as the INS calls them, "aliens"—formally admitted to the United States in the end-of-century year 2000.

Leaving aside, for the moment, the vexed matter of illegal immigrants, the question "How many immigrants came to America in that year?" can be answered in various ways, with vastly different numbers. The number most frequently cited for the year 2000 is 849,807: that is, the number of persons formally admitted to the United States as, in the language of the INS, immigrants. And as long as we are dealing with legal definitions, that number is sufficient. But if we ask "How many people came to America in 2000?" very different numbers have to be considered.

One is 34,539,889: this is the number of persons formally admitted to the United States, adding, again in the language of the INS, 33,690,082 nonimmigrants to the 849,807 immigrants. To be sure, 90.5 percent are "visitors for pleasure or business," almost all of whom leave fairly quickly. But embedded among the visitors are some who manage to change their status legally, as well as probably a majority of the estimated 275,000 new illegal immigrants who enter every year. These change from legal "visitors" to illegal immigrants if they are still in the country when their visas expire. We might also call them "visa overstayers" to differentiate them from those who came in as surreptitious entrants or what the INS terms "EWIs," persons who "entered without inspection."

But the remaining 9.5 percent of nonimmigrants, amounting to 3,178,957 individuals—more than three times the number of the year's legal "immigrants"—entered the United States legally in a bewildering number of categories, most with the possibility of changing their legal category from nonimmigrant to immigrant at some future date. It would be more precise to call most of these people "potential legal immigrants," a term that might also apply to all the illegal immigrants in the country at any time. The INS calls the process of changing from one category to another "adjustment of status." During 2000 an absolute majority of the 849,807 legal "immigrants"—442,405 or 52 percent—were not, in the normal sense of the word, immigrants in 2000. Rather, they were persons who in some prior year had been admitted in a nonimmigrant category or who had entered illegally, and had their status legally changed in 2000. The INS knew that 152,696 of its change-of-status "immigrants" for 2000 had entered in the 1990s, and that 26,151 persons had entered before 1990, but it was unable to tell in what year 217,522 persons awarded resident status in 2000 had entered the country. This amounted to more than half—53 percent—of the adjustment for 2000.[26]

Not quite 250,000 of the adjusters were family-sponsored; nearly 85,000 were employment-based; and some 60,000 were refugees and asylees. Another 40,000 were in fact refugees, but they were allowed in under other programs, chiefly NACARA.[27] Thus a third, serious number to be considered is 3,586,359: 407,402 new immigrant arrivals plus 3,178,957 new potential immigrant arrivals.*

And, to inject a ridiculous note, one could also say that 500,000,000 people actually came to America in 2000: that is the total number of border crossings by non-U.S. citizens in 2000 as estimated by serious researchers. They were mostly Mexicans and Canadians who came briefly to shop, work, study, and play, and many individuals made literally hundreds of regular border crossings. Theoretically such border crossers stay within twenty-five miles of the border: some of them do become illegal immigrants.[28] I mention this figure only to underscore how irresponsible it is to speak about controlling our borders.

We know a great deal, statistically, about both immigrants and nonimmigrants, and almost nothing, apart from common knowledge, about casual border crossers. Let us begin with what the INS calls "immigrants" as shown in Table 12.2a. Combining "family-sponsored" and "immediate relatives" plus the small group of "children born abroad to alien residents" we see that just over two-thirds—584,159 or 68.7 percent—gained admission because they were related to people who were already here. One-eighth of the INS "immigrants"—107,024 persons or 12.6 percent—were "employment-based." To be sure, some of the latter group had relatives here, and many of the former came to work, but we are concerned with how they got in. Almost a ninth—92,786 persons—were "refugees," "asylees," "NACARA immigrants," or "parolees" admitted for humanitarian reasons or reasons of state. The remaining 7.6 percent were divided among the 50,000 "diversity immigrants" (lottery winners), 12,000 persons whose previous removal orders were cancelled usually as a result of acts of Congress, such as NACARA, and 269 persons who had successfully applied under the registry provisions of the law. This last group had been illegally in

---

*To be sure, there are categories among the "potential immigrants" from which very few persons are able to change their status, for example those on transit visas: 437,671 persons in 2000.

the country since before January 1, 1972, and were not ineligible for immigrant status and therefore were able to apply for and receive what can be called an amnesty *in petto.** Finally there were 911 persons whom the INS was unable to classify.

TABLE 12.2a
IMMIGRANTS ADMITTED BY MAJOR CATEGORY
OF ADMISSION, 2000

Category

All Categories	849,807
New Arrivals	407,402
Adjustments of status	442,405
Preference Immigrants	342,304
Family-sponsored Immigrants	235,280
Employment-based Preferences	107,024
Immediate Relatives of U.S. Citizens	347,870
Refugees and Asylees	65,941
Refugees	59,083
Asylees	6,858
Other Immigrants	93,271
Diversity Programs	50,945
NACARA	23,641
Cancellation of removal	12,349
Parolees	3,201
Children born abroad to alien residents	1,009
Registry, entry prior to 1/1/72	269
Miscellaneous	911

Source: Adapted from INS, 2000 *Statistical Yearbook,* Table 4, p. 29.

Taking all the year's immigrants as a group, as Table 12.2b shows, 55.5 percent were female, 44.5 percent male. Like most groups of migrants they were clustered in the middle years of life with more than two-fifths of each gender between twenty and thirty-nine years of age, and very few either under ten or over sixty years of age.

*When I explained this to my daughter, a very practical business executive, she responded: "I see. The government figures that if you can survive in this country long enough, you deserve citizenship." That is a good instrumental interpretation, but not one used by Congress.

TABLE 12.2b
IMMIGRANTS ADMITTED BY AGE AND GENDER, 2000

	Female	%	Male	%
Total	470,854	55.5	378,259	44.5
Under 10	44,366	9.4	40,752	10.8
10–19	74,750	15.9	77,862	20.6
20–39	219,389	46.6	164,896	43.6
40–59	95,081	20.2	68,322	18.1
60+	36,132	7.7	5,444	6.7
Unknown age	1,136	—	983	—
Unknown Gender	694			

Source: Adapted from INS, *Statistical Yearbook 2000*, Table 12, p. 62.

Table 12.2c shows where the immigrants came from. Two-fifths of all immigrants came from North America, with half of them, one fifth of all legal immigrants, coming from Mexico. Most of the rest of the North Americans were either from the Caribbean (88,198 or 10.3 percent) or from Central America (64,442 or 7.8 percent). If the geographical concept of circum-Caribbean is used, and immigrants from Colombia, Guyana, and Venezuela are added in, that region's percentage of all "immigrants" amounts to just over a fifth. Propinquity clearly has its advantages.

TABLE 12.2c
IMMIGRANTS ADMITTED BY REGION AND
MAJOR NATION, 2000

Region/Country	Number	% of Total
All Countries	849,807	
Europe	132,480	15.6
Russia	17,110	
Ukraine	15,810	
United Kingdom	13,385	
Bosnia-Herzegovina	11,828	
Asia	265,400	31.2
China (PRC)	45,652	
Philippines	42,474	

Region/Country	Number	% of Total
Vietnam	26,747	
Korea	15,830	
Pakistan	14,585	
Africa	*44,731*	*5.3*
Nigeria	7,853	
Egypt	4,461	
Ghana	4,344	
Ethiopia	4,061	
Morocco	3,636	
Oceania	*5,136*	*0.6*
Australia	2,059	
Fiji	1,487	
New Zealand	972	
North America	*344,805*	*40.6*
Mexico	173,919	20.5
(Caribbean)	88,198	10.3
(Central America)	66,442	7.8
Nicaragua	24,029	
El Salvador	22,578	
Haiti	22,364	
Cuba	20,831	
Dominican Republic	17,536	
Canada	16,210	
Jamaica	16,000	
South America	*56,074*	*6.6*
Colombia	14,498	
Peru	9,613	
Brazil	6,959	
Guyana	5,746	
Venezuela	4,716	

Source: Adapted from INS, *2000 Statistical Yearbook*, Table 11, p. 54.

Just under a third, 31.2 percent, came from Asia, with 54.7 percent of all Asians, or 145,288, coming from the top five nations: the People's Republic of China, the Philippines, Vietnam, Korea, and Pakistan. Europe accounted for nearly one immigrant in six, 15.6 percent, with Eastern European nations dominating, while South America (56,074), Africa (44,731) and Oceania (808) combined had only about an eighth, 12.5 percent.

A very different pattern of geographical distribution occurred in the diversity program, which had overcome its origins as a thinly disguised affirmative action program for Western Europeans in general and Irish in particular. In 2000, the diversity program limit was 50,000. It was now intended to provide opportunities to get immigrant visas to persons who lived in countries with relatively few recent immigrants. A country from which as many as 50,000 persons had come in the past five years is ineligible to participate in the diversity program. Each of the eligible countries is assigned to one of six regions and limits are determined by the INS for each region. The limits are calculated annually using a formula based on immigrant admissions during the preceding five years and the population total of the region. The maximum visa limit per country is 3,850.

The regional numbers and percentages for the 50,000 diversity admissions of 2000 were:

Europe: 25,585 (48.3 percent)—more than 85 percent of European visas went to winners in Eastern European nations;

Asia: 7,244 (14.2 percent);

Africa: 15,810 (31 percent), which was just over a third of all immigrants from Africa, so the program increased African immigration by just over 50 percent;

North and South America: just over 1,200 diversity visas each, a total of 4.8 percent;

Oceania: 808, 1.5 percent.[29]

The INS's "nonimmigrant" categories are shown in Table 12.3. The whole category underwent spectacular growth in recent years, while the annual number of actual immigrants has never exceeded maximums established early in the twentieth century, when the population was about a third of that in 2000. As late as 1980 the total number of nonimmigrants never significantly exceeded 8 million in any one year. In the intervening twenty years, most of which were marked by Barbara Jordan's "furor" over immigration, annual "immigration," as measured by the INS, ranged relatively narrowly between 544,000 in 1984 and 916,000 in 1996.* In that same twenty-year period the numbers of nonimmigrants more than tripled to some 33.7 million persons, a phenomenon little discussed in the press or Congress.

*This ignores the swollen IRCA amnesty years of 1989–92, which are analyzed elsewhere.

TABLE 12.3
NONIMMIGRANTS ADMITTED BY MAJOR CATEGORY OF ADMISSION, 2000

Category			*Adjustment of Status, 2000*
All Categories		33,690,082	442,405
Temporary visitors for business and pleasure		30,511,125	75,553
Students	659,081		
Students' spouses and children	40,872		
	699,953	699,953	16,161
Employment and business based		1,731,123	
Temporary workers and trainees	543,950		
" " spouses and children	128,993		
	672,943	672,943	44,598
Intra-company transferees	294,658		
" " spouses and children	132,105		
	426,763	426,763	12,467
Exchange visitors	304,225		
" " spouses and children	45,518		
	349,743	349,743	2,867
Treaty traders, investors & families		168,214	NR
NAFTA workers		113,460	NR
Other categories		745,881	
Transit aliens		437,671	NR
Foreign government & NATO officials		152,363	NR
International representatives		97,555	NR
International media		33,918	NR
Fiancés(ées) of U.S. citizens		23,671	12,047
Other and unknown		703	703

Source: Adapted from INS, *2000 Statistical Yearbook*, Table 35, p. 142.

As noted, the bulk of these, the 30.5 million tourists, need not concern us, although we should remind ourselves that in all probability a couple of hundred thousand or more simply stayed on as illegal immigrants; and in 2000, for example, some 75,000 persons who had previously entered as "visitors for pleasure or business" were able to adjust their status to "resident aliens" and thus became immigrants in the eyes of the INS. Still the overwhelming majority of visitors depart on or before the expiration of their visas. That still leaves nearly 3.3 million persons legally admitted to the United States for longer periods than the then-typical six-month visitor's visa. Most of these are in categories that are subject to future "adjustment."

Nearly 700,000 students and their families entered on visas that are good until they complete their degree(s) and may be extended for postgraduate training and employment. Every year large numbers of them are able to adjust their status: more than 16,000 did so in 2000; almost a quarter were Chinese.

In 2000 more than half of all student visas, 55.3 percent, were used by Asians, with Japanese, Chinese, Koreans, and Indians accounting for more than 70 percent of the subset.* It is clear that Chinese students in particular have a great propensity to adjust their status, aided in part by the previously noted Chinese Student Protection Act of 1992.

The fact that many students from lesser-developed nations manage to stay on in the United States and other more-developed nations has long been described as a "brain drain" on their homelands and, to a lesser degree, as a "brain gain" for the host nations. Recently, however, students, professionals, and technological entrepreneurs from India and China have been moving back and forth, so the term "brain circulation" is becoming appropriate.[30]

One misleading aspect of the State Department/INS data on foreign students is that it understates significantly the numbers of students from both Canada and Mexico, which are reported at 18,478 and 17,698 respectively. These figures ignore the significant number of students who lived close enough to the border to be commuters and who did not, in 2000, need to have student visas. Students and their families are the most numer-

---

* The student visa data, compiled by the State Department, merged students from the PRC and Taiwan as "Chinese" but listed those from Hong Kong separately. The adjustment of status data, compiled by the INS, which did not have a "one China" policy, lists them separately. I call students from all three places Chinese, but students of Chinese ethnicity from other places are included in the figures of their nation of nationality; *e.g.*, the nearly 5,000 students admitted from Singapore in 2000.

ous single group of long-term nonimmigrants, which are listed and enumerated in Tables 12.3 and 12.4.[31]

TABLE 12.4
TEMPORARY WORKERS ADMITTED, 2000

Type	*Number*
Registered nurses (H-1A)	565
Specialty workers (H-1B)	355,605
Agricultural workers (H-2A)	33,292
Nonagricultural workers (H-2B)	51,462
Industrial trainees (H-3)	3,208
Exchange visitors (J-1)	304,225
Intracompany transferees (L-1)	294,658
Workers with extraordinary ability (O-1)	21, 746
Helpers of O-1 workers (O-2)	3,627
Internationally recognized athletes/entertainers (P-1)	40,920
Artists in exchange programs (P-2)	4,227
Artists in culturally unique programs (P-3)	11,230
Workers in cultural exchange programs (Q-1)	2,726
Workers in religious occupations (R-1)	15,342
NAFTA workers (TN)	91,279
Total	1,234,112

Source: INS, *Statistical Yearbook*, 2000, Table 37, p. 150.

Of all these groups the most controversial are specialty workers who enter on H-1B visas. Congress has enacted particularly nontransparent legislation about them.* The American Competitiveness and Workforce Improvement Act of 1998 increased the number of new H-1B visas from 65,000 to 115,000 in fiscal years 1999 and 2000, and reduced it slightly to 107,500 for 2001.[32] In October 2000, Congress, in the American Competitiveness in the Twenty-first Century Act (ACA21), retroactively provided that any H-1B petitions filed after March 22, 2000 (the day the previously legislated cap of 115,000 had been reached), and before September 1, 2000, regardless of when approved, would not count toward the 115,000 cap. Instead these would be counted as if they had occurred during the INS's fiscal year 2000, which ended on September 30, 2000: all told,

---

*It was necessary to read and construe four separate footnotes and two seemingly contradictory tables in the INS *Statistical Yearbook*, 2000, to write the following paragraph. See fns. 1, 6, and 7, pp. 131–32 and fn. 1, Table F, p. 131, and Table 37, p. 150, of that volume.

365,000 H-1B visas were approved in fiscal 2000.[33] Thus, although the law still stated that the cap on new H-1B applications for 2000 was 115,000, it was overridden without being repealed. In addition, neither ACA21 nor any prior law put a cap on renewals of H-1B visas, although there was a theoretical six-year limitation for any one worker. In effect, this has meant that there is no way to discover how many H-1B visa holders are legally in the country. The INS admits that it is clueless about this and many other details concerning H-1B workers: it knows even less about H-2A and H-2B workers, and still less about the 129,000 dependents of temporary workers admitted in 2000.

The H-1B workers are the aristocracy and the H-2A and H-2B workers are plebeians, although some H-2B workers are overseas students who come here during their vacations. An employer's request for H-1B workers requires a separate petition for each worker sought, and, although the requirements are stiff and the petitions must be approved by the Department of Labor and the INS, the great preponderance of petitions submitted, 257,640—82.6 percent—were stamped approved. H-1B nonimmigrants are approved for a maximum of three years, with a maximum three-year extension possible. About 53 percent of the petitions approved in 2000 were new as opposed to continuing. Almost half, 44 percent, of these new H-1B workers, however, were already in the United States in some other nonimmigrant category.

The greatest occupational concentration of H-1B workers—some 42 percent—was in computer and computer-related industries. Asian Indians dominate this group: in INS terminology, 37 percent of all new 2000 H-B1 "beneficiaries" were born in India, had a bachelor's or master's degree, and were in a computer-related occupation. And not just the Indians were well educated. Ninety-eight percent of all H-1B workers had bachelor's degrees, 41 percent had achieved master's degrees, 3 percent had professional degrees, while 7 percent held doctorates. Indians loomed large in the computer sector and in the whole H-1B program in 2000: they were 29 percent of all H-1B workers. The next-largest group, amounting to some 32,000, came from the United Kingdom, while there were 17,000 Chinese (PRC, Taiwan, and Hong Kong combined), 15,000 French, 14,000 Germans, and 11,000 Japanese. No other nation provided as many as 10,000 H-1B workers.

H-1B workers are well compensated. The highest-paid were a few fashion models earning a median annual salary of $130,000; the lowest-paid H-1B workers were educators under twenty-five years of age, whose median wage was $28,000. For all H-1B workers the median annual salary was $52,800.[34]

If we look at compensation by nation of origin, those from Western nations received higher compensation than those from Asian nations. Workers from the United Kingdom, Canada, France, and Germany received median salaries of $70,000, $66,000, $57,000, and $55,000, respectively, while the highest-paid group of Asian workers, the Indians, received on average only $54,000; lower-paid Asian workers from the PRC, Taiwan, and Japan received median salaries of $53,000, $47,000, and $36,000, respectively. Older and more experienced workers tended to get higher pay.

We have no data regarding the gender of H-1B workers, but there is every reason to believe that the entire group was dominated by males: the INS data for all temporary workers and trainees show that 77 percent were male; similar percentages were registered for all nontourist "nonimmigrant" entrants.

The INS is almost completely silent about temporary workers with H-2A and H-2B visas. As with most visas for temporary employment, the employer, not the worker, applies and those visas are for jobs at the lower end of the economic ladder. The best indication of this is the places from which the H-2 workers come. In 2000 there were almost 85,000 H-2 workers: 33,000 agricultural workers (H-2A) and 51,000 nonagricultural (H-2B). Eighty-two percent of the agricultural workers came from Mexico, and another 13 percent from other parts of North America. There is a little more diversity among the nonagricultural temporary workers, but North America and Mexico still provided disproportionate shares: Mexicans constituted a little more than half of the total with another quarter from the rest of North America. The remaining 22 percent were widely distributed, largely among Western nations. Most of the 98 Austrians, for example, were probably employed at ski resorts.[35]

Immigration After 9/11

The business as usual described in the previous chapter was a far cry from the situation that prevailed at the beginning of the century, although, superficially, the numbers of "immigrants" were not that different. In the first decade of the century, 1901–10, 8,795,386 immigrants entered the United States: in the final decade, 1991–2000, the number supplied by the INS was 9,095,417. That similarity, of course, is an illusion, a chimera deliberately fostered by the Aesopian language of the immigration statutes crafted by legislators and bureaucrats.

As late as the first years of the twentieth century, immigration to the United States was a relatively simple affair, unless you were Chinese or had an immediately apparent disqualifying physical or mental defect. The vast majority of the nearly 9 million immigrants came to work or to join working family members already present in the United States, and probably a third of them returned to Europe, whence almost all of them came. Those who came as visitors, as opposed to casual border crossers, mostly traveled in first class and were not even enumerated, much less classified: their presumed class and social standing were all the identification they needed. There was no such thing as an American visa.

One apparent relative constant is the amount of emigration from the United States; that is "immigrants," both citizen and noncitizen, who have left. The government has never been enthusiastic about counting them. Emigration is perhaps the most "un-American" act, according to the standard mythos. There was no tabulation at all of persons emigrating from the United States until 1908 and the government discontinued counting emigrants in 1957. However, the most sophisticated estimates suggest that over the course of the century, about three "emigrants" left for every ten "immigrants" who arrived. For the first nine decades of the century the notion is that a total of 37.9 million "immigrants" arrived and 11.9 million departed, giving a net "immigration" of 26 million, an annual net average of about 290,000.[1]

Apart from the actual difference in numbers, perhaps nothing so clearly and simply demonstrates the increased complexity of coming to America in our own time, as opposed to a century ago, than the ports of entry. In 1901, and for many years after that, immigration meant New York City and Ellis Island: in the century's first year 80 percent of all immigrants landed either on Ellis Island or on one of the piers of New York proper.[2] In 2000 ports had become airports and New York's airports (including the one in Newark, New Jersey, just across the Hudson) received the most, 6.2 million, or some 18 percent, of all "immigrants" and "nonimmigrants." Seven other entry points took in more than a million foreigners each. In rank order they were: Miami, 4.4; Los Angeles, 3.6; Honolulu, 2.0; Chicago, 1.7; San Francisco, 1.7; Agana (Guam), 1.2; and Atlanta, 1.1. Entry points were so widely distributed that the fourteen largest accounted for a little less than four-fifths of the total, about 78 percent.[3]

The number and variety of these end-of-century locations indicate both where immigrants are coming from—Asia and Latin America—and where in the United States they are settling. In 1900 the predominantly European immigration settled chiefly in the northeastern and north central states in the area bounded by Boston and Baltimore on the Atlantic Coast to the Mississippi River. In 2000 two-thirds of all immigrants resided in one of six states: California, New York, Florida, Texas, Illinois, and New Jersey, and one-fifth of them settled in either New York City or Los Angeles.

Despite these contrasts—which, it seems to me, overwhelm the continuities—as the twenty-first century began it was reasonable to assume, as most of us usually do, that the future would, in most respects, resemble the past. Yet there were also good reasons to believe that the new president might bring a more realistic approach to immigration with him from Texas, particularly with regard to policies affecting Mexico and Mexican immigration.

The stated immigration policies of the first seven and a half months of the administration of George W. Bush represented a very different approach from those of his immediate predecessors regardless of party. Bush made it clear that the administration saw Mexico as a partner rather than a threat. He held a "summit" with the new president of Mexico, Vicente Fox, who later addressed the U.S. Congress. Although much of Bush's initial notions about immigration as articulated in his first budget message were typical immigration-reform rhetoric—strengthen border control and enforcement, detain and remove illegal aliens, restructure the INS—his remarks about immigration were prefaced by an extremely sympathetic passage:

> The United States is a Nation of immigrants. Unfortunately, today when new immigrants arrive on our shores, their first experience is often one of frustration and anxiety. The Administration believes that legal immigrants should be greeted with open arms, rather than endless lines. We must be responsive to those who seek to immigrate to this country by legal means, and to those who have emigrated and now seek to become U.S. citizens.[4]

In addition, the administration clearly floated trial balloons suggesting that some kind of a general amnesty was in the works.

But the September 11, 2001, terrorist attacks on the World Trade Center and the Pentagon put immigration liberalization on hold and may well have triggered or exacerbated an enduring economic downturn. Although many persons insisted that 9/11, as it came to be called, "changed everything," it is now clear that in spite of the traumatic shock of the attack, color-coded terrorist alerts, a brief recession, and a distinct slowing of the national economy, the same economic and social forces that had produced the burgeoning of American immigration in the last half of the twentieth century were continuing.

The one victory for hard-line immigration reformers was the abolition of the INS, which was put out of its misery on March 1, 2003. Ironically the "sin" that was the final nail in the INS's coffin was not of its doing. The Saudi perpetrators of the 9/11 attacks entered the United States either on student visas or under the Visa Waiver program: though the INS advised Congress against adopting the latter program, it took the blame for its use by the terrorists. The INS was folded into the new conglomerate Department of Homeland Security (DHS) and trisected into separate entities: a Bureau of Customs and Border Protection (BCBP), a Bureau of Immigration and Customs Enforcement (BICE), and a Bureau of Citizenship and

Immigration Services (BCIS).* All reported to the DHS Undersecretary for Border and Transportation Security, Asa Hutchinson, a fifty-two-year-old former Republican congressman from Arkansas and graduate of Bob Jones University. On assuming his post Hutchinson promised great changes and seemed to believe that all of the immigration-control problems could be solved, eventually, by better communication, improved organization, and more automated equipment.[5] Hutchinson had made similar promises—without noticeably positive results—when he left Congress to become Director of the Drug Enforcement Administration in August 2001.

The man Bush originally appointed as Commissioner of the INS, James W. Ziglar, issued a warning in a newspaper "op-ed" piece on the occasion of the INS's demise. Noting that after 9/11 "the nation has understandably placed unprecedented focus on law enforcement and border security," Ziglar pointed out that

> while this focus on national security is appropriate and wise, there is also a continuing need for immigration officials in the Department of Homeland Security to maintain, and even strengthen, the INS' traditional service function. Indeed, the Department of Homeland Security should consider taking advantage of the opportunity to begin a dialogue on our immigration policies and find new ways to better assimilate immigrants into our culture. This will not be easy, and it is not a natural fit for this new department. The law creating the Department of Homeland Security spells out its security mission in great detail. But the role this agency will play in serving immigrants and visitors—a role that helps to boost our economy, enrich our culture and secure our moral standing in the world—is barely mentioned.[6]

Ziglar's concerns may have been triggered by the prosecutorial posture of his successor as INS commissioner, Michael Garcia. A federal prosecutor for nine years, Garcia became head of BICE in March 2003.[†]

It was fairly clear that although the administrative deck had been reshuffled, the same cards are in play and most of the same rules still apply. As one of its last acts in late February the INS issued what *Immigration Daily* called a "Welcome" brochure explaining the new acronyms to immigration law-

---

*INS employees speculated, in the weeks before the shift, whether they were going to be assigned to the "keep 'em out" bureaus or to the "let 'em in" bureau.

†Gossip in Washington reported that during Garcia's initial INS briefing he was informed that the INS's malfunctioning SEVIS system, intended to track foreign students, was indicating that 120,000 students were not in compliance with new regulations. Garcia wanted to know why they hadn't all been arrested.

yers. By and large, the former INS employees did the same old jobs in the new administrative structure.[7]

Although most of the proponents of the "abolition" of the INS and its encapsulation within the new conglomerate DHS claimed that this consolidated the administration of immigration more rationally, such was not the case. Not only was the trifurcation of functions a violation of most of the maxims of administrative theory, but there were still four other government departments — State, Labor, Justice, and Health and Human Services — that retained important responsibilities for immigrant selection and processing. A more rational reorganization would have created a separate cabinet department for immigration and placed the Washington officials dealing with immigration in one building under unified leadership instead of parceling them out all over town and inserting them into an organization in which immigration is, at best, a stepchild.

One apparent result of the turmoil within the INS in the months before the reshuffle was the cessation of data about the number of immigrants and nonimmigrants admitted. As of mid-March 2003, there were data about post–9/11 deportations and removals but none about post–9/11 admissions. It seems clear, however, that despite the difficulties faced by persons who are or look "Middle Eastern," immigration was fairly heavy. This was confirmed, at least in part, by a regular Census Bureau report on the foreign-born population, issued in March 2003, which indicated that in the eight months immediately following 9/11 immigration flows, both legal and illegal, were similar to those of the 1990s. In the two years since the 2000 census, the percentage of foreign-born in the population had risen from 11.1 percent to 11.5 percent.[8]

That this was the case under the unsettled conditions then prevailing is testimony to the continuing attraction of the United States as a place to work and live, and of a growing awareness of immigration's vital significance to the functioning of the American economy. As Federal Reserve Chairman Alan Greenspan noted:

> Immigration . . . could prove an even more potent antidote for slowing growth in the working-age population. As the influx of foreign workers in response to the tight labor markets of the 1990s showed, immigration does respond to labor shortages.[9]

The real population threat for mature economies is not the old Malthusian bugaboo of too many people, but instead the shortage of workers, skilled and unskilled, in the so-called first world, the inevitable result of falling birthrates and extended life spans. The following pair of demographic graphs for foreign-born and native-born Americans as of March 2002 shows where the extra workers are coming from. Nations like Germany and Japan, which have no tradition of immigration and are highly resistant to it, are much more likely to suffer from these shortages—which can have devastating effects on social insurance programs—than does an immigrant country like the United States. Simply put, the nativist approach to immigration, which sees it as a threat, is not only illiberal but, if adopted, could be disastrous to the entire economy.[10]

CHART 13.1

POPULATION BY NATIVITY, AGE, AND SEX: 2002

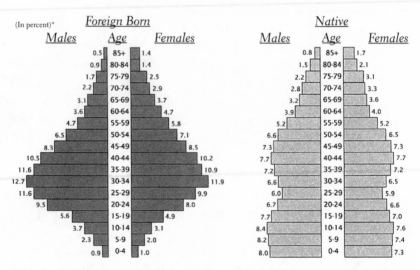

*Each bar represents the percent of the foreign-born (native) population who were within the specified age group and of the specified sex.
Source: U.S. Census Bureau, Current Population Survey, March 2002.

Since more and more persons are becoming aware of the force of this argument, the appeals of nativists of all kinds have been weakened. One would have expected 9/11, plus the economic downturn, to have had devastating effects on immigration flows and attitudes toward immigration. But as Doris Meissner noted, "The single most remarkable development post–September 11, from an immigration standpoint, is that we had no debate or serious effort to shut down immigration."[11] The long-term view, of course, may be very different.

It will be years, if not decades, before we can properly assess the impact and significance of the injustices that the American government inflicted ◉ on immigrants who were prosecuted and persecuted because of their origins, not their activities, in the twenty months following 9/11, twenty months during which not a single act of foreign terrorism occurred in the United States. For a long time it was almost impossible to obtain any accurate information about how many immigrants had been detained, but on June 2, 2003, the Department of Justice's Inspector General, Glenn A. Fine, issued a devastating report on the arrest and confinement of 762 immigrants "in connection with the FBI terrorism investigation," available on his office's website. While many were discovered to be in the country illegally—mostly visa overstayers—and were eventually deported, not one was even charged with anything in connection with the events of 9/11 or any other terrorist activity.

Many were held for months, deprived of the right to counsel, verbally and physically abused, tried, and in some cases deported in secret. It was a shocking revelation of the DoJ's violations of its own rules. The Department's spin-lady, public affairs director Barbara Comstock, insisted that:

> Under these unprecedented and extraordinary circumstances, the law was scrupulously followed and respected while aggressively protecting innocent Americans from another terrorist attack.

But legal scholar David Cole, writing in the next Sunday's *Washington Post*, pointed out that the Attorney General was determined to have "preventive" law and:

> [since] in the criminal justice system, individuals cannot be arrested and tried in secret . . . Ashcroft turned to immigration law . . . to arrest people on no charges at all, and to hold them for many weeks before they were charged and given any hearing before a judge . . . The American public would not stand for such measures if they were applied broadly. Had Ashcroft locked up hundreds of U.S. citizens unconnected to terrorism under similar conditions, the political and legal reaction would have been swift and sharp. But foreign nationals do not vote. And by targeting foreigners, the government reassures the citizenry that "our" rights need not be sacrificed in the name of national security; it is enough to sacrifice "their" rights.

While some may think that this is a storm in a teacup—analogies with World War II incarceration of Japanese Americans are overblown if understandable—it is merely one more bitter fruit of policies begun as part of Chinese exclusion. To quote Lucy Salyer again:

> [In the struggle to exclude Chinese] government officials . . . persuaded Congress and the Supreme Court that the nation's gates could be effectively guarded only if they were allowed full authority and discretion over immigration policy without interference from the federal courts.

Notes

1. The Beginnings of Immigration Restriction, 1882–1917

1. E. P. Hutchinson, *Legislative History of American Immigration Policy, 1798–1965* (Philadelphia: University of Pennsylvania Press, 1981), chs. 2 and 3.
2. For the concept of settler societies see the work of the Australian scholar Donald Denoon, especially *Settler Capitalism: The Dynamics of Dependent Developing in the Southern Hemisphere* (New York: Cambridge University Press, 1983).
3. Address to the Members of the Volunteer Association of Ireland, December 2, 1783. John C. Fitzpatrick, ed., *The Writings of George Washington* (Washington: GPO, 1931), 27: 254. At the end of the Truman administration a federal commission used the phrase "whom we shall welcome" as the title of its pro-immigration report (see ch. 6).
4. James D. Richardson, ed., *Messages and Papers of the Presidents* (Washington: Bureau of National Literature and Art, 1903), 4: 41.
5. Act of Mar. 26, 1790 (1 *Stat* 103). Although who could become naturalized went virtually unchanged, the time required for naturalization yo-yoed. The 1790 act required two years; in 1795 it was upped to five; in 1798, as part of the Alien and Sedition Acts furor, it was boosted to fourteen years. In 1802 the Jeffersonians went back to five years, where it has remained.
6. For two examples see Roger Daniels, "Heco, Joseph" and "Wing, Yung" in John A. Garraty, ed., *American National Biography* (New York: Oxford University Press, 2000).
7. Act of Mar. 2, 1819 (3 *Stat.* 488). There had been a similar provision in the Alien Act of 1798, but that act expired in 1800.
8. John Higham, *Strangers in the Land: Patterns of American Nativisim, 1860–1925* (New Brunswick, NJ: Rutgers University Press, 1955), 4.

9. Leonard W. Labaree, ed., *The Papers of Benjamin Franklin* (New Haven: Yale University Press, 1961), 4: 234. For a different view see Philip Gleason, "Trouble in the Colonial Melting Pot," *Journal of American Ethnic History* 20 (Fall 2000).

10. *Smith v. Turner* and *Norris v. Boston*, 48 U.S. 283 (1849).

11. Tyler Anbinder, *Nativism and Slavery: The Northern Know Nothings and the Politics of the 1850s* (New York: Oxford University Press, 1991) is the best account, but for the broader picture of early nineteenth-century religious nativism the pioneering account by Ray Allen Billington, *The Protestant Crusade, 1800–1860* (New York: Macmillan, 1938) is still of value.

12. Donald L. Kinzer, *An Episode in Anti-Catholicism: The American Protective Association* (Seattle: University of Washington Press, 1964).

13. The act of Apr. 9, 1866, provided that "All persons born in the United States and not subject to any foreign power, excluding Indians not taxed, are declared to be citizens of the United States," but as it was not litigated its meaning is not clear.

14. Nineteen statutes or parts of statutes amended the naturalization law prior to the act of July 14, 1870, but none affected the statutory limitation of naturalization to whites only. James H. Kettner, *The Development of American Citizenship, 1608–1870* (Chapel Hill: University of North Carolina Press, 1978) is the best guide to naturalization law prior to 1870, but largely ignores practice.

15. Najia Aarim, *Chinese Immigrants, African Americans, and Racial Anxiety in the United States, 1848–82* (Urbana: University of Illinois Press, 2003) is a brilliant revisionist analysis of the racism of the era.

16. Winfield J. Davis, *History of Political Conventions in California, 1849–1892* (Sacramento: California State Library, 1893), 265, 260, 307–8.

17. William M. Mallory, comp., *Treaties, Conventions, International Acts, Protocols, and Agreements between the United States of America and Other Powers, 1776–1909* (Washington: GPO, 1910), 1: 234–6.

18. Henry George, New York *Tribune*, May 1, 1869.

19. Reproduced in John R. Commons et al., eds., *A Documentary History of American Industrial Society* (Cleveland: A. H. Clark, 1910), 9: 81.

20. Lennie A. Cribbs, "The Memphis Chinese Labor Convention, 1869," *West Tennessee Historical Society Papers* (1983): 176–83. See also the leading work on Chinese in the South, Lucy M. Cohen, *Chinese in the Post–Civil War South: A People Without a History* (Baton Rouge: Louisiana University Press, 1984).

21. Letter, Pixley to Sumner, Apr. 28, 1870, Sumner mss., Harvard, as printed in Gerald Stanley, "Frank Pixley and the Heathen Chinese," *Phylon* 40 (1979): 224–28.

22. The foregoing may be found in the *Congressional Globe* for July 2 and 4, 1870, 4819–5177; Sumner's remarks are conveniently printed in Charles Sumner, *The Works of Charles Sumner* (Boston: Lee and Shepard, 1880), 13: 474–98.

23. Letter, Douglas to Sumner, July 6, 1870, as cited in Benjamin Quarles *Frederick Douglass* (New York: Associated Publishers, 1948), 254.

24. Frederick Rudolph, "Chinamen in Yankeedom: Anti-Unionism in Massachusetts in 1870," *American Historical Review* 53 (1947): 1–29. Andrew Gyory, *Closing the*

Gate: Race, Politics, and the Chinese Exclusion Act (Chapel Hill: University of North Carolina Press, 1998) contains a fine account of anti-Chinese labor activism in the East combined with what seems to me a tendentious attempt to exculpate labor. For a better analysis see Aarim, *Chinese Immigrants.*

25. Commons, *Documentary History,* 9: 241, 257–67.
26. Roger Daniels, *The Politics of Prejudice: The Anti-Japanese Movement in California and the Struggle for Japanese Exclusion* (Berkeley: University of California Press, 1962), 30.
27. Grant's message is in Richardson, *Messages,* 7: 288.
28. The Page Act is 18 *Stat.* 477. George Anthony Peffer, *If They Don't Bring Their Women Here: Chinese Female Immigration before Exclusion* (Urbana: University of Illinois Press, 1999).
29. Anti-Chinese planks in national party platforms were numerous. Ignoring minor parties, the Democrats and the Republicans had anti-Chinese planks in 1876, 1880, 1888, and 1904. Kirk H. Porter and Donald B. Johnson, comps., *National Party Platforms* (Urbana: University of Illinois Press, 1970), *passim.*
30. The very large committee report is U.S. Congress, Senate, *Report of the Joint Special Committee to Investigate Chinese Immigration.* Report 689 (Washington: GPO, 1877). Quotations at iii–viii.
31. Richardson, *Messages,* 7: 514–20.
32. Malloy, *Treaties,* 1: 237–39.
33. Richardson, *Messages,* 8: 112–18.
34. 22 *Stat.* 58.
35. 23 *Stat.* 115.
36. 25 *Stat.* 504.
37. Richardson, *Messages,* 8: 630–35.
38. 130 U.S. 581, also known as *Chae Chan Ping v. U.S.*
39. 27 *Stat.* 25.
40. 149 *U.S.* 698. Two similar analyses of the case are Charles J. McClain, Jr., *In Search of Equality: The Chinese Struggle Against Discrimination in Nineteenth Century America* (Berkeley: University of California Press, 1994), 203–13, and Lucy E. Salyer, *Laws Harsh as Tigers: Chinese Immigrants and the Shaping of Modern Immigration Law* (Chapel Hill: University of North Carolina Press, 1995), 47–58. See Roger Daniels, "Ah Sin and His Lawyers," *Reviews in American History* 23 (1995): 472–77.
41. See correspondence published in the *Congressional Record,* 53rd Congress, 1st Session, 2422, 2444.
42. George E. Paulsen, "The Gresham-Yang Treaty," *Pacific Historical Review* 37 (1968): 281–97.
43. 28 *Stat.* 7.
44. 32 *Stat.* 176. Extension of the exclusion act to Hawaii was effected by Sec. 101 of 31 *Stat.* 143, which gave Chinese aliens in Hawaii a year to get a certificate and provided that, even with a certificate, such aliens could not enter "any State, Territory, or District of the United States." However, a few Hawaiian Chinese had

acquired Hawaiian citizenship and, under other sections of this act, became U.S. citizens. In addition Chinese born in Hawaii after Apr. 29, 1900, were citizens of the U.S.

45. Christian G. Fritz, "A Nineteenth Century 'Habeas Corpus Mill': The Chinese before the Federal Courts in California," *American Journal of Legal History* 32:4 (1988): 347–72. For cases outside California see John R. Wunder, "Anti-Chinese Violence in the American West, 1850–1910," pp. 212–35 in J. McLaren et al., *Law for the Elephant, Law for the Beaver* (Regina, Sask.: Canadian Plains Research Center, 1992). See also the works cited in n. 18, above.

46. 28 *Stat.* 7.

47. Xiaojian Zhao, *Remaking Chinese America: Immigration, Family, and Community, 1940–1965* (New Brunswick: Rutgers University Press, 2002).

48. A good brief account, with oral testimony, of the paper sons phenomenon is in Victor and Brett de Bary Nee, *Longtime Californ': A Documentary Study of an American Chinatown* (New York: Pantheon, 1973). For details see several of the essays in Sucheng Chan, ed., *Entry Denied: Exclusion and the Chinese Community in America, 1882–1943* (Philadelphia: Temple University Press, 1991). For paper daughters see Judy Yung, *Unbound Feet: A Social History of Chinese Women in San Francisco* (Berkeley: University of California Press, 1995).

49. 46 *Stat.* 581.

50. Alan M. Kraut, *Silent Travelers: Germs, Genes, and the "Immigrant Menace"* (New York: Basic Books, 1994) is an analysis of the medical aspects of European immigration.

51. Roger Daniels, "No Lamps Were Lit for Them: Angel Island and the Historiography of Asian American Immigration," *Journal of American Ethnic History* 17 (1997): 4–18.

52. Salyer, *Laws Harsh as Tigers*, 247–48.

2. The 1920s: The Triumph of the Old Nativism

1. 22 *Stat.* 214.

2. 23 *Stat.* 322 and 24 *Stat.* 414. I describe the text as amended. Martin A. Foran (1844–1921), a representative from Cleveland, was its sponsor.

3. The law originally included the phrase "or relative or personal friend" after "his family," but that was repealed in 1891.

4. 26 *Stat.* 1084.

5. For example, immigration is ignored in both Frederick Jackson Turner's ubiquitous essay, "The Significance of the Frontier in American History," and in Henry Steele Commager's "watershed" concept spelled out at the beginning of *The American Mind: An Interpretation of American Thought and Character since the 1880's* (New Haven: Yale University Press, 1850).

6. United States Immigration Commission, *Reports of the Immigration Commission* (Washington: GPO, 1911), 1: 24.

7. James Bryce, *The American Commonwealth* (New York, Macmillan, 1988), 2: 473.

8. Barbara Miller Solomon, *Ancestors and Immigrants* (Cambridge, MA: Harvard University Press, 1956), 102, 111, 147.
9. Solomon, *Ancestors*, 102.
10. Solomon, *Ancestors*, 111.
11. Solomon, *Ancestors*, 102, 147.
12. E. P. Hutchinson, *Legislative History of American Immigration Policy, 1798–1865* (Philadelphia: University of Pennsylvania Press, 1981), 101.
13. Kirk H. Porter and Donald B. Johnson, comps., *National Party Platforms* (Urbana, University of Illinois Press, 1970), 266, 271, 295, 303.
14. James D. Richardson, ed., *Messages and Papers of the Presidents* (Washington: Bureau of National Literature and Art, 1903), 9: 758–61.
15. Hutchinson, *Legislative History*, 124.
16. Lewis L. Gould, *The Presidency of William McKinley* (Lawrence: The Regents Press of Kansas, 1980), 30–31 and Richardson, *Messages*, 10: 15. Gould seems not to see any discrepancy between the platform and McKinley's careful utterances.
17. *Congressional Record*, 55th Congress, 1st Session, 11r; 2nd Session, 688–89; 3rd Session, 196–97.
18. For Natal see Robert A. Huttenback, *Racism and Empire: White Settlers and Colored Immigrants in the British Self-Governing Colonies, 1830–1910* (Ithaca, NY: Cornell University Press, 1976), 141. For Australia see Charles A. Price, *The Great White Walls Are Built* (Canberra: Australian National University Press, 1974). Roger Daniels, "The Growth of Restrictive Immigration Policies in the Colonies of Settlement before World War II," in Robin Cohen, ed., *The Cambridge Survey of World Migration* (Cambridge: Cambridge University Press, 1995), 39–43 is a comparative survey.
19. Edward N. Saveth, *American Historians and European Immigrants, 1875–1925* (New York: Columbia University Press, 1948).
20. Taft's veto message and Nagel's letter may be found in *Congressional Record* 49 (Feb. 17, 1913): 3269–70.
21. Arthur S. Link, *Wilson: The Road to the White House* (Princeton: Princeton University Press, 1947), 381.
22. Woodrow Wilson, *A History of the American People* (New York: Harper, 1902), 5: 212–13.
23. Albert Shaw, ed., *The Messages and Papers of Woodrow Wilson* (New York: Review of Reviews, 1917), 1: 96.
24. See his posthumously published autobiography, *The Path I Trod: The Autobiography of Terence V. Powderly* (New York: Columbia University Press, 1940). A number of indexed passages relate to McKinley.
25. *New York Times*, Jan. 10, 1899, p. 1. There is a follow-up on p. 9 the following day.
26. Powderly's biases can most conveniently be seen in his Annual Reports as immigration commissioner.
27. *Report of the Secretary of the Treasury, 1897* (Washington: GPO, 1897), iii.
28. *Report of the Secretary of the Treasury, 1900* (Washington: GPO, 1900), xlvii.

29. Congressional Research Service, Library of Congress, *History of the Immigration and Naturalization Service* (Washington: GPO, 1980), 13. For the creation of the Border Patrol see 43 *Stat.* 1049.

30. Fiorello H. La Guardia, *The Making of an Insurgent: An Autobiography: 1882–1919* (Philadelphia: Lippincott, 1948), 64. La Guardia's biographers tend to disseminate this myth.

31. Few scholars have noted this. For an exception see Gavan Daws, *Shoal of Time* (Honolulu: University of Hawaii Press, 1966), 293.

32. James E. Kerr, *The Insular Cases: The Role of the Judiciary in American Expansion* (Port Washington: NY: Kennikat, 1982); Finley Peter Dunne, *Mr. Dooley's Opinions* (New York: R. H. Russell, 1901), 26.

33. Joint Resolution 5, 55th Congress, 2d Session, 30 *Stat.* 750.

34. 31 *Stat.* 141.

35. Ernest H. Gruening, *Many Battles: The Autobiography of Ernest Gruening* (New York: Liveright, 1973), 230.

36. The Foraker Act is 31 *Stat.* 77.

37. 39 *Stat.* 951.

38. José A. Cabranes, *Citizenship and the American Empire* (New Haven: Yale University Press, 1979).

39. 32 *Stat.* 825; 34 *Stat.* 596; 37 *Stat.* 737.

40. 34 *Stat.* 596.

41. 32 *Stat.* 1213.

42. Letter, Roosevelt to Lloyd C. Griscom, July 15, 1905, Elting E. Morison, ed., *The Letters of Theodore Roosevelt* (Cambridge, MA: Harvard University Press, 1951), 4: 1274–75.

43. Richardson, *Messages*, 10: 1164–67.

44. Richardson, *Messages*, 10: 7388–89.

45. Philip C. Jessup, *Elihu Root* (New York: Dodd, Mead, 1938), 2: 19.

46. *San Francisco Examiner*, May 18, 1905.

47. Metcalf's report is U.S. Congress, Senate, *Japanese in the City of San Francisco, Cal.* 59th Congress, 2d Session, Sen. Doc. 147 (Washington: GPO, 1907).

48. U.S. Department of State, *Foreign Relations of the United States, 1924* (Washington: GPO, 1939), 339–69.

49. 34 *Stat.* 898, Sec. 1, last proviso.

50. U.S. Immigration Commission, *Reports* 1: 47, has Dillingham's original plan.

51. 39 *Stat.* 874.

52. Louis F. Post, *The Deportations Delirium of Nineteen-Twenty: A Personal Narrative of an Historic Official Experience* (Chicago: C. H. Kerr, 1923). It must be noted that the post-war deportations—3,068 in fiscal 1919, 2,762 in fiscal 1920, and 4,514 in fiscal 1921—were soon dwarfed by post-1924 deportations, which ran between 10,000 and 20,000 every year between 1926 and 1933. Jane Perry Clark, *Deportation of Aliens from the United States to Europe* (New York: Columbia University Press, 1931) is still the best work on deportation.

53. John Higham, *Strangers in the Land: Patterns of American Nativism, 1860–1925* (New Brunswick, NJ: Rutgers University Press, 1955), p. 309.

54. Hutchinson, *Legislative History,* 175 ff.

55. The 1921 act and its extension are 42 *Stat.* 5 and 42 *Stat.* 540.

56. Porter and Johnson, *National Party Platforms,* 249, 265, 276.

57. Charlotte Erickson, "Some Thoughts on the Social and Economic Consequences of the Quota Acts," *European Contributions to American Studies* (Neth.) 10 (1986): 28–46 is particularly perceptive and thoughtful about long-range consequences.

58. Higham, *Strangers,* ch. 10.

59. The Cable Act is 42 *Stat.* 1021; the act that ended denaturalization of wives of Asian aliens is 46 *Stat.* 854.

60. The 1921 law had exempted aliens who had lived one year in a New World nation; it was raised to five years in 1922. 42 *Stat.* 5 and 42 *Stat.* 540.

61. For details, see Roger Daniels, *The Politics of Prejudice: The Anti-Japanese Movement in California and the Struggle for Japanese Exclusion* (Berkeley: University of California Press, 1962), ch. 7.

62. For Chinese merchants see Roger Daniels, *Asian America: Chinese and Japanese in the United States since 1850* (Seattle: University of Washington Press, 1988), 91–92.

63. For a sketch of Carr and an analysis of his views see Richard Breitman and Alan M. Kraut, *American Refugee Policy and European Jewry, 1933–1945* (Bloomington: Indiana University Press, 1987), 29–39. Carr had helped Rep. Albert Johnson in the preparation of the quota acts, and his letters to the congressman contain such statements as: "the great mass of aliens passing through Rotterdam . . . are Russian Poles or Polish Jews of the usual ghetto type . . . They are filthy unamerican and often dangerous in their habits." Carr, letter to Johnson, Dec. 4, 1920, as cited by Patricia R. Evans, " 'Likely to Become a Public Charge': Immigration in the Backwaters of Administrative Law, 1882–1933," unpublished Ph.D. diss., George Washington University, 1987. Theodore A. Wilson, "Carr, Wilbur John." http://www.anb.org/articles/06/06-00092.html; *American National Biography Online,* February 2000, ignores Carr's well-known nativism.

64. Messersmith to Secretary of State, Feb. 27, 1925 and Ralph C. Busser to Department of State, Mar. 2, 1925, both cited in Evans, ". . . Public Charge," pp. 178–80.

65. The language of the statute was deliberately obscure: "The annual quota of any nationality . . . shall be a number which bears the same ratio to 150,000 as the number of inhabitants in continental United States in 1920 having that national origin (ascertained as herein provided in this section) bears to the number of inhabitants in continental United States in 1920, but the minimum quota of any nationality shall be 100" [Sec. 11 (b)].

66. 43 *Stat.* 153. The national origins provision was originally scheduled to go into effect in 1927 but the data were not ready then, so the 2 percent of 1890 quota was extended to 1929.

67. Cf. Congressional Research Service. *History of the INS*, 34–37.
68. Presidential Proclamation 1872, March 22, 1929; William S. Myers and Walter H. Newton, *The Hoover Administration: A Documented Narrative* (New York: Scribner, 1936), 376. It allocated 152,588 quota spaces. Four "Asian" countries, China, India, Japan, and Siam, each received 100 quota spaces, but no Asian person could use them.

3. No New Deal for Immigration

1. For example see Stephan Thernstrom, ed., *Harvard Encyclopedia of American Ethnic Groups* (Cambridge, MA: Harvard University Press), 493. (Hereafter *HEAEG*.)
2. Kirk H. Porter and Donald B. Johnson, comps., *National Party Platforms* (Urbana: University of Illinois Press, 1970), 289.
3. Hoover's annual messages may be found conveniently in U.S. Department of State, *Foreign Relations of the United States* (hereafter *FRUS*) in the opening pages of the first volume of each year. The quoted passages appear in *FRUS*, 1929, 1: xxv; *FRUS*, 1930, 1: xvi; *FRUS*, 1931, 1: xxii. The campaign quotation is from William S. Myers and Walter H. Newton, *The Hoover Administration: A Documented Narrative* (New York: Scribner, 1936), 509.
4. 22 *Stat.* 214.
5. George Kiser and David Silverman, "Mexican Repatriation during the Great Depression," *Journal of Mexican American History* 3 (1973) at footnote 12.
6. Robert A. Divine, *American Immigration Policy* (New Haven: Yale University Press, 1957), 62. The policy was discussed in *The New York Times*, Jan. 16, 1929.
7. Cited by Divine, *Immigration Policy*, 78. For Hoover's announcement see Myers, *Hoover Administration*, 44–45.
8. Box quoted from *Congressional Record* [hereafter *CR*] (Feb. 9, 1928), 2817–18; Garner from U.S. Congress, House Committee on Immigration and Naturalization, *Immigration from Western Hemisphere* (Washington: GPO 1930), 61.
9. Divine, *Immigration Policy*, 66.
10. Carlos Cortés, "Mexicans," *HEAEG*, 702.
11. California, Governor, *Mexicans in California* (San Francisco, 1930), 171.
12. James B. Lane and Edward J. Escobar, *Forging a Community: The Latino Experience in Northwest Indiana, 1919–1975* (Chicago: Cattails Press, 1987), 13–14.
13. Albert Camarillo, *Chicanos in a Changing Society: From Mexican Pueblos to American Barrios in Santa Barbara and Southern California, 1848–1930* (Cambridge, MA: Harvard University Press, 1979), 163.
14. Abraham Hoffman, *Unwanted Mexican Americans in the Great Depression* (Tucson: University of Arizona Press, 1974), 150.
15. George J. Sánchez, "The 'New Nationalism,' Mexican Style: Race and Progressivism in Chicano Political Development during the 1920s," 229–44 in W. Deverell and T. Sitton, eds., *California Progressivism Revisited* (Berkeley: University of California Press, 1994), 239–40.

16. George Martin, *Madame Secretary: Frances Perkins* (Boston: Houghton Mifflin, 1976), 31–38.
17. Porter and Johnson, *National Party Programs*, 276.
18. "Campaign Address on Progressive Government at the Commonwealth Club, San Francisco, Calif. September 23, 1932," 1: 750 in Samuel I. Rosenman, comp., *The Public Papers and Addresses of Franklin D. Roosevelt* (New York: Random House, 1938).
19. "Campaign Address on a Program for Unemployment and Long-Range Planning, Boston, Mass., October 31, 1932," in *ibid.*, 842–55 at 854. For attempts to reform the immigration bureaucracy, see Martin, *Madame Secretary*, 292–94 and *passim*.
20. Rosenman, *FDR Public Papers*, "... Extemporaneous Remarks before the Daughters of the American Revolution," 8: 258–60.
21. Barbara M. Posadas and Roland L. Guyotte, "Unintentional Immigrants: Chicago's Filipino Foreign Students Become Settlers, 1900–1941," *Journal of American Ethnic History* 9:2 (1990): 26–48.
22. Mary Dorita Clifford, "The Hawaiian Sugar Planters Association and Filipino Exclusion," in Josepha M. Saniel, ed., *The Filipino Exclusion Movement, 1927–1935* (Quezon City: University of the Philippines, 1967), 28.
23. *Los Angeles Times*, Feb. 2, 1930.
24. Barrows testimony from H. Brett Melendy, *Asians in America: Filipinos, Koreans and East Indians* (Boston: Twayne, 1977), 66.
25. C. M. Goethe, "Filipino Immigration Viewed as a Peril," *Current History*, January 1934, 354. He had earlier been concerned about Mexican immigration: see his "The Influx of Mexican Amerinds," *Eugenics*, January 1929, 9.
26. *Buck v. Bell*, 247 U.S. 200 at 207 (1927).
27. *California Statutes* 50 (1993): 561. Other western states soon followed.
28. American Federation of Labor, *Proceedings, 1928, "List of Resolutions"* (Washington, 1928).
29. U.S. Congress, House, Committee on Immigration and Naturalization, *Hearings on Exclusion of Immigration from the Philippine Islands* (71st Congress, 2d Session, Washington: GPO, 1930), 187.
30. *CR* 76: 1761 (Jan. 13, 1933).
31. 48 *Stat.* 456.
32. 49 *Stat.* 478–9; it was renewed in 1939 by 53 *Stat.* 1133, and remained on the books until 1952. H. Brett Melendy, "California's Discrimination Against Filipinos, 1927–1935," in Saniel, *Filipino Exclusion*, 9–10.
33. Arthur D. Morse, *While Six Million Died: A Chronicle of American Apathy* (New York: Random House, 1968).
34. Walter Z. Laqueur, *The Terrible Secret: Suppression of the Truth about Hitler's "Final Solution"* (Boston: Little, Brown, 1980).
35. Mondale speech text, Office of the Vice President's Press Secretary, July 1979, for release Saturday, July 21, 5:00 P.M.
36. Carter speech as reported in *The New York Times*, July 29, 1979.

37. 18 *Stat.* 477 (1882) is the first of many.
38. 48 *Stat.* 926. In the era of the American Civil War there was a special use of the word *refugee*, as in the Bureau of Freedmen, Refugees, and Abandoned Lands, which is ignored here. The 1923 bill (S. 4092) referred to "any homeless person of the Armenian race" who had fled from Turkey. See *CR* 64: 3037–38.
39. 39 *Stat.* 874, Sec. 3.
40. Letters, Moley to Marguerite LeHand, April 4, 1936, and Hull to Roosevelt, April 21, 1936, as printed in Edgar B. Nixon, ed., *Franklin D. Roosevelt and Foreign Affairs* (Cambridge, MA: Harvard University Press, 1969), 3:278–80, 282–83.
41. Letters, Lehman to Roosevelt, Nov. 1, 1935, and June 15, 1936, and Roosevelt to Lehman, Nov. 13, 1935 and July 2, 1936, in Nixon, *FDR & Foreign Affairs*, 3: 50–52, 64–66, 123–24, 341–43.
42. 43 *Stat.* 153, Sec. 4 (d).
43. Avra Warren, not to be confused with George Warren of the President's Advisory Committee on Political Refugees, is a shadowy figure about whom little is known. See the index of Breitman and Kraut, *American Refugee Policy*, for some notion of his activities.
44. Roosevelt to Lehman, Nov. 12, 1935, as cited in Nixon, ed., *FDR & Foreign Affairs*, 3: 65.
45. Meyer, "The Refugee Scholars Project of the Hebrew Union College," in B. W. Korn, ed., *A Bicentennial Fetschrift for Jacob Rader Marcus* (New York: Ktav, 1976), 359–75.
46. Diary entry for Feb. 6, 1938, as cited by Donald Schwartz, "Long Breckinridge," *ANB.*
47. For examples of fruitless searches for a "smoking gun" see Breitman and Kraut, *American Refugee Policy*, 126. For Johnson's philo-Semitism, see Spencer C. Olin, *California's Prodigal Sons: Hiram Johnson and the Progressives, 1911–1917* (Berkeley: University of California Press, 1968).
48. Rosenman, *FDR Public Papers* (1938 volume), 169.
49. Rosenman, *FDR Public Papers* (1938 volume), 170–71.
50. Divine, *Immigration Policy*, 98.
51. For the Wagner-Rogers bills see Barbara McDonald Stewart, *United States Government Policy on Refugees from Nazism, 1933–1940* (New York: Garland, 1982), ch. 12. The Laura Delano quotation is from the manuscript diary of State Department official Jay P. Moffat, May 25, 1939, as cited by Stewart, 532. This, and all other references to Jewish refugee matters, were omitted from the published version of the diary. Nancy H. Hooker, ed., *The Moffat Papers: Selections from the Diplomatic Journals of Jay Pierrepont Moffat, 1919–1943* (Cambridge, MA: Harvard University Press, 1956).
52. For a scholarly account see Breitman and Kraut, *American Refugee Policy*, 70–73, 232; for a journalistic account filled with human interest, see Gordon Thomas and Max Morgan Witts, *Voyage of the Damned* (New York: Stein & Day, 1974).
53. Rosenman, *FDR Public Papers* (1938), 602–4.

54. David S. Wyman, *Paper Walls: America and the Refugee Crisis* (Amherst: University of Massachusetts Press, 1968), 209, 217–19. If anything, Wyman's figures may be a bit high, but the total cannot be computed with accuracy.

4. World War II and After: The Barriers Begin to Drop

1. See, for example, the State Department–inspired article by Samuel Lubell, "War by Refugee," *Saturday Evening Post*, Mar. 29, 1941.
2. For the latest analysis see Louise London, *Whitehall and the Jews, 1933–1948: British Immigration Policy and the Holocaust* (Cambridge: Cambridge University Press, 2000). For Churchill see Peter and Leni Gillman, *Collar the Lot!: How Britain Interned and Expelled Its Wartime Refugees* (New York: Quartet Books, 1980).
3. See examples cited in John Christgau, *"Enemies": World War II Alien Internment* (Ames: Iowa State University Press, 1985), 50–85 and Harvey Strum, "Jewish Internees in the American South, 1942–1945," *American Jewish Archives* 42 (1980): 27–48. For Canada see Paula Jean Draper, "Muses Behind Barbed Wire: Canada and the Interned Refugees," 271–81 in J. C. Jackman and C. M. Borden, eds., *The Muses Flee Hitler: Cultural Transfer and Adaptation, 1930–1945* (Washington: Smithsonian Institution Press, 1983).
4. The veto message is in *Congressional Record* 86: 4157.
5. Reorganization Plan No. V, 5 *Federal Register* 2223; George Martin, *Madam Secretary: Frances Perkins* (Boston: Houghton Mifflin, 1976), 442.
6. 54 *Stat.* 670.
7. 54 *Stat.* 1137.
8. Robert A. Divine, *American Immigration Policy* (New Haven: Yale University Press, 1957), 102–3; Cynthia Jaffee McCabe, " 'Wanted by the Gestapo: Saved by America'—Varian Fry and the Emergency Rescue Committee," 79–91 in Jackman, *Muses*; Varian Fry, *Surrender on Demand* (New York: Random House, 1945).
9. Divine, *American Immigration Policy*, 103.
10. United Nations Relief and Rehabilitation Administration, *UNRRA: The History of the United Nations Relief and Rehabilitation Administration* (New York: Columbia University Press, 1950).
11. John Morton Blum, ed., *From the Morgenthau Diaries: Years of War, 1941–1945* (Boston: Houghton Mifflin, 1967), 220–27; Blum, *Morgenthau and Roosevelt* (Boston: Houghton Mifflin, 1970), 531–33.
12. Rosenman, *FDR Public Papers* (1944 volume), 48–53.
13. There is no monographic study of the War Refugee Board. Volume 11 of David S. Wyman, ed., *America and the Holocaust* (New York: Garland, 1989–91) is devoted to War Refugee Board "Weekly Reports." Verne Newton, ed., *FDR and the Holocaust* (New York: St. Martin's, 1996) contains essays by scholars representing a broad spectrum of opinion.
14. Rosenman, *FDR Public Papers* (1944 volume), 163–65.
15. Rosenman, *FDR Public Papers* (1944 volume), 168–72.

16. Sharon R. Lowenstein, *Token Refuge: The Story of the Jewish Refugee Shelter at Oswego, 1944–1946* (Bloomington: Indiana University Press, 1986). See also the memoir by Ruth Gruber, *Haven: The Untold Story of 1,000 World War II Refugees* (New York: Coward-McCann, 1983). She was a special assistant to Interior Secretary Harold L. Ickes. Lowenstein seems not to have seen FDR's cable to Murphy.

17. Presidential proclamations 2525, 2526, and 2563 of Dec. 7, Dec. 8, 1941, and July 17, 1942.

18. Presidential proclamation 2527, Jan. 14, 1942.

19. Francis Biddle, *In Brief Authority* (Garden City, NY: Doubleday, 1962), 207.

20. Department of Justice, Federal Bureau of Investigation, Reference Document 4014, "APPREHENSIONS December 7, 1941 to June 3, 1945." But the annual report of the Department of Justice for 1943 shows apprehensions of 7,459 aliens; 4,092 Japanese, 2,384 Germans, 794 Italians, and 199 "others." Biddle's memoir says "about 16,000 were arrested" (*In Brief Authority*, 209). The INS was apologetic about its camps. In writing about a Texas camp, N. D. Collaer claimed, improbably, that "except for the 10-foot wire fence that surrounded the facility, the Crystal City camp resembled any thriving and bustling southwestern town" (Collaer, "The Crystal City Internment Camp" *INS Monthly Review* 5 [Dec. 1947]: 77). The best account of an American internment camp is John J. Culley, "The Santa Fe Internment Camp and the Justice Department Program for Enemy Aliens." 57–71 in Daniels et al., *Japanese Americans from Relocation to Redress*. (Salt Lake City: University of Utah Press, 1986). For the special camp for families see Karen L. Riley, *Schools Behind Barbed Wire: The Untold Story of Wartime Internment and the Children of Arrested Enemy Aliens* (Lanham, MD: Rowman & Littlefield, 2002).

21. For the political implications see John W. Jeffries, *Testing the Roosevelt Coalition: Connecticut Society and Politics in the Era of World War II* (Knoxville: University of Tennessee Press, 1979). Stephen Fox, *The Unknown Internment: An Oral History of the Internment of the West Coast Italian Americans during World War II* (Boston: Twayne, 1990) describes and magnifies the travails of his protagonists. Three essays in Kay Saunders and Roger Daniels, *Alien Justice: Wartime Internment in Australia and North America* (St. Lucia, Queensland: University of Queensland Press, 2000) provide useful capsule studies. Jörg Nagler on Germans, George E. Pozzetta on Italians, and Culley on enemy alien control.

22. Roger Daniels, *Prisoners Without Trial: Japanese in World War II* (New York: Hill & Wang, 1993). For fuller documentation see Daniels, *Concentration Camps, USA: Japanese Americans and World War II* (New York: Holt, Rinehart & Winston, 1972). For the very different experience of the 150,000 Japanese Americans of Hawaii, see Dennis M. Ogawa and Evarts C. Fox, Jr., "Japanese Internment and Relocation: The Hawaii Experience," 131–34 in Daniels et. al., *Japanese Americans*.

23. C. Harvey Gardiner, *Pawns in a Triangle of Hate: The Peruvian Japanese and the United States* (Seattle: University of Washington Press, 1981). Seiichi Higashide,

Adios to Tears: The Memoirs of a Japanese Peruvian Internee in U.S. Concentration Camps, 2nd ed. (Seattle: University of Washington Press, 2000). Max Paul Friedman, *Nazis and Good Neighbors: The United States Campaign against the Germans of Latin America in World War II* (New York: Cambridge University Press, 2003) is the source for the precise numbers in the text.

24. U.S. Congress, House, Committee on Foreign Relations, *Hearings on House Resolution 350 and House Resolution 352* (Washington: GPO, 1943), 23.

25. Donald E. Collins, *Native American Aliens: Disloyalty and Renunciation of American Citizenship by Japanese Americans during World War II* (Westport, CT: Greenwood, 1985) and John Christgau, "Collins versus the World: The Fight to Restore Citizenship to Japanese American Renunciants of World War II," *Pacific Historical Review* 54 (1985): 1–31. For the judge see Eric L. Muller, *Free to Die for Their Country: The Story of the Japanese American Draft Resisters in World War II* (Chicago: University of Chicago Press, 2001).

26. 39 *Stat.* 847.

27. Letter, Herbert C. Hoover to Felix Frankfurter, June 14, 1918, National Archives, RG 85, File No. 54261/202 as cited in George C. and Martha W. Kiser, eds., *Mexican Workers in the United States: Historical and Political Perspectives* (Albuquerque: University of New Mexico Press, 1979), 13–14.

28. Lawrence A. Cardoso, "Labor Emigration to the Southwest, 1916 to 1920: Mexican Attitudes and Policy," *Southwestern Historical Quarterly* 79 (1979): 400–16 and Otey M. Scruggs, "The First Mexican Labor Program," *Arizona and the West* 2 (1960): 318–26.

29. The WW II bracero program was initially ratified by 57 *Stat.* 70. The literature is very large. A place to begin is Wayne D. Rasmussen, *A History of the Emergency Farm Labor Supply Program, 1943–1947* (Washington: GPO, 1951). A table showing annual numbers and nationalities is printed in Congressional Research Service, *U.S. Immigration Law and Policy* (Washington: GPO, 1979), Table 3, p. 40. See comments in ch. 7.

30. Barbara A. Driscoll, *The Tracks North: The Railroad Bracero Program of World War II* (Austin: University of Texas Press, 1999). For a masterful brief survey of the whole guestworker phenomenon, see Cindy Hahamovitch, "Creating Perfect Immigrants: Guestworkers of the World in Historical Perspective," *Labor History* 44 (February 2003): 69–95.

31. A four-year legal effort involving several lawsuits is encountering great legal difficulties and, as I write in early 2003, it seems as if only congressional action will be of any use. Even more outrageous was what happened to the railroad braceros. They, like other railroad workers, had to pay money into the Railway Retirement Board. After the war the State Department tried to get the board to return the braceros' contributions. The board refused. Eventually the U.S. and Mexico agreed to apply the funds to Mexico's Lend Lease debt to the U.S. The workers got nothing. Driscoll, *The Tracks North*, 163–65.

32. Much of the following derives from Fred W. Riggs, *Pressures on Congress: A Study of the Repeal of the Chinese Exclusion* (New York: King's Crown, 1950)

and Roger Daniels, *Asian America: Chinese and Japanese in the United States since 1850* (Seattle: University of Washington Press, 1988).

33. Letter, Richard J. Walsh to Miller Freeman, May 14, 1943, Miller Freeman mss., University of Washington Archives, Seattle. The earliest wartime public call for repeal that I have seen was in Walsh's magazine, *Asia and the Americas*, February 1942.

34. *Saturday Evening Post*, Oct. 23, 1943. The figure of 107 was inaccurate.

35. Rosenman, *FDR Public Papers* (1943), 429–30.

36. U.S. Congress, House, Committee on Immigration and Naturalization, *Repeal of the Chinese Exclusion Acts. Hearings* . . . (Washington: GPO, 1943), 108–16.

37. Gallup polls data in Riggs, *Pressures*, 230, n. 69.

38. Rosenman, *FDR Public Papers* (1943), 548.

39. For State Department programs see Wilma Fairbank, *America's Cultural Experiment in China, 1942–1949* (Washington: GPO, 1976); for stranded Chinese see ch. 8.

40. 59 *Stat.* 659.

41. 60 *Stat.* 339.

42. 60 *Stat.* 975.

43. Xiaojian Zhao, *Remaking Chinese America: Immigration, Family, and Community, 1940–1965* (New Brunswick, NJ: Rutgers University Press, 2002), traces and analyzes the demographic and social impact of this immigration.

44. 60 *Stat.* 415; Proclamation No. 2696.

45. D. W. Meinig, "A Prospectus for Geographers and Historians," *American Historical Review* 43 (1978): 1201.

46. 60 *Stat.* 415.

47. Robert Shaplen, "One Man Lobby," *New Yorker*, Mar. 24, 1951, 35.

48. R. Narayanan, "Indian Immigration and the India League of America," *Indian Journal of American Studies* 2 (1972): 1–29; CR 79: 6933.

49. Premdatta Varma, *Indian Immigrants in USA: Struggle for Equality* (New Delhi: Heritage Publishers, 1995) and Roger Daniels, *History of Indian Immigration to the United States: An Interpretive Essay* (New York: The Asia Society, 1989).

50. D. S. Saund, *Congressman from India* (New York: Dutton, 1960).

5. Admitting Displaced Persons: 1946–1950

1. The IRO began its work in 1946, as a part of UNRRA, but survived it. Before it was succeeded by the Office of the High Commissioner for Refugees in 1952 it had resettled perhaps one million persons. Louise W. Holborn, *The International Refugee Organization, a Specialized Agency of the United Nations: Its History and Work, 1946–1952* (London: Oxford University Press, 1956).

2. 61 *Stat.* 214.

3. Constitution of the International Refugee Organization, Annex I.

4. Martin Blumenson, ed., *The Patton Papers* (Boston: Houghton Mifflin, 1972),

751; Leonard Dinnerstein, *America and the Survivors of the Holocaust* (New York: Columbia University Press, 1982), 47.

5. Dinnerstein, *Survivors*, 49.

6. Clarence G. Lasby, *Project Paperclip: German Scientists and the Cold War* (New York: Atheneum, 1971). Theodore Saloutos, *Human Scientific and Technical Capabilities at Holloman Air Force Base: Their Origins and Development* (Holloman AFB, NM: Historical Branch, Office of Information, Air Force Missile Development Center, Air Research and Development Command, United States Air Force, 1960).

7. 63 *Stat.* 208. "Administration of the Central Intelligence Agency," Sec. 8, June 29, 1949.

8. Dinnerstein, *Survivors*, 34–38. Cf. Harry S. Truman, *Memoirs* (Garden City, NY: Doubleday, 1955), 1: 311. See also Judah Nadich, *Eisenhower and the Jews* (New York: Twayne, 1953). There is nothing on the 1945 situation of DPs in any of John M. Blum's work on Morgenthau.

9. Department of State, *Bulletin*, 13 (Sep. 30, 1945): 456–63. It is reprinted in Dinnerstein, *Survivors*, 291–305.

10. Louise London, *Whitehall and the Jews, 1933–1948: British Immigration Policy and the Holocaust* (Cambridge: Cambridge University Press, 2000) contains a good account of post-war policy.

11. Dinnerstein, *Survivors*, 273–90, has given us a necessarily inconclusive statistical synopsis, which I have summarized, that is probably as close to accuracy as we are likely to get.

12. Letter, Hirschmann to La Guardia, June 16, 1946, as cited in Dinnerstein, *Survivors*, 59.

13. Robert W. Ross, *So It Was True: The American Protestant Press and the Persecution of the Jews* (Minneapolis: University of Minnesota Press, 1980), 213.

14. As cited by Dinnerstein, *Survivors*, 114.

15. Truman directive, Dec. 22, 1945. It was drafted in the White House by Samuel I. Rosenman, then Truman's special counsel, and Joseph W. Beck, executive director of the National Refugee Service. See Sharon R. Lowenstein, "National Refugee Service," 374–82 in Michael N. Dobkowski, ed., *Jewish American Voluntary Organizations* (Westport, CT: Greenwood, 1986), and Amy Zahl Gottlieb, "Refugee Immigration: The Truman Directive," *Prologue* 13 (Spring 1981): 5–18.

16. As cited by Dinnerstein, *Survivors*, 115.

17. For the 1940s situation, see Dinnerstein, *Survivors*, 115ff.

18. As cited by Dinnerstein, *Survivors*, 248.

19. Board members included Barry Bingham, William J. Donovan, David Dubinsky, James A. Farley, Marshall Field, Virginia Gildersleeve, William Green, Palmer Hoyt, Fiorello La Guardia, Herbert Lehman, Msgr. Luigi Ligutti, Philip Murray, John Nuveen, Jr., Edward A. O'Neal, Jacob Potofsky, Joseph Proskauer, A. Philip Randolph, John J. Raskob, Eleanor Roosevelt, Lessing Rosenwald, Mrs.

Harper Sibley, Edward Stettinius, Charles P. Taft, Walter Van Kirk, Edward E. M. Warburg, Sinclair Weeks, and Walter White.

20. *Public Papers of the Presidents of the United States, Harry S. Truman, 1952–3* (Washington: GPO, 1966), 10.

21. Letter, George Perrine to Stratton, Apr. 18, 1947, as cited in David Kenney, *A Political Passage: The Career of Stratton of Illinois* (Carbondale: Southern Illinois University Press, 1990), 52–53.

22. Dinnerstein, *Survivors*, 184.

23. David M. Reimers, *Still the Golden Door: The Third World Comes to America* (New York: Columbia University Press, 1985), 12.

24. United States Displaced Persons Commission, *Memo to America: The DP Story* (Washington: GPO, 1952), hereafter cited as *DP Story*. The report was based on the work of Stuart Portner, its chief historian.

25. *DP Story*, 274–94.

26. Allan W. Austin, "From Concentration Camp to Campus: A History of the National Japanese American Student Relocation Council, 1942–1946," Ph.D. diss., U. of Cincinnati, 2001, will soon be published by the University of Illinois Press.

27. Mark Wyman, *DP: Europe's Displaced Persons, 1945–1951* (Philadelphia: Balch Institute, 1985), 198.

28. *DP Story*, 72–76 describes a processing "pipeline" of sixteen steps.

29. 64 *Stat.* 219. For war criminals and others admitted to the United States see Alan S. Rosenbaum, *Prosecuting Nazi War Criminals* (Boulder: Westview Press, 1993) and Allan A. Ryan, Jr., *Quiet Neighbors: Prosecuting Nazi War Criminals in America* (San Diego: Harcourt Brace Jovanovich, 1984).

30. The supposed security checks were made by the FBI, the CIA, the Counter Intelligence Corps, U.S. Army, which allegedly had a twenty-one-step investigative process, the Army's Provost Marshal General for Germany, the Berlin Document Center, a special investigation for DPs whose origin was in the Soviet sphere, by INS inspectors overseas, by consular officials, plus special liaison investigations with British intelligence, the French Sûreté, and the Italian Questra. *DP Story*, 100.

31. *DP Story*, 366 gives an admittedly incomplete figure of 393,542. The INS later calculated 409,696. INS, *Annual Report, 1965* (Washington: GPO, 1966), 30.

32. The statistical material that follows comes from the 30 tables in *DP Story*, 363–76.

33. *DP Story*, 350.

34. *DP Story*, 353.

6. The Cold War and Immigration

1. U.S. Congress, House, Committee on Immigration and Naturalization, *Hearings before Subcommittee 1* (Washington: GPO, 1945).

2. 64 *Stat.* 987.

3. Robert A. Divine, *American Immigration Policy, 1924–1952* (New Haven: Yale University Press, 1957), 164.

4. New York: Harper, 1950.

5. United States Displaced Persons Committee, *Memo to America: The DP Story* (Washington: GPO, 1952), 353–54.

6. U.S. Congress, *Joint Hearings before the Subcommittees of the Committees on the Judiciary* (Washington: GPO, 1951).

7. Colin Holmes, *John Bull's Island: Immigration and British Society, 1871–1971* (Basingstoke, UK: Macmillan Education, 1988), 221. See also Dilip Hiro, *Black British, White British* (London: Eyre & Spottiswoode, 1971), 8–10, and Nicholas Deakin et al., *Colour, Citizenship, and British Society, based on the Institute of Race Relations Report* (London: Panther Books, 1970), 44–45.

8. 66 *Stat.* 26.

9. The "Texas proviso" is Section 274, subsection (a) of the McCarran-Walter Act or *INA*.

10. The McCarran-Walter Act or the Immigration and Nationality Act of 1952, here-after *INA*, is 66 *Stat.* 163. For additional details see Divine, *American Immigration Policy*, 171–86, and E. P. Hutchinson, *Legislative History of American Immigration Policy, 1798–1965* (Philadelphia: University of Pennsylvania Press, 1981), 297–313.

11. As cited in Divine, *American Immigration Policy*, 181.

12. *Public Papers of the Presidents of the United States: Harry S. Truman* (Washington: GPO, 1966), 1952–53 volume, 441–47.

13. Philip B. Perlman (1890–1960), former solicitor general, and Earl G. Harrison were chair and vice-chair. Members included Rev. Thaddeus F. Gulixson, president of a Lutheran seminary, Msgr. John O'Grady of Catholic Charities, and Clarence Pickett of the American Friends Service Committee.

14. President's Commission on Immigration and Naturalization, *Whom We Shall Welcome* (Washington: GPO, 1953), The awkward title comes from a 1783 statement by George Washington: "The bosom of America is open to receive not only the opulent and respectable stranger but the oppressed and persecuted of all nations who we shall wellcome [sic] to a participation in all rights and privileges, if by decency and propriety of conduct they appear to merit the enjoyment."

15. *Public Papers, Truman*, 1952–53, 209–16.

16. As printed in Bernard M. Ziegler, ed., *Immigration: An American Dilemma* (Boston: D. C. Heath, 1953), 112–13.

17. Frank D. Bean, Georges Vernez, and Charles B. Keely, *Opening and Closing the Doors: Evaluating Immigration Reform and Control* (Santa Monica: Rand, 1989), xv. Statement by Victor H. Palmieri.

18. Further power was given to the president under subsection (e) of the same section which authorized him to suspend, by proclamation, "for such period as he may deem necessary . . . the entry of all aliens or any class of aliens . . . or im-

pose . . . any restrictions he may deem appropriate." Although never yet used, this is one of the more sweeping grants of presidential power on the statute books.

19. Letter, Hull to Roosevelt, Apr. 21, 1936, as printed in Edgar B. Nixon, ed., *Franklin D. Roosevelt and Foreign Affairs* (Cambridge, MA: Harvard University Press, 1969), 3: 282–83.

20. 67 *Stat.* 400.

21. 71 *Stat.* 679.

22. *Public Papers of the Presidents, Dwight D. Eisenhower, 1960* (Washington: GPO, 1961), 308–10. Historians of the period have largely ignored immigration and immigration policy. For example, in an otherwise most useful book, Gary W. Riechard, *Politics as Usual: The Era of Truman and Eisenhower* (Arlington Heights, IL: Harlan Davidson, 1988) there is no discussion of immigration at all. The terms "immigration," "refugee," and "displaced person" do not appear in the index. There are two references to the McCarran Internal Security Act, none to the McCarran-Walter Immigration Act.

23. 72 *Stat.* 419 and 72 *Stat.* 699.

24. 74 *Stat.* 504.

25. Leo Pap, *The Portuguese Americans* (Boston: Twayne, 1981), 95. The largest single concentration of Portuguese Americans is in Massachusetts.

26. Robert F. Kennedy, "Introduction," to the revised and enlarged edition (New York: Harper & Row, 1964).

7. Lyndon Johnson and the End of the Quota System

1. Kirk H. Porter and Donald Johnson, *National Party Platforms, 1940–1968* (Urbana: University of Illinois Press, 1970), 577–78, 620.

2. 76 *Stat.* 191.

3. 75 *Stat.* 350.

4. For his own account see *The Open Society* (New York: Simon and Schuster, 1968).

5. Kennedy, letter to House and Senate, July 23, 1963 in *Public Papers of the Presidents of the United States, John F. Kennedy, 1963* (Washington: GPO, 1964), 594–97.

6. Michael O'Brien, *Philip Hart: The Conscience of the Senate* (East Lansing: Michigan State University Press, 1995) makes no mention of immigration or the 1965 act, also known as the Hart-Celler Act.

7. Robert Dallek, *Lone Star Rising: Lyndon Johnson and His Times, 1908–1960* (New York: Oxford University Press, 1991), 58–70. Dallek draws much of his information on this topic from Louis S. Gomolak, "Prologue: LBJ's Foreign Affairs Background, 1908–1948," Ph.D. diss., University of Texas, 1989.

8. *New York Times*, Mar. 20, 1992 (Feighan's obituary).

9. U.S. Congress, Senate, Subcommittee on Immigration and Naturalization of the Committee on the Judiciary, *Immigration Hearings* (89th Congress, 1st Session, Washington: GPO, 1965), 67. Curiously, Ervin, in his memoirs, makes no men-

tion of immigration bills. *Preserving the Constitution: The Autobiography of Senator Sam Ervin* (Charlottesville, VA: Michie, 1984). Dick Dabney, *A Good Man: The Life of Sam J. Ervin* (Boston: Houghton Mifflin, 1976), 42, 90, 228–29, is explicit about his prejudices against some immigrants.

10. A detailed account of its passage is in David M. Reimers, *Still the Golden Door: The Third World Comes to America*, 2nd ed. (New York: Columbia University Press, 1992), ch. 1.

11. Allen J. Matusow, *The Unraveling of America: A History of Liberalism in the 1960s* (New York: Harper & Row, 1984).

12. *Public Papers of the Presidents, Lyndon B. Johnson, 1965* (Washington: GPO, 1967), 1039–40.

13. Elliott R. Barkan, "Whom Shall We Integrate? A Comparative Analysis of the Immigration and Naturalization Trends of Asians Before and After the 1965 Immigration Act (1951–1978)," *Journal of American Ethnic History* 1: 3 (Fall 1983): 29–57.

14. Immigration and Naturalization Service, *1997 Statistical Yearbook of the Immigration and Naturalization Service* (Washington: GPO, 1999), 199–203.

15. For a brief summary see Roger Daniels, *Coming to America: A History of Race and Ethnicity in American Life*, 2nd ed. (New York: HarperCollins, 2002), 126 ff. The indispensable work on classic Irish immigration is Kerby A. Miller, *Emigrants and Exiles: Ireland and the Irish Exodus to North America* (New York: Oxford University Press, 1985).

16. Linda Dowling Almeida, *Irish Immigrants in New York City* (Bloomington: Indiana University Press, 2001) contains a good account of "New Irish." She uses a conservative estimate of 50,000 illegal Irish.

17. Francis X. Clines, "The New Illegals: The Irish," *New York Times Magazine*, Nov. 20, 1988.

18. Congressional Research Service, *U.S. Immigration Law and Policy* (Washington: GPO, 1979), Table 3, 40. See also U.S. Department of Agriculture, *Termination of the Bracero Program* (Washington: GPO, June 1956).

19. Richard Griswold del Castillo and Richard A. García, *César Chavez: A Triumph of Spirit* (Norman: University of Oklahoma Press, 1995), 42–44.

20. INS, *Annual Report, 1970* (Washington: GPO, 1970), 11.

8. Immigrants from Other Worlds: Asians

1. Robert W. Gardner, Bryant Robey, and Peter C. Smith, "Asian Americans: Growth, Change, and Diversity," *Population Bulletin* 40:4 (1985): Table 2, p. 8. In those years only four groups—Japanese, Chinese, Filipinos, and Koreans—were enumerated, although Koreans were not separately tabulated in 1960. Inclusion of Koreans and Asian Indians, the only other Asian ethnic group of any size, might have raised the 1960 count by 100,000.

2. Leon F. Bouvier and Anthony Agresta, "Projections of the Asian American Population, 1980–2030," in Gardner et al., "Asian Americans: Growth, Change, and

Diversity," Table 16, 37. Their estimates of the size of individual ethnic groups missed the mark by even greater percentages. They assumed that there would be almost 2.1 million Filipinos and only 1.7 million Chinese in 2000; the census numbers were 1.85 million Filipinos and 2.43 million Chinese.

3. U.S. Census Bureau, Census 2000 Redistricting (Public Law 94-171) Summary File, Tables PL1 and PL2. These figures are roughly comparable with previous censuses. The 2000 census, however, recorded mixed ancestry for the first time. Almost 11.9 million persons reported some Asian ancestry, some 4.2 percent of the total population. See Census 2000 Summary File 1 (SF 1) 100-Percent Data: QT-P7 Race Alone or in Combination for . . . Asian[s]: 2000.

4. INS, *1999 Statistical Yearbook*, Chart K, 170.

5. Even worse is the "Asian and Pacific Islander" category. Marian A. Smith, "INS Administration of Racial Provisions in U.S. Immigration and Nationality Law since 1898," *Prologue* 34 (Summer 2002): 90–105, is a path-breaking essay.

6. William Wei, *The Asian American Movement* (Philadelphia: Temple University Press, 1993).

7. Lisa Lowe, *Immigrant Acts: On Asian American Cultural Politics* (Durham, NC: Duke University Press, 1996).

8. Eric Liu, *The Accidental Asian: Notes of a Native Speaker* (New York: Random House, 1998), 80.

9. U.S. Department of Commerce, Bureau of the Census, 1990 Census of Population, *Asians and Pacific Islanders in the United States*, 1990 CP-3-5 (Washington: GPO, 1993) and *Nonwhite Population by Race*, PC (2)-1C.

10. Pyong Gap Min, *Caught in the Middle: Korean Communities in New York and Los Angeles* (Berkeley: University of California Press, 1996).

11. For Chinese American men, see U.S. Selective Service System, Special Monograph 10, *Special Groups* (Washington: GPO, 1953), 2: 13. For women see Xiaojian Zhao, *Remaking Chinese America: Immigration, Family, and Community, 1940–1965* (Philadelphia: Temple University Press, 2002), 60–66.

12. 58 *Stat.* 659, 60 *Stat.* 339, and 67 *Stat.* 400.

13. Rose Hum Lee, "The Recent Immigrant Chinese Families of the San Francisco-Oakland Area," *Journal of Marriage and the Family* 18 (1956): 14–24. For Lee see Henry Yu, *Thinking Orientals: Migration, Contact, and Exoticism in Modern America* (New York: Oxford University Press, 2001), 125–33 and *passim*.

14. A somewhat similar picture is painted in the most somber fictional portrait of Chinese American family life in this era, Louis Chu's *Eat a Bowl of Tea* (New York: Lyle Stuart, 1961).

15. Zhao, *Remaking Chinese America*, 80–93: most of Zhao's numerical analysis comes from her large sample of INS files.

16. Zhao, *Remaking Chinese America*, 141–42. Letter printed in *Chung Sai Yat Po* for Oct. 13, 1950. The translations are Zhao's.

17. Much of what follows is based on Rose Hum Lee, "The Stranded Chinese in the United States," *Phylon* 19 (1958): 180–94. The topic of "stranded Chinese" is one that needs a fuller exploration.

18. Wilma Fairbank, *America's Cultural Experiment in China, 1942–1949* (Washington: GPO, 1976).

19. Roger Daniels, "Yung Wing," http://www.anb.org/articles/09/09-00834.html; *American National Biography Online*, February 2000.

20. Weili Ye, *Seeking Modernity in China's Name: Chinese Students in the United States, 1900–1927* (Stanford: Stanford University Press, 2001) is the best modern account. Y. C. Yang, *Chinese Intellectuals and the West, 1872–1949* (Chapel Hill: University of North Carolina Press, 1966), views the phenomenon in a Chinese context. Edward C. Cieslak, *The Foreign Student in American Colleges: A Survey and Evaluation of Administrative Problems and Practices* (Detroit: Wayne University Press, 1955), recounts the bureaucratic structure and Leo A. Orleans, *Chinese Students in America: Policies, Issues and Numbers* (Washington: National Academy Press, 1988) focuses on the late twentieth century. For women see Huping Ling, "A History of Chinese Female Students in the United States, 1880s–1990s," *Journal of American Ethnic History*, 16 (Spring 1977): 81–109.

21. Diane Mei Lin Mark and Ginger Chih, *A Place Called Chinese America* (Dubuque, IA: Kendall/Hunt, 1982), 105–7. The book is copyright by the Organization of Chinese Americans, Inc.

22. Stephen G. Marshall, "Wang, An"; http://www.anb.org/articles/13/13-02154.html; *American National Biography Online*, February 2000.

23. Him Mark Lai, "The Kuomintang in Chinese American Communities before World War II," 170–212 in Sucheng Chan, ed., *Entry Denied: Exclusion and the Chinese Community in America, 1882–1943* (Philadelphia: Temple University Press, 1991). For the other side of the coin see his "To Bring Forth a New China, To Build a Better America: The Chinese Marxist Left in America," *Chinese America: History & Perspectives*, 1992, 3–82.

24. As cited in Stanford M. Lyman, "Red Guard on Grant Avenue: The Rise of Youthful Rebellion in Chinatown," in his *The Asian in the West* (Reno: Western Studies Center, University of Nevada, 1970), 117.

25. E. J. Kahn, *The China Hands: America's Foreign Service Officers and What Befell Them* (New York: Viking, 1975), 38. Kahn's text ignores Drumright's Hong Kong career but does examine his later tenure in Taipei.

26. Him Mark Lai, "Unfinished Business: The Chinese Confession Program," 47–57 in *The Repeal and Its Legacy: Proceedings of the Conference of the 50th Anniversary of the Repeal of the Exclusion Acts, Nov. 12–14, 1993* (San Francisco: Chinese Historical Society of America, 1994); Mae M. Ngai, "Legacies of Exclusion: Illegal Chinese Immigration during the Cold War Years," *Journal of American Ethnic History* 18: 1 (Fall 1998): 3–35; and Zhao, *Remaking Chinese America*, 176–84, are all improvements on earlier accounts. See, for example, Harry H. L. Kitano and Roger Daniels, *Asian Americans: Emerging Minorities* (Englewood Cliffs, N.J., 1988), 43–4. See also Roger Daniels. *Asian America: Chinese and Japanese in the United States since 1850* (Seattle: University of Washington Press, 1989), 307–9.

27. Ngai, "Legacies of Exclusion"; earlier accounts of the Chuck case by Mark and Chih, *A Place Called . . .* , 104, and Victor and Brett de Bary Nee, *Longtime Californ': A Documentary Study of an American Chinatown* (New York: Pantheon, 1973), 213–17 describe the attack on the left and its consequences, but do not use the term "confession program."

28. Ngai, "Legacies of Exclusion," 25.

29. Ngai, "Legacies of Exclusion," 3 and Table 1, 22.

30. Zhao, *Remaking Chinese America*, 183.

31. Ngai, "Legacies," 26; Zhao, *Remaking*, 182–83. While my narrative stresses their differences, these scholars agree on most points and each has advanced our knowledge significantly.

32. *Newsweek*, Dec. 6, 1982, 39 ff; Peter I. Rose, "Asian Americans: From Pariahs to Paragons," 181–212 in Nathan Glazer, ed., *Clamor at the Gates: New American Immigration* (San Francisco: ICS Press, 1985).

33. Educational data from Bureau of the Census, *1990 Census of Population, Asians and Pacific Islanders in the United States*, 1990 CP-3-5 (Washington: GPO, 1993), Table 3. This volume is the source for all 1990 census data cited in this chapter.

34. E. G. Ravenstein, "The Laws of Migration," *Journal of the Royal Statistical Society* 52 (1889): 21–30.

35. The best general account, but with an East Coast focus, is Peter Kwong, *Forbidden Workers: Illegal Chinese Workers and American Labor* (New York: New Press, 1997). See also his many articles, especially "Impact of Chinese Human Smuggling on the American Labor Market," 235–56 in David Kyle and Rey Koslowski, *Global Human Smuggling: Comparative Perspectives* (Baltimore: Johns Hopkins University Press, 2001) and articles in that volume by Zai Liang/Wenzhen Ye and by Ko-Lin Chin.

36. Leon Stein, *The Triangle Fire* (Philadelphia: Lippincott, 1962) is the classic account.

37. Xiaolan Bao, *Holding Up More Than Half the Sky: Chinese Women Garment Workers in New York City, 1948–92* (Urbana: University of Illinois Press, 2001).

38. Mitchell T. Maki, Harry H. L. Kitano, and S. Megan Berthold, *Achieving the Impossible Dream: How Japanese Americans Obtained Redress* (Urbana: University of Illinois Press, 1999).

39. For an early account of the spread of the concept see: Harry H. L. Kitano and Stanley Sue, "The Model Minorities," *Journal of Social Issues* 29 (1973): 1–9.

40. William Petersen, "Success Story, Japanese American Style," *New York Times Magazine*, Jan. 6, 1996, 20–21. His book, elaborating it, is *Japanese Americans: Oppression and Success* (New York: Random House, 1971).

41. The fullest account is Regina F. Lark, "They Challenged Two Nations: Marriages between Japanese Women and American G.I.s, 1945 to the Present," Ph.D. diss., University of Southern California, 1999. See also Evelyn Nakano Glenn, *Issei, Nisei, War Bride: Three Generations of Japanese American Women in*

Domestic Service (Philadelphia: Temple University Press, 1986) and "The Truth About Japanese War Brides," *Ebony*, March 1952, 17–25.

42. See, for example, several articles in the 2001 Holiday Issue (December) of the *Pacific Citizen*, the organ of the Japanese American Citizens League. Many Nikkei think that this is a Japanese word, but it is originally Hawaiian. "**hapa** 1. Portion, fragment, part (Eng. *half*). 2. Of mixed blood, person of mixed blood." Mary Kawena Pukui and Samuel H. Elbert, *Hawaiian Dictionary: Hawaiian-English, English-Hawaiian*, revised and enlarged edition (Honolulu: University of Hawaii Press, 1986), 58. I owe this explanation and reference to Prof. Eileen Tamura of the University of Hawaii-Manoa.

43. Unless otherwise noted, data in this section come from Barbara M. Posadas, *The Filipino Americans* (Westport, CT: Greenwood, 1959) or the census and INS documents cited above.

44. As noted previously, since the INS records immigrants by nationality, Chinese who emigrated from places other than China, Hong Kong, and Taiwan are not included in the Chinese totals by the INS but are included in the census data.

45. End of century data from *Asian Migration News*, April 2002.

46. Cris Pristay, "Nurse Shortage in U.S. Drains Philippine Pool," *Wall Street Journal*, July 18, 2002.

47. "Arroyo to thank Filipinos in U.S. for boosting economy," *Asia Pulse*, Nov.16, 2001.

48. For details see two books by the major historian of Korean Americans, Wayne Patterson, *The Korean Frontier in America: Immigration to Hawaii, 1896–1910* (Honolulu: University of Hawaii Press, 1988), and *The Ilsei: First-generation Korean Immigrants in Hawai'i, 1903–1973* (Honolulu: University of Hawaii Press, 2000).

49. Bong-youn Choy, *Koreans in America* (Chicago: Nelson-Hall, 1979), 146–49.

50. Elting E. Morison, ed., *The Letters of Theodore Roosevelt* (Cambridge: Harvard University Press, 1951), 4: 1112.

51. Richard C. Allen, *Korea's Syngman Rhee: An Unauthorized Portrait* (Rutland, VT: Charles E. Tuttle, 1960), and Chong-Sik Lee, *Syngman Rhee: The Prison Years of a Young Radical* (Seoul: Yonsei University Press, 2001).

52. Two English-language memoirs give some account of Korean immigrant life before the 1950s: Sucheng Chan, *A Pioneer Korean Family in America, 1905–Present* (Seattle: University of Washington Press, 1990) and Wayne Patterson, ed., *The Golden Mountain: The Autobiography of a Korean Immigrant, 1895–1960* (Urbana: University of Illinois Press, 1995).

53. Hyung-ju Ahn, *Between Two Adversaries: Korean Interpreters at Japanese Alien Enemy Detention Camps during World War II* (Fullerton: Oral History Program, California State University, Fullerton, 2002).

54. Kinoaki Matsuo, *How Japan Plans to Win* (Boston: Little, Brown, 1942).

55. Ji-Yeon Yuh, *Beyond the Shadow of Camptown: Korean Military Brides in America* (New York: New York University Press, 2002); Bok-Lim C. Kim "Asian Wives of U.S. Servicemen: Women in Shadows," *Amerasia Journal* 4: 1 (1977): 91–115,

and *Women in Shadows: A Handbook for Service Providers Working with Asian Wives of U.S. Military Personnel* (La Jolla, CA: National Committee Concerned with Asian Wives of U.S. Servicemen, 1981); see also Haeyun Juliana Kim, "Voices from the Shadows: The Lives of Korean War Brides," *Amerasia Journal* 17: 1 (1991): 15–30.

56. INS, *1997 Statistical Yearbook*, Table 15, 57.
57. For historical accounts of Hinduism in North America see Carl T. Jackson, *Vedanta for the West: The Ramakrishna Movement in the United States* (Bloomington: Indiana University Press, 1994). See also Roger Daniels, *History of Indian Immigration to the United States: An Interpretive Essay* (New York: The Asian Society, 1989).
58. Karen Isaksen Leonard, *Making Ethnic Choices: California's Punjabi Mexican Americans* (Philadelphia: Temple University Press, 1992) and Bruce La Brack, *The Sikhs of Northern California, 1904–1975* (New York: AMS Press, 1988) are excellent for the early twentieth century.

9. Immigrants from Other Worlds: Latinos

1. U.S. Census Bureau, *Current Population Survey, March 2000* (Washington: Ethnic and Hispanic Statistics Branch, Population Division, Mar. 6, 2001).
2. Leonard Schlup, "Pacheco, Romualdo"; http://www.anb.org/articles/05/05005-80.html; *American National Biography Online*, February 2000.
3. Albert Camarillo, "Latin Americans: Mexican Americans and Central Americans," in Mary K. Cayton et al., eds., *Encyclopedia of American Social History* (New York: Scribner, 1993), 2: 856.
4. Hubert Howe Bancroft, *Retrospection: Political and Personal* (New York: The Bancroft Company, 1912), 345–74, lays out his racial prejudices conveniently.
5. Water, too, immigrated/emigrated across the southern border in ways too complex to delineate here. See the pioneering work of Norris Hundley, *Dividing the Waters: A Century of Conflict Between the United States and Mexico* (Berkeley: University of California Press, 1966) and *The Great Thirst: Californians and Water—A History* (Berkeley: University of California Press, 2001).
6. Carey McWilliams, *Factories in the Field: The Story of Migratory Farm Labor in California* (Boston: Little, Brown, 1939) should be supplemented with Clete Daniel, *Bitter Harvest: A History of California Farm Workers, 1870–1941* (Berkeley: University of California Press, 1982) and Devra Weber, *Dark Sweat, White Gold: California Farm Workers, Cotton, and the New Deal* (Berkeley: University of California Press, 1994).
7. Gilbert C. Gonzalez, *Labor and Community: Mexican Citrus Worker Villages in a Southern California County, 1900–1950* (Urbana: University of Illinois Press, 1994).
8. Richard Gribble, "Varela y Morales, Félix Francisco"; http://www.anb.org/articles/08/08-01582.html; *American National Biography Online*, February 2000. For an account of Varela's New York ministry see Jay P. Dolan, *The Immigrant Church:*

New York's Irish and German Catholics, 1815–1865 (Baltimore: Johns Hopkins University Press, 1975).

9. Gary Mormino and George Pozzetta, *The Immigrant World of Ybor City: Italians and Their Latin Neighbors in Tampa, 1885–1985* (Urbana: University of Illinois Press, 1987).

10. María Cristina García, *Havana USA: Cuban Exiles and Cuban Americans in South Florida, 1959–1994* (Berkeley: University of California Press, 1996).

11. Elizabeth Llorente, "N.J. Cubans Moving On: Other States Beckon with Jobs, Retirement," Bergen (N.J.) *Record*, Mar. 1, 2002.

12. Fabiola Santiago, "Separated Yet Together, Exiles Span Many Lands," *Miami Herald*, Dec. 29, 1998.

13. John F. Stover, "Flagler, Henry Morrison"; http://www.anb.org/articles/10/10-00559.html; *American National Biography Online*, February 2000.

14. David M. Reimers, *Still the Golden Door: The Third World Comes to America*, 2nd ed. (New York: Columbia University Press, 1992), 168–69.

15. Stephen Fidler, "New migrants spur growth in remittances," *Financial Times* (London), May 17, 2001.

16. Nancy Foner, *From Ellis Island to JFK: New York's Two Great Waves of Immigration* (New Haven: Yale University Press, 2000), 12.

17. This and the preceding paragraphs are from a summary in *Migration News* (Davis: University of California, November 1996), electronic edition. It is an invaluable compilation.

10. Refugees and Human Rights: Cubans, Southeast Asians, and Others

1. Tracy S. Voorhees, *Interim Report to the President on the Cuban Refugee Problem* (Washington: GPO, 1960).

2. 72 *Stat.* 419, Act of July 25, 1958 granted admission for permanent residence to Hungarian parolees of at least two years residence in the U.S. if the alien had been admissible at the time of original entry.

3. Bertolt Brecht, "Concerning the Label Emigrant," in J. Willett and R. Mannheim, eds., *Bertolt Brecht, Poems, Part Two 1929–1938* (London: Methuen, 1976), 301.

4. Publications focusing on Operation Pedro Pan include: Tracy S. Voorhees, *Interim Report . . .* ; United States, Children's Bureau, *Cuba's Children in Exile* (Washington: GPO, 1967); Bryan O. Walsh, "Cuban Refugee Children," *Journal of Interamerican Studies and World Affairs* 13 (July–October 1971), 378–415. Josefina Leyva, *Operación Pedro Pan: el éxodo de los niños cubanos* (Coral Gables, FL: Editorial Ponce de León, 1993); María Cristina García, *Havana USA: Cuban Exiles and Cuban Americans in South Florida, 1959–1994* (Berkeley: University of California Press, 1996), 21 ff.; Victor Andres Triay, *Fleeing Castro: Operation Pedro Pan and the Cuban Children's Program* (Gainesville: University Press of Florida, 1998); and Yvonne M. Conde, *Operation Pedro Pan: The Untold Exodus of 14,048 Cuban Children* (New York: Routledge, 1999).

5. Walsh, "Cuban Refugee Children," 379 says that "14,048" unaccompanied children came between the Jan. 3, 1961, break in diplomatic relations and the Missile Crisis of October 1962, and some have used that as the total number of children, but Walsh makes clear that there were some children before that and that a federally-funded Cuban children's program continued into the 1970s. Of the 14,048, 6,486 received foster care in the federal program.

6. *The New York Times*, Nov. 11, 2002, and Montse Armengou and Ricard Belis, *Los niños perdidos del franquismo* (Madrid: Plaza & Janés, 2002).

7. See, for example, "Cuba—And Now the Children," *Time* (Oct. 6, 1961), 41.

8. Walsh, "Cuban Refugee Children," reports that there were already a number of unaccompanied Cuban children in the Miami area before the Pedro Pan operation began on Dec. 26, 1960.

9. García, *Havana USA*, 23–25.

10. Children's Bureau, *Cuba's Children*, 6.

11. Joan Didion, *Miami* (New York: Simon and Schuster, 1987). Curiously, García. *Havana USA*, published nine years later, ignores Didion, but has an informative section on *Areito*, 201–4. Triay, *Fleeing Castro*.

12. Conde, *Operation Pedro Pan*, xii.

13. *Public Papers of the Presidents of the United States, Lyndon B. Johnson, 1965* (Washington: GPO, 1967), 2: 1038.

14. Walsh, "Cuban Refugee Children," 386–87.

15. The Cuban Adjustment Act is Pub. L. 89–732, Nov 2, 1966, 80 *Stat.* 1161, as amended by Pub. L. 94–571, Sec. 8, Oct. 20, 1976, 90 *Stat.* 2706; Pub. L. 96–212. Title II. Sec. 203 (i) Mar. 17, 1980, 94 *Stat.* 108.

16. Robert M. Levine, *Tropical Diaspora: The Jewish Experience in Cuba* (Gainesville: University of Florida Press, 1993); Alfonso Chardy, "As Jews Dwindle in Cuba, They Flourish in Miami," *Miami Herald*, Sept. 22, 1990, as cited in García, *Havana USA*, 43–44.

17. For the evolution of the larger concept, see T. Christopher Jesperson, "Human Rights," in Alexander DeConde et al., eds., *Encyclopedia of American Foreign Policy*, 2nd ed. (New York: Scribner, 2002), 2:173–85 and its bibliography.

18. The 1980 law is 94 *Stat.* 102.

19. Alex Larzelere, *The Cuban Boatlift* (Washington: National Defense University Press, 1988).

20. García, *Havana USA*, 65.

21. Jimmy Carter, *Public Papers of the Presidents of the United States, 1980* (Washington: GPO), 1: 834.

22. The Refugee Education Assistance Act is 94 *Stat.* 1799.

23. See Heriberto Dixon, "The Cuban-American Counterpoint: Black Cubans in the United States," *Dialectical Anthropology* 13 (1988): 227–39.

24. Larzelere, *Cuban Boatlift*, 434–35. He reproduces charts that appeared in the *New York Times*, Nov. 25, 1987, under the headline "What Happened to the Marielitos?"

25. Presidential Press Conference Transcript, Office of the [White House] Press Secretary, Nov. 7, 2002.
26. *Miami Herald*, Nov. 9, 2002. *Federal Register*, Nov. 13, 2002, vol. 67, no. 219, pp. 68923–68926.
27. INS, *1999 Statistical Yearbook* (Washington: GPO, 2002), Table 27, 100–6.
28. Michel S. Laguerre, *Diasporic Citizenship: Haitian Americans in Transnational America* (New York: St. Martin's, 1998), 1: 68. Mami E. Locke gives his name as "Homer A. Plessy" in her *American National Biography* essay, and mentions no Haitian American connection. Mamie E. Locke, "Plessy, Homer Adolph"; http://www.anb.org/articles/11/11-00692.html; *American National Biography Online*, February 2000.
29. Michel S. Laguerre, "Haitians," in Stephan Thernstrom, ed., *Harvard Encyclopedia of American Ethnic Groups* (Cambridge: Harvard University Press, 1980), 446–49.
30. *Migration News*, December 2000.
31. For European refugees from Asia see David Kranzler, *Japanese, Nazis, and Jews: The Jewish Refugee Community of Shanghai, 1938–1945* (New York: Yeshiva University Press, 1976) and Marcia R. Ristaino, *Port of Last Resort: Diaspora Communities of Shanghai* (Stanford: Stanford University Press, 2001).
32. John K. Whitmore, "Chinese from Southeast Asia," 81–101 in David W. Haines, ed., *Refugees in America in the 1990s: A Reference Handbook* (Westport, CT: Greenwood, 1996), is the best account I know.
33. Scott McConnell, *Leftward Journey: The Education of Vietnamese Students in France, 1919–1939* (New Brunswick, NJ: Transaction, 1989).
34. Lecture, Miami University, Nov. 13, 2002.
35. U.S. Department of Commerce, Bureau of the Census, QT-P7, "Race Alone . . . Asian . . . 2000," *Data Set: Census 2000. Summary File 1 (SF 1) 100-Percent Data*. Bureau of Census Web site, 2002.
36. Jeremy Hein, *From Vietnam, Laos, and Cambodia: A Refugee Experience in the United States* (New York: Twayne, 1995), Table 4.3, 55, for 1975 and 1990. For 2000 see the data set cited in n. 33.
37. For two highly sensitive works allowing refugees to speak for themselves see Usha Welaratna, *Beyond the Killing Fields: Voices of Nine Cambodian Survivors in America* (Stanford: Stanford University Press, 1993) and Sucheng Chan, ed., *Not Just Victims: Conversations with Cambodian Community Leaders in the United States* (Urbana: University of Illinois Press, 2003).
38. Hein, *From Vietnam, Laos, and Cambodia*, 158.
39. Jimmy Carter, *Keeping Faith: Memoirs of a President* (New York: Bantam Books, 1982), 209.

11. Immigration Reform: Myths and Realities

1. Lyndon B. Johnson, *Public Papers of the Presidents of the United States, 1965* (Washington: GPO, 1967), 2: 1038.

2. Lawrence H. Fuchs, "Immigration Reform in 1911 and 1981: The Role of Select Commissions," *Journal of American Ethnic History* 3: 1 (1983): 58–89. Labeling the Dillingham Commission as "reform" is an anachronism although consonant with 1980s usages.

3. Theodore Hesburgh, *God, Country, Notre Dame* (New York: Doubleday, 1990), 277.

4. Theodore Hesburgh, "Enough Delay on Immigration," *New York Times*, Mar. 20, 1986.

5. Rowan in Cincinnati *Enquirer*, June 21, 1986; Simpson in *The Washington Post*, Apr. 28, 1981. For Simpson's salty and simplistic views of almost everything see his *Right in the Old Gazoo: What I've Observed in a Lifetime of Scrapping with the American Press* (New York: William Morrow, 1997).

6. Hesburgh, *God, Country, Notre Dame*, 278.

7. *Public Papers of the Presidents, Ronald W. Reagan, 1981.* "Statement on United States Immigration and Refugee Policy," July 30, 1981 (Washington: GPO, 1982), 676–77.

8. *The Washington Post*, Apr. 28, 1981.

9. *Public Papers of the Presidents: Ronald Reagan, 1986* (Washington: GPO, 1989), 1521.

10. IRCA is 100 *Stat.* 3359.

11. INS, *Statistical Yearbook, 1988* (Washington: GPO, 1989), Table 60, 109.

12. INS, *Statistical Yearbook, 1988*, Table 61, 110.

13. Charles Dickens, *Oliver Twist*, ch. 51.

14. "U.S. Border Patrol History." INS Wesbsite, accessed Nov. 28, 2002. http://www.ins.usdoj.gov/graphics/lawenfor/bpatrol/bphistorya.htm

15. See, for example, INS Fact Sheet, "INS' Southwest Border Strategy," May 1, 1999. Cf. INS, *Statistical Yearbook, 1988*, Tables 55–56, 207–10, and 241.

16. See the informed discussion in "Operation Hold the Line in Texas," *Migration News*, March 1994.

17. For the INS view of the program see Testimony of Michael D. Cronin, Assistant Commissioner for Inspections, Immigration and Naturalization Service, before the House Judiciary Committee, Subcommittee on Immigration and Claims, regarding the Visa Waiver Pilot Program, June 17, 1997. Typescript, INS Historical Reference Library. I have this document courtesy of the INS historian, Marian Smith.

18. 45 *Stat.* 1512.

19. For a description see INS, *Statistical Yearbook, 1997*, Appendix 3, 10.

20. Nicholas Laham, *Ronald Reagan and the Politics of Immigration Reform* (Westport, CT: Praeger, 2000), 172–73.

21. Christopher Mitchell, "Changing the Rules: The Impact of the Simpson/Rodino Act on Inter-American Diplomacy," 177–89 in Georges Vernez, ed., *Immigration and International Relations* (Santa Monica, CA: Rand Corporation, 1990). Quotation at 183.

12. *"Controlling Our Borders"*: *Struggles over Immigration Policy*

1. David M. Reimers, *Unwelcome Strangers: American Identity and the Turn Against Immigration* (New York: Columbia University Press, 1998).

2. For Jordan's comments, see *Migration News*, May 1994. For the reports and other materials generated by the U.S. Commission on Immigration Reform (1990–1997) see: http://www.utexas.edu/lbj/uscir/

3. A description of each appears in INS, *Statistical Yearbook, 1997*, Appendix 1, 19–26.

4. 106 *Stat.* 1969 and 106 *Stat.* 3316.

5. 103 *Stat.* 2099.

6. 104 *Stat.* 4978.

7. An implementation act for each was necessary: 102 *Stat.* 1876 and 107 *Stat.* 2057.

8. Section 302 of the 1990 act.

9. Anna O. Law, "The Diversity Visa Lottery—A Cycle of Unintended Consequences in United States Immigration Policy," *Journal of American Ethnic History* 21 (Summer 2002): 1–29 is excellent.

10. The Maxwell School Report may be found online at: http://www.govexec.com/gpp/reportcard.htm.

11. Interview, Migration Policy Institute, December 2002.

12. U.S. Department of Justice, Immigration and Naturalization Service, "INS Commissioner Doris Meissner Announces Departure." News release, Oct. 18, 2000.

13. There is a good summary in the perceptive essay by the German scholar Herbert Dittgen, "The American Debate about Immigration in the 1990s: A New Nationalism After the Cold War?," 197–225 in Knud Krakau, ed., *The American Nation, National Identity, Nationalism* (Münster, Germany, 1997).

14. "Hot Lines and Hot Tempers," *Time*, Nov. 28, 1994.

15. *Los Angeles Times*, Sept. 14, 1999.

16. *The Economist* (London), July 13, 1996.

17. 110 *Stat.* 1214; 110 *Stat.* 2105; and 110 *Stat.* 3009.

18. George Thomas Kurian, ed., *The Encyclopedia of the Republican Party* and *The Encyclopedia of the Democratic Party* (Armonk, NY: Sharpe Reference, 1997, 2002), 2: 800 and 4: 838.

19. *Public Papers of the Presidents, William J. Clinton, 1996* (Washington: GPO, 1998), 1731.

20. 111 *Stat.* 270.

21. 111 *Stat.* 2193.

22. 112 *Stat.* 575.

23. 112 *Stat.* 1998.

24. Detailed series of California election returns may be consulted on the excellent high-tech Web sites of the California Secretary of State.

25. Steven Greenhouse, "Labor Urges Amnesty for Legal Immigrants," *New York Times*, Feb. 17, 2000.

26. INS, *Statistical Yearbook* 2000, Table 11.
27. INS, *Statistical Yearbook* 2000, Table 5.
28. Palmer Morrel-Samuels, "Measuring Illegal Immigration at U.S. Border Stations by Sampling from a Flow of 500 Million Travelers," *Population and Environment* 23 (January 2002): 285–302.
29. INS, *Statistical Yearbook* 2000, 16 and Table 8, 44–51.
30. Several of the essays in Peter H. Koehn and Xiao-huang Yin, eds., *The Expanding Roles of Chinese Americans in U.S.-China Relations* (Armonk, NY: M. E. Sharpe, 2002), illuminate some of these questions with regard to China and Chinese. For the development of these kinds of international interactions within the computer industry see the work of AnnaLee Saxenian, most recently *Local and Global Networks of Immigrant Professionals in Silicon Valley* (San Francisco: Public Policy Institute of California, 2002).
31. INS, *Statistical Yearbook* 2000, Glossary, 291. Not all categories were in use in 2000.
32. 112 *Stat.* 2681.
33. For an informed critique of the IT industry lobbying that and of the H-1B program generally, see Paul Donnelly, "H-1B is Just Another Subsidy," *Computer World*, July 22, 2002.
34. Workers in the four largest occupational categories, which employed almost 83 percent of the 235,000 H-1B workers whose salary data we have, earned the following median amount:

Job	Number of H-B1 Workers	Median Annual Compensation
Computer-related	138,383	$55,000
Architecture, Surveying, and Engineering	28,297	58,000
Administrators	16,518	40,795
Educators	10,900	35,000

35. INS, *Statistical Yearbook* 2000, Table 38.

Epilogue: Immigration After 9/11

1. Robert Warren and Ellen Percy Kraly, *The Elusive Exodus: Emigration from the United States* (Washington: Population Reference Bureau, 1985) and INS, *Statistical Yearbook* 2000, 271.
2. *Annual Report of the Commissioner General of Immigration, 1901* (Washington: GPO, 1902), 1.
3. INS, *Statistical Yearbook* 2000, Table 39.
4. George W. Bush, Budget Message, Feb. 28, 2001. www.whitehouse.gov/news/usbudget/blueprint/buddoc.html [85–86]. The printed version is ISBN 0-16-050683-2 (Washington: GPO, 2002).
5. Asa Hutchinson, "Improvements Are Coming," *Immigration Daily* (ILW.com), Feb. 25, 2003.

6. James W. Ziglar, "Let's Not Forget Our Immigration Duties," *Miami Herald,* Mar. 4, 2003. Ziglar resigned Nov. 30, 2002, after the impending switch of INS to DHS had been announced.

7. The "new" BCIS Web site, http://www.immigration.gov/graphics/index.htm, is clearly a clone of the old INS Web site. A headline assured users that "INS Transitions Into DHS; All Customer Services Remain in Place." Mark Krikorian, in his chortling obituary, "INS, R.I.P.: Into the Dustbin of History," *National Review Online,* Feb. 28, 2003, is clearly unaware of the continuity.

8. Diane Schmidley, *The Foreign-Born Population in the United States: March 2002.* Current Population Reports, P20–539 (Washington: U.S. Census Bureau, 2003).

9. Testimony of Chairman Alan Greenspan, *Aging Global Population,* Before the Special Committee on Aging, U.S. Senate, Feb. 27, 2003. http://www.federalreserve.gov/

10. Roger Daniels, "Two Cheers for Immigration," 5–69 in Roger Daniels and Otis L. Graham, *Debating American Immigration* (Lanham, MD: Rowman & Littlefield, 2001).

11. Interview, Migration Policy Institute, December 2002.

Bibliography

Aarim, Najia. *Chinese Immigrants, African Americans, and Racial Anxiety in the United States, 1848–82*. Urbana: University of Illinois Press, 2003.

Ahn, Hyung-ju. *Between Two Adversaries: Korean Interpreters at Japanese Alien Enemy Detention Camps during World War II*. Fullerton: Oral History Program, California State University, Fullerton, 2002.

Allen, Richard C. *Korea's Syngman Rhee: An Unauthorized Portrait*. Rutland, VT: Charles E. Tuttle, 1960.

Almedia, Linda Dowling. *Irish Immigrants in New York City*. Bloomington: Indiana University Press, 2001.

American Federation of Labor. *Proceedings, 1928*. Washington, 1928.

Anbinder, Tyler. *Nativism and Slavery: The Northern Know Nothings and the Politics of the 1850s*. New York: Oxford University Press, 1991.

Annual Report of the Commissioner General of Immigration, 1901. Washington: GPO, 1902.

Anon., "The Truth About Japanese War Brides." *Ebony*, March 1952, 17–25.

Armengou, Montse and Richard Belis. *Los Niños Perdidos del Franquismo*. Madrid: Plaza & Janés, 2002.

Austin, Allan W. *From Concentration Camp to Campus: Japanese American Students and World War II*. Urbana: University of Illinois Press, forthcoming.

Bancroft, Hubert Howe. *Retrospection: Political and Personal*. New York: The Bancroft Company, 1912.

Bao, Xiaolan. *Holding Up More Than Half the Sky: Chinese Women Garment Workers in New York City, 1948–92*. Urbana: University of Illinois Press, 2001.

Barkan, Elliott R. "Whom Shall We Integrate? A Comparative Analysis of the Immigration and Naturalization Trends of Asians Before and After the 1965 Immigration Act (1951–1978)." *Journal of American Ethnic History* 1:3 (Fall 1983): 29–57.

Bean, Frank D., Georges Vernez, and Charles B. Keely. *Opening and Closing the Doors: Evaluating Immigration Reform and Control.* Santa Monica: Rand, 1989.

Bernard, William S. *American Immigration Policy: A Reappraisal.* New York: Harper, 1950.

Biddle, Francis. *In Brief Authority.* Garden City, NY: Doubleday, 1962.

Billington, Ray Allen. *The Protestant Crusade, 1800–1860.* New York: Macmillan, 1938.

Blum, John Morton. *Morgenthau and Roosevelt.* Boston: Houghton Mifflin, 1970.

———, ed. *From the Morgenthau Diaries: Years of War, 1941–1945.* Boston: Houghton Mifflin, 1967.

Blumenson, Martin, ed. *The Patton Papers.* Boston: Houghton Mifflin, 1972.

Breitman, Richard and Alan M. Kraut. *American Refugee Policy and European Jewry, 1933–1945.* Bloomington: Indiana University Press, 1987.

Bryce, James. *The American Commonwealth.* New York: Macmillan, 1891.

Cabranes, José A. *Citizenship and the American Empire.* New Haven: Yale University Press, 1979.

California. Governor. *Mexicans in California.* San Francisco, 1930.

Camarillo, Albert. *Chicanos in a Changing Society: From Mexican Pueblos to Mexican Barrios in Santa Barbara and Southern California, 1848–1930.* Cambridge, MA: Harvard University Press, 1979.

———. "Latin Americans: Mexican Americans and Central Americans." In Mary K. Cayton et al., eds. *Encyclopedia of American Social History.* New York: Scribner, 1993, 2: 855–72.

Cardoso, Lawrence A. "Labor Emigration to the Southwest, 1916 to 1920: Mexican Attitudes and Policy." *Southwestern Historical Quarterly* 79 (1979): 400–16.

Carter, Jimmy. *Keeping Faith: Memoirs of a President.* New York: Bantam Books, 1982.

Centre for Contemporary Cultural Studies. *The Empire Strikes Back: Race and Racism in 70s Britain.* London: Hutchinson, 1982.

Chan, Sucheng, ed. *Entry Denied: Exclusion and the Chinese Community in America, 1882–1943.* Philadelphia: Temple University Press, 1991.

———, ed. *Not Just Victims: Conversations with Cambodian Community Leaders in the United States.* Urbana: University of Illinois Press, 2003.

——— and Mary Lee Paik. *A Pioneer Korean Family in America, 1905–Present.* Seattle: University of Washington Press, 1990.

Choy, Bong-youn. *Koreans in America.* Chicago: Nelson-Hall, 1979.

Christgau, John. "Collins versus the World: The Fight to Restore Citizenship to Japanese American Renunciants of World War II." *Pacific Historical Review* 54 (1985): 1–31.

———. *"Enemies": World War II Alien Internment.* Ames: Iowa State University Press, 1985.

Chu, Louis. *Eat a Bowl of Tea.* New York: Lyle Stuart, 1961.

Cieslak, Edward C. *The Foreign Student in American Colleges: A Survey and Evaluation of Administrative Problems and Practices.* Detroit: Wayne University Press, 1955.

Clark, Jane Perry. *Deportation of Aliens from the United States to Europe.* New York: Columbia University Press, 1931.

Clifford, Mary Dorita. "The Hawaiian Sugar Planters Association and Filipino Exclusion." In Josepha M. Saniel, ed. *The Filipino Exclusion Movement, 1927–1935.* Quezon City: University of the Philippines, 1967.

Clines, Francis X. "The New Illegals: The Irish." *New York Times Magazine,* November 20, 1988.

Cohen, Lucy M. *Chinese in the Post–Civil War South: A People Without a History.* Baton Rouge: Louisiana State University Press, 1984.

Collaer, N. D. "The Crystal City Internment Camp." *INS Monthly Review* 5 (December 1947): 77.

Collins, Donald E. *Native American Aliens: Disloyalty and Renunciation of American Citizenship by Japanese Americans during World War II.* Westport, CT: Greenwood, 1985.

Commager, Henry Steele. *The American Mind: An Interpretation of American Thought and Character since the 1880's.* New Haven: Yale University Press, 1950.

Commons, John R. et al., eds. *A Documentary History of American Industrial Society,* 11 vols. Cleveland: A. H. Clark, 1910.

Conde, Yvonne M. *Operation Pedro Pan: The Untold Exodus of 14,048 Cuban Children.* New York: Routledge, 1999.

Congressional Research Service, Library of Congress. *History of the Immigration and Naturalization Service.* Washington: GPO, 1980.

———. *U.S. Immigration Law and Policy.* Washington: GPO, 1979.

Corbett, F. Scott. *Quiet Passages: The Exchange of Civilians between the United States and Japan during the Second World War.* Kent, OH: Kent State University Press, 1987.

Cortés, Carlos. "Mexicans." In S. Thernstrom, ed., *The Harvard Encyclopedia of American Ethnic Groups.* Cambridge, MA: Harvard University Press, 1980.

Cribbs, Lennie A. "The Memphis Chinese Labor Convention, 1869." *West Tennessee Historical Society Papers* (1983): 176–83.

Culley, John J. "The Santa Fe Internment Camp and the Justice Department Program for Enemy Aliens." 57–71 in R. Daniels et al., *Japanese Americans from Relocation to Redress.* Salt Lake City: University of Utah Press, 1986.

Dabney, Dick. *A Good Man: The Life of Sam J. Ervin.* Boston: Houghton Mifflin, 1976.

Dallek, Robert. *Lone Star Rising: Lyndon Johnson and His Times, 1908–1960.* New York: Oxford University Press, 1991.

Daniel, Clete. *Bitter Harvest: A History of California Farm Workers, 1870–1941.* Berkeley: University of California Press, 1982.

Daniels, Roger. "Ah Sin and His Lawyers." *Reviews in American History* 23 (1995): 472–77.

——. *Asian America: Chinese and Japanese in the United States since 1850.* Seattle: University of Washington Press, 1988.

——. *Coming to America: A History of Race and Ethnicity in American Life,* 2nd ed. New York: HarperCollins, 2002.

——. *Concentration Camps, USA: Japanese Americans and World War II.* New York: Holt, Rinehart and Winston, 1972.

——. "The Growth of Restrictive Immigration Policies in the Colonies of Settlement before World War II." 39–43 in Robin Cohen, ed., *The Cambridge Survey of World Migration.* Cambridge: Cambridge University Press, 1995.

——. *History of Indian Immigration to the United States: An Interpretive Essay.* New York: The Asia Society, 1989.

——. "No Lamps Were Lit for Them: Angel Island and the Historiography of Asian American Immigration." *Journal of American Ethnic History* 17 (1997): 4–18.

——. *The Politics of Prejudice: The Anti-Japanese Movement in California and the Struggle for Japanese Exclusion.* Berkeley: University of California Press, 1962.

——. *Prisoners Without Trial: Japanese Americans in World War II.* New York: Hill & Wang, 1993.

——. "Two Cheers for Immigration." 5–69 in Roger Daniels and Otis L. Graham, *Debating American Immigration.* Lanham, MD: Rowman & Littlefield, 2001.

Davis, Winfield J. *History of Political Conventions in California, 1849–1892.* Sacramento: California State Library, 1893.

Daws, Gavan. *Shoal of Time.* Honolulu: University of Hawaii Press, 1966.

Deakin, Nicholas, et al. *Colour, Citizenship, and British Society, Based on the Institute of Race Relations Report.* London: Panther Books, 1970.

Denoon, Donald. *Settler Capitalism: The Dynamics of Dependent Development in the Southern Hemisphere.* New York: Cambridge University Press, 1983.

Dickens, Charles. *Oliver Twist.* Chapter 51.

Didion, Joan. *Miami.* New York: Simon and Schuster, 1987.

Dinnerstein, Leonard. *America and the Survivors of the Holocaust.* New York: Columbia University Press, 1982.

Dittgen, Herbert. "The American Debate about Immigration in the 1990s: A New Nationalism After the Cold War?" 197–225 in Knud Krakau, ed., *The American Nation, National Identity, Nationalism.* New Brunswick, NJ: Transaction, 1997.

Divine, Robert A. *American Immigration Policy.* New Haven: Yale University Press, 1957.

Dixon, Heriberto. "The Cuban-American Counterpoint: Black Cubans in the United States." *Dialectical Anthropology* 13 (1988): 227–39.

Dolan, Jay P. *The Immigrant Church: New York's Irish and German Catholics, 1815–1865.* Baltimore: Johns Hopkins University Press, 1975.

Donald, David H. *Charles Sumner and the Rights of Man.* New York: Knopf, 1970.

Draper, Paula Jean. "Muses Behind Barbed Wire: Canada and the Interned Refugees." 271–81 in J. C. Jackman and C. M. Borden, eds., *The Muses Flee Hitler: Cultural Transfer and Adaptation, 1930–1945.* Washington: Smithsonian Institution Press, 1983.

Driscoll, Barbara A. *The Tracks North: The Railroad Bracero Program of World War II.* Austin: University of Texas Press, 1999.

Dunne, Finley Peter. *Mr. Dooley's Opinions.* New York: R. H. Russell, 1901.

Erickson, Charlotte. "Some Thoughts on the Social and Economic Consequences of the Quota Acts." *European Contributions to American Studies* (Neth.) 10 (1986): 28–46.

Ervin, Sam J. *Preserving the Constitution: The Autobiography of Sam Ervin, Jr.* Charlottesville, VA: Michie, 1984.

Evans, Patricia R. " 'Likely to Become a Public Charge': Immigration in the Backwaters of Administrative Law, 1882–1933." Ph. D. dissertation, George Washington University, 1987.

Fairbank, Wilma. *America's Cultural Experiment in China, 1942–1949.* Washington: GPO, 1976.

Fitzpatrick, John C., ed. *The Papers of George Washington*, vol. 27. Washington: GPO, 1931.

Foner, Nancy. *From Ellis Island to JFK: New York's Two Great Waves of Immigration.* New Haven: Yale University Press, 2000.

Fox, Stephen. *The Unknown Internment: An Oral History of the Internment of the West Coast Italian Americans during World War II.* Boston: Twayne, 1990.

Friedman, Max Paul. *Nazis and Good Neighbors: The United States Campaign against the Germans of Latin America in World War II.* New York: Cambridge University Press, 2003.

Fritz, Christian G. "A Nineteenth Century 'Habeas Corpus Mill': The Chinese before the Federal Courts in California." *American Journal of Legal History* 32: 4 (1988): 347-720.

Fry, Varian. *Surrender on Demand.* New York: Random House, 1945.

Fuchs, Lawrence H. "Immigration Reform in 1911 and 1981: The Role of Select Commissions." *Journal of American Ethnic History* 3:1 (1983): 58–89.

García, María Cristina. *Havana USA: Cuban Exiles and Cuban Americans in South Florida, 1959–1994.* Berkeley: University of California Press, 1996.

Gardiner, C. Harvey. *Pawns in a Triangle of Hate: The Peruvian Japanese and the United States.* Seattle: University of Washington Press, 1981.

Gardner, Robert W., et al. "Asian Americans: Growth, Change, and Diversity." *Population Bulletin* 40 (1985): 4.

Garraty, John A., ed. *American National Biography*, 20 vols. New York: Oxford University Press, 2000.

Gibson, Campbell and Emily Lennon. "Historical Census Statistics on the Foreign-born Population of the United States: 1850–1990." Population Division Working Paper No. 15. Washington: U.S. Bureau of the Census, February 1999.

Gillman, Peter and Leni Gillman. *Collar the Lot!: How Britain Interned and Expelled Its Wartime Refugees.* New York: Quartet Books, 1980.

Gleason, Philip. "Trouble in the Colonial Melting Pot." *Journal of American Ethnic History* 20 (Fall 2000): 3–17.

Glenn, Evelyn Nakano. *Issei, Nisei, War Bride: Three Generations of Japanese American Women in Domestic Service.* Philadelphia: Temple University Press, 1986.

Goethe, C. M. "Filipino Immigration Viewed as a Peril." *Current History,* January 1934, 354.

———. "The Influx of Mexican Amerinds." *Eugenics,* January 1929, 9.

Gomolak, Louis S. "Prologue: LBJ's Foreign Affairs Background, 1908–1948." Ph.D. dissertation, University of Texas, 1989.

Gonzalez, Gilbert C. *Labor and Community: Mexican Citrus Worker Villages in a Southern California County, 1900–1950.* Urbana: University of Illinois Press, 1994.

Gottlieb, Amy Zahl. "Refugee Immigration: The Truman Directive." *Prologue* 13 (Spring 1981): 5–18.

Gould, Lewis L. *The Presidency of William McKinley.* Lawrence: The Regents Press of Kansas, 1980.

Griswold del Castillo, Richard and Richard A. García. *César Chavez: A Triumph of Spirit.* Norman: University of Oklahoma Press, 1995.

Gruber, Ruth. *Haven: The Untold Story of 1,000 World War II Refugees.* New York: Coward-McCann, 1983.

Gruening, Ernest H. *Many Battles: The Autobiography of Ernest Gruening.* New York: Liveright, 1973.

Gyory, Andrew. *Closing the Gate: Race, Politics, and the Chinese Exclusion Act.* Chapel Hill: University of North Carolina Press, 1998.

Haan, Kilsoo, translator and editor. *How Japan Plans to Win.* Written by Kinoaki Matsuo. Boston: Little, Brown, 1942.

Hahamovitch, Cindy. "Creating Perfect Immigrants: Guestworkers of the World in Historical Perspective." *Labor History* 44 (February 2003): 69–95.

———. *The Fruits of Their Labor: Atlantic Coast Farmworkers and the Making of Migrant Poverty, 1870–1945.* Chapel Hill: University of North Carolina Press, 1997.

Hein, Jeremy. *From Vietnam, Laos, and Cambodia: A Refugee Experience in the United States.* New York: Twayne, 1995.

Hesburgh, Theodore. *God, Country, Notre Dame.* New York: Doubleday, 1990.

———. "Enough Delay on Immigration." *The New York Times,* March 20, 1986.

Higashide, Seiichi. *Adios to Tears: The Memoirs of a Japanese Peruvian Internee in U.S. Concentration Camps,* 2nd ed. Seattle: University of Washington Press, 2000.

Higham, John. *Strangers in the Land: Patterns of American Nativism, 1860–1925.* New Brunswick, NJ: Rutgers University Press, 1955.

Hiro, Dilip. *Black British, White British*. London: Eyre & Spottiswoode, 1971.

Hoffman, Abraham. *Unwanted Mexican Americans in the Great Depression*. Tucson: University of Arizona Press, 1974.

Holborn, Louise W. *The International Refugee Organization, a Specialized Agency of the United Nations: Its History and Work, 1946–1952*. London: Oxford University Press, 1956.

Holmes, Colin. *John Bull's Island: Immigration and British Society, 1871–1971*. Basingstoke, UK: Macmillan Education, 1988.

Hooker, Nancy H., ed. *The Moffat Papers: Selections from the Diplomatic Journals of Jay Pierrepont Moffat*. Cambridge, MA: Harvard University Press, 1956.

Hundley, Norris. *Dividing the Waters: A Century of Conflict Between the United States and Mexico*. Berkeley: University of California Press, 1966.

——. *The Great Thirst: Californians and Water—A History*. Berkeley: University of California Press, 2001.

Hutchinson, Asa. "Improvements Are Coming." *Immigration Daily* (ILW.com), Feb. 25, 2003.

Hutchinson, E. P. *Legislative History of American Immigration Policy, 1798–1865*. Philadelphia: University of Pennsylvania Press, 1981.

Huttenback, Robert A. *Racism and Empire: White Settlers and Colored Immigrants in the British Self-Governing Colonies, 1830–1910*. Ithaca, NY: Cornell University Press, 1976.

Jackman, J. C. and C. M. Borden, eds. *The Muses Flee Hitler: Cultural Transfer and Adaptation, 1930–1945*. Washington: Smithsonian Institution Press, 1983.

Jackson, Carl T. *Vedanta for the West: The Ramakrishna Movement in the United States*. Bloomington: Indiana University Press, 1994.

Jeffries, John J. *Testing the Roosevelt Coalition: Connecticut Society and Politics in the Era of World War II*. Knoxville: University of Tennessee Press, 1979.

Jesperson, T. Christopher. "Human Rights." In Alexander DeConde et al., eds., *Encyclopedia of American Foreign Policy*, 2nd ed. New York: Scribner, 2002, 2: 173–85.

Jessup, Philip C. *Elihu Root*, 2 vols. New York: Dodd, Mead, 1938.

Kahn, E. J. *The China Hands: America's Foreign Service Officers and What Befell Them*. New York: Viking, 1975.

Kennedy, Robert F. "Introduction" to John F. Kennedy, *A Nation of Immigrants*, revised and enlarged edition. New York: Harpers, 1964.

Kenney, David. *A Political Passage: The Career of Stratton of Illinois*. Carbondale: Southern Illinois University Press, 1990.

Kerr, James E. *The Insular Cases: The Role of the Judiciary in American Expansion*. Port Washington, NY: Kennikat, 1982.

Kettner, James H. *The Development of American Citizenship, 1608–1870*. Chapel Hill: University of North Carolina Press, 1978.

Kim, Bok-Lim C. "Asian Wives of U.S. Servicemen: Women in Shadows." *Amerasia Journal* 4:1 (1977): 91–115.

——. *Women in Shadows: A Handbook for Service Providers Working with Asian Wives of U.S. Military Personnel.* La Jolla, CA: National Committee Concerned with Asian Wives of U.S. Servicemen, 1981.

Kim, Haeyun Juliana. "Voices from the Shadows: The Lives of Korean War Brides." *Amerasia Journal* 17:1 (1991): 15–30.

Kinzer, Donald L. *An Episode in Anti-Catholicism: The American Protective Association.* Seattle: University of Washington Press, 1964.

Kiser, George C. and Martha W. Kiser, eds. *Mexican Workers in the United States: Historical and Political Perspectives.* Albuquerque: University of New Mexico Press, 1979.

Kiser, George C. and David Silverman. "Mexican American Repatriation during the Great Depression." *Journal of Mexican American History* 3 (1973): 139–64.

Kitano, Harry H. L. and Roger Daniels. *Asian Americans: Emerging Minorities.* Englewood Cliffs, N.J., 1988.

—— and Stanley Sue. "The Model Minorities." *Journal of Social Issues* 29 (1973): 1–9.

Koehn, Peter H. and Xiao-huang Yin, eds. *The Expanding Roles of Chinese Americans in U.S.-China Relations.* Armonk, NY: M. E. Sharpe, 2002.

Kranzler, David. *Japanese, Nazis, and Jews: The Jewish Refugee Community of Shanghai, 1938–1945.* New York: Yeshiva University Press, 1976.

Kraut, Alan. *Silent Travelers: Germs, Genes, and the "Immigrant Menace."* New York: Basic Books, 1994.

Kurian, George Thomas, ed. *The Encyclopedia of the Republican Party; The Encyclopedia of the Democratic Party.* Armonk, NY: Sharpe Reference, 1997.

——. *Supplement to the Encyclopedia of the Republican Party and the Encyclopedia of the Democratic Party.* Armonk, NY: Sharpe Reference, 2002.

Kwong, Peter. *Forbidden Workers: Illegal Chinese Workers and American Labor.* New York: New Press, 1997.

——. "Impact of Chinese Human Smuggling on the American Labor Market." 235–56 in David Kyle and Rey Koslowski, eds., *Global Human Smuggling: Comparative Perspectives.* Baltimore: Johns Hopkins University Press, 2001.

Labaree, Leonard W., ed. *The Papers of Benjamin Franklin,* vol. 4. New Haven: Yale University Press, 1959.

La Brack, Bruce. *The Sikhs of Northern California, 1904–1975.* New York: AMS Press, 1988.

La Guardia, Fiorello H. *The Making of an Insurgent: An Autobiography: 1882–1919.* Philadelphia: Lippincott, 1948.

Laguerre, Michel S. *Diasporic Citizenship: Haitian Americans in Transnational America.* New York: St. Martin's, 1998.

——. "Haitians." In Stephan Thernstrom, ed., *Harvard Encyclopedia of American Ethnic Groups.* Cambridge: Harvard University Press, 1980, 446–49.

Laham, Nicholas. *Ronald Reagan and the Politics of Immigration Reform.* Westport, CT: Praeger, 2000.

Lai, Him Mark. "The Kuomintang in Chinese American Communities before World War II." 170–212 in Sucheng Chan, ed., *Entry Denied: Exclusion and the Chinese Community in America, 1882–1943.* Philadelphia: Temple University Press, 1991.

——. "To Bring Forth a New China, To Build a Better America: The Chinese Marxist Left in America." *Chinese America: History & Perspectives,* 1992, 3–82.

——. "Unfinished Business: The Chinese Confession Program." 47–57 in *The Repeal and Its Legacy: Proceedings of the Conference on the 50th Anniversary of the Repeal of the Exclusion Acts.* Nov. 12–14, 1993. San Francisco: Chinese Historical Society of America, 1994.

Lane, James B. and Edward J. Escobar. *Forging a Community: The Latino Experience in Northwest Indiana, 1919–1975.* Chicago: Cattails Press, 1987.

Lark, Regina F. "They Challenged Two Nations: Marriages between Japanese Women and American G.I.s, 1945 to the Present." Ph.D. dissertation, University of Southern California, 1999.

Laqueur, Walter Z. *The Terrible Secret: Suppression of the Truth about Hitler's "Final Solution."* Boston: Little, Brown, 1980.

Larzelere, Alex. *The Cuban Boatlift.* Washington: National Defense University Press, 1988.

Lasby, Clarence G. *Project Paperclip: German Scientists and the Cold War.* New York: Atheneum, 1971.

Law, Anna O. "The Diversity Visa Lottery—A Cycle of Unintended Consequences in United States Immigration Policy." *Journal of American Ethnic History* 21 (Summer 2002): 1–29.

Lee, Chong-Sik. *Syngman Rhee: The Prison Years of a Young Radical.* Seoul: Yonsei University Press, 2001.

Lee, Rose Hum. "The Recent Immigrant Chinese Families of the San Francisco-Oakland Area." *Journal of Marriage and the Family* 18 (1956): 14–24.

——. "The Stranded Chinese in the United States." *Phylon* 19 (1958): 180–94.

Leonard, Karen Isaksen. *Making Ethnic Choices: California's Punjabi Mexican Americans.* Philadelphia: Temple University Press, 1992.

Levine, Robert M. *Tropical Diaspora: The Jewish Experience in Cuba.* Gainesville: University of Florida Press, 1993.

Leyva, Josefina. *Operación Pedro Pan: El Éxodo de los Niños Cubanos.* Coral Gables, FL: Editorial Ponce de León, 1993.

Ling, Huping. "A History of Chinese Female Students in the United States, 1880s—1990s." *Journal of American Ethnic History* 16 (Spring 1977): 81–109.

Link, Arthur S. *Wilson: The Road to the White House.* Princeton: Princeton University Press, 1947.

Liu, Eric. *The Accidental Asian: Notes of a Native Speaker.* New York: Random House, 1998.

London, Louise. *Whitehall and the Jews, 1933–1948: British Immigration Policy and the Holocaust.* Cambridge: Cambridge University Press, 2000.

Lowe, Lisa. *Immigrant Acts: On Asian American Cultural Politics.* Durham, NC: Duke University Press, 1996.

Lowenstein, Sharon R. "National Refugee Service." 374–72 in Michael N. Dobkowski, ed., *Jewish American Voluntary Organizations.* Westport, CT: Greenwood, 1986.

———. *Token Refuge: The Story of the Jewish Refugee Shelter at Oswego, 1944–1946.* Bloomington: Indiana University Press, 1986.

Lubell, Samuel. "War by Refugee." *Saturday Evening Post,* Mar. 29, 1941.

Lyman, Stanford M. *The Asian in the West.* Reno: Western Studies Center, University of Nevada, 1970.

Magliari, Michael. "Caminetti, Anthony." *American National Biography.* New York: Oxford University Press, 2000.

Maki, Mitchell T., Harry H. L. Kitano, and S. Megan Berthold. *Achieving the Impossible Dream: How Japanese Americans Obtained Redress.* Urbana: University of Illinois Press, 1999.

Malloy, William M. *Treaties, Conventions, International Acts, Protocols and Agreements Between the United States and Other Powers, 1776–1909,* 2 vols. Washington: GPO, 1910.

Mark, Diane Mei Lin and Ginger Chih. *A Place Called Chinese America.* Dubuque, IA: Kendall/Hunt, 1982.

Martin, George. *Madame Secretary: Frances Perkins.* Boston: Houghton Mifflin, 1976.

Matusow, Allen J. *The Unraveling of America: A History of Liberalism in the 1960s.* New York: Harper & Row, 1984.

McCabe, Cynthia Jaffee. " 'Wanted by the Gestapo: Saved by America'—Varian Fry and the Emergency Rescue Committee." 79–91 in J. C. Jackman and C. M. Borden, eds., *The Muses Flee Hitler: Cultural Transfer and Adaptation, 1930–1945.* Washington: Smithsonian Institution Press, 1983.

McClain, Charles J., Jr. *In Search of Equality: The Chinese Struggle Against Discrimination in Nineteenth-Century America.* Berkeley: University of California Press, 1994.

McConnell, Scott. *Leftward Journey: The Education of Vietnamese Students in France, 1919–1939.* New Brunswick, NJ: Transaction, 1989.

McWilliams, Carey. *Factories in the Field: The Story of Migratory Farm Labor in California.* Boston: Little, Brown, 1939.

Meinig, D. W. "A Prospectus for Geographers and Historians." *American Historical Review* 43 (1978): 1186–1205.

Melendy, H. Brett. *Asians in America: Filipinos, Koreans and East Indians.* Boston: Twayne, 1977.

———. "California's Discrimination Against Filipinos, 1927–1935." In Josepha M. Saniel, ed., *The Filipino Exclusion Movement, 1927–1935.* Quezon City: University of the Philippines, 1967.

Meyer, Michael A. "The Refugee Scholars Project of the Hebrew Union College." In B. W. Korn, ed., *A Bicentennial Festschrift for Jacob Rader Marcus.* New York: Ktav, 1976.

Miller, Kerby A. *Emigrants and Exiles: Ireland and the Irish Exodus to North America.* New York: Oxford University Press, 1985.

Min, Pyong Gap. *Caught in the Middle: Korean Communities in New York and Los Angeles.* Berkeley: University of California Press, 1996.

Mitchell, Christopher. "Changing the Rules: The Impact of the Simpson/Rodino Act on Inter-American Diplomacy." 177–89 in Georges Vernez, ed., *Immigration and International Relations.* Santa Monica, CA: Rand Corporation, 1990.

Morison, Elting E., ed. *The Letters of Theodore Roosevelt,* 8 vols. Cambridge, MA: Harvard University Press, 1951.

Mormino, Gary and George Pozzetta. *The Immigrant World of Ybor City: Italians and Their Latin Neighbors in Tampa, 1885–1985.* Urbana: University of Illinois Press, 1987.

Morrel-Samuels, Palmer. "Measuring Illegal Immigration at U.S. Border Stations by Sampling from a Flow of 500 Million Travelers." *Population and Environment* 23 (January 2002): 285–302.

Morse, Arthur D. *While Six Million Died: A Chronicle of American Apathy.* New York: Random House, 1968.

Muller, Eric L. *Free to Die for Their Country: The Story of the Japanese American Draft Resisters in World War II.* Chicago: University of Chicago Press, 2001.

Myers, William S. and Walter H. Newton. *The Hoover Administration: A Documented Narrative.* New York: Scribner, 1936.

Nadich, Judah. *Eisenhower and the Jews.* New York: Twayne, 1953.

Nee, Victor and Brett de Bary Nee. *Longtime Californ': A Documentary Study of an American Chinatown.* New York: Pantheon, 1973.

Newton, Verne, ed. *FDR and the Holocaust.* New York: St. Martin's, 1996.

Ngai, Mae M. "Legacies of Exclusion: Illegal Chinese Immigration during the Cold War Years." *Journal of American Ethnic History* 18:1 (Fall 1998): 3–35.

Nixon, Edgar B., ed. *Franklin D. Roosevelt and Foreign Affairs,* 10 vols. Cambridge, MA: Harvard University Press, 1969.

O'Brien, Michael. *Philip Hart: The Conscience of the Senate.* East Lansing: Michigan State University Press, 1995.

Ogawa, Dennis and Evarts C. Fox, Jr. "Japanese Internment and Relocation: The Hawaii Experience." 131–34 in R. Daniels et al., *Japanese Americans from Relocation to Redress.* Salt Lake City: University of Utah Press, 1986.

Olin, Spencer C. *California's Prodigal Sons: Hiram Johnson and the Progressives, 1911–1917.* Berkeley: University of California Press, 1968.

Orleans, Leo A. *Chinese Students in America: Policies, Issues and Numbers.* Washington: National Academy Press, 1988.

Pap, Leo. *The Portuguese Americans.* Boston: Twayne, 1981.

Patterson, Wayne. *The Ilsei: First-generation Korean Immigrants in Hawai'i, 1903–1973.* Honolulu: University of Hawaii Press, 2000.

———. *The Korean Frontier in America: Immigration to Hawaii, 1896–1910.* Honolulu: University of Hawaii Press, 1988.

——, ed. *The Golden Mountain: The Autobiography of a Korean Immigrant, 1895–1960.* Urbana: University of Illinois Press, 1995.

Paulsen, George E. "The Gresham-Yang Treaty." *Pacific Historical Review* 37 (1968): 281–97.

Peffer, George Anthony. *If They Don't Bring Their Women Here: Chinese Female Immigration before Exclusion.* Urbana: University of Illinois Press, 1999.

Petersen, William. *Japanese Americans: Oppression and Success.* New York: Random House, 1971.

——. "Success Story, Japanese American Style." *New York Times Magazine.* Jan. 6, 1996, 20–21.

Pilkington, Hilary. *Migration, Displacement, and Identity in Post-Soviet Russia.* New York: Routledge, 1938.

Pitkin, Thomas M. *Keepers of the Gate: A History of Ellis Island.* New York: New York University Press, 1975.

Porter, Kirk H. and Donald B. Johnson, comps. *National Party Platforms.* Urbana: University of Illinois Press, 1970.

Posadas, Barbara M. *The Filipino Americans.* Westport, CT: Greenwood, 1959.

—— and Roland L. Guyotte. "Unintentional Immigrants: Chicago's Filipino Foreign Students Become Settlers, 1900–1941," 9:2 (1990): 26–48. *Journal of American Ethnic History.*

Post, Louis F. *The Deportations Delirium of Nineteen-Twenty: A Personal Narrative of an Historical Official Experience.* Chicago: C. H. Kerr, 1923.

Powderly, Terence V. *The Path I Trod: The Autobiography of Terence V. Powderly.* New York: Columbia University Press, 1940.

President's Commission on Immigration and Naturalization. *Whom We Shall Welcome.* Washington: GPO, 1953.

Price, Charles A. *The Great White Walls Are Built.* Canberra: Australian National University Press, 1974.

Public Papers of the Presidents of the United States. Harry S. Truman. 1952–3. Washington: GPO, 1966.

Public Papers of the Presidents of the United States. Jimmy Carter. 1980. Washington: GPO, 1981.

Public Papers of the Presidents of the United States. John F. Kennedy. 1963. Washington: GPO, 1964.

Public Papers of the Presidents of the United States. Lyndon B. Johnson. 1965. Washington: GPO, 1967.

Public Papers of the Presidents of the United States. Ronald Reagan, 1981; . . . 1986. Washington: GPO, 1983, 1989.

Public Papers of the Presidents of the United States. William J. Clinton. 1996. Washington: GPO, 1998.

Pukui, Mary Kawena and Samuel H. Elbert. *Hawaiian Dictionary: Hawaiian-English, English-Hawaiian.* Revised and enlarged edition. Honolulu: University of Hawaii Press, 1986.

Quarles, Benjamin. *Frederick Douglass.* New York: Associated Publishers, 1948.

Rasmussen, Wayne D. *A History of the Emergency Farm Labor Supply Program, 1943–1947.* Washington: GPO, 1951.

Ravenstein, E. G. "Laws of Migration." *Journal of the Royal Statistical Society* 52 (1889): 21–30.

Reichard, Gary W. *Politics as Usual: The Era of Truman and Eisenhower.* Arlington Heights, IL: Harlan Davidson, 1988.

Reimers, David M. *Still the Golden Door: The Third World Comes to America.* New York: Columbia University Press, 1985.

——. *Unwelcome Strangers: American Identity and the Turn Against Immigration.* New York: Columbia University Press, 1998.

Richardson, James D., ed. *Messages and Papers of the Presidents,* 10 vols. Washington: Bureau of National Literature and Art, 1903.

Riggs, Fred W. *Pressures on Congress: A Study of the Repeal of Chinese Exclusion.* New York: King's Crown, 1950.

Riley, Karen L. *Schools Behind Barbed Wire: The Untold Story of Wartime Internment and the Children of Arrested Enemy Aliens.* Lanham, MD: Rowman & Littlefield, 2002.

Ristaino, Marcia R. *Port of Last Resort: Diaspora Communities of Shanghai.* Stanford: Stanford University Press, 2001.

Rose, Peter I. "Asian Americans: From Pariahs to Paragons." 181–212 in Nathan Glazer, ed., *Clamor at the Gates: New American Immigration.* San Francisco: ICS Press, 1985.

Rosenbaum, Alan S. *Prosecuting Nazi War Criminals.* Boulder: Westview Press, 1993.

Rosenman, Samuel I., comp. *The Public Papers and Addresses of Franklin D. Roosevelt,* 13 vols. New York: various, 1938–50.

Ross, Robert W. *So It Was True: The American Protestant Press and the Persecution of the Jews.* Minneapolis: University of Minnesota Press, 1980.

Rudolph, Frederick. "Chinamen in Yankeedom: Anti-Unionism in Massachusetts in 1870." *American Historical Review* 53 (1947): 1–29.

Ryan, Allan A., Jr. *Quiet Neighbors: Prosecuting Nazi War Criminals in America.* San Diego: Harcourt Brace Jovanovich, 1984.

Saloutos, Theodore. *Human Scientific and Technical Capabilities at Holloman Air Force Base: Their Origins and Development.* Holloman AFB, NM: Historical Branch, Office of Information, Air Force Missile Development Center, Air Research and Development Command, United States Air Force, 1960.

Salyer, Lucy E. *Laws Harsh as Tigers: Chinese Immigrants and the Shaping of Modern Immigration Law.* Chapel Hill: University of North Carolina Press, 1995.

Sánchez, George J. *Becoming Mexican American: Ethnicity, Culture and Identity in Chicano Los Angeles, 1900–1945.* New York: Oxford University Press, 1993.

——. "The 'New Nationalism,' Mexican Style: Race and Progressivism in Chicano Political Development during the 1920s." 229–44, in W. Deverell and T. Sitton, eds., *California Progressivism Revisited*. Berkeley: University of California Press, 1994.

Saniel, Josepha M., ed. *The Filipino Exclusion Movement, 1927–1935*. Quezon City: University of the Philippines, 1967.

Saund, D. S. *Congressman from India*. New York: Dutton, 1960.

Saunders, Kay and Roger Daniels. *Alien Justice: Wartime Internment in Australia and North America*. St. Lucia, Queensland: University of Queensland Press, 2000.

Saveth, Edward N. *American Historians and European Immigrants, 1875–1925*. New York: Columbia University Press, 1948.

Saxenian, AnnaLee. *Local and Global Networks of Immigrant Professionals in Silicon Valley*. San Francisco: Public Policy Institute of California, 2002.

Schmidley, Dianne. *The Foreign-Born Population in the United States: March 2002*. Current Population Reports, P20–539. Washington: U.S. Census Bureau, 2003.

Schwartz, Abba P. *The Open Society*. New York: Simon and Schuster, 1968.

Scruggs, Otey M. "The First Mexican Labor Program." *Arizona and the West* 2 (1960): 318–26.

Shaplen, Robert. "One Man Lobby." *New Yorker*, Mar. 24, 1951.

Shaw, Albert. *The Messages and Papers of Woodrow Wilson*. New York: Review of Reviews, 1917.

Simpson, Alan K. *Right in the Old Gazoo: What I've Observed in a Lifetime of Scrapping with the American Press*. New York: William Morrow, 1997.

Smith, Marian L. "INS Administration of Racial Provisions in U.S. Immigration and Nationality Law Since 1898." *Prologue* 34 (Summer 1902): 90–105.

Solomon, Barbara Miller. *Ancestors and Immigrants*. Cambridge, MA: Harvard University Press, 1956.

Stanley, Gerald. "Frank Pixley and the Heathen Chinese." *Phylon* 40 (1979): 224–28.

Stein, Leon. *The Triangle Fire*. Philadelphia: Lippincott, 1962.

Stewart, Barbara McDonald. *United States Government Policy on Refugees from Nazism, 1933–1940*. New York: Garland, 1992.

Strum, Harvey. "Jewish Internees in the American South, 1942–1945." *American Jewish Archives* 42 (1980): 27–48.

Sumner, Charles. *The Works of Charles Sumner*, 10 vols. Boston: Lee and Shepard, 1870–1883.

Svejda, George J. *Castle Garden as an Immigrant Depot*. Washington: GPO, 1968.

Thernstrom, Stephan, ed. *The Harvard Encyclopedia of American Ethnic Groups*. Cambridge, MA: Harvard University Press, 1980.

Thomas, Gordon and Max Morgan Witts. *Voyage of the Damned*. New York: Stein & Day, 1974.

Triay, Victor Andres. *Fleeing Castro: Operation Pedro Pan and the Cuban Children's Program*. Gainesville: University Press of Florida, 1998.

Truman, Harry S. *Memoirs*, 2 vols. Garden City, NY: Doubleday, 1955.

Turner, Frederick Jackson. *The Frontier in American History*. New York: H. Holt & Co., 1920.

United Nations Relief and Rehabilitation Administration. *UNRRA: The History of the*

United Nations Relief and Rehabilitation Administration. New York: Columbia University Press, 1950.

U.S. Children's Bureau. *Cuba's Children in Exile.* Washington: GPO, 1967.

U.S. Congress. *Joint Hearings before the Subcommittees of the Committees on the Judiciary.* Washington: GPO, 1951.

U.S. Congress. House. Committee on Foreign Relations. *Hearings on House Resolution 350 and House Resolution 352.* Washington: GPO, 1943.

U.S. Congress. House. Committee on Immigration and Naturalization. *Hearings Before Subcommittee 1.* Washington: GPO, 1945.

——. *Hearings on Exclusion of Immigration from the Philippine Islands.* 71st Congress, 2d Session, Washington: GPO, 1930.

——. *Immigration from the Western Hemisphere.* Washington: GPO, 1930.

——. *Repeal of the Chinese Exclusion Acts. Hearings.* Washington: GPO, 1943.

U.S. Congress. Senate. Subcommittee on Immigration and Naturalization of the Committee on the Judiciary. *Immigration Hearings.* Washington: GPO, 1965.

U.S. Congress. Senate. *Japanese in the City of San Francisco, Cal.* 59th Congress, 2d Session, Sen. Doc. 147. Washington: GPO, 1907.

U.S. Congress. Senate. *Report of the Joint Special Committee to Investigate Chinese Immigration.* Report 689. Washington: GPO, 1877.

U.S. Department of Agriculture. *Termination of the Bracero Program.* Washington: GPO, June 1956.

U.S. Department of Commerce. Bureau of the Census. 1990 Census of Population. *Asians and Pacific Islanders in the United States.* 1990 CP-3-5. Washington: GPO, 1993.

——. *Current Population Survey, March 2000.* Washington: Ethnic and Hispanic Statistics Branch, Population Division, March 6, 2001.

——. *Nonwhite Population by Race.* PC (2)-1C. Washington: GPO, 1993.

——. QT-P7. "Race Alone . . . Asian . . . 2000." *Data Set: Census 2000. Summary File 1 (SF-1) 100-Percent Data.* Bureau of Census Web site, 2002.

U.S. Department of Justice. *Annual Report, 1943.* Washington: GPO, 1944.

U.S. Department of State. *Bulletin* 13. Sept. 30, 1945.

——. *Foreign Relations of the United States.* Washington: GPO, various years.

United States Displaced Persons Commission. *Memo to America: The DP Story.* Washington: GPO, 1952.

U.S. Immigration Commission. *Reports of the Immigration Commission,* 41 vols. Washington: GPO, 1911.

U.S. Immigration and Naturalization Service. *Statistical Yearbook of the Immigration and Naturalization Service.* Washington: GPO, various years.

U.S. Immigration and Naturalization Service. *Annual Report, 1970.* Washington: GPO, 1970.

U.S. Selective Service System. Special Monograph 10. *Special Groups.* Washington: GPO, 1953.

Varma, Premdatta. *Indian Immigrants in USA: Struggle for Equality.* New Delhi: Heritage Publishers, 1995.

Voorhees, Tracy S. *Interim Report to the President on the Cuban Refugee Problem.* Washington: GPO, 1960.

Walker, Francis A. "Immigration." *Yale Review* 1 (1892): 131–35.

——. "Restriction of Immigration." *Atlantic Monthly* 67 (1896): 822–29.

Walsh, Bryan O. "Cuban Refugee Children." *Journal of Interamerican Studies and World Affairs* 13 (July–October 1971): 378–415.

Warren, Robert and Ellen Percy Kraly. *The Elusive Exodus: Emigration from the United States.* Washington: Population Reference Bureau, 1985.

Weber, Devra. *Dark Sweat, White Gold: California Farm Workers, Cotton, and the New Deal.* Berkeley: University of California Press, 1994.

Wei, William. *The Asian American Movement.* Philadelphia: Temple University Press, 1993.

Welarata, Usha. *Beyond the Killing Fields: Voices of Nine Cambodian Survivors in America.* Stanford: Stanford University Press, 1993.

Whitmore, John K. "Chinese from Southeast Asia." 81–101 in David W. Haines, ed., *Refugees in America in the 1990s: A Reference Handbook.* Westport, CT: Greenwood, 1996.

Willett, John and Ralph Mannheim, eds. *Bertolt Brecht, Poems.* London: Methuen, 1976.

Wilson, Woodrow. *A History of the American People,* 5 vols. New York: Harper, 1902.

Wunder, John R. "Anti-Chinese Violence in the American West, 1850–1910." 212–35 in J. McLaren et al., *Law for the Elephant, Law for the Beaver.* Regina, Sask.: Canadian Plains Research Center, 1992.

Wyman, David S. *The Abandonment of the Jews.* New York: Pantheon, 1984.

——. *Paper Walls: America and the Refugee Crisis, 1938–1941.* Amherst: University of Massachusetts Press, 1968.

Wyman, Mark. *DP: Europe's Displaced Persons, 1945–1951.* Philadelphia: Balch Institute, 1985.

Yang, Y. C. *Chinese Intellectuals and the West, 1872–1949.* Chapel Hill: University of North Carolina Press, 1966.

Ye, Weili. *Seeking Modernity in China's Name: Chinese Students in the United States, 1900–1927.* Stanford: Stanford University Press, 2001.

Yu, Henry. *Thinking Orientals: Migration, Contact, and Exoticism in Modern America.* New York: Oxford University Press, 2001.

Yuh, Ji-Yeon. *Beyond the Shadow of Camptown: Korean Military Brides in America.* New York: New York University Press, 2002.

Yung, Judy. *Unbound Feet: A Social History of Chinese Women in San Francisco.* Berkeley: University of California Press, 1995.

Zhao, Xiaojian. *Remaking Chinese America: Immigration, Family, and Community, 1940–1965.* New Brunswick: Rutgers University Press, 2002.

Ziegler, Bernard M., ed. *Immigration: An American Dilemma.* Boston: D. C. Heath, 1953.

Ziglar, James W. "Let's Not Forget Our Immigration Duties." *Miami Herald,* Mar. 4, 2003.

Index